THE Mycenaean FEAST

EDITED BY

James C. Wright

American School of Classical Studies at Athens
Princeton 2004

This volume is also published as issue 73:2 (2004)
of *Hesperia: The Journal of the American School of
Classical Studies at Athens* (ISSN 0018-098X).

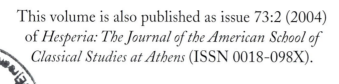

Cover illustration: **Pylos megaron fresco: procession.** Drawing Piet
de Jong, Piet de Jong Papers; photo I. Ioannidou and L. Bartzioti.
Courtesy American School of Classical Studies at Athens

Cover design: Mary Jane Gavenda, Publications Management

To order, contact:
(in North America)   (outside North America)
The David Brown Book Company   Oxbow Books
www.davidbrownbookco.com   www.oxbowbooks.com
Tel. 800-791-9354   Tel. +44 (0) 1865-241-249

Library of Congress Cataloging-in-Publication Data

The Mycenaean Feast / edited by James C. Wright.
    p. cm.
    "This volume is also published as issue 73:2 (2004) of Hesperia: The
Journal of the American School of Classical Studies at Athens (ISSN 0018-
098X)."—t.p. verso.
    Includes bibliographical references.
    ISBN 0-87661-951-0 (alk. paper)
    1. Civilization, Mycenaean. 2. Greece—Antiquities. 3. Food habits—
Greece—History—To 1500. I. Wright, James C., 1946–

DF220.5.M89 2004
394.1′2′09388—dc22   2004046237

Contents

Preface

In recent years, archaeologists have tackled an increasingly diverse range of social and political questions about prehistoric communities in the Aegean. The present volume contributes to this trend as scholars take a close look at the evidence for ritual feasting and drinking ceremonies in the Mycenaean world. In seven essays and an introduction, James Wright and his colleagues present a wealth of detail about feasting, drawing on many sources: large deposits of drinking and serving vessels, massive accumulations of animal bones, depictions in fresco and on painted pottery, and Linear B documents from Pylos, Thebes, and Knossos. The geographical and chronological limits of discussion are expansive, as the authors investigate traditions of feasting on mainland Greece, Crete, and Cyprus from the Late Bronze Age to the Iron Age. The implications of ethnographic and archaeological accounts of feasting from around the world are also considered. The contributors to this volume pay special attention to the ways in which, in the Mycenaean world, these ritual ceremonies serve as arenas where alliances among the elite are forged and legitimized, prestige is acquired, and cultural identity formed. The complex role of feasting within the Mycenaean economy and social structure is closely studied, as is the relationship between Homer's accounts of banqueting and the Late Bronze Age archaeological record.

The genesis of this project was a colloquium organized by Wright and Sharon Stocker for the 103rd Annual Meeting of the Archaeological Institute of America in Philadelphia in January 2002. After attending the session and hearing the enthusiastic discussion that followed, I invited the organizers to submit the papers to *Hesperia*, the journal of the American School of Classical Studies at Athens, for publication as a special theme-issue. The colloquium coincided not only with the upsurge of sociocultural studies in Aegean prehistory, but also with the changing focus of the publications program of the American School (see editorials in *Hesperia* 69, 2000; and 73, 2004). One explicit goal is that *Hesperia* reflect the recent expansion of disciplinary approaches taken to the study of the ancient Mediterranean while also representing the broad spectrum of research undertaken at the American School itself. Publication of an occasional issue devoted to a theme of current interest was thus endorsed, and *The Mycenaean Feast*, after passing peer review, appeared as *Hesperia* 73:2.

Because the subject of Mycenaean feasting is of interest to a potentially wider readership than *Hesperia* subscribers—Aegean prehistorians,
anthropologists, and others intrigued by the wider social aspects of eating
and drinking—ASCSA Publications decided to publish the volume con-
currently as a freestanding book. In doing so, we have made minimal
changes to the articles themselves; the primary differences between the
present volume and the journal version pertain to format and the renum-
bering of pages.

Many individuals deserve thanks for bringing this volume to light:
Jim Wright, above all, who coordinated the project and collected and shaped
the subsequent articles; and the other contributors, who sustained their
initial enthusiasm for the project and met increasingly demanding dead-
lines with good humor. Brian Hayden and Jeremy Rutter reviewed the
original submissions, and their insightful comments contributed significantly to the final versions. A later addition to the volume, by Thomas Palaima, benefited from review by John Bennet, John Papadopoulos, and the
late Paul Rehak. For editorial assistance I thank Camilla MacKay, Priscilla
Murray, and Molly Richardson, and especially my hardworking colleagues
in ASCSA Publications, Sarah George Figueira, Carol Stein, and Timo-
thy Wardell. I am also grateful to Carol Hershenson and Natalia Vogeikoff-
Brogan for assistance with illustrations, Eleni Hasaki and Zina Gianno-
poulou for checking Greek citations, and Mary Jane Gavenda for designing
a wonderful cover for the book.

Tracey Cullen
Editor, *Hesperia*

Contributors

Elisabetta Borgna, Dipartimento di Storia e Tutela dei Beni Culturali, Università di Udine, Via Petracco 8, 33100 Udine, Italy; elisabetta_borgna@yahoo.it

Mary K. Dabney, Department of Classical and Near Eastern Archaeology, Bryn Mawr College, Bryn Mawr, Pennsylvania 19010-2899, USA; mdabney@brynmawr.edu

Jack L. Davis, Department of Classics, University of Cincinnati, Cincinnati, Ohio 45221-0226, USA; jack.davis@uc.edu

Paul Halstead, Department of Archaeology, University of Sheffield, Sheffield S1 4ET, United Kingdom; P.Halstead@sheffield.ac.uk

Thomas G. Palaima, Department of Classics, University of Texas at Austin, 1 University Station C3400, Austin, Texas 78712-0308, USA; tpalaima@mail.utexas.edu

Susan Sherratt, Ashmolean Museum, Beaumont Street, Oxford OX1 2PH, United Kingdom; sue.sherratt@ashmus.ox.ac.uk

Louise Steel, Department of Archaeology, University of Wales, Lampeter, Ceredigion SA48 7ED, United Kingdom; l.steel@lamp.ac.uk

Sharon R. Stocker, Department of Classics, University of Cincinnati, Cincinnati, Ohio 45221-0226, USA; stockesr@email.uc.edu

Patrick Thomas, Department of Archaeology and Art History, University of Evansville, Evansville, Indiana 47722-0001, USA; pt4@evansville.edu

James C. Wright, Department of Classical and Near Eastern Archaeology, Bryn Mawr College, Bryn Mawr, Pennsylvania 19010-2899, USA; jwright@brynmawr.edu

ABBREVIATIONS

AA = Archäologischer Anzeiger

Aegaeum = Aegaeum. Annales d'archéologie égéenne de l'Université de Liège

Aevum = Aevum. Rassegna di scienze storiche, linguistiche, e filologiche

Ägypten und Levante = Ägypten und Levante. Zeitschrift für ägyptische Archäologie und deren Nachbargebiete

AJA = American Journal of Archaeology. The Journal of the Archaeological Institute of America

AM = Mitteilungen des Deutschen Archäologischen Instituts, Athenische Abteilung

AmerAnt = American Antiquity

American Anthropologist = American Anthropologist. The Journal of the American Anthropological Association

AnnÉconSocCiv = Annales. Économie, sociétés, civilisations

Antiquity = Antiquity. A Quarterly Review of Archaeology

AntK = Antike Kunst

Archaeologica = Archaeologica, or Miscellaneous Tracts Relating to Antiquity

ArchDelt = Ἀρχαιολογικὸν Δελτίον

ArchEph = Ἀρχαιολογικὴ Ἐφημερίς

ArchHom = Archaeologia Homerica, ed. F. Matz and H. G. Buchholz, Göttingen 1967–

ArchKorrBl = Archaeologisches Korrespondenzblatt

ASAtene = Annuario della Scuola archeologica di Atene e delle Missioni italiane in Oriente

BAR = British Archaeological Reports

BAR-IS = British Archaeological Reports, International Series

BASOR = Bulletin of the American Schools of Oriental Research

BCH = Bulletin de correspondance hellénique

BICS = Bulletin of the Institute of Classical Studies of the University of London

BSA = Annual of the British School at Athens

CAJ = Cambridge Archaeological Journal

CÉFR = Collection de l'École française de Rome

CMS = Corpus der minoischen und mykenischen Siegel

CQ = Classical Quarterly

CretChron = Κρητικὰ χρονικά. Κείμενα καὶ μελέται τῆς κρητικῆς
  ἱστορίας

CronCatania = Cronache di archeologia e di storia dell'arte, Università di
  Catania

CurrAnthr = Current Anthropology

DenkschrWien = Österreichische Akademie der Wissenschaften, Wien,
  Philosophisch-historische Klasse. Denkschriften

Eirene = Eirene. Studia graeca et latina

EntrHardt = Fondation Hardt pour l'étude de l'antiquité classique.
  Entretiens sur l'antiquité classique

Environmental Archaeology = Environmental Archaeology. The Journal
  of Human Palaeoecology

Eranos = Eranos. Acta philologica suecana

ÉtCrét = Études crétoises

Gymnasium = Gymnasium. Zeitschrift für Kultur der Antike und
  humanistische Bildung

Hesperia = Hesperia. The Journal of the American School of Classical
  Studies at Athens

Hydra = Hydra. Working Papers in Middle Bronze Age Studies

Incunabula graeca = Incunabula graeca. Collana dell'Istituto per gli studi
  micenei ed egeo-anatolici del Consiglio nazionale delle ricerche di
  Roma

IrAnt = Iranica antiqua

JAnthArch = Journal of Anthropological Archaeology

JAS = Journal of Archaeological Science

JdI = Jahrbuch des Deutschen Archäologischen Instituts

JFA = Journal of Field Archaeology

JMA = Journal of Mediterranean Archaeology

JPR = Journal of Prehistoric Religion

JRGZM = Jahrbuch des Römisch-germanischen Zentralmuseums,
  Mainz

Kadmos = Kadmos. Zeitschrift für vor- und frühgriechische Epigraphik

Ktema = Ktema. Civilisations de l'Orient, de la Grèce, et de Rome
  antiques

Minos = Minos. Revista de filología e egea

Mnemosyne = Mnemosyne. Bibliotheca classica batava

MonAnt = Monumenti antichi

NatGeogRes = National Geographic Research

OJA = Oxford Journal of Archaeology

OpAth = Opuscula atheniensia

Orientalia = Orientalia. Commentarii periodici Pontificii Instituti
  Biblici, Rome

PCPS = Proceedings of the Cambridge Philological Society

Prakt = Πρακτικὰ τῆς ἐν Ἀθήναις Ἀρχαιολογικῆς Ἑταιρείας

PZ = Prähistorische Zeitschrift

Qedem = Qedem. Monographs of the Institute of Archaeology, Hebrew
     University of Jerusalem
RA = Revue archéologique
RDAC = Report of the Department of Antiquities, Cyprus
RÉA = Revue des études anciennes
RivFil = Rivista di filologia e d'istruzione classica
RStFen = Rivista di studi fenici
ScAnt = Scienze dell'antichità. Storia, archeologia, antropologia
SIMA = Studies in Mediterranean Archaeology
SIMA-PB = Studies in Mediterranean Archaeology and Literature.
     Pocketbook
SkrAth = Skrifter utgivna av Svenska Institutet i Athen
SMEA = Studi micenei ed egeo-anatolici
SymbOslo = Symbolae osloenses
TAPS = Transactions of the American Philosophical Society
WorldArch = World Archaeology
ZfA = Zeitschrift für Archäologie
ZivaAnt = Ziva antika. Antiquité vivante
ZPE = Zeitschrift für Papyrologie und Epigraphik

CHAPTER I

THE MYCENAEAN FEAST: AN INTRODUCTION

James C. Wright

In 2001, I participated in a conference on the culture and cuisine of the prehistoric Aegean, sponsored by the Department of Prehistory and Archaeology at the University at Sheffield.[1] Many of the papers focused in one way or another on feasting, and I realized that the archaeological remains of feasting were more abundant than I had suspected. Especially interesting was the amount of evidence from different sources that elucidated feasting in Mycenaean society. I decided that it would be worthwhile to organize a conference on that subject, and, initially collaborating with Sharon Stocker, proposed a session entitled "The Mycenaean Feast" for the 103rd Annual Meeting of the Archaeological Institute of America (AIA), to be held in Philadelphia in January 2002. We wished to demonstrate that the archaeological record was sufficiently rich to allow the identification and characterization of the practice of feasting in Mycenaean times. We therefore invited colleagues to contribute papers approaching this issue from a number of perspectives, using several varieties of evidence: iconographic, artifactual, textual, faunal, and contextual (actual deposits).[2]

The papers presented in Philadelphia included one by Jack Davis and Stocker on the evidence from the Palace of Nestor at Pylos; another on a deposit from Tsoungiza by Mary Dabney, Paul Halstead, and Patrick Thomas; one by Lisa Bendall on the textual and archaeological evidence from Pylos; and my own investigation of the problem of identifying feasting from tomb assemblages, as depicted on frescoes, and from other sources. If these papers succeeded in characterizing a distinctive "Mycenaean" practice, that practice could be further defined by contrasting it with those from cultures in contact with the Mycenaeans. Thus, we also invited Elisabetta Borgna to talk about Minoan feasting, with special reference to the evidence from Phaistos, and Louise Steel to discuss feasting in Late Bronze Age Cyprus. Both were charged to consider how practices in their areas were affected by Mycenaean customs of feasting, and to what extent local practices continued or even resisted the introduction of new practices. Robin Hägg served as the respondent and compared and contrasted the Late Bronze Age evidence with later Greek practices of feasting and sacrifice. Afterward, the participants agreed that it would be worthwhile to rework our papers and present them for publication, and Tracey Cullen suggested we consider publishing them as a special issue of *Hesperia*.

1. I wish to thank Paul Halstead and Jack Davis for reading a draft of this introduction, providing useful references, and making valuable suggestions.

2. Abstracts of the papers delivered as part of "The Mycenaean Feast: An Archaeological Colloquium" at the AIA Annual Meeting in Philadelphia in 2002 are published in *AJA* 106 (2002), pp. 272–273.

In the course of pulling this volume together, changes were made. Bendall's paper will appear in the publication of the Sheffield Conference and therefore is not included here.[3] I invited Thomas Palaima to contribute a paper that treated the Linear B evidence, an exceptionally rich and fundamental source of information. A study of feasting in the Homeric epics and during the Iron Age was needed to round out the subject, and Susan Sherratt accepted the challenge. Together, the authors survey the different kinds of evidence for feasting during the Mycenaean era, set this evidence in the context of feasting practices among interdependent cultures, and consider the difficult issue of a tradition and its transformation as the "civilization" that practiced it becomes only a practice of memory.

Thematic conferences are common in the discipline of Aegean pre- and protohistory, and have dealt with subjects such as invasions and migrations,[4] the "Minoan thalassocracy,"[5] death and burial customs,[6] the state,[7] warfare,[8] religion,[9] urbanism,[10] and economy and politics[11]—to name only a few. Fewer have been solely concerned with the Mycenaeans,[12] and fewer yet have chosen a theme that is a specific social practice. The reason for this may be that archaeologists are not comfortable exploring social practices, which are difficult to document through the material record. For example, if it is difficult for archaeologists to reconstruct religion, even in the abstract, it is more difficult, if not altogether questionable, to try to understand highly social practices such as marriage, kinship, and feasting. That we make the effort to do so today represents the extent to which we have made sufficient advances in our examination of evidence. Addressing these issues has required overcoming skepticism about the limits of archaeological inquiry,[13] and the development of methods of analysis that move beyond traditional concerns with typology, chronology, and distribution. This renewed interest in recovering social aspects of ancient societies is functional in that it reflects a desire to know how and for what purpose objects were created and employed by humans; it also, however, grows out of our increasing recognition that the issues of production and consumption that have interested us for decades are products of the social agency of individuals and of corporate bodies.[14]

Skeptics of archaeology's ability to explain past events base their concern on the unbridgeable maw that separates the material past from the present. The conceptual gap lies between the material remains of the past and the intentions and actions of humans who created them, and it is argued that it can be bridged through the use of ethnographic and ethnoarchaeological analogy. This argument, however, rests on the assumption that humans acted in the past in much the same manner in which they do today. If archaeology is ever to contribute to our understanding of the past, it is necessary that we employ analogy. In this sense, archaeology, like other interpretive disciplines of the humanities, is a "theoretically informed practice."[15] Ethnography is fundamental to such an archaeology, but, as Comaroff and Comaroff claim, it must be an ethnography that bears

> the imprint of contemporary debates, of assumptions and
> claims profoundly questioned, of the impossibility of ironic
> detachment. . . . [It] must also assert a faith that the human world,

3. Bendall, forthcoming. The papers from this conference will appear in Halstead and Barrett, forthcoming.

4. Crossland and Birchall 1974.

5. Hägg and Marinatos 1984.

6. Laffineur 1987; Hägg and Nordquist 1990; Branigan 1998.

7. Laffineur and Niemeier 1995.

8. Laffineur 1999a.

9. Hägg and Nordquist 1990; Laffineur and Hägg 2001.

10. Branigan 2001.

11. Voutsaki and Killen 2001.

12. Shelmerdine and Palaima 1984; Voutsaki and Killen 2001.

13. Leach 1977; Patrik 1985; Shanks and Tilley 1987; Hodder 1991.

14. Giddens 1984.

15. Comaroff and Comaroff 1992, p. x.

post-anything and -everything, remains the product of discernible social and cultural processes: processes partially indeterminate yet, in some measure, systematically determined; ambiguous and poly-valent, yet never utterly incoherent or meaningless; open to multiple constructions and contest, yet never entirely free of order—or the reality of power and constraint.[16]

The authors go on to argue that ethnography "is indispensable to the pro-duction of knowledge about all manner of social phenomena. Indeed . . . no humanist account of the past or present can (or does) go very far with-out the kind of understanding that the ethnographic gaze presupposes."[17] In the study of feasting, the fundamental value of ethnography is evident in a recent volume edited by Michael Dietler and Brian Hayden on the archaeology and ethnography of feasting;[18] ethnographic and archaeologi-cal accounts from around the globe provide rich and varied examples on which to draw. The articles demonstrate the extent to which some human activities have a universal quality and they also counter simplistic explana-tions by broadening the choices of probable interpretations, sometimes even offering contradictory ones.[19]

In studying the practice of feasting, archaeologists devise and utilize methods of analysis that lead to a direct assessment of specific human activities. This is most apparent in faunal analysis, in which the compara-tive, ethnoarchaeological study of butchering now permits declarative as-sessments of the purposes of different kinds of butchering marks and bone treatment and disposal.[20] Increasingly, the analysis of residues in vessels allows us to determine, with varying degrees of precision, the contents of vessels and the ways in which vessels were used in food production.[21] Simi-larly, studies of deposits can lead to precise histories of deposition, for example through attention to palaeoentomological evidence, the remains of which can indicate the presence of organic waste in which insects thrived during the spring and summer months.[22]

It is also possible to reconstruct from palaeobotanical and zoological remains the very wide range of foodstuffs consumed at feasts. In feasting deposits at Cahokia in southern Illinois, for example, Pauketat and his colleagues found evidence of corn, bottle gourd, squash, sunflower, sump-weed, chenopod, maygrass, erect knotweed, four varieties of nuts, grape, and many fruits (persimmon, strawberry, plum, bramble, elderberry, night-shade, blackhaw, mulberry, sunflower), along with greens and small grains (amaranth, purslane, panicoid grasses, carpetweed, and spurges).[23] At the Mycenaean sanctuary at Ayios Konstantinos, Hamilakis and Konsolaki identified sheep, goat, cattle, pig, red deer, mouse/rat, rock dove, bird, and fish.[24] Comparative study of ceramic vessel forms and their quantities in deposits elucidates similarities and differences between feasting deposits and domestic ones, as demonstrated by Pauketat et al. in their analysis of vessels from Cahokia and by Pappa and colleagues in a study of the drink-ing cups from Makriyalos in Macedonia.[25] As noted, chemical analysis of contents also promises identification of specific foodstuffs prepared in ves-sels.[26] A particularly valuable source of information is textual, as observed by Schmandt-Besserat in her review of feasting in the ancient Near East,

16. Comaroff and Comaroff 1992, p. xi.

17. Comaroff and Comaroff 1992, p. xi.

18. Dietler and Hayden 2001.

19. Orme 1981, p. 284.

20. Binford 1981; Speth 1983; O'Connor 1998. I thank Paul Halstead for supplying these references.

21. Tzedakis and Martlew 1999.

22. Pauketat et al. 2002, pp. 261–263.

23. Pauketat et al. 2002, pp. 265–266.

24. Hamilakis and Konsolaki 2004, p. 142.

25. Pauketat et al. 2002, pp. 268–269; Pappa et al., forthcoming.

26. Tzedakis and Martlew 1999; McGovern et al. 1999; McGovern 2003.

and as is well known from the rich documentation of the *deipnon* and *symposion* in ancient Greece.[27] For the study of Mycenaean feasting, the Linear B texts from Thebes, Pylos, and Knossos have proven especially important. These examples demonstrate the array of information available to archaeologists investigating this fundamental human social practice.

It is perhaps the strength of the textual evidence for the Mycenaean feast that gives the greatest credibility to the collection of papers in this volume. These papers provide a material substance to the bureaucratic shorthand of the texts. The Linear B documents are notations of palace scribes, found in their briefest form on sealings that accompanied groups of texts or objects,[28] and more fully on the tablets collected in archives.[29] These records do not contain specific references to "feasts" but rather indicate them indirectly.[30] Thus, Killen, following on the work of Piteros, Olivier, and Melena, showed how the clay sealings from Thebes that documented the provisioning of animals for sacrifice or slaughter were related to similar documents from Knossos and Pylos.[31] Taken together, the records provide powerful evidence for large-scale feasts.

In a further study of this subject, Killen associated the well-known Ta series tablets from Pylos with the auditing of feasting equipment in the palace.[32] These tablets list bronze vessels that had been stored, record their condition, and list other equipment, including tables, chairs, and stools, different kinds of ceramic serving vessels, and axes and knives. Although the interpretation relies on circumstantial associations, it represents a powerful argument for feasting and its importance in activities at the palace, as Palaima's chapter in this volume demonstrates. The provisioning and preparation for feasts, especially large-scale events sponsored by the palace, had a major impact on many sectors of the economy and society. When one considers the many types of vessels, implements, furnishings, and foodstuffs employed in a feast, and the large number of animals involved,[33] the magnitude of Mycenaean feasting becomes apparent. Killen suggests this by stating that the importance of the feast was for "holding together the fabric of the society" and he goes on to claim that "the provision of feasts was felt to be one of the duties of the monarch: part of what he gave in reciprocity, as it were, for the services and taxes which the subjects provided him with; and feasts also clearly played an important role in ensuring the continuing good-will of important state officials and of the subordinate nobility."[34] We may observe in passing that the faunal deposit of a feast at Neolithic Makriyalos may have been so large as to require the slaughter of all the cattle, pigs, and sheep/goats of the entire region,[35] and Halstead and Isaakidou (see also Stocker and Davis, this volume) estimate

27. Schmandt-Besserat 2001, pp. 397–399. For *deipnon* and *symposion,* see Murray 1990, p. 6; Lissarrague 1990.

28. Piteros, Olivier, and Melena 1990; for general discussion of seals and sealings, see the contributions in Palaima 1990 and Palaima 1984, 1987, 1988, 1996, 2000a, b.

29. For a general introduction to the tablets, see Chadwick 1987, esp. pp. 33–43; also Chadwick 1958; Olivier 1967; Ventris and Chadwick 1973; Palaima 1988; Bennet 2001, pp. 27–33.

30. Compare the discussion of the Homeric term δαίς in Sherratt's contribution to this volume.

31. Piteros, Olivier, and Melena 1990, pp. 171–184. Killen 1994, pp. 71–76; see also Killen 1992.

32. Killen 1998.

33. Isaakidou et al. 2002; Stocker and Davis, this volume.

34. Killen 1994, p. 70.

35. Pappa et al., forthcoming.

that the total number of persons fed at a feast at Pylos was "enough, by the rules of thumb of modern British receptions, to feed several thousand guests."[36] These calculations help us appreciate the widespread impact of feasting on the economy of the Mycenaean palaces, and they also make clear how many areas of scribal activity were affected by feasting.

In this regard Palaima's contribution to this volume marks a significant advance on previous scholarship. He examines the tablets for evidence of the administrative structure of feasting by focusing on the role of individuals, notably the "collectors," in the administration of feasting; by indicating the larger context of feasting within the practice of sacrifice and worship at sanctuaries; and by considering the geographical and political implications posed by the tablets. From his study we learn that feasting was administered in similar fashion by the palaces at Knossos, Pylos, and Thebes; it was part of a highly centralized palace bureaucracy that had firm control of territories and provincial localities up to 100 km distant; and that state feasting was sponsored not only at the major palaces, but also at secondary centers or localities within them. Monitoring of feasting was also important within the hierarchies of bureaucratic attention. As Palaima notes, feasting was an activity in which the *wanax* was centrally involved. Furthermore, in his discussion of the Ta series from Pylos, he observes that the inventorying of festal equipment fell under the purview of one of the most important scribes. On the assumption that different sets of texts are closely interrelated, he is able to look at the records of thrones and stools for details of the seating arrangement of high officials.

This textual information supports the interpretation of evidence from Tsoungiza by Dabney, Halstead, and Thomas in this volume. They argue that a feast held at Tsoungiza, a minor settlement in the territory of Mycenae, was connected with the palace or its representatives. Equally, the archaeological evidence from the Palace of Nestor presented here by Stocker and Davis confirms Palaima's textual exegesis. The authors show that the locations of feasting deposits around the palace, especially in the Archives Complex, relate to large-scale feasts sponsored by the state and probably also to the seating of highly ranked individuals.

If the centrality of the feast among the social practices of the Mycenaeans is evident, then we should inquire about the impact of feasting on the structure and organization of the society. The texts focus on feasting that was politically and economically significant enough to be recorded. Feasting, however, surely operated at levels and in areas outside the purview of the palaces. In this regard, the ethnographic study of feasting is particularly helpful. We learn that feasts occur throughout the year. They are performed by every social group—from the family to an entire society—by kin, moiety and sodality, and individuals acting through all kinds of personae. The occasions include any event from birth to death that people choose to celebrate. Clarke's list of occasions for Akha feasts is illustrative: to honor ancestors, mark the naming of a newborn, cure sickness, honor butchers, for workmen as a penalty, for purification, to mark a gate rebuilding, honor the Lords of the Earth, mark the harvest, announce the new year, on occasion of an annual drama, for a wedding, for a new house, to mark menopause, and on occasion of a funeral.[37] It is little wonder, in

36. Halstead and Isaakidou, forthcoming; see also Isaakidou et al. 2002.
37. Clarke 2001, p. 153.

consequence, that the reasons proposed for feasting have been equally varied, with different observers emphasizing different aspects of the feast.[38] Some have seen feasts as mechanisms for redistribution, others as means for demonstrating heritable holdings and status, while many claim that they demonstrate and amplify prestige. It is evident that feasts were not merely performed for practical and social benefit, but also for theological and liturgical reasons—in order, for example, to maintain the cosmic order. The result, however, as Hayden emphasizes, is practical,[39] and his list of nine benefits of feasting is a powerful statement about the degree to which this social practice permeates the many dimensions of human activities.[40] According to Hayden, feasts

1. mobilize labor;
2. create cooperative relationships within groups or, conversely, exclude other groups;
3. create cooperative alliances between social groups (including political support between households);
4. invest surpluses and generate profits;
5. attract desirable mates, labor, allies, or wealth exchanges by advertising the success of the group;
6. create political power (control over resources and labor) through the creation of a network of reciprocal debts;
7. extract surplus produce from the general populace for elite use;
8. solicit favors; and
9. compensate for transgressions.

We are not yet in the position of being able to identify which of the many possible reasons for feasting are those most relevant to Mycenaean society. Killen has argued that, among tablets from Pylos, Ta 711 refers to preparations for a feast upon the appointment of a new magistrate, and Un 138 "records the provisions for a banquet held 'on the initiation of the king' (*mu-jo-me-no e-pi wa-na-ka-te, /muiomenôi epi wanaktei/*)."[41] Palaima discusses other tablets that link feasting with the *wanax*, which is to be expected among the records of the palace, but surely other motivations for feasting occurred, both within the palace and among communities outside it.

In their study of the deposit from the rural settlement at Tsoungiza, Dabney, Halstead, and Thomas suggest that it was from a feast that was a community celebration marking a relationship between the community and the palace, but there is no strong evidence to indicate more precisely the reason for this feast. I had earlier proposed that the deposit at Tsoungiza represented a rural shrine,[42] but the faunal remains and analysis of the ceramics now strongly suggest a feast with a religious component, which raises a question about the identification of religious centers outside the palaces.[43] Evidence from the recently excavated shrine complex at Ayios Konstantinos on Methana may give reason to investigate whether feasts were regularly held at religious centers,[44] but we cannot yet be more precise about the nature of these centers. Nonetheless, this probability should cause excavators and researchers to look again at the remains from identified sanctuary sites for any evidence of feasting that might have been over-

38. Hayden 2001, pp. 28–35; Perodie 2001, pp. 187–188.

39. Hayden 2001, pp. 28–35.

40. Hayden 2001, pp. 29–30.

41. Killen 1998, p. 422; see also Piteros, Olivier, and Melena 1990, pp. 171–184; and Killen 1994.

42. Wright 1994, pp. 69–70.

43. Wright 1994, pp. 63–72.

44. Hamilakis and Konsolaki 2004.

looked. Places where this would be especially worthwhile are Mycenae, Tiryns, Asine, Amyklai, Epidauros, Delphi, Aigina, and Ayia Triada at Ayios Vassilios.

It remains difficult to identify the reasons for feasting, since, as Clarke's list above (p. 5) indicates, in most instances they are not specific to locales and many of his occasions that might take place in a domestic setting would be equally appropriate at a sanctuary. Sanctuaries are often the locales of special feasts, especially when the deity of the sanctuary is celebrated at a specific time of the year, such as the onset of the new year, the harvest, or some other natural phenomenon marked by celebration. The Linear B texts that record activities, dedications, offerings, and landholdings at shrines and to particular deities are therefore candidates for thinking about ways to specify the occasions of feasting.

Homer is of great value in this matter, as the often-cited festival to Poseidon in book III of the *Odyssey* illustrates. The epics also provide many specific occasions for feasting. As Sherratt observes in her contribution to this volume, feasting and fighting are the two most frequent activities described in the *Iliad* and the *Odyssey*. In her analysis we are confronted with the longstanding problem of whether we can use the epics to understand the Mycenaeans, and if so, how. The crux of this issue rests on whether or not there are sufficient similarities in the structures of Mycenaean and Homeric society to warrant comparison. Comparative study of feasting practice may be a particularly fruitful way of revealing societal structure. In both Mycenaean and Homeric society, feasting is predominantly a male activity in a warrior society. The warrior tradition was established during the Middle Bronze Age and was accentuated during the Early Mycenaean period (Middle Helladic III–Late Helladic II) as aggrandizing elites competed with each other and between different localities.[45] The symbolism employed by these groups bespeaks their roles as hunters and warriors and is reflected in the iconography shared among the peer-polity palace centers on the mainland and the islands.[46]

Feasting was a central practice in the process of sociopolitical evolution. As Sherratt's comparative examination of Mycenaean and Homeric feasting shows, many of the types of animals sacrificed and eaten, and the practices of cooking and types of equipment employed, are similar, but there remain significant differences, and she concludes that the feasts in Homer's epics primarily describe practices of the Early Iron Age. As she indicates, Homeric feasts are also celebrated on many different occasions, by different social groups, and with different levels of inclusion. In the studies presented here, there is little evidence to suggest such variety, nor can we say much about the different occasions for feasting. Instead, much of what we present is the residue of elite feasting. Nonetheless, progress has been made. Stocker and Davis suggest that at the Palace of Nestor at least two levels of feasting took place, one public and another private and also associated with important ritual practice. In my survey, I argue that the association of the bronze tripod with cooking game such as venison and boar was restricted to elite hunting groups who took their feasting equipment with them to their graves. We hope that future work will focus on refining our understanding of the feast. Some occasions that we might

45. Acheson 1999; Deger-Jalkotzy 1999; Davis and Bennet 1999.
46. Hiller 1999; Kontorli-Papadopoulou 1999; Laffineur 1999b.

search for are agricultural feasts (planting, harvest), initiation feasts, and funerary feasts, and we are challenged to imagine what kinds of evidence would best demonstrate the occurrence of these feasts and to develop methods for recovering such information.

Borgna grapples with issues of social structure and organization in detail in her comparative study of Minoan and Mycenaean traditions of feasting. It is her contention that feasting, especially its material representation in pottery selection and usage, actively promotes social structure and that archaeologists, through judicious examination of the evidence, can make strong statements about a society and its transformations. By analyzing many contexts on Crete from the Early Bronze Age through the end of the Late Bronze Age, she makes a strong argument that Minoan society was corporate in structure and that more vertical and hierarchical relationships became apparent through the influence of Mycenaean culture. Feasting in Mycenaean society, she argues, was from the beginning focused on individual reciprocity among aggrandizing elites operating in competitive arenas. For this reason she believes that the customs of feasting and drinking associated with Mycenaean funerary practice reflect an exclusive practice among kin and social peers that is different from feasting in Crete. Of particular interest is Borgna's attention to the locales of feasting: interior and exterior, centralized and dispersed. These, she believes, can be recognized through the study of feasting contexts in settlements and in mortuary spaces. More attention to this issue in the different cultural settings of the Aegean and eastern Mediterranean would be valuable, as is demonstrated by Steel's discussion of the location of feasting debris in Cypriot contexts, in building X at Kalavasos-Ayios Dhimitrios and, especially, in the well deposits near the sanctuary at Kouklia.

Hayden's list of the potential benefits of feasting signifies the dynamic nature of the feast. The broad spectrum of categories covered by the list illustrates the central role that feasting has as a social activity in the formation and maintenance of societies, and thereby points to ways to explore both the evolution of a society as well as the social and cultural dynamics of the relations of power. In the essays that follow, these issues are broached in general terms. In my overview, I explore the ways in which tracing the development of feasting as a formal practice allows us to confront issues in the formation of a Mycenaean cultural identity. The observations I make are amplified by the studies of Cretan and Cypriot feasting practices by Borgna and Steel, who describe and interpret the evidence for "native" feasting practices on these islands before the advent of Mycenaean influence. The contrasts between traditional Minoan and Cypriot practices, on the one hand, and the Mycenaean feast, on the other, are also explored. Minoan feasting expresses the horizontal, group-reinforcing structure of Minoan communities; on Cyprus a more eclectic tradition seems to develop drawing from Anatolia, the Levant, and the Aegean. The authors' identification of Mycenaean elements in Minoan and Cypriot contexts reinforces the notion that the Mycenaean feast was an exclusive custom tied to competition for status and power among elites.

This last point is particularly evident in the study of the pottery, as Borgna argues, and as Steel illustrates in her discussion of the Cypriot attention to the Mycenaean krater. The krater, as a container for wine, strongly symbolizes the importance of drinking within these elite groups. It, like the drinking cup, became an icon of the warrior society of the Iron Age, with its codes of honor, as examined by Sherratt in her study of Homeric feasting. Through these studies, the evolving and changing form of feasting appears to be a sensitive gauge of changes in sociopolitical structure, and a useful way to think about continuity through periods of transformation, such as the postpalatial transition to the Iron Age (Late Helladic/Late Minoan IIIC through the Protogeometric period).

In terms of Mycenaean social structure, however, there is much more to explore. None of these papers, for example, considers the role of gender in feasting. The differentiation of social groups within palace society also needs more attention, as Stocker and Davis note in their study of feasting at the Palace of Nestor.[47] Furthermore, we should address questions about the organization and social divisions within such feasts, of other kinds of feasting, and of feasting not sponsored by the palace, and the methods for doing this are well within our grasp: careful documentation of context, collection of organic remains through sieving and flotation, analysis of soils, and biomolecular investigation for organic residues of comestibles.[48] In her contribution to the publication of the Sheffield Conference, Bendall pursues some of these issues through a spatial analysis of the areas of feasting and the varying contexts of pottery storage in different areas of the palace.[49] Both Borgna's and Steel's considerations of "native" Minoan and Cypriot traditions of feasting provide a context for thinking about the feast as an expression of identity and, as Borgna emphasizes, of the structural relations within a society. Here again, issues of power relations and gender are relevant and may be fruitfully explored in further research.

The contributions to this volume, therefore, do not represent a comprehensive survey of the practice of feasting in Mycenaean society or the many ways that feasting can be studied to provide insight into the society. They offer, nonetheless, powerful and richly detailed evidence from a variety of sources for Mycenaean feasting. The authors make it clear that feasting was an important activity from the beginning of Mycenaean society until its end and was fundamentally linked to the formation and maintenance of Mycenaean identity. They show how the practice of feasting evolved and, to some extent, how it differed (or how the importance of it differed) from locality to locality and region to region. Although our sources are strongly weighted in favor of Pylos and its territory, feasting seems to have been similarly constructed and practiced at other Mycenaean palace centers as well—certainly Knossos, Mycenae, and Thebes. The contrast of Mycenaean practices with those of cultures with whom the Mycenaeans were in contact confirms the general character of Mycenaean feasting and makes clear the way in which the manipulation of social practices is fundamental to the formation and maintenance of power relations within communities. Material culture in this sense is a sensitive and extremely rich source of information about ancient societies and the specific social practices that define their structure and identity.

In closing, I wish to thank the Institute for Aegean Prehistory for providing funds to bring the participants in the AIA colloquium to Philadelphia in 2002. I thank Tracey Cullen for inviting us to submit these

47. See also Isaakidou et al. 2002.
48. Tzedakis and Martlew 1999; McGovern et al. 1999; McGovern 2003.
49. Bendall, forthcoming.

papers for publication in *Hesperia;* she has moved this project along with patience and a firm hand. She and her colleagues at the American School of Classical Studies Publications Office have brought a level of professionalism and attention to detail that uphold high standards unusual in this age, though long a tradition at *Hesperia.* Jeremy Rutter and Brian Hayden, the *Hesperia* reviewers, have held us to the highest scholarly standards: if these papers succeed in their arguments and have merit in their presentation, it is due in large part to the thoughtful and exceptionally detailed attention they paid to the manuscripts in draft form. We are grateful to all of the above for their help in improving each offering. Finally, to all of the participants, I express my personal thanks for their joining in this undertaking and making their contributions reflect the work of the group.

REFERENCES

Acheson, P. 1999. "The Role of Force in the Development of Early Mycenaean Polities," in Laffineur 1999a, pp. 97–104.

Bendall, L. M. Forthcoming. "Fit for a King? Hierarchy, Exclusion, Aspiration, and Desire in the Social Structure of Mycenaean Banqueting," in Halstead and Barrett, forthcoming.

Bennet, J. 2001. "Agency and Bureaucracy: Thoughts on the Nature and Extent of Administration in Bronze Age Pylos," in Voutsaki and Killen 2001, pp. 25–37.

Binford, L. 1981. *Bones: Ancient Men and Modern Myths,* New York.

Branigan, K., ed. 1998. *Cemetery and Society in the Aegean Bronze Age* (Sheffield Studies in Aegean Archaeology 1), Sheffield.

———. 2001. *Urbanism in the Aegean Bronze Age* (Sheffield Studies in Aegean Archaeology 4), Sheffield.

Chadwick, J. 1958. "The Mycenaean Filing System," *BICS* 5, pp. 1–5.

———. 1987. *Linear B and Related Scripts* (Reading the Past 1), London.

Clarke, M. 2001. "Akha Feasting: An Ethnoarchaeological Perspective," in Dietler and Hayden 2001, pp. 144–167.

Comaroff, J., and J. Comaroff. 1992. *Ethnography and the Historical Imagination,* Boulder.

Crossland, R. A., and A. Birchall, eds. 1974. *Bronze Age Migrations in the Aegean: Archaeological and Linguistic Problems in Greek Prehistory,* Park Ridge, N.J.

Davis, J. L., and J. Bennet. 1999. "Making Mycenaeans: Warfare, Territorial Expansion, and Representations of the Other in the Pylian Kingdom," in Laffineur 1999a, pp. 105–120.

Deger-Jalkotzy, S. 1999. "Military Prowess and Social Status in Mycenaean Greece," in Laffineur 1999a, pp. 121–131.

Dietler, M., and B. Hayden, eds. 2001. *Feasts: Archaeological and Ethnographic Perspectives on Food, Politics, and Power,* Washington, D.C.

Giddens, A. 1984. *The Constitution of Society,* Berkeley.

Hägg, R., and N. Marinatos, eds. 1984. *The Minoan Thalassocracy: Myth and Reality. Proceedings of the Third International Symposium at the Swedish Institute in Athens* (*SkrAth* 4°, 32), Stockholm.

Hägg, R., and G. C. Nordquist, eds. 1990. *Celebrations of Death and Divinity in the Bronze Age Argolid. Proceedings of the Sixth International Symposium at the Swedish Institute at Athens* (*SkrAth* 4°, 40), Stockholm.

Halstead, P., and J. C. Barrett, eds. Forthcoming. *Food, Cuisine, and Society in Prehistoric Greece* (Sheffield Studies in Aegean Archaeology 5), Sheffield.

Halstead, P., and V. Isaakidou. Forthcoming. "Faunal Evidence for Feasting: Burnt Offerings from the Palace of Nestor at Pylos," in Halstead and Barrett, forthcoming.

Hamilakis, Y., and E. Konsolaki. 2004. "Pigs for the Gods: Burnt Animal Sacrifices as Embodied Rituals at a Mycenaean Sanctuary," *QJA* 23, pp. 135–151.

Hayden, B. 2001. "Fabulous Feasts: A Prolegomenon to the Importance of Feasting," in Dietler and Hayden 2001, pp. 23–64.

Hiller, S. 1999. "Scenes of Warfare and Combat in the Arts of Aegean Late Bronze Age: Reflections on Typology and Development," in Laffineur 1999a, pp. 319–330.

Hodder, I. 1991. *Reading the Past: Current Approaches to Interpretation in Archaeology,* New York.

Isaakidou, V., P. Halstead, J. Davis, and S. Stocker. 2002. "Burnt Animal Sacrifice in Late Bronze Age Greece: New Evidence from the Mycenaean 'Palace of Nestor,' Pylos," *Antiquity* 76, pp. 86–92.

Killen, J. T. 1992. "Observations on the Thebes Sealings," in *Mykenaïka. Actes du IXe Colloque international sur les textes mycéniens et égéens organisé par le Centre de l'antiquité grecque et romaine de la Fondation hellénique des recherches scientifiques et l'École française d'Athènes* (*BCH* Suppl. 25), ed. J.-P. Olivier, Paris, pp. 365–380.

———. 1994. "Thebes Sealings, Knossos Tablets, and Mycenaean State Banquets," *BICS* 39, pp. 67–84.

———. 1998. "The Pylos Ta Tablets Revisited," pp. 421–422, in F. Rougemont and J.-P. Olivier, eds., "Recherches récentes en épigraphie créto-mycénienne," *BCH* 122, pp. 403–443.

Kontorli-Papadopoulou, L. 1999. "Fresco Fighting-Scenes as Evidence for Warlike Activities in the LBA Aegean," in Laffineur 1999a, pp. 331–339.

Laffineur, R., ed. 1987. *Thanatos: Les coutumes funéraires en Égée à l'âge du Bronze. Actes du Colloque de Liège* (*Aegaeum* 1), Liège.

———. 1999a. *Polemos: Le contexte guerrier en Égée à l'âge du Bronze. Actes de la 7e Rencontre égéenne international, Université de Liège* (*Aegaeum* 19), Liège.

———. 1999b. "De Mycènes à Homère: Réflexions sur l'iconographie

guerrière mycénienne," in Laffineur 1999a, pp. 313–317.

Laffineur, R., and R. Hägg, eds. 2001. *Potnia: Deities and Religion in the Aegean Bronze Age. Proceedings of the 8th International Aegean Conference, Göteborg* (*Aegaeum* 22), Liège.

Laffineur, R., and W.-D. Niemeier, eds. 1995. *Politeia: Society and State in the Aegean Bronze Age. Proceedings of the 5th International Aegean Conference, Heidelberg* (*Aegaeum* 12), Liège.

Leach, E. 1977. "A View from the Bridge," in *Archaeology and Anthropology: Areas of Mutual Interest* (*BAR* Suppl. 19), ed. M. Spriggs, Oxford, pp. 161–176.

Lissarrague, F. 1990. *The Aesthetics of the Greek Banquet: Images of Wine and Ritual,* trans. A. Szegedy-Maszak, Princeton.

McGovern, P. E. 2003. *Ancient Wine: The Search for the Origins of Viticulture,* Princeton.

McGovern, P. E., D. L. Glusker, R. A. Moreau, A. Nuñez, C. W. Beck, E. Simpson, E. D. Butrym, L. J. Exner, and E. C. Stout. 1999. "A Feast Fit for King Midas," *Nature* 402, pp. 863–864.

Murray, O., ed. 1990. *Sympotica: A Symposium on the Symposion,* Oxford.

O'Connor, T. P. 1998. "On the Difficulty of Detecting Seasonal Slaughterings of Sheep," *Environmental Archaeology* 3, pp. 5–11.

Olivier, J.-P. 1967. *Les scribes de Cnossos: Essai de classement des archives d'un palais mycénien* (Incunabula graeca 17), Rome.

Orme, B. 1981. *Anthropology for Archaeologists: An Introduction,* London.

Palaima, T. G. 1984. "Scribal Organization and Palatial Activity," in Shelmerdine and Palaima 1984, pp. 31–39.

———. 1987. "Mycenaean Seals and Sealings in Their Economic and Administrative Contexts," in *Tractata Mycenaea. Proceedings of the Eighth International Colloquium on Mycenaean Studies, Ohrid,* ed. P. H. Ilievski and L. Crepajac, Skopje, pp. 249–266.

———. 1988. *The Scribes of Pylos* (Incunabula graeca 87), Rome.

———. 1990. "Origin, Development, Transition, and Transformation: The Purposes and Techniques of Administration in Minoan and Mycenaean Society," in *Aegean Seals, Sealings, and Administration. Proceedings of the NEH-Dickson Conference, Austin* (*Aegaeum* 5), ed. T. G. Palaima, Liège, pp. 83–104.

———. 1996. "Sealings as Links in an Administrative Chain," in *Administration in Ancient Societies. Proceedings of Session 218 of the 13th International Congress of Anthropological and Ethnological Sciences, Mexico City,* ed. P. Ferioli, E. Fiandra, and G. G. Fissore, Turin, pp. 37–66.

———. 2000a. "Transactional Vocabulary in Linear B Tablet and Sealing Administration," in *Administrative Documents in the Aegean and Their Near Eastern Counterparts,* ed. M. Perna, Turin, pp. 261–276.

———. 2000b. "The Palaeography of Mycenaean Inscribed Sealings from Thebes and Pylos: Their Place within the Mycenaean Administrative System and Their Links with the Extra-Palatial Sphere," in *Minoisch-mykenische Glyptik: Stil, Ikonographie, Funktion. V. Internationales Siegel-Symposium, Marburg* (*CMS* Beiheft 6), ed. W. Müller, Berlin, pp. 219–238.

Pappa, M., P. Halstead, K. Kotsakis, and D. Urem-Kotsou. Forthcoming. "Evidence for Large-Scale Feasting at Late Neolithic Makriyalos, N. Greece," in Halstead and Barrett, forthcoming.

Patrik, L. 1985. "Is There an Archaeological Record?" in *Advances in Archaeological Method and Theory* 8, ed. M. Schiffer, Orlando, pp. 27–62.

Pauketat, T. R., L. S. Kelly, G. F. Fritz, N. H. Lopinot, S. Elias, and E. Hargrave. 2002. "The Residues of Feasting and Public Ritual at Early Cahokia," *AmerAnt* 67, pp. 257–279.

Perodie, J. R. 2001. "Feasting for Prosperity: A Study of Southern Northwest Coast Feasting," in Dietler and Hayden 2001, pp. 185–214.

Piteros, C., J.-P. Olivier, and J. L. Melena. 1990. "Les inscriptions en linéaire B des nodules de Thèbes

(1982): La fouille, les documents, les possibilités d'interprétation," *BCH* 114, pp. 103–184.

Schmandt-Besserat, D. 2001. "Feasting in the Ancient Near East," in Dietler and Hayden 2001, pp. 391–403.

Shanks, M., and C. Tilley. 1987. *Reconstructing Archaeology: Theory and Practice,* Cambridge.

Shelmerdine, C. W., and T. G. Palaima, eds. 1984. *Pylos Comes Alive: Industry and Administration in a Mycenaean Palace. Papers of a Symposium,* New York.

Speth, J. D. 1983. *Bison Kills and Bone Counts: Decision Making by Ancient Hunters,* Chicago.

Tzedakis, Y., and H. Martlew, eds. 1999. *Minoans and Mycenaeans: Flavours of Their Time,* Athens.

Ventris, M., and J. Chadwick. 1973. *Documents in Mycenaean Greek,* 2nd ed., Cambridge.

Voutsaki, S., and J. Killen, eds. 2001. *Economy and Politics in the Mycenaean Palace States* (Cambridge Philological Society, Suppl. 27), Cambridge.

Wright, J. C. 1994. "The Spatial Configuration of Belief: The Archaeology of Mycenaean Religion," in *Placing the Gods: Sanctuaries and Sacred Space in Ancient Greece,* ed. S. E. Alcock and R. Osborne, Oxford, pp. 37–78.

CHAPTER 2

A Survey of Evidence
for Feasting in
Mycenaean Society

James C. Wright

ABSTRACT

The study of feasting on the Greek mainland during the Middle and Late Bronze Age provides insights into the nature of Mycenaean society. Grave goods demonstrate changes in feasting and drinking practices and their importance in the formation of an elite identity. Cooking, serving, and drinking vessels are also recorded in Linear B documents. Feasting scenes appear in the frescoes of Crete and the islands, and the Mycenaeans adapt this tradition for representation in their palaces. Feasting iconography is also found in vase painting, particularly in examples of the Pictorial Style. Mycenaean feasting is an expression of the hierarchical sociopolitical structure of the palaces.

INTRODUCTION

In this paper I survey the artifactual evidence for Mycenaean feasting, including pottery, bronze vessels, frescoes, Linear B ideograms, and painted representations on pottery and other terracotta artifacts.[1] There is no generally accepted definition of feasting: some scholars prefer a definition that encompasses most occasions of the consumption of food and drink; others argue for a more restrictive one.[2] For the purposes of this investigation, I define feasting as the formal ceremony of communal eating and drinking to celebrate significant occasions. I exclude the quotidian partaking of food and drink that is carried out for biological or fundamental social reasons, such as eating with family or casually with acquaintances, friends, and colleagues—activities that do not include any perceived reciprocity. Material evidence for either eating or drinking may indicate feasting, but one must scrutinize the evidence closely to determine whether the remains are the result of formal and ritual activities not involving feasting. For example,

1. I am indebted to the two *Hesperia* reviewers, Brian Hayden and Jeremy Rutter, for their sharp-eyed criticism and many excellent suggestions for changes and improvements. I thank Lyvia Morgan for insightful comments and useful bibliography, and Maria Shaw for comments and encouragement and for providing Figure 8. I am also grateful to Elisabetta Borgna, Mary Dabney, Paul Halstead, Yannis Hamilakis, and Dimitri Nakassis for suggestions and help.

2. Dietler and Hayden 2001b, pp. 3–4; Clarke 2001, pp. 150–151.

people frequently use vessels to make offerings to deities or perform rituals, such as toasting or leaving food remains for the dead, and these vessels are not *a priori* evidence for feasting, unless the remains are so substantial that they indicate unusual consumption of food or drink.[3] I intend to argue closely on the basis of good evidence for feasting as a common but variably performed ritual, remains from which are recoverable by archaeologists.

It is not my purpose to examine the organic residues and archaeological deposits of feasts, especially since that is the subject of two other chapters in this volume.[4] Instead, the information collected for this research is that which to our eyes presents consistent patterns of form and decoration, of assemblage, and of context and deposition, evidence that represents a style peculiar to the practice of feasting and formal drinking during the era we define as Mycenaean. By "Mycenaean" I mean the assemblage of artifacts that constitutes the characteristic archaeological culture that originates on the mainland of Greece in the late Middle Bronze Age, finds its fullest expression in the palaces during Late Helladic (LH) IIIA–B, and can be traced through the postpalatial LH IIIC period.[5] Different scholars will define differently the chronological and geographical range of this culture, but probably will not disagree that it takes recognizable form about 1600–1550 B.C. and ends about 1100–1050 B.C.; is characterized by settlements with palaces and writing in Linear B; and in its broadest extent encompasses coastal Thessaly, central Greece, the Peloponnese, Crete, the Aegean islands, and perhaps some settlements on the western Anatolian coast.

In this chapter I necessarily consider evidence from Crete and the Aegean islands, since much of what we characterize as Mycenaean is derived from the earlier palace-based societies of Middle and Late Bronze Age Crete and the island cultures of the Aegean. Identifying the formative processes through which these were incorporated into Mycenaean culture, however, has proven difficult and confusing.[6] The essays by Borgna and Steel in this volume treat the subject of the Mycenaean feast on Crete and Cyprus, where previous indigenous traditions of feasting can be documented. The authors confront the problem of the adaptation of distinctive, perhaps essential, elements of the Mycenaean feast during periods of strong Mycenaean influence on these islands. These discussions consider the feasting tradition as an elite one, and that is no less the case for this study. One can argue that the consistency of the elite practice of feasting creates a richer and more patterned material record than that produced by nonelite practice.

Feasting, by virtue of its bringing people together in the biological act of eating, is a social activity that binds a group through sharing. Feasting is also a formal ceremonial practice that differentiates host from guest, and youth from elder, and affirms other status distinctions. As a social practice feasting is dynamic, and archaeologists attempting to reconstruct a feasting tradition must also pay attention to the sociopolitical trajectory of the society under study. I argue here that feasting is an important ceremony instrumental in the forging of cultural identity. Most explanations of the

3. Although, as a number of the authors in this volume argue (see esp. the chapters by Borgna and Palaima), libations and offerings to deities and mortuary rituals involving drinking vessels may not be distinguishable from the practice of feasting, in either the artifactual record or texts. See below, n. 59.

4. See the chapters by Stocker and Davis; and Dabney, Halstead, and Thomas.

5. There is a long history to the term "Mycenaean," from Furtwängler and Loeschcke's use of it (1886; Furtwängler 1879) to Davis and Bennet's recent examination (1999, p. 112). For its origins, see Dickinson 1977, pp. 15–16; the issue was also recently reviewed by Bennet 1999.

6. See Vermeule 1975, pp. 1–6, 50–51; Dickinson 1977, pp. 15–16, 107–110; Kilian-Dirlmeier 1986, pp. 159, 196–198; Kilian 1988, pp. 292–293; Wright 1995b.

formation of pre- and protohistoric Aegean cultures are based on assumptions of degree of interaction, particularly through modes of production and exchange, including exchanges of information.[7] Hodder, however, argues that in general such interaction models have been used mechanistically and that the concentration on economic transactions has resulted in an inadequate account of cultural formation and change.[8] He maintains that models of social identity and interaction better explain the sources of and processes behind cultural formation and change. Through ethnoarchaeological studies he demonstrates that expressions of group identity as manifest in material culture are highly variable and subject to many different impetuses, particularly social strategies and conceptual frameworks that range across various orders of sociopolitical integration.[9] These identities are manipulated and mutable and result in material expressions that are ephemeral, yet loaded with meaning. Consequently, the degree of consistency and distribution of material assemblages cannot be assessed merely according to mechanical articulations of economic interactions, but instead have to be understood as the material displays of other kinds of social activity, many of which relate to the expression and reaffirmation of individual identity and membership in groups. Feasting is one such activity.

Archaeologists attempt to define a culture by "reading" the material remains of groups who have adopted a stylistic vocabulary representing their common social customs.[10] This material expression comes into being largely as a social process that evolves as it is practiced. Feasting is a fundamental social practice that marks most celebrations of life stages and natural cycles when people gather and in varying ways display, reaffirm, and change their identities as individuals and as members of groups. It is an integral part of ritual and religious practice, occurring nearly universally as a component of other activities; the universality of its practice underscores its importance in the formation of identity.[11] Wiessner has provided insight into the process of identity formation in several ethnographic studies that examine the social meanings and uses of style.[12] Particularly useful is her distinction between two forms of display that lead to the formation of identity: "assertive" and "emblemic." Assertive display represents the active process of identity formation and is concerned with the activities of leaders, or individuals competing for leadership, who use objects as a part of their competitive display. Emblemic display results when a common set of symbolic expressions is achieved and becomes an expression of group identity.[13]

Identities are formed, expressed, affirmed, and changed through many social activities, especially those that bring groups together for celebration, which are usually accompanied by feasting.[14] As Wiessner points out:

> Feasting involves food sharing and food distribution. Food sharing appears to have its roots in the parent-child relationship and thus can be a way of expressing affection and extending familial behavior to distant or non-kin in order to bond larger groups. By contrast, food distribution, which often requires returns at a later date, creates temporary imbalance between food donors and recipients and permits the construction of inequality.[15]

7. Dickinson 1977; Cherry and Davis 1982; Bennet and Galaty 1997, pp. 90–96; Bennet 1999.

8. Hodder 1982, pp. 8–9, 185–190, 202–203; cf. Earle and Ericson 1977; Plog 1976; Wobst 1977.

9. See, e.g., Hodder 1982.

10. Hodder 1978, pp. 185–229; and see, e.g., Baines and Yoffee 1998.

11. Other activities that relate to identity formation and often incorporate feasting include hunting, warfare, craft activities, worship, agriculture, and animal husbandry.

12. See, e.g., Wiessner 1983, 1989.

13. Wiessner 1983, pp. 257–258.

14. On ways that cuisine expresses cultural identity, see Elias 1978; Loraux 1981; Goody 1982; Murray 1990, 1996; Schmitt Pantel 1990; Dietler 2001; Hayden 2001a.

15. Wiessner 2001, p. 116.

Identity, difference, and obligation are primary social manifestations of cuisine, and, as many scholars have observed, the construction of rules of etiquette further refines these distinctions.[16]

Davis and Bennet have recently recommended that to answer the question of who the Mycenaeans are, we examine "the mechanisms that lay behind the creation of the Mycenaeans."[17] Their conclusion is that "the formation of a Mycenaean material culture appears to have been the result of a process, whereby specific regional traditions achieved supra-regional prominence and were elevated gradually to a status as the dominant styles accepted by the elite who governed Mycenaean kingdoms."[18] Missing from this observation, however, is a specific anatomy of this process at work. Feasting is a very significant activity in the formation of Mycenaean culture because, as noted above, it is nearly always linked to other social activities, whether hunting or harvesting, worship or initiation. Feasting as a preeminent social celebration consistently provides an arena for the display of styles. In part this is because it is effective in encompassing all members of a social group and even those outside it, while still reserving special places for subgroups (especially elites) to differentiate themselves. In other words, feasting allows for the reinforcement of egalitarian horizontal relationships while simultaneously facilitating the construction of hieratic or hierarchical and vertical ones.[19]

As Hayden points out, feasts have many practical benefits: creating cooperative relationships, alliances, and political power; mobilizing labor; and extracting and investing surpluses.[20] All of these activities of feasting are instrumental to the formation of complex societies. The communicative aspect of this process of social formation involves the creation and reproduction of styles that symbolize the dominant group, not merely through monosemic emblems but also through polysemic ones that represent salient activities and structural relations of the group. These styles are expressed iconographically and are part of the construction of a society's cosmology, of the proper relationships among people, society, and nature.[21]

The process of identity formation is an act of recording and, in stylistic terms, of constructing an iconographic synthesis, as Panofsky defined the phrase.[22] Such a synthesis necessarily excludes certain information, particularly aspects of activities not selected for inclusion in emblemic display, since recording is a proprietary act governed by social custom, by sociopolitical and ideological hierarchies, and prescribed by convention, tradition, dogma, and ritual action. In this way, as Davis and Bennet note, "specific regional traditions achieved supra-regional prominence,"[23] though the resulting "dominant styles" are not merely passively accepted, but rather utilized and actively practiced, and hence inherently mutable. Consequently, what the modern observer can hope to achieve through the analysis of the archaeologically recovered material and written record of feasting is an

16. See, e.g., Elias 1978; Douglas and Isherwood 1979; Goody 1982; Wright, forthcoming a.

17. Davis and Bennet 1999, p. 113.

18. Davis and Bennet 1999, p. 114; cf. Baines and Yoffee (1998, pp. 233–236), who argue that elites control cultural reproduction through the creation and reproduction of style.

19. Feinman 1998, p. 107; Dietler 1999, pp. 141–142; Hayden 2001a, pp. 28–42.

20. Hayden 2001a, pp. 29–30. For a thorough analysis of the ethnographic evidence, see Hayden 1995.

21. Turner 1967; Bourdieu 1980, pp. 52–79, 122–134. For a critique, see Bell 1992, pp. 187–196; for a discussion of the role of style in states and civilizations, see Baines and Yoffee 1998, pp. 252–259.

22. Panofsky 1939, pp. 3–17.

23. Davis and Bennet 1999, p. 114.

understanding, however imperfect, of an iconography characteristic primarily of Mycenaean palace society. Aspects of feasting that are not specifically controlled or influenced by the palaces might also be apparent, but they are harder to discern, in large part for lack of redundancy in the archaeological record. A good example is provided in the chapter in this volume by Dabney, Halstead, and Thomas concerning a deposit at Tsoungiza, the interpretation of which depends in part on the artifactual connection with objects known primarily from palatial contexts. The variability and ubiquitous nature of feasting in any society means that feasts will leave variable archaeological traces; only those that are created through repetition and the relatively consistent utilization of identifiable remains are left for us to interpret with a high degree of probability.[24]

Representation of feasting may be understood as part of the very practice of feasting. It is also a part of the tradition that the Mycenaeans drew upon from Neopalatial Crete and the islands of the Aegean. An iconography of feasting in the palaces may have developed by LH IIIA but is only fully developed in the LH IIIB frescoes of the main building at Pylos (see below). By examining the development of this iconography, we will understand better the processes through which, over generations of interaction, elite groups came to control and administer the palace centers. As Davis and Bennet state, "Mycenaean material culture came to define the elite of those palaces and of the territories they controlled and influenced."[25]

Largely missing from this analysis is evidence for the multiple forms of feasting, and the social and ritual nuances of the practice of feasting that transpired during the Late Bronze Age in the Aegean. Such information will probably be better preserved in feasting deposits, as Pauketat and his colleagues have recently demonstrated for feasting at Cahokia in the lower Mississippi Valley.[26] But it may well be that by sketching the outlines of feasting as a general phenomenon of Mycenaean palace society, directions for future research will be indicated that may lead to a more detailed and subtle understanding of this fundamental social act.

DRINKING RITUALS

The evidence for drinking rituals is preserved in archaeological contexts where an abundance of drinking vessels or the deposition of special vessels indicates extraordinary activity, for example, cups and chalices from the sanctuary at Kato Syme on Crete (Fig. 1).[27] Special vessels, some of which are for drinking, were found in the mortuary context of the Shaft Graves at Mycenae. Their intended function, however, is not clear, since their deposition may be attributed to a number of intentions, including the request of the deceased to inter them, the fulfillment of ritual obligations associated with the afterlife, or as tokens given by the burying group, perhaps representing the deceased's status. There are two ways to decide among these possibilities: to establish whether the deposition of drinking vessels (or other vessels associated with feasting) was a customary mortuary practice of the group being studied[28] and to search for possible symbolic meanings of the vessels, both as iconographic conventions and as icons within a particular cultural activity.[29] A suitably large and chronologically broad set of comparanda is necessary to determine customary mortuary practices,

24. See Clarke 2001, pp. 158–162; Knight 2001, p. 321.

25. Davis and Bennet 1999, p. 115.

26. Pauketat et al. 2002.

27. Lebessi and Muhly 1987; 1990, pp. 324–327.

28. Hamilakis 1998.

29. Panofsky 1939, pp. 3–17; on the symbolism of drinking, see Jellinek 1977; Dietler 1990.

Figure 1. Pottery chalice from Kato Syme. After Lebessi and Muhly 1990, p. 325, fig. 11:a

and their variation over time. The discovery of symbolic meaning is complicated both by the fragmentary preservation of representations and by the probability that vessels are part of a variety of practices with different meanings, not all of which involve drinking and eating.

To identify a customary set of artifacts, I restrict myself here to the examination of a Mycenaean drinking service formed at the beginning of the Late Bronze Age. Its appearance is marked by the merging of indigenous pottery forms with exogenous ones, and by a shift from pottery to metal. The acquisition of imported pottery, especially drinking vessels, is a sign of differentiated social status. The acquisition of exotic items within Mycenaean society was centered primarily on sources in the Aegean, especially Crete. Even before the onset of the Middle Bronze Age, imported cups and jugs appeared at settlements such as Lerna. The preference for drinking vessels in these contexts might have resulted from practices of competitive drinking in which display would have enhanced social standing.[30] The data unfortunately provide neither quantitative measures nor consistent contexts to demonstrate this case.

In mortuary contexts of the later Middle Bronze Age, drinking vessels predominate (Table 1). Because of the heterogeneity of local customs during this period, numerous morphological and decorative variations can be identified, but the predominance of cups and jugs and the preference for specific drinking vessels (kantharos, straight-sided cup, and goblet)

30. In the settlement of Lerna, abundant evidence exists for exotic drinking and serving vessels from the very beginning of the Middle Helladic (MH) period, significantly from the House of the Post Holes, with six Minoan imports (Zerner 1978, pp. 60–62); and deposit D 602, outside this house, contained Minoanizing cups and a Minoan jug. Deposit D 597, which is described as a street outside house BS, disclosed a fine Minoanizing cup with barbotine decoration, while house BS itself contained a Minoanizing angular cup, three Minoan imports of Middle Minoan (MM) IA date, and two Cycladic imported bowls (Zerner 1978, pp. 66–74). Floor 2 of house BS contained both Minoanizing and Minoan imports—mostly cups, but also a barbotine jar and a notable number of other craft items (Zerner 1978, pp. 75–81; see also the finds from the courtyard and street, pp. 88–94). The various MH I occupation levels of house 24 revealed a variety of Minoanizing and Minoan pottery along with other craft items (Zerner 1978, pp. 99–109). Rooms 44 and 45 within the complex of house 98A date to MH I and contained Minoan imports (Zerner 1978, pp. 121–126), while house 98A of late Lerna VA contained a Minoan collar-necked jar in room 1 and a Cycladic bowl in room 2 (Zerner 1978, pp. 112–119). Unfortunately, there is insufficient published information about the domestic deposits of the later phases of the Middle Bronze Age to ascertain whether this fondness for exotic items continued within these household areas or in the settlement in general.

TABLE 1. DISTRIBUTION OF MH VESSELS AT SELECTED MAINLAND CEMETERIES

Legend (symbol size): ●=1 ●=2 ●=3 ●=4 ●=5 ●=6 ●=7 ●=8 ●=9

Site and Burial	Open Forms						Closed Forms		
	Generalized cup	Straight-sided cup	Shallow cup	"Paneled" cup	Goblet	Kantharos form	Jar form	Bridge-spouted jar	Jug form
Asine									
B12						●			
B15	●				●	●			
B30	●								●
B32	●					●			●
LT-18	●								●
1971-2									●
1971-10						●			
1971-15	●					●	●		
1971-3	●	●		●	●	●	●	●	●
Argos									
Gamma 82	●					●			●
Delta 161	●					●			●
Delta 1, 132	●	●							●
Delta 1,137	●				●				●
Gamma 22	●				●				●
Gamma 61	●	●							●
Gamma 2	●	●				●			●
Gamma 27	●								●
Gamma 29	●	●	●		●		●		
Prosymna									
I	●						●		●
III					●				
IV	●				●				●
XIII	●				●				
XVI	●								●
XVII	●								●
XVIII	●								●
XIX	●	●							●
XX	●	●							●
XXI	●	●	●				●		●
XXIV							●		●
XXVI									●
XXVIII						●			
XXXI	●					●			●
Corinth									
1	●								●
2	●								●
3							●		
5	●					●	●		●
6									●
7	●								
8	●					●			●
9						●			
10		●							
11	●								●
13	●								●

Sources: Asine: *Asine* II, pp. 33–63; Nordquist 1987, pp. 128–136; Argos: Dietz 1991; Prosymna: Blegen 1937, pp. 30–50; Corinth (North Cemetery): *Corinth* XIII, pp. 6–12.

Figure 2. Gold kantharos from Mycenae, Grave Circle A, shaft grave IV. Photo A. Frantz (AT 308), courtesy American School of Classical Studies at Athens

probably indicate a concern to provide the deceased with vessels needed for drinking.[31] In burial assemblages at the end of the Middle and beginning of the Late Bronze Age, such as grave 1971-3 at Asine and the Shaft Graves at Mycenae, these indigenous forms are increasingly standardized morphologically and decoratively, and imported vessels as well as vessels influenced in shape and form by foreign ones are also found (Tables 2, 3). This transition is accompanied by a replacement of pottery in high-status burials by luxurious vessels made by specialized craftspersons working in gold, silver, and bronze, as indicated in Tables 4–6. Examples include a gold kantharos (Fig. 2) and "Nestor's cup" from grave IV of Grave Circle A at Mycenae;[32] the latter combines the Vapheio cup shape, the chalice stem, and the handles of a kantharos. From the same tomb comes a composite Helladic-Minoan silver goblet, with its carinated shape and a Minoan niello floral scene (Fig. 3).[33]

I addressed this phenomenon in an earlier study, in which I emphasized that this shift reflects

> an amplification of traditions which were already a part of indigenous behavior; thus, foreign objects are introduced alongside prestigious items of local origin. Accompanying these objects must be a change of behavior that explains their presence. . . . The prestige enhancement that accompanies the introduction of foreign but not altogether new ceremonies of drinking, and the social distance expressed by the luxurious vessels used in the ceremonies are fundamental aspects of the emergence of chiefly groups at developing Mycenaean centers. Hybrid vessels incorporate all these elements and document the syncretistic nature of early Mycenaean social and political ideology.[34]

I was concerned in that paper to show that the emergence of a service of this type resulted from the desire of elites to display their elevated status and from efforts to consolidate power, and I compared this process to the adoption of Greek and Etruscan drinking customs by the Celts as demonstrated by Dietler and Arnold.[35] This issue has also been explored by Clark and Blake in a study of the adoption of foreign ceramics by aggrandizing elites in Lowland Mesoamerica during the Early Formative period.[36]

31. Wright, forthcoming a.
32. Davis 1977, pp. 183–186, cat. no. 63.
33. Davis 1977, pp. 208–220, cat. no. 83; for gardens, see Shaw 1993.
34. Wright 1995a, pp. 294–295; see also Palmer 1994, 1995.
35. Dietler 1990, pp. 375–380, 382–390; Arnold 1999.
36. Clark and Blake 1994.

TABLE 2. DISTRIBUTION OF POTTERY IN GRAVE CIRCLE B

Burial	Open Forms — Cup forms							Kantharoi		Closed Forms — Jar forms								Jug forms						
	Generalized cup form	Straight-sided matt-ptd	Straight-sided "Minoan"	Conical/paneled	Semiglobular matt-ptd	Semiglobular "Minoan"	Goblet	Shallow w/o foot matt-ptd	Carinated with foot	Generalized jar form	Plain jar	Hole-mouth and spouted	LH I jar	"Cycladic" jar	Hydria & stamnos	Amphora	Amphoriskos	Generalized jug form	LH I squat	Spouted jar/jug	"Cycladic" spouted jug	"Minoan" spouted jug	Cut-away spout matt-ptd	Askos
Z male weapons		●					●	●												●			●	
H male weapons	●						●	●															●	
I early		●						●															●	
I late male weapons							●					●			●	●		●						
Λ 2, S. side																							●	
Λ 2, N. side	●									●														
Ξ early							●		●									●						
Ξ late							●									●		●						●
P	●						●	●																
B male weapons							●					●		●		●								
E fill				●			●																	
Λ fill			●				●								●									
Λ male weapons	●			●			●								●			●						
N roof							●				●						●				●			●
Y female							●								●		●							●
MYC 58 female		●		●	●		●		●	●													●	
Δ fill	●						●								●			●						
A male weapons							●		●						●			●					●	
E inside, later															●									
K								●							●								●	
Λ 1								●							●									
N later male															●									
Π							●											●					●	
K-112								●							●								●	
M early	●						●			●	●	●				●								●
N							●																	
Γ male weapons		●	●	●	●	●	●	●	●	●					●		●	●	●		●	●	●	●
Δ							●						●	●	●			●						
O				●			●	●				●			●	●								●

Sources: Mylonas 1973; Graziadio 1988.

TABLE 3. DISTRIBUTION OF POTTERY IN GRAVE CIRCLE A

Burial	Open Forms — Cup forms					Kantharoi			Closed Forms — Jar forms									Jug forms			
	One-handled carinated	Straight-sided	Conical/paneled	Semiglob., everted rim	Goblet	Shallow without foot	Carinated with foot	Carinated with pedestal	Hemispherical	Hole-mouth	Krater	Spherical bridge-spouted	One-handled squat	Alabastron	Piriform	Hydria & stamnos	Amphora/amphoriskos	One-handled	Spouted jar/jug	Cut-away spout	Askos
I	●			●		●			●						●					●	
II										●			●							●	
III				●									●					●		●	
IV							●											●	●		
V														●	●						
VI		●	●		●		●				●	●				●	●	●		●	●

Source: Karo 1930–1933, pp. 41–165, 251–258.

TABLE 4. GOLD AND SILVER VESSELS FROM THE SHAFT GRAVES AT MYCENAE

Burial (circle and grave number)	Open Forms					Closed Forms				Misc.	
	Basin	Cup	Goblet	Kantharos	Krater	Amphoriskos	Jug	Jar	Pyxis	Rhyton	Situla
A I	■	■					■				
A II		■									
A III		■	■			■	■		■		
A IV		■	■	■	■	■	■	■		■	
A V		■	■				■				■
A VI		■									
B I 327		■									
B A 325							■				
B Δ 326		■									
B Γ 35		■									
B N 325		■									

■ =1 ■ =2 ■ =3 ■ =4 ■ =5 ■ =6 ■ =7 ■ =8 ■ =9
■ =10 ■ =11 ■ =12 ■ =13 ■ =14 ■ =15

Source: Davis 1977, pp. 125–251.

They too emphasize that in order for the symbolic meaning of foreign items to be transferred to a community, it must be expressed in a familiar material code. In the case they study, the foreign technology of ceramics is introduced by clay vessels imitating the shape of gourd vessels current in the community. Significant to the present study, the vessels introduced through this transference of medium were those used for serving and drinking liquids. Rising elites at Early Mycenaean centers must similarly have expressed new customs through familiar forms (for example, the use of the kantharos—a two-handled carinated cup—for serving wine)

Figure 3. Niello goblet from Mycenae, Grave Circle A, shaft grave IV.
After Marinatos and Hirmer 1973, pl. 186, courtesy Hirmer Verlag

TABLE 5. DISTRIBUTION OF GOLD AND SILVER VESSELS IN MAINLAND GREECE

Legend (dot size = number of vessels): •=1, •=2, •=3, •=4, •=5, •=6, •=7, •=8, •=9, •=10, •=11, •=12

Period	Context		Stemmed shallow cup	Shallow cup	Semiglob. cup	Stemmed Vapheio cup	Cup, Vapheio	Cup, conical	Goblet	Kantharos	Krater	Amphoriskos, lidded	Jar, miniature	Jug	Pyxis, cylindrical	Rhyton	Situla
							Open Forms					**Closed Forms**				**Misc.**	
MH III	Mycenae	B, A 325												•			
LH I	Mycenae	B, I 327					•										
		B, Δ 326					•										
		B, Γ 357					•										
		B, Γ 358					•										
		B, N 389					•										
		A, II					•		•						•		
		A, III	•	•	•	•	• (large)		• (large)	•	•	•	•	•			
		A, IV					• (largest)					•		• (large)		•	
		A, V		•	•		•		•					•			•
		A, VI					•										
		A, I					• •										
LH II	Vapheio	Tholos		•			•										
	Peristeria	Tholos III		•			•										
	Kazarma	Tholos		•													
	Marathon	Tholos		•										•			
	Kokla	Tholos		•				•	• (large)								
LH IIIA	Tholos	Tomb 12															
	Dendra	Tomb 10		• (large)		•	• •		• (large)								
		Tomb 9		•	•						•						
		Tomb 2			•												
	Acrop. Treasure				•				• (large)								
LH III	Mycenae	Tomb 78		•													
		Tomb 24		•													
	Pylos	Palace			•				•								
	Patras	Pherai															
	Kalamata	Kampos		•						•							
	Mycenae	Chamber tomb							•								
	Routsi	Tholos					•										

Source: Davis 1977, passim.

23

TABLE 6. DISTRIBUTION OF PRIMARY DEPOSITS OF BRONZE VESSELS IN THE AEGEAN

Legend: ●=1 ●=2 ●=3 ●=4 ●=5 ●=6 ●=7 ●=8 ●=9 ●=10

Period	Site	Cup	Cup/bowl, broad rim	Kylix	Bowl	Basin	Lekane	Krater	Pan	Cauldron/kettle	Tripod kettle	Ladle	Pitcher	Hydria	Amphora	Lamp	Brazier	Sieve
										Open Forms			**Closed Forms**			**Misc.**		
LM I–II	Mallia, Grammatikakis		●			●				●	●		●	●				
	Knossos, basement cell by Stepped Portico		●		●	●							●					
	Mochlos		●		●	●												
	Knossos, house SE of South House									●	●		●					
	Kato Zakros, palace, room 45a					●					●		●		●	●	●	
	Knossos, NW Treasure House		●										●					
	Thera Δ 3	●				●							●	●				
	Thera Δ 16								●								●	
	Knossos, Unexplored Mansion	●				●											●	
	Tylissos	●								●								
MH III–LH II	Mycenae, B, grave E					●	●						●					
	Mycenae, A, grave VI					●							●					
	Mycenae, A, grave V		●	●	●	●		●		●			●	●				
	Mycenae, A, grave IV	●				●		●	●	●			●					
	Mycenae, A, grave III	●	●		●			●	●	●								
	Mycenae, A, grave I					●							●					
	Vapheio											●					●	
LH IIB–LH IIIA	Dendra tomb 2				●	●	●		●	●			●	●	●	●		●
	Asine tomb I,5		●		●	●			●	●			●	●				
	Tragana tholos I,1				●	●				●								●
	Nichoria tholos				●	●	●						●		●			●
	Dendra tomb 12					●	●						●	●				
	Mycenae tomb 47	●					●		●				●					●
	Tragana tholos I,2				●		●		●	●					●			
LM II–LM IIIA	Sellopoulo 3				●	●	●						●			●		
	Sellopoulo 4.III	●	●			●	●			●			●			●		
	Archanes A	●					●	●	●	●			●	●	●			
	Zapher Papoura 14		●	●	●	●	●		●	●	●	●	●	●		●		●
	Phaistos 8						●		●	●			●					●
	Zapher Papoura 36						●			●				●				

Source: Matthäus 1980, pp. 63, 65, 69, 70, figs. 5–8.

while introducing new forms (Minoan shapes and decorative schemes, for instance) in rare materials. In this fashion these elites adopted Minoan luxury items while adapting them for their own social ends.[37]

Tables 5 and 6 display the wide distribution across mainland Greece of vessels of gold, silver, and bronze that were produced at specialized workshops on Crete, the Cyclades, and the mainland and can reasonably be associated with drinking.[38] It is also clear in comparing Tables 2–6 that,

37. On Minoan feasting, see Moody 1987; Hamilakis 1999; Rutter, forthcoming.

38. Davis 1977; Matthäus 1980; on metal drinking vessels in the Near East, see Moorey 1980.

Figure 4 *(top).* **Silver vessels from Dendra tomb 10, shaft II.** After Persson 1942, p. 88, fig. 99; courtesy Swedish Institute at Athens

Figure 5 *(bottom).* **Set of "tinned" pottery from Dendra.** After Persson 1942, p. 92, fig. 103; courtesy Swedish Institute at Athens

while the earlier Grave Circle B at Mycenae contained large numbers of ceramic drinking vessels (especially goblets), in the later Circle A where bronze, silver, and gold drinking vessels are common and widely distributed, ceramic ones are less well represented. The preference for metal Vapheio cups among open forms is notable (Table 5).

In Mycenaean society, drinking rituals achieved standard expression through certain vessel shapes, beginning with the Vapheio cup and shallow cup, both of which were popular ceramic shapes during LH II and IIIA, also appearing in gold and silver (Table 5).[39] These were replaced by the kylix during LH IIIA.[40] Particularly worthy of notice is a set of LH IIIA silver drinking vessels (shallow cup, small and large goblets) found in tomb 10, shaft II, of the cemetery at Dendra (Fig. 4, Table 5). In the contemporary tholos at Kokla another set of silver goblets, along with a silver shallow cup and three silver conical cups, was found, while the Acropolis Treasure from Mycenae contains four golden goblets and a semiglobular cup (Table 5).[41] Sets such as these were emulated in clay and "tinned" to resemble silver or gold; these appear at Dendra (Fig. 5), in the Athenian Agora, and elsewhere.[42] The appearance of these sets coincides significantly with the ascendance of the kylix form.[43]

39. See discussion in Davis 1977; Wright, forthcoming a.

40. In pottery as well as metal: Mountjoy 1986, pp. 64–66. The notion of potters producing matching sets of vessels for use as a service has been little explored (see MacGillivray 1987 for examples from protopalatial Crete). Thus, the producers of Ephyraean ware

made matching goblets and pitchers (Mountjoy 1983; 1999, pp. 57–58) and one can speak of sets of Zygouries pottery of LH IIIB1 date. I thank J. Rutter for advice on this point.

41. Persson 1942, pp. 87–95; Demakopoulou 1990, 1993, 1997; on the Acropolis Treasure, see Davis 1977, pp. 291–296.

42. Immerwahr 1966; Gillis 1991, 1992, 1994, 1996, 1997; other examples come from Athens, Knossos, Mycenae, and Ialysos.

43. Matthäus 1980, p. 340; Mountjoy 1986, pp. 64–66. The changing composition of these sets is part of the process of the establishment of an etiquette; see Wright, forthcoming a.

FEASTING EQUIPMENT

If the sets of drinking vessels described above are presumed to have been used in feasting ceremonies, it would be profitable to survey primary deposits of bronze vessels in domestic and mortuary contexts, for these deposits present a wide array of vessels associated with the cooking and serving of food. Their distribution is presented above in Table 6, which includes vessels from selected contexts dating between Late Minoan (LM) I and IIIA and MH III–LH IIIA. The following tombs consistently provided the broadest groups of vessels: chamber tomb 14 at Zapher Papoura, near Knossos (Fig. 6);[44] tholos A at Archanes;[45] Asine chamber tomb I, 5;[46] Dendra chamber tomb 2;[47] and the tholos tomb at Nichoria.[48] The groups included vessels that we would expect were used for feasting: tripod and cylindrical kettles, lekanes (convex conical, spouted bowls), lamps, basins, bowls, cups, pitchers, pans, hydrias (water jars), and amphoras (two-handled storage jars for liquids). Overall the morphological variation among shapes is considerable. Some variation can be attributed to the production of different workshops and to the presence of heirlooms,[49] but it may be due in part to their uses for different types of preparation or, perhaps, for particular occasions (see below).

The Shaft Graves at Mycenae represent a special case. Few graves (B epsilon, and A I, III, IV, V) contained any quantity of bronze vessels (Table 6), and their concentration reflects a selective gathering from different producers throughout the Aegean.[50] The people who deposited these vessels showed a particular preference for kettles, pitchers, hydrias, pans, and kraters (large mixing bowls for liquids). This collection differs from other contemporary assemblages, admittedly less well known, that come largely from Minoan domestic contexts. Although the difference may be primarily one of context, it could suggest that the Shaft Grave assemblages manifest a developing Mycenaean taste, especially since, as we shall see, they relate to peculiarities in fresco painting that Morgan has attributed to nascent Mycenaean preferences.[51]

Many of these vessels show signs of wear and repair, and, therefore, cannot have been made expressly for the mortuary rite but were either owned by the deceased or given by the mourners. Either way these culinary items symbolize the feast and announce the significance of feasting to the burying group. The combination of these vessels for use in drinking and preparing and serving food—in ceramic, bronze, silver, and gold—demonstrates a dramatic increase in feasting equipment beginning at the end of the Middle Bronze Age, focused on a small group of high-status burials. This indication of feasting continues but is represented more widely in wealthy burials among the many chamber tombs throughout the mainland and on Crete (LM and LH II–III). These developments are accompanied by an elaboration of shapes and forms. Although it is difficult to quantify a specific service of vessels, by LH IIIA the following appear together most frequently: kettles, lekanes, basins, bowls, pitchers, pans, hydrias, amphoras, and cups (see below, Fig. 7:226, for an ideogrammatic representation of a service). This integration of drinking vessels and equip-

44. Evans 1906.
45. Sakellarakis 1970; Sakellarakis and Sakellarakis 1991, p. 84.
46. Frödin 1938.
47. Persson 1942.
48. Wilkie 1992.
49. Matthäus 1980, p. 66; Palaima 2003.
50. Matthäus 1980, pp. 341–342.
51. Morgan 1990, pp. 257–258.

Figure 6. Bronze vessels from tomb 14 at Zapher Papoura. After Evans 1906, pl. 89

ment for feasting in the deposition of metal vessels with the deceased is not necessarily proof that the two activities were bound together; there could always have been a distinction between feasting and drinking. Feasting can be either an inclusive or an exclusive activity, as we know from many sources from classical antiquity and modern ethnography.[52] The presence of feasting equipment in a tomb no doubt represents the ability of the deceased to sponsor feasts, and may also indicate memorable occasions of sponsorship and a reputation for hospitality. Drinking is a specialized and often exclusive activity that occurs either in the context of feasts (consider the difference between *deipnon* and *symposion*[53]) or on an individual basis. The presence of drinking vessels in a tomb, especially of silver and gold (but also of bronze or "tinned" clay), may refer to the status of the deceased as one who shares drinks with special companions.

The practice of depositing valuable metal vessels in tombs from the late Middle through the Late Bronze Age in the Aegean indicates the value attached both to the objects and to the activities they symbolize. Their significant early appearance in elite burials on the mainland and their continuing predominance, especially in the Argolid and Messenia, suggest a Mycenaean custom. Attention has been given to the appearance of similar burials on Crete, primarily around Knossos, and, even if not the burials of occupying Mycenaean overlords, they strongly indicate the

52. See Murray 1996 for discussions of Dark Age, Classical, Hellenistic, and royal Persian feasting; for the Near East in general, see Dentzer 1971, esp. pp. 240–256; for Macedonia, see Borza 1983; for Hallstatt, see Dietler 1999.

53. Murray 1990, p. 6.

acceptance of Mycenaean customs for elite burials at this time.[54] As status markers these assemblages denote what Dietler and Hayden term the "diacritical" feast, i.e., one that is marked by sumptuary display.[55] Metal kettles and basins found in these deposits are larger than their ceramic counterparts and therefore may indicate the ability of the occupant to sponsor substantial feasts that would have served sociopolitical as well as economic purposes.[56] As durable goods of high value they record a personal and social history and can be the source and inspiration for narrative. Caution is recommended in our chronological and typological examination of these deposits, since they may contain heirlooms or objects acquired outside the network of generally recognized exchange. Given their value and utility, these mortuary objects were often inventoried while they were in use,[57] a topic pursued in the following section.

LINEAR B EVIDENCE

In the Linear B records, vessels are recorded and denoted by ideograms representing a wide range of shapes and types (Fig. 7, Table 7). The ideograms are a shorthand designation accompanying written text, which often includes the vessel name. Not every mention of vessels in the tablets can be associated with feasting. Some—MY Ge 602–604, KN K 773+ 1809—are concerned with activities of production.[58] A long list of tablets record offerings to deities of amphoras filled with honey (KN Fs 8v; KN Gg 10, 701–711, 713+994, 995+7370, 5007, 5184, 5548, 5637+8243, 7232, 7371, 7372, 7792), which may be exclusively a dedication but could also be used in feasts.[59] Other texts with vessel ideograms provide no clear textual context (KN K 774–776, 778; KN K 829+874, 877[+]1052, 7353, 7363; KN U 521+712, 7501), though some are associated with things sacred (KN K 875) or are perhaps simply inventories (KN K 700).

Not all ideograms of drinking vessels found in Table 7 are concerned with feasting. For example, the ideograms for chalice, goblet, and bowl on Tn 316 from Pylos record offerings to deities on a tablet that is strictly

54. Preston (1999) compares LM II monumental burials to burials of LH I–II; see also Popham 1973; Popham and Catling 1974; Matthäus 1983; Kilian-Dirlmeier 1985; and Löwe 1996.

55. Dietler 2001, pp. 85–88; Hayden 2001a, pp. 35–42.

56. The largest kettles are as much as 0.50 m in diameter, although they average about 0.30 m; ceramic examples range from 0.12 to 0.20 m (see n. 177, below). In volumetric terms the clay tripods, if they average 0.15 m in diameter and are 0.075–0.10 m in depth, would hold between 1,237 and

1,767 cc, while the average bronze tripod (diameter 0.30 m, depth 0.15–0.20 m) would hold between 10,603 and 14,138 cc, an eightfold difference in capacity. The tripods may be important for differentiating between large-scale feasts, such as those at Pylos (discussed by Stocker and Davis, this volume), and more restricted feasting for a privileged group that may have enjoyed special foods. Bronze tripods may have been used for such special feasting, but also as part of the activities of larger feasts. The problem here is determining what the tripods were used for, a question discussed below in the

context of their representation in frescoes.

57. Cf. Hayden 2001a, pp. 40–41.

58. Bennett 1958, pp. 79–82; 1962; Shelmerdine 1985, pp. 49–50, 117.

59. Y. Hamilakis (pers. comm.) points out that it is difficult to distinguish offerings from feasting items; see also Hamilakis and Konsolaki 2004, pp. 143–148. See also Sacconi 2001. B. Hayden notes (pers. comm.) that in contemporary Buddhist temples "offerings are often made to Buddha, but they are actually used by the priests for their upkeep and perhaps for feasting."

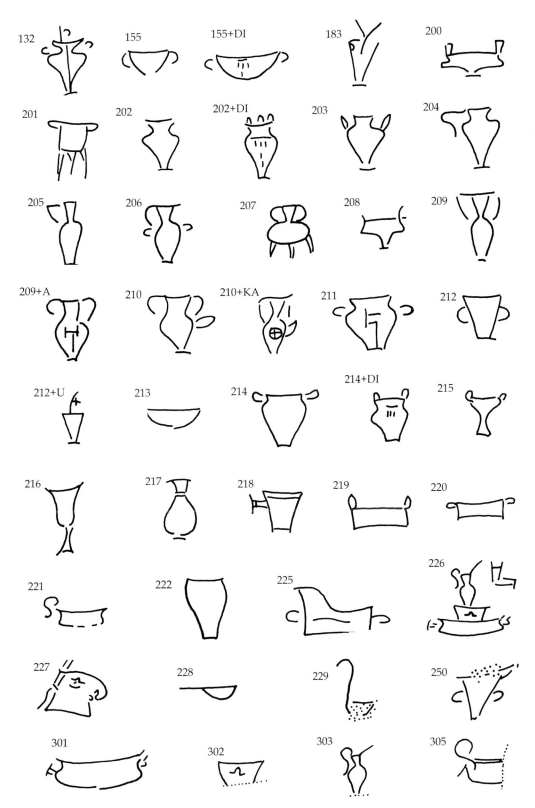

Figure 7. Ideograms of vessels in Linear B. Adapted from Vandenabeele and Olivier 1979, passim

TABLE 7. DISTRIBUTION OF IDEOGRAMS ON SELECTED LINEAR B TABLETS

No.	Shape Name	PY Ta 641	PY Ta 709.1,3	PY Ta 711	PY Ta 316	PY Tn 996.1,3,4	PY Un 2,4	MY Ge 602-604	MY Ue 661.1	KN Fs 8v	KN Gg 10	KN Gg 701	KN Gg 702	KN Gg 703-704	KN Gg 705-710	KN Gg 711	KN Gg 713+994	KN Gg 995+7370	KN Gg 5007	KN Gg 5184	KN Gg 5548	KN Gg 5637+8243	KN Gg 7232	KN Gg 7371	KN Gg 7372	KN Gg 7792	KN K 93a	KN K 434.1	KN K 700.1,2	KN K 740.2	KN K 773+1809	KN K 774	KN K 775	KN K 776+bis b (=1810)	KN K 778	KN K 829+874	KN K 872.3b	KN K 873.1,2,3	KN K 875.6	KN K 877[+]1052	KN K 5526	KN K 7353	KN K 7363	KN K 7599+8440	KN K 8244	KN U 521+712	KN U 1053bis (=1812)	KH U 7501	KN Uc 160
301	Basin																										■																						
219	Basin, angular					■																					■																						
155+D1	Bowl w/ handle																																															
155	Bowl w/ handle/pannier							■	■																																							
211a	Bowl w/ 2 handles																																					■					■					
213	Bowl w/o handle				■																																												■
200	Bowl, pedestal, 2 handles		■																																							■						
216	Chalice				■																																											
302	Conical bowl																																															
183	Conical vase																											■															■					■	
250	Conical vase					■																																										
212	Conical vase w/ handles					■																													■						■								
212+U	Conical vase w/o handles																														■	■																■
208	Cup w/o handle					■																																										
221	Cup, one-handle																												■									■											
218	Vapheio cup																																															
215	Goblet				■																										■																	
214+D1	Jar (di-pa) w/ 2 handles																																															
214	Jar (pa-ko-to) w/ 2 handles		■																																													
210	Stirrup jar																													■																			
210+KA	Stirrup jar																																			■													
228	Dipper		■																																														
229	Dipper																																																
226	Feasting sets																											■	■																■				
217	Flask																											■	■																				
202+D1	Amphora										■	■	■	■	■																																	
209	Amphora					■										■	■	■	■	■	■	■	■	■																								
209+A	Amphora																							■	■										■	■								■			■
202	Amphora (di-pa): 0, 3, 4 handles	■																									■																					
132	Amphoroid																																																
211b	Amphoroid						■			■																																							
203	Stamnos (qe-to)	■																																															
206	Hydria					■																																										
204	Pitcher			■		■																																										
205	Pitcher				■	■																																										
303	Pitcher w/ spout																																																
222	Pithoid vase																																																
227	Rhyton																																													■				
207	Tripod glob. flask w/ 2 handles																																					■											
201	Tripod kettle	■																																															
225	Bathtub	■																																															

Sources: Bennett and Olivier 1973; *CoMIK* I, III, IV; Vandenabeele and Olivier 1979, passim.

religious.[60] The appearance of the chalice and goblet ideograms on Tn 316 is unique, and the bowl ideogram appears only infrequently. These ideograms do not appear on tablets associated with feasting (e.g., Ta 709 and Tn 996). The Ta series from Pylos, Killen has suggested, "record an audit of the palace's equipment for banqueting."[61] He believes that they mark the appointment of the important magistrate, the *da-mo-ko-ro*.[62] The audit includes lists of vessels such as tripod kettles, amphoras, kraters, basins, bowls, and jugs, among other forms and variants, especially on tablets Ta 641 and 709. To these we should also add tablets from Knossos that denote special vessels or even sets of them (KN Gg 5637+8243, Uc 160, K 93, K 740, and K 872).[63]

As an economic activity feasting drew heavily on the resources of the palace and required considerable logistical planning, as Killen points out in his article on state-sponsored banquets, in which he analyzes sealings from Thebes and their relationship to tablets from Pylos and Knossos.[64] In these documents Killen argues that cattle, pigs, and goats/sheep, which were requisitioned and fattened, were intended for feasts, and that other documents record the preparation of equipment for a state-sponsored feast. In advance of any large-scale feast, palace officials must have had animals brought in from distant grazing and foraging areas and penned up where fodder was provided before they were taken for slaughter.[65] Similarly, vessels for the preparation of the feast would be readied for use, checked for condition, and defective ones noted. Stores of pottery vessels also would be inventoried or requisitioned.[66] In addition, as Killen and Palaima note, other tablets in the Ta series record items such as furniture and instruments probably used for slaughter (axes and swords or knives).[67] A tablet especially indicative of the collection and recording of feasting equipment is KN K 93, with ideograms *219, *226, *301, *302, and *303 (Fig. 7:219, 226, 301–303), which records a service of vessels that were kept together.[68]

The ideograms on these tablets relied on shorthand for noting items. For the archaeologist who collects artifacts from domestic and funerary contexts, a disjuncture exists between the Linear B ideograms and the range of objects known to us. The ideograms for vessels do not lend themselves to a literal reading as they were strongly modified by textual description and vary both in execution and type.[69] How, then, can we relate them to the many artifacts we find in the palaces and tombs? Here we face the classic problem of trying to read the ideograms as markers within our own system of transcription and translation, instead of attempting to understand how they were used by the scribes to signify meaning to themselves and to

60. See Palaima 1999, and this volume; Sacconi 1987.

61. Killen 1998, p. 421.

62. Killen 1998.

63. A fuller textual consideration of this matter is found in Palaima, this volume.

64. Killen 1994; Piteros, Olivier, and Melena 1990.

65. Killen 1994; for this procedure in an ethnographic setting, see Hayden 2001b.

66. Isaakidou et al. 2002; Wright 1994; Galaty 1999a, 1999b; Whitelaw 2001 (I would like to thank J. Rutter for reminding me of this recent study).

67. Killen 1992; 1994, p. 80; 1998.

The tablets in question are Ta 716 and 722; see Palaima, this volume.

68. Vandenabeele and Olivier 1979, pp. 271–273.

69. Bennett and Olivier 1973, pp. 231, 235; Ventris and Chadwick 1973, passim; Matthäus 1980, pp. 78–79; Palaima 2003, pp. 193–198.

other scribes.[70] It is clear that the addition of Linear B signs within certain ideograms (e.g., *202, see Fig. 7) modifies their meaning,[71] and we know from texts where the vessel form has been written out, e.g., PY Ta 641 and 709, that the ideogram in some instances needs supplementing with words to convey a more specific meaning.[72] This is a significant scribal convention in that it allows us to recognize that the standard set of ideograms was too small to represent all the cognitive types of vessels employed in the palace—a classic problem of typology without taxonomy.[73] Matthäus, in categorizing the corpus of bronze vessels from Bronze Age Greece, created a typology with a bewildering array of types and variants according to form, shape, size, and decorative and functional aspects—a classification much greater than what one sees represented on painted pottery or in frescoes and ideograms, a scheme that leads the contemporary analyst to despair when attempting to determine functional and symbolic relationships.[74] Similarly, no scribe in antiquity could have worked with such a typology, for every variation in the objects could never be registered in bureaucratic discourse. Nevertheless, the ancient scribes at Pylos and Knossos had to account for each vessel, and they devised ways of adding description to the ideograms that accounted for the variation and enabled them to refer to specific vessels.

This digression concerns an important issue of method. As Matthäus recognized, we are obligated when studying preserved metal vessels, and in some instances ceramic ones, to relate them to texts discussing those vessels.[75] To recover meaning from the texts, we must learn to read them, not merely translate them, and, in the structuralist sense, acknowledge the iconographic tradition that underlies the ideograms. This iconography informs other modes of representation: painted vessels in frescoes, painted vessels on vessels, and depictions of vessels in use. While there is no one-to-one correspondence between actual vessels and their ideogrammatic representation, a relatively consistent usage among different forms of representation may inform us as to what the Mycenaeans were saying about feasting through such depictions.

70. Matthäus 1980, p. 78.

71. Ventris and Chadwick 1973, p. 324, fig. 16; Vandenabeele and Olivier 1979, pp. 185 *(*155)*, 190 *(*212)*, 196 *(*123)*, 205–206 *(*211)*, 234 *(*202)*, 259 *(*209)*, and 266 *(*210)*.

72. For example, *202 and its variants with and without handles: Vandenabeele and Olivier 1979, pp. 234–239; Ventris and Chadwick 1973, pp. 330–331 *(*232)*, 336 *(*236)*; Bennett and Olivier 1973, p. 231; see also the discussion by Sherratt, this volume.

73. See Rice 1987, p. 284; Whallon and Brown 1982; Adams and Adams 1991; Sinopoli 1991, pp. 49–67.

74. For example, Matthäus (1980, pp. 82–118) categorized kettles into nine types, each with subtypes and variants: 1) kettles with walls of multiple sheets; 2) two-handled kettles with single-part walls; 3) round-bottomed kettles with carination; 4) kettles with shoulder carination; 5) kettles with ring handles; 6) MM tripod kettles; 7) cylindrical tripod kettles with horizontal handles; 8) round-bottomed tripod kettles with collar rim; and 9) round-bottomed tripod kettles with incurved rim.

75. Matthäus 1980, p. 80. In his discussion Matthäus observes that in cases where a vessel form appears as an ideogram but is unknown in clay, we can conclude that it exists in metal, e.g., *201—tripod kettles with ring handles—but the reverse is not true. As he points out, if the tablets recorded very large numbers of vessels (hundreds or thousands), then it would be clear that they are inventories of clay vessels; without such quantification one cannot tell whether ceramic or metal vessels are referred to. Consider in this regard that Pylos tablet Tn 996, which lists a few metal vessels, was found in pantry room 20, which contained 522 clay pots (Wright 1984, pp. 23–24; see also Mountjoy 1993, pp. 81–82).

The Linear B documents appear to indicate that feasting was an important activity that occurred with enough frequency and required such specialized implements that an inventory was necessary. As Palaima argues, some of the items used in feasting were heirlooms and had narrative, historical, personal, and prestige values.[76] Others were simply large clay vessels that needed to be on hand for use.[77] The attention given to recording implements used in feasting is not unlike the preservation of important residues of feasting, such as the burned cattle bones from the Archives Room at Pylos discussed by Stocker and Davis elsewhere in this volume. Ethnographical and historical studies of feasting have documented how communities record feasts; for example, the Akha of northern Thailand display water buffalo horns and pig mandibles.[78] Hayden observes that these are records of a "community's ability to sponsor such events."[79] Without textual records, however, it is unclear that remains recovered archaeologically could be interpreted in this manner; they might just as well advertise the wealth or historical position of a powerful person or group within the community.[80] In this regard, Killen's conclusion that the Mycenaean texts refer to feasts that marked the transition of magistracies is only one of a number of possible interpretations of feasting as a practice, and we cannot extend his classification of Mycenaean palatial feasts as "state sponsored" to all archaeologically discovered instances of feasting. Indeed, there is no reason to believe that all of the feasts recorded in the texts need to have been sponsored by the state.[81]

DISTRIBUTION PATTERNS

Material evidence for feasting is not found universally throughout the mainland. For the early period, it is largely restricted to a few tombs in the Argolid and in southwestern Messenia; later, it is distributed more widely around the Argolid and Messenia. Evidence is much less abundant in Lakonia, Attica, Boiotia, and Thessaly.[82] In Lakonia, for example, only the Vapheio tholos of LH II date contained any feasting equipment, and not in large quantity, although the effects of robbing must be taken into account.[83] In Achaia in the western Peloponnese, a tomb at Katarraktis provided a silver bowl, a hemispherical bronze bowl, a bowl with wishbone handle, and a carinated bowl.[84] In central Greece at Thebes, excavations in a storeroom on the acropolis turned up a few bronze vessels of probable LH IIIA1 date: a two-handled bowl, piriform jug, and broad-rimmed

76. Palaima 2003, and this volume.

77. Säflund 1980, p. 239; Wright 1984, pp. 23–26; Galaty 1999a; 1999b, pp. 45–49, 69–72, 77–80; Whitelaw 2001, pp. 52–62, 71–76.

78. Hayden 2001a, p. 55, figs. 2.7, 2.8; Clarke 2001. Of interest in this regard is a deposit of seven wild boar mandibles, apparently pierced through

for hanging, found during 1995–1997 rescue operations of the Kadmeia, Thebes, in a LH IIIB2 deposit in room 2; see Snyder and Andrikou 2001.

79. Hayden 2001a, p. 55.

80. Hayden 2001a, pp. 57–58.

81. I thank D. Nakassis for this insight.

82. I wish to thank J. Rutter for

urging me to look at this problem of distribution and attempt to explain it.

83. In bronze there are two jugs, a ladle, and a brazier; in silver, a ladle and some fragments; and in gold, the two famous cups (Matthäus 1980, pp. 32–33).

84. Papadopoulos 1979, pp. 277–280.

bowl.[85] Additional hoards scattered throughout the mainland, on the Acropolis in Athens, at Anthedon and Orchomenos in Boiotia, and at Kalydon in Aitolia add slightly to the evidence.[86]

Most of these instances date between the periods LH IIB and LH IIIA, when major deposits of feasting equipment appear in chamber tombs on Crete. At this time the Mycenaeans were establishing themselves as overlords of the Cretan palaces, and the contemporaneous spread of feasting assemblages in elite tombs on the mainland and at major centers on Crete is surely indicative of the strength this custom had attained among high-status and powerful groups, as Borgna explores in her essay in this volume.[87] The absence of such evidence during the earlier, formative period between MH III and LH II is indicative of the various regional trajectories on the mainland as communities made the transition from "transegalitarian" to more highly organized entities such as chiefdoms or states.[88] The matter may be understood in terms of Dickinson's suggestion that Mycenae had a "special relationship" with Crete,[89] that is, that for elites in the Argolid and Messenia the act of feasting—as well as representing it—was an important and self-conscious display of aggrandizement that may have had its origins in their relationship to court life in palatial Crete.[90]

That it was less important in other regions to display the capability to feast may indicate that different customs of aggrandizement evolved in different areas (or equally that aggrandizing behavior was discouraged for social and ideological reasons in some areas, or that certain communities lacked the resources and social connections to amass the conspicuous wealth such behavior would require).[91] As I have argued elsewhere,[92] during the formative stage of development of Mycenaean society, variation would have been the norm, and there is no compelling reason for different social groups to represent their identities in the same way. At the height of Mycenaean society in LH III, feasting was widely practiced, becoming part of the emblemic identity of Mycenaean polities. It is likely that the representation of feasting in frescoes began at this time (see below).

The archaeological and textual evidence for feasting demonstrates in general its importance for the formation of political and economic ties by rising elites during the formative era of Mycenaean society. In many areas the social act of feasting was probably independent of and preceded the formation of the Mycenaean "state." Feasting in these areas would have functioned not merely for the advancement of political goals, but as an older custom for kin groups and factions within the community to mark occasions of importance, promote solidarity within the feasting group,

85. Matthäus 1980, p. 14.

86. Matthäus 1980, pp. 53–58.

87. See also Kilian-Dirlmeier 1985; Matthäus 1983; Popham and Catling 1974.

88. The term "transegalitarian" is used by Hayden (1995) to refer to the many stages of complexity in societies in transition from egalitarian to chiefdom, and gives a more nuanced meaning to what traditionally has

been described as "tribe." This topic is discussed at length in Wright, forthcoming b.

89. Dickinson 1977, p. 54.

90. Wright 1995a, pp. 290–292; 1995b, p. 72.

91. In her masterful publication of the "shaft-grave" tomb at Kolonna on Aigina, including a comparative study of high-status MH tombs, Kilian-Dirlmeier (*Alt-Ägina* IV.3) shows that

as early as MH II there emerged elite burials with exotic and luxury artifacts similar to grave goods, yet distinctive. It is at this time, as I argue elsewhere (Wright 2001; forthcoming a, b), that there emerged among elites in different regions ways of competing that were not governed by rules determining the kinds of items most appropriate to represent elite status.

92. Wright 2001; forthcoming a, b.

demonstrate superior economic and social resources, and, only at the level of the chiefdom and state, to offer tribute.[93]

In some regions, notably the Argolid and Messenia, feasting would have been manipulated by elites as an effective way to mobilize labor, promote allegiance to the leader, and make alliances with other powerful groups. It was probably not always institutionalized, however, but rather was carried out and sponsored by individuals and groups at all levels of society. These functional aspects of feasting surely remained important for all social orders after the formation of the state-level institutions of the Mycenaean palaces. That the evidence for feasting ranges widely, although variously, from the Middle through the Late Bronze Age and broadly from Minoan Crete through the islands and on the mainland, indicates development and change in the customs of feasting. Yet there was continuity in the act, as is documented by the presence of heirlooms among the assemblages—both those preserved in tombs and those noted in Linear B.[94] In a consideration of the iconographic evidence provided by frescoes, these issues (along with attendant problems) become much clearer.

FRESCOES

Frescoes that illustrate feasting or the preparation for feasts appear from the beginning to the end of the Late Bronze Age (LM I on Crete through LH IIIB on the Greek mainland) and are found in many contexts: the so-called villas of Neopalatial Crete, buildings at settlements on the islands (of Late Cycladic I date), and in the Mycenaean palaces. These widely diverse chronological and geographic contexts provide room for a number of interpretations. The use of evidence from the Cretan Neopalatial period to help fill out the picture of Mycenaean feasting in the later Late Bronze Age might, methodologically, be questioned. We need to examine whether what appears iconographically apprehensible and consistent, at Panofsky's level of iconographic synthesis as described above,[95] is indeed the same among the posited cultural entities of Crete, the Cycladic islands, and the mainland, and whether that meaning changed as these individual cultural groups developed, as Morgan has emphasized.[96]

Militello has recently observed that the problem is complicated by the uncertainty that much of the evidence we have can even be read at the initial and necessary pre-iconographic level.[97] It is unclear how to identify and name representations of animals, insects, fantastic creatures, vegetation, and architecture until we understand the conventions of representation. Not only are we uncertain what the *Realien* of fresco representation are, but due to the polysemic nature of representation in the different media of fresco, pottery painting, writing, and so forth, there remains the probability of different meanings and structures of meaning.[98] In this study, however, I am primarily concerned with the meanings of Mycenaean expression rather than those of Minoan or Cycladic production, and I have the benefit of textual sources and several comprehensively studied types of artifacts. One might infer backward from meanings gleaned from Mycenaean evidence to develop an explanation of the cultural practices of the islands or Crete; for example, one might posit that, since Mycenaeans

93. See Hayden 2001a, pp. 54–58.

94. Heirlooms in the Shaft Graves are discussed by Palaima 2003; those in tomb assemblages in general are documented by Matthäus 1980, pp. 341–342. The references in PY Ta 641 to "Cretan" tripods made by specific crafts persons surely document heirlooms (see Palaima 2003).

95. Panofsky 1939.

96. Morgan 1985, 1989.

97. *Haghia Triada* I, pp. 245–246; see also Morgan's (1989) discussion of ambiguity.

98. *Haghia Triada* I, p. 246; Morgan 1989.

curated special items such as the Cretan-made bronze tripods inventoried in Ta 641.1, there is a historical connection in usage and meaning from perhaps LM/LH I to LH IIIB. Such arguments, however, are open to the objection that whatever historical narrative was attendant on an object for Mycenaeans need bear no relation to the meaning it held either for its Minoan producer or for any similar object produced for and used by Minoans during LM I and II. For this reason, I restrict my discussion of Cretan and Cycladic frescoes to pointing out structural differences between frescoes from the Neopalatial and Mycenaean eras.

Strong evidence exists from tomb assemblages and Linear B tablets that items made in the earlier phase of Mycenaean culture, i.e., LH I–II, continued to be used during the palatial periods. Such evidence justifies the assertion that a certain consistency of meaning and practice prevailed—at both the functional and social level. I suggest that this continuity has to do with the interactions of Early Mycenaean elites as they competed with each other in their own regions as well as in other regions that were sources for prestigious craft goods (e.g., vessels of precious metal).[99] This history of interactions ultimately explains the formation of the homologous Mycenaean peer polities distinguished by common architectural forms, pottery manufacture, language of documentation (and in the courts of the palaces, the language of discourse), and legends of ancestors, heroes, and deities. While Mycenaean frescoes were derived from representations and conventions of Minoan and Cycladic painting, the Mycenaeans adapted these for their own purposes. We should be aware that what might be specifically understandable from Linear B texts—that feasts were sponsored by the state or *wanax* to mark royal activities—may not be understood directly from the frescoes without a consideration of specific iconographic evidence and architectural context.[100]

Illustration of activities that appear to be related to feasting begins in LM I in the form of miniature frescoes from Tylissos on Crete and Ayia Irini on Kea. Fragments from Tylissos reconstructed by Shaw (Fig. 8) are organized in two registers, the lower of which shows males moving in a file, one of whom holds one end of a pole on his shoulder from which a large jar is suspended. Elements of architecture suggest a setting for the action.[101] At Ayia Irini a series of fragments of miniature frescoes from rooms 18 and 20 of the Northeast Bastion have been reconstructed by Morgan as showing a festival outside the walls of a seaside town (Fig. 9). She compares them to the miniature fresco from the West House at Akrotiri on Thera and to that from Tylissos, while noting that the Ayia Irini frescoes have many elements that foreshadow Mycenaean painting.[102] In the fresco men are depicted standing over tripod kettles. Abramovitz has suggested that one man is carrying to the kettle a large brown object from what might be a red table, and she wonders if this may be understood as venison from the hunt.[103] Morgan observes that the cauldron has "black burn marks . . . showing that the men are cooking."[104]

In other fragments from Ayia Irini, men are shown coming from left and right in a procession, which Morgan compares to the hilltop scene in the north fresco from the West House at Akrotiri.[105] Some individuals, who are part of a procession, carry items in their hands or suspended from poles; a large jar hangs from one, while an amorphous object hangs from

99. Wright 1995b; and see discussion above.

100. I thank L. Morgan for clarifying this point.

101. Shaw 1972.

102. Morgan 1990, p. 258; 1995; 1998, pp. 202–205.

103. Abramowitz 1980, p. 62, cat. nos. 90–95; for scenes of the hunt see p. 61, cat. nos. 83–89.

104. Morgan 1998, p. 204.

105. Morgan 1990, p. 257; 1998, p. 204; Abramowitz 1980, pp. 58–59, cat. nos. 66–82.

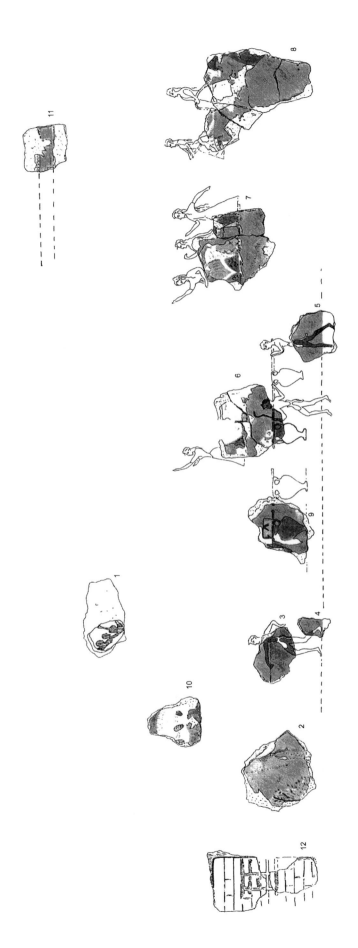

MCS 1972

Figure 8. Fresco from Tylissos: feasting scene. After Shaw 1972, p. 184, fig. 13, with additional details by M. Shaw

Figure 9. Fresco from Ayia Irini: feasting scene. After Morgan 1998, p. 209, fig. 6

another.[106] One fragment shows a male with a large head, who Abramowitz thought may be a dwarf,[107] although Morgan does not single the figure out for discussion. A group of fragments that Morgan believes come from the western end of the south wall, or from the west wall, depict a helmeted hunter carrying a deer slung from a pole. Other fragments from the west wall, larger in scale than the scene with the men and kettles, show dogs running to the south pursuing deer.[108] Morgan emphasizes that these scenes show horses and chariots, the earliest such representations in fresco.[109]

Morgan's comments suggesting a special affinity between the Kea scenes and Mycenaean frescoes bear closer inspection.[110] During LH III such scenes were still being painted in Mycenaean palaces. Scattered around the palace grounds and within the palace rooms at Pylos are fresco fragments that recall those from Ayia Irini. From a second-story room (probably above hall 46) fragments combine to show men and dogs from the hunt accompanying other men carrying tripods (Fig. 10), presumably to cook the meat.[111] This reconstructed scene includes fragments showing men and dogs hunting deer,[112] and, significantly, from the southwest wall (which collapsed into the small rooms to the side of the flanking corridor) came large-scale fragments, including a scene with deer and papyrus.[113] A fragment from the northwest fresco dump shows a robed man apparently holding a dead animal by the legs (Fig. 11).[114] The similarity of these scenes to those from Ayia Irini suggests a relationship between hunting scenes

106. Abramowitz 1980, p. 59, cat. nos. 66, 68, 70.

107. Abramowitz 1980, p. 58, cat. no. 65, pl. 4:b.

108. Morgan 1998, p. 204; Abramowitz 1980, pp. 61–62, cat. nos. 106–113; I thank L. Morgan for discussing this scene with me.

109. Morgan 1998, pp. 204–205. J. Rutter points out (pers. comm.) that

these are not the earliest Bronze Age representations of horses, however, since the depictions of horses on the grave stelai from Mycenae are probably earlier; see Mylonas 1973, p. 33, cat. no. A-490, pl. 12; dated to LH I by Graziadio (1988, p. 371).

110. Morgan 1990; 1998, p. 205.

111. *Palace of Nestor* II, pp. 68–70, frr. 16–17H43, 19–20H43, and

21H48; pp. 107–108, frr. 12–14C43.

112. *Palace of Nestor* II, pp. 205–207, 212, pl. M.

113. Fr. 36C17: *Palace of Nestor* II, pp. 118–119, 195, pls. 61, 62, 136, G; see also Lang's discussion of the northwestern wall, p. 196.

114. *Palace of Nestor* II, pp. 43–44, 49, 74–75, fr. 31Hnws, c, pls. 22, N.

Figure 10. Fresco from Pylos: men, dogs, and tripods. After *Palace of Nestor* II, pl. 122; courtesy Princeton University Press and the University of Cincinnati

Figure 11. Fresco from Pylos: hunters. After *Palace of Nestor* II, pl. N; courtesy Princeton University Press and the University of Cincinnati

and those showing the preparation of a feast, an opinion already expressed by Morgan in her treatment of the Ayia Irini frescoes.[115]

The presence of deer in these frescoes is worthy of notice, although given the frequent appearance of deer in Aegean art, perhaps we should not be overly surprised.[116] Of special interest in this regard is the stag in a LM III fresco from Ayia Triada on Crete published by Militello; a lyre-player is also depicted, suggesting that a feasting scene may have been represented.[117] Additional evidence that venison was a regular part of the feast is provided by archaeozoological analyses from Pylos, Tsoungiza, and Ayios Konstantinos on Methana,[118] and by Linear B sources; Bennet, in noting deer on seal impressions and on two tablets from Pylos (Cr 591, 868+875), suggested that they were contributions to feasts by elites.[119] We must consider possible restrictions on the consumption of hunted foods by elites, a point recently made by Hamilakis.[120] For a later period, we are told by Athenaeus (1.17–18) that King Cassander was not permitted to recline at dinner and had to remain sitting, since he had never speared a boar without the use of a net.[121] He adds that the heroes of Homer feasted on nothing but meat, which they prepared for themselves. It seems, therefore, within the bounds of probability that game such as venison and boar, both products of the hunt, may have been restricted in distribution, prepared differently than domesticated animals, and consumed only by those who had participated in the rituals of the hunt.[122]

Game meats have a tough fiber with high albumin content and they also contain much gristle and tendon, which is best made edible by boiling; Athenaeus (14.656) reports that the Athenians preferred to boil pig as it takes away the rawness of the meat and softens it.[123] The boiling of pig is also mentioned in the *Iliad* (21.362–364), but, as Sherratt discusses in her contribution to this volume, this method of cooking is not otherwise attested by Homer. A large quantity of beef was distributed at Mycenaean feasts, but while it was roasted over an open flame, meat from the hunt was boiled and distributed to a more exclusive audience, and the tripod would have been the appropriate vessel for such preparation.[124] It is reasonable to

---

115. Morgan 1998, p. 204: "The relationship of these scenes—deer hunt, hunter, chariot, cauldron—therefore makes sense in terms of hunting for the feast."

116. Pylos: *Palace of Nestor* II, pp. 104–106, frr. 1–2C2, 3C20, 4C19, 5C63, 6Cnw; Ayia Irini: Abramowitz 1980, pp. 61–62; Tiryns: *Tiryns* II, pp. 140–154, figs. 60, 61; Ayia Triada: *Haghia Triada* I, pp. 139–142, pls. I, L. They are also frequently depicted on seals, for which see Erlenmeyer and Erlenmeyer 1956, 1957; but also Younger 1988, pp. xi–xii, xvii–xix, on the problem of distinguishing quadrupeds. J. Rutter points out (pers. comm.) "that deer are second only to bulls as the most popular zoomorphic pattern

in Mycenaean pictorial vase painting, and the kraters on which both bulls and deer appear are likely to have played some role in Mycenaean (or Mycenaean-derived, as on Cyprus) feasting." See also Kontorli-Papadopoulou 1996, pp. 121–122.

117. *Haghia Triada* I, pp. 139–142, 287–288.

118. Isaakidou et al. 2002; Stocker and Davis, this volume; Dabney, Halstead, and Thomas, this volume; Hamilakis and Konsolaki 2004.

119. Bennet 2001, pp. 34–35; cf. Melena 1997a, p. 284; 1997b, p. 163, for the recent join.

120. Hamilakis 2003; I thank Y. Hamilakis for drawing this article to my attention.

121. Murray 1996, p. 16.

122. Hamilakis 2003; Becker (1999) has found that the bones of deer at Plataia Magoula Zarkou were treated differently than those of domestic animals; I thank Y. Hamilakis for directing me to this article.

123. I thank Phyllis Bober for clarification of this point; Speth (2004) argues that the boiling of meat, especially the bones for their marrow, significantly increases the nutrient content by releasing fats.

124. A possible reason both for prizing bronze tripods and making them larger than ceramic ones; see above, n. 56, and also Sherratt (this volume) for further discussion of tripod vessels.

think that one type of Mycenaean feast was restricted to elites who were members of hunter-warrior groups and who used bronze tripods and other equipment found in their tombs for the preparation and consumption of meats of the hunt. It is also possible that within large-scale, state-sponsored banquets such as suggested by Killen (see above) and reconstructed from the remains at Pylos (Stocker and Davis, this volume), there may have occurred smaller exclusive feasts among groups of high-status palace officials and nobility.

Morgan's restoration of the Ayia Irini fragments reflects the paratactic arrangement of scenes in the miniature frescoes from the West House at Akrotiri, where, as Sarah Morris has argued, the whole can be read as a narrative.[125] Her restoration also presumes that a corpus of miniature frescoes served as a major source for Mycenaean painters, who continued to paint them in the palatial period, as Shaw has often observed.[126] Other sources, of course, could have influenced the Mycenaeans, not least Egyptian painting, as has frequently been pointed out.[127] The inferences drawn by these comparisons, however, are based upon highly fragmentary evidence, the contexts and associations of which are not sufficiently clear to prove the linkages between the Neopalatial and Mycenaean traditions, let alone from elsewhere. As Cain has recently cautioned,[128] in studies of Aegean iconography scholars tend to reach a consensus based more upon the history of discourse than upon any renewed critical examination of the evidence.

The evidence presented so far has three components: 1) an argument, based on artifact distributions, that certain vessels were used by elites in feasting; 2) three epigraphic arguments, one of which cites the slaughtering of fattened animals as evidence of state-sponsored feasts, another that interprets inventories of vessels as the equipment of feasting, and a third that posits that feasts occurred in conjunction with the installation of state officials; and 3) an argument based on fresco iconography that involves at least three scenes—men and dogs hunting deer and bringing the kill home (and at Kea showing horses and chariots), preparations for the feast where men are cooking what appears to be meat in tripods, and men in procession, with some carrying large vessels that might be presumed to hold wine or some other refreshment. The last two scenes may take place near architectural settings.

Two additional frescoes are significant for an examination of the question of feasting: the fresco from the megaron unit at Pylos (Figs. 12, 13) and the Campstool Fresco from Knossos (see below, Fig. 15), both of which show figures thought to be eating and drinking, seated in chairs with X-shaped cross-pieces. The Pylos fragments have been interpreted by Lang and McCallum as forming part of a decorative program of the entrance rooms to the central megaron, consisting of a procession leading a bull into the antechamber of the megaron, presumably for sacrifice (Fig. 12),[129] and continuing into the megaron proper, to the right as one approaches the throne. On a fragment from the foyer (hall 5) of this procession, men carry indeterminate objects, one of which is described by Lang as "the upright of a rectangular frame which rests on his shoulder cushioned by a large white pillow" (perhaps a stool?), while others depict furniturelike and hornlike objects (cf. the Linear B text KN K(1) 872).[130] Other individuals carry

125. Morris 1989, pp. 515, 534–535; 2000; Cain 2001, pp. 29–33.

126. Shaw 1980, 1996, 1999.

127. Most recently, Hiller 1996, esp. pp. 91–92; and Rehak 1998.

128. Cain 2001, p. 46; see also Rehak 1998, 2000.

129. *Palace of Nestor* II, pp. 192–196; McCallum 1987a, 1987b.

130. *Palace of Nestor* II, p. 64; see also p. 193, frr. 5–6H5.

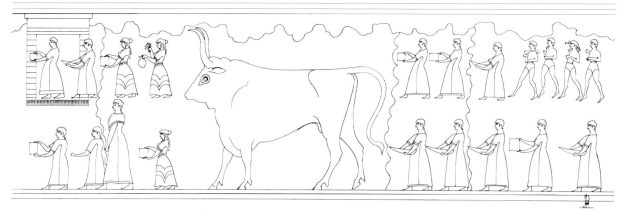

Figure 12. Pylos megaron fresco: procession. Drawing Piet de Jong, Piet de Jong Papers; photo I. Ioannidou and L. Bartzioti. Courtesy American School of Classical Studies at Athens

a variety of items in the procession: pyxides or baskets, large shallow bowls, and a lamp stand.[131]

On the wall of the megaron itself is the famous scene showing the lyre-player, bull, and individuals seated on campstools on either side of a three-legged table (Fig. 13). The entire scene brings to mind other procession frescoes from Knossos, Pylos, Tiryns, and Thebes where figures carry similar items.[132] The goal of the processions is uncertain. Was it for presentation of tribute or part of a festival that ended in sacrifice and feasting? Or a combination of these? The restored bull in the Pylos fresco evokes the sacrifice depicted on the Ayia Triada sarcophagus (Fig. 14), in which a bull is strapped to a table, his blood collected in a tapered cylindrical vase that is similar to those in the scene on the other side of the sarcophagus, where women empty vases into a krater placed between two poles surmounted by double axes.[133] Below the table are two goats, seemingly oblivious to the fact that their turn is next.

In the Pylos megaron fresco, the upper bodies of the figures seated across the table from each other are missing. To associate these two fragments with the Campstool Fresco, details of which are shown here (Fig. 15), we must reconcile their interpretations. The Campstool Fresco is too fragmentary to reconstruct the whole scene, and care must be taken not to read too much into it. Evans interpreted it as pairs of seated males facing each other and exchanging "loving cups."[134] In his view the fragments of females represent the "Mother Goddess." The interpretation of the "loving cups" is derived from the two fragments illustrated here, which show the base and foot of what appear to be a chalice and a two-handled goblet of LM IIIA type.[135] In 1959 Platon reconstructed the entire scene in two

131. *Palace of Nestor* II, pp. 66–68, 81, 193, 198, frr. 8–9H5, 47H13, 49Hnws.

132. Immerwahr 1990, pp. 114–118.

133. *Palace of Nestor* II, pl. 53, fr. 19C6; *Haghia Triada* I, pp. 295–296; see also Sakellarakis 1970, pp. 178–188. Other representations of sacrifice are known from signet rings and seals, and thoroughly discussed by Sakellarakis (1970, pp. 166–178). Lang (*Palace of*

Nestor II, pp. 26, 80) suggested that fr. 18C5 in the vestibule may represent a scene of bull sacrifice, but she doubted that fr. 19C6 in the Throne Room was a bull (p. 99); see also pp. 109–110. Stocker and Davis (this volume, p. 70, n. 47) draw attention to an unpublished restudy of this fragment that dismisses its identification as a bull.

134. *PM* IV.2, pp. 381–396; see

Hiller 1999 for an investigation of Egyptian parallels to this scene.

135. The chalice is reconstructed in Evans's diagram (*PM* IV.2, p. 390, fig. 325), and is based on the appearance of a distinct flattish base of the bowl attached to a slender stem, which then rises vertically forming the wall of the chalice. For the form, see Mountjoy 1999, p. 352.

Figure 13. Pylos megaron fresco: lyre player, sacrificial bull, and banqueters.
K. E. Leaman, after McCallum 1987a,
pl. 10; courtesy L. R. McCallum

Figure 14. Ayia Triada sarcophagus.
Photo A. Frantz (CR 13), courtesy
American School of Classical Studies at
Athens

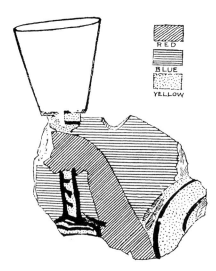

Figure 15. Details of the Campstool Fresco from Knossos. Adapted from *PM* IV.2, pp. 389–390, figs. 324, 325

registers and argued that the juxtaposition of seated figures facing each other was incorrect.[136] Because the angle of the hand extending the vessel worked better when restored to a standing figure, he proposed that standing individuals offered vessels to those seated. In 1964 Cameron published a new study; he did not follow all of Platon's suggestions, and declined to offer a restoration, although he convincingly demonstrated that some of the figures (e.g., "La Parisienne") are larger than others, so that the two registers of the frieze may conceivably merge into one.[137] Immerwahr accepted that the figures were part of a religious scene and that "La Parisienne" was standing.[138]

In a recent study of Aegean painting, Shaw includes the Campstool Fresco in the category of feasting scenes, but there is no direct evidence that these fragments illustrate a feast.[139] As Shaw notes, there are details common to feasting scenes, such as seated men dressed in robes decorated with diagonal stripes sitting on campstool-type chairs. She does not believe the figures in the Campstool Fresco are divinities for the following reasons: they seem to be paired as equals, with different figures (including "La Parisienne") wearing dresses with the same decorations, and deities in Aegean art are not usually depicted receiving offerings directly from humans.[140] Other illustrations of seated deities do exist. The most complete, and presumably earliest, is the gold signet ring from the Tiryns Treasure (Fig. 16).[141] Here a robed figure with a rolled crown or cap sits on a campstool that has a back. The figure's feet rest on a footstool and the right hand holds out a chalice as four genii process forward, each holding out a jug. This figure must be a deity, since both the falcon behind and the genii presenting would not be appropriate for a mere mortal.

In support of the notion that deities are represented in similar scenes is a fragment of a terracotta figure from the sanctuary at Amyklai; it preserves a left hand grasping the stem of a vessel, which Demakopoulou interprets as a kylix.[142] The head of a snake(?) is attached to the hand and appears to be heading toward the kylix. This supports the interpretation of the figure as a deity. Another representation is painted on a vessel from

136. Platon 1959.
137. Cameron 1964; see Marinatos 1993, p. 55, fig. 44, for an illustration of Cameron's reconstruction.
138. Immerwahr 1990, p. 95.
139. Shaw 1997, p. 496.
140. M. C. Shaw (pers. comm.).
141. Sakellariou 1964, p. 179.
142. Demakopoulou 1982, pp. 55–56.

Figure 16. Ring from Tiryns. After Marinatos and Hirmer 1973, pl. 207, courtesy Hirmer Verlag

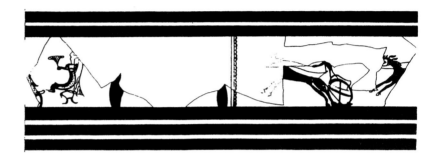

Figure 17. Scene on chariot krater from Tiryns. After Kilian 1980, p. 23, fig. 2

143. Kilian 1980, p. 22, n. 10; the findspot is unknown but surely the vessel was not funerary. Kilian claims it is an amphoroid krater.

144. Kilian 1980, pp. 30–31; Immerwahr (1990, p. 154), however, demurs.

145. Steel 1999, p. 806.

146. Platon 1971, pp. 6, 65, 132–148; Persson 1931, p. 52; Karo 1930–1933, cat. nos. 600, 854; an exception is the clay Sykes chalice, probably from Cyprus: see Karageorghis 1957.

147. The handleless bowl ideogram is found on only two other Linear B documents: KN K 7353 and KN Uc 160 (Vandenabeele and Olivier 1979, p. 183).

148. Lang's thoughtful consideration of the problem of distinguishing deities from humans (*Palace of Nestor* II, pp. 57–61) is worth considering in this context.

Tiryns;[143] it shows a figure seated in a chair holding a kylix by its stem while chariots race around the vessel (Fig. 17). Kilian advocates the interpretation of this scene as a deity at funeral games,[144] although Steel has recently argued for a more general interpretation, urging that it be understood merely as a "scene denoting an aristocratic lifestyle."[145]

These alternative interpretations caution against adopting any single one. The common display of a goblet or chalice, however, is significant and is open to further analysis. The Tiryns ring presents a complete scene, and there can be no mistaking it as a presentation to a deity. Here, as elsewhere, the chalice is firmly associated with divinities. It rarely appears in archaeological contexts, and when it does it is made of marble, alabaster, or gold and is found in special contexts such as the Treasure Room at Zakros on Crete, the Shaft Graves at Mycenae, and the tholos at Dendra in the Argolid.[146] Especially important is the unique appearance of the chalice and goblet in the Linear B tablets (see Fig. 7:215, 216). They appear only in Tn 316 at Pylos, which we have seen interpreted as a text recording the dedication of offerings to deities at their shrines. Similarly, three gold goblets and seven gold bowls are uniquely offered to deities.[147] Associations of the chalice and the goblet conform to their co-occurrence on the Campstool Fresco and to the terracotta figure from Amyklai, as well as illustrations mentioned earlier. Notwithstanding Shaw's concerns about the interpretation of the Campstool Fresco, all these examples must be considered as representations of formal ceremonies of presentation to deities. It seems likely that the accepted convention was to depict deities seated while they received honors or tribute, signified by these special vessels.[148] The chalice and goblet thus appear to be signs of divine participation in the feast, and the connection between the portrayal of these vessels and their use by elites may demonstrate the special relationship with the gods enjoyed by these high-status individuals.

Although the megaron fresco at Pylos permits an association between procession, sacrifice, and feasting, and at Ayia Irini it is probable that the preparation for feasting is accompanied by a procession, it is unclear if that is the case for other depicted processions, such as the Procession Fresco and the Grand Staircase Fresco at Knossos. Therefore, a distinction between formal palace-centered ceremonial processions and feasting must be preserved.[149] Procession frescoes are a complex genre with many sources (Crete, Egypt, the Near East),[150] and may have been intended for a variety of purposes. Some could be processions of tribute, and others of sacrifice, which might include a feasting scene.[151] The representations of large formal processions in the Mycenaean palaces at Pylos, Tiryns, and Thebes may draw on the tradition recognized in the great Procession Fresco at Knossos and the frescoes at Xeste 4 at Akrotiri,[152] but they may also have been adapted for Mycenaean purposes, as the procession into the megaron complex at Pylos illustrates (see Fig. 12).[153] The complex at Pylos, as several scholars have observed,[154] is part of a program of decoration that unifies each megaron suite.

No matter which iconographic tradition the Mycenaeans were drawing on (large-scale or miniature, Cretan or island or Egyptian), they transformed it for their own purposes and used it especially to organize an elaborate meaning around and within the megaron units at Tiryns, Thebes, Mycenae, and Pylos.[155] These programs and their constituent iconographic ensembles express the hierarchical character of Mycenaean society, which began with the appropriation of Minoan and island cultural forms by Early Mycenaean chiefs (mostly from the Argolid and Messenia) and concluded with the focused iconography of the political culture of the palaces. Depictions of feasting per se are hardly the goal of these programs, since the feast was being actively celebrated by living participants, whether in the megaron or in the palace courts. Scenes showing people seated at a table are self-conscious and rare reproductions of these practices.

149. The procession frescoes differ in size: Mycenaean ones, such as those from Xeste 4 at Akrotiri on Thera and the Procession Fresco from Knossos, are large, whereas those from Ayia Irini are miniature. In general the Mycenaean examples are not only large, but also, with the exception of that from Pylos, contain only women, which distinguishes them from the island and Cretan examples (*Palace of Nestor* II, pp. 51–62; Immerwahr 1990, pp. 114–121). Immerwahr also observes differences in dress: the Mycenaean ones more often represent the flounced skirt, whereas the example from Knossos has a bordered robe and apparently depicts priestesses or deities in contrast to the mainland Greek females, who are bearing pyxides and flowers, as if they were votaries (cf. Boulotis 1987). Lang, however, suggests that the Mycenaeans did not distinguish between deity and priestess, and she states (*Palace of Nestor* II, pp. 58–60) "that it would seem best, therefore, to think of the regular processions (Thebes, Tiryns, Pylos) as going toward an altar or shrine and being composed at the same time of priestesses about to make offerings and goddesses flocking in to bestow their favors."

150. *Palace of Nestor* II, pp. 58–61; Immerwahr 1990, pp. 114–121; Boulo-

tis 1987; Hiller 1996; Rehak 1998.

151. Hägg 1985, pp. 210–214; Boulotis 1987, esp. pp. 151–154.

152. Boulotis (1987, p. 155) argues persuasively that the Procession Fresco at Knossos is purely Minoan and must date to about LM II, a position followed by Immerwahr (1990).

153. McCallum 1987a, 1987b; *Palace of Nestor* II; Hägg 1985, 1995, 1996.

154. Kilian 1984; Hägg 1985, pp. 216–217; 1996; McCallum 1987a; Davis and Bennet 1999.

155. For an interpretation of the complex at Thebes as a megaron, see Kilian 1987, p. 207.

Aegean frescoes provide a rich but fragmentary and generalized picture of feasting across cultures and over generations. The early examples are found exclusively in Minoan "villas" or the mansions of wealthy islanders and consequently offer a restricted, elite view that need not be representative of the practices of feasting throughout the society. This limitation notwithstanding, these examples provide considerable insight into the elements of feasting: the probable hunting of game, especially deer; the preparation for the feast through the readying of cooking equipment and the transport of refreshments; and the setting of the scene of feasting outside monumental structures. This picture of Minoan and Cycladic feasts does not permit us to determine their purpose, whether for creating alliances and fostering cooperation, for economic gain, or for sumptuary display.[156] Boulotis has suggested, however, that we should pay attention to any evidence that these activities were regulated by a sacred calendar.[157]

As Borgna has argued, it is likely that Minoan feasting was conceived as an activity that reinforced solidarity among age-old communities.[158] Certainly feasting equipment belonged to the elite, whether those of palaces or villas, and they would have most likely sponsored and benefited from feasts.[159] It is probable that the acquisition of bronze, silver, and gold vessels by aggrandizing Mycenaean elites during the beginning years of the Late Bronze Age resulted from their participation in such festivals while on Crete. Their reenactment of formal feasting in their mainland communities, however, seems to have been a much more exclusive activity that was oriented toward competitive display initially for the purposes of promoting solidarity within their retinue and to gain political support and forge alliances as they expanded their control.[160] Feasting was a means of mobilizing labor, which became a major concern as Mycenaean chiefs began to mount major construction projects, such as monumental underground "tholos" tombs and Cyclopean stone fortifications,[161] and manage large-scale drainage and farming operations, as at Kophini near Tiryns and in the Kopaic basin. It is equally reasonable that feasting may have been carried out to mark the change of magistracies, as Killen argues,[162] since the focus of such feasting again reinforced the hierarchical sociopolitical structure of the Mycenaean palace societies. At the same time, as Dabney, Halstead, and Thomas argue elsewhere in this volume, feasting in the territories of the Mycenaean polities could have continued to serve the purposes of elites as they expanded networks of obligation for alliance building, for extending political and ideological dominance, and for economic purposes.

156. Hayden 2001a, pp. 29–42; 1995, pp. 26–28, fig. 3.

157. Boulotis 1987, p. 153, and esp. n. 40.

158. Borgna 1997, 1999, and this volume; see also Moody 1987; Rutter, forthcoming. Morgan (1998, p. 205) argues that the frescoes at Ayia Irini are local productions representing local ceremonies.

159. This is evident in the distribution of equipment in the palaces and "villas" (e.g., Mallia, Knossos, Tylissos) and in elite tombs, as at Archanes, around Knossos, and at Phaistos.

160. Borgna, this volume; Davis and Bennet 1999.

161. Wright 1987.

162. Killen 1994.

REPRESENTATIONS ON POTTERY

The majority of scenes on pottery that show a variety of vessels, and may indicate assemblages used in commensal activities, derive from the eastern Aegean and Cyprus, and thus may not be strictly representative of Aegean social conventions at the end of the Late Bronze Age. Since this area was largely implicated in the Mycenaean political economy, it is likely that iconographic traditions were derived from Mycenaean practice, but we cannot exclude consideration of other practices, such as those from the Near East, as Steel reminds us in her discussion of Cypriot feasting.[163] The iconography may have also been influenced by a myriad of local conventions, whether older practices of feasting on Crete (for which see Borgna, this volume), continuing traditions of feasting among residents of the islands and the western coast of Anatolia, or the multicultural society of Cypriot polities (see Steel, this volume).

The most complex of these representations is on a fragmentary krater from Enkomi (Fig. 18). A procession led by two robed figures riding in a chariot, with another robed person walking behind, is depicted. The robes are spotted. The walking figure has a baldric strapped across his chest from which hangs a long sword in a scabbard. He is attended by a nude servant who walks behind, holding a sunshade in his left hand and a small staff in his right. Clearly these implements are markers of rank and give the impression that this is a formal procession. Painted on the background around the armed walking man are a dipper, jug, chalice, krater, and conical rhyton. These vessels may be depicted as appropriate for a drinking ceremony, which might have included feasting, and their placement in the background may be an adopted convention, seen also, for example, in the scene on the Ayia Triada sarcophagus (Fig. 14).[164] It is significant that the scene occurs on a krater and that the drinking assemblage depicted is that which appears at the time of the palaces. The hint from the Ayia Irini frescoes that horse-drawn chariots may have been part of these procession scenes permits the conclusion that by the end of the Late Bronze Age a specialized iconography of drinking had evolved.

A similar fragment, probably from another krater, preserves the head and shoulders of a robed man, and on the background are painted a thin-necked, beak-spouted jug and a crosshatched hemispherical dipper.[165] A looping cable is suspended above the man's head and a painted curving line in front is broken away. It is likely that this display of vessels is a way of symbolizing a drinking service, owned by elites and used in rituals, both commensal and religious. This painted assemblage can be contrasted with ideogram *226* from Knossos tablet K 93 (Fig. 7:226). The difference is that painting these vessels on kraters emphasizes the predominant role played by the krater and dipper in drinking activities by elites at this time, a matter explored by Steel and by Sherratt in this volume.[166]

Another krater fragment, of advanced LH IIIC date from Lefkandi in Euboia, shows a two-handled bowl.[167] Large and small legs indicate that the scene also contained people. A krater from a tomb at Pigadi on Karpathos depicts an instrument (a rattle or sistrum?), wheel, pilgrim flask, and two high-handled kylikes—a special collection of artifacts whose pur-

163. Steel, this volume; see also Joffe 1998.

164. Long 1974.

165. Vermeule and Karageorghis 1982, p. 196, cat. no. and pl. III.22.

166. See also Steel 1998, 1999.

167. Vermeule and Karageorghis 1982, p. 223, cat. no. and pl. XI.66.

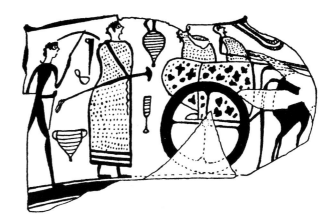

Figure 18. Detail from Enkomi krater. Adapted from Furumark 1941, p. 435, fig. 75

pose is unknown since not enough is preserved to reconstruct the scene.[168] A conical rhyton from the cemetery at Kameiros on Rhodes is even less easily understood.[169] It illustrates a high-handled kylix in the midst of a group of three standing boars (or men dressed as boars). It is possible that it represents a ritual dance, perhaps associated with the boar hunt. Whether or not it can be associated with feasting remains to be demonstrated.

Other representations do not readily add to our understanding of feasting since they are explicitly associated with mourning the dead. For example, a LM IIIB painted terracotta larnax from a chamber tomb at Episkopi, Ierapetra, Crete, depicts standing individuals raising kylikes.[170] Another from Tanagra in Boiotia shows a person raising a kylix or goblet while another individual raises both hands in an apparent gesture of mourning.[171] In this regard the frequent appearance of smashed drinking vessels, primarily kylikes and angular bowls, in the dromoi of chamber tombs should be considered; such an activity may have been part of a mourning feast or represent a more restricted ritual marking the final separation of the deceased.[172]

CONCLUSIONS

A distinct Mycenaean society emerged on the mainland of Greece between 1600 and 1400 B.C., demonstrated by a consistent stylistic and iconographic system of representation, of which feasting is one important aspect. From initial displays of high-status vessels, such as the gold and silver drinking vessels from the Shaft Graves at Mycenae, a broader pattern of display developed, particularly through the deposition of bronze feasting equipment in elite tombs distributed widely over the areas of Mycenaean dominance. These practices are signs of the competitive and somewhat disparate nature of social formation among various elite groups. This competition eventually led to the adoption of a common Mycenaean style and iconography at the time of the founding of the palaces and is displayed in the program of frescoes and records of Linear B tablets and sealings in the palaces at Pylos, Thebes, Mycenae, and Knossos.

Mycenaean feasting is characterized by several practices: the hunting of deer; fattening and gathering of sheep (and goats), pigs, and cattle; probable boiling of meat in tripods; delivery of large vessels holding a liquid

168. Vermeule and Karageorghis 1982, p. 228, cat. no. and pl. XII.28.

169. Vermeule and Karageorghis 1982, p. 227, cat. no. and pl. XII.17. See also Benzi 1992, pp. 109–110, 413, pl. 130:a, b. I thank J. Rutter for this reference.

170. Kanta 1980, pp. 150–153; Watrous 1991, p. 301.

171. From tomb 36: Spyropoulos 1973, p. 21, pl. 10:b; Immerwahr 1995, p. 116, fig. 7.5:a.

172. Cavanagh and Mee 1998, p. 115.

(probably wine);[173] processions near architectural settings (fortifications and large buildings); processions with bulls; the sacrifice of cattle, sheep, and goats; the collection of large bronze vessels and implements specific for feasts; the collection of specific serving and drinking vessels made of bronze, silver, and gold (and complementary ceramic forms); the apparent dedication of burned animal bones and other gifts to deities; and, finally, the preservation of feasting equipment and sacred debris. Analysis of the vessel forms and of their representation indicates particular emphasis on drinking, which results about the time of the founding of the palaces in LH IIIA in a ritual of the consumption of wine that is characterized by the use of a krater for holding (and mixing?) the wine, a dipper, and a goblet, kylix, or angular bowl for drinking.

Just as earlier Minoan and Cycladic feasting practices influenced the tastes of mainland elites at the beginning of the Late Bronze Age, the Mycenaean feast found favor in many areas with which the Mycenaeans were in contact. In this manner the iconography of feasting spread through-out the area of Mycenaean influence in the Aegean and eastern Mediter-ranean, continuing even after the demise of the mainland palace centers. This is the period when the symbols of the feast are widely illustrated on painted pottery, especially on Cyprus, as Steel eloquently shows in her contribution to this volume.

It is apparent that drinking is an important part of feasting activities, evident from the drinking vessels found in tombs and, as the studies by the other contributors to this volume demonstrate, in feasting deposits. Many depictions of drinking represent activities that are largely independent of feasting (such as honoring divinities and the dead). Drinking as a central activity of feasting is consistent with its historic function of aggrandize-ment by elites for whom rituals of drinking were associated with social strategies for consolidating their leadership and building the allegiance of a retinue. The practices of feasting and drinking gave hosts and guests alike opportunities for signaling their positions and status. Murray argues that in Classical times particular types of feasting can be identified and that among the Macedonians a type of feasting emerged that expressed hierarchy among the elites who surrounded the royal household.[174] The organization of these feasts reflected social position, with main partici-pants in the principal rooms and others seated (or reclined) in outer halls and courtyards.[175] Something like this arrangement may have been taking place in the Mycenaean palaces.

Grandiose displays by Mycenaean elites, in particular those reflected by burials in the Shaft Graves at Mycenae between MH III and LH I–II, were necessary early on to establish positions of dominance and display hospitality. Sponsored feasts were probably held exclusively for their kin, important retainers, and allied peers. The importance of this activity is registered by the appearance in tombs of the great metal vessels used for preparing and serving feasts. Over time this activity became evident in other categories—as deposits of cooking vessels in tombs and in domestic contexts, as records in Linear B, and in frescoes.

As Mycenaean society became more complex, social divisions emerged. Some evidence suggests that those striving to achieve status were eager to demonstrate their ability to command the resources of feasting or to par-

173. On wine, see Palmer 1994, 1995; and for barley wine and spiced wines, see McGovern 2003, pp. 262–276.

174. Murray 1996, pp. 16–25.

175. See especially Athenaeus's description (12.538) of the marriage feast of Alexander in 324 B.C. at Persepolis (Murray 1996, p. 20); see also Ath. 1.17–18.

ticipate in feasts, as can be surmised from the emulation of elite expressions of feasting through the compromised value of items such as ceramic imitations of metal vessels. For the less wealthy, participating in a feast exhibited an alternative kind of value, measured in terms of social distance. In this way feasting reflects the expansion of a Mycenaean social identity tied to the emerging political and economic needs of the palaces.

For the elites, however, the ability to sponsor feasts represented real economic value.[176] The size and importance of a feast denote the amount of surplus the sponsor can draw on, which is symbolized through particular vessels, such as the bronze tripod kettles displayed in the assemblages of bronze cooking and serving vessels found in so many tombs of the elite (Table 6). Since the surplus is collected from agricultural activities, its economic dimension is both geographically and demographically broad. Any substantial feast affected directly and indirectly a large and diverse population throughout the territory held by a community, as Palaima indicates in this volume in his study of the Linear B evidence. Therefore, the sponsor of a feast demonstrates the ability to bring together large groups (through coalitions and alliances), to mobilize labor, and to command surplus and distribute it. The sponsor gains in prestige through these activities and advances his family, lineage, and allies both within and beyond the community.

The bronze tripod kettle may have been selected so often for representation because it symbolizes the necessary wealth to command technologically superior craft items that were instrumental in the preparation of elite feasts, especially diacritical ones.[177] The special attention accorded the tripod kettle is amplified by textual references to Cretan-made kettles, and by the appearance of heirloom kettles (e.g., the Cretan kettle from grave IV of Circle A at Mycenae).[178] The tripod was selected early on as an important sign of wealth and prestige in historic Greece, with dedications occurring as early as the 10th century at sanctuaries.[179] The vessel has probably always been accorded symbolic value, since it was manufactured throughout the Late Bronze Age and into the Iron Age without a break, especially on Cyprus,[180] and becomes an icon in Classical times, as Jones has recently argued.[181] Heirlooms carry a history of their own, which can be related by participants in a feast. Through such storytelling, participants and sponsors can assert and establish claims of status back through the generations and, in passing the tales on, look into the future.

A feast must have food, and meat of course is highly regarded due to its cost and associations with the hunt. Thus we see three other aspects of the feast represented and recorded: the hunt, procession, and sacrifice. In Aegean art the hunt centers on deer and boar. The boar hunt has not been considered in this review because as of yet there are no clear associations with any of the feasting scenes.[182] It may be that the boar hunt was a separate activity, reserved for the elite and, as we know from later sources,[183] a sign of manhood and therefore a restricted rite of passage. The hunting of deer, however, is frequently represented. Textual evidence and zooarchaeological remains indicate that it was associated with feasting.[184] The hunt may be understood as one way—an aboriginal way—of provisioning meat and thus identified exclusively with peer hunters and warriors, and perhaps with cooking in a tripod.

176. Wiessner 2001, pp. 117–119.

177. Bronze tripod kettles range in size from 0.20 to 0.53 m in diameter, with most clustering around 0.30 m, in contrast to the standard ceramic Mycenaean tripod, which ranges from 0.12 to 0.20 m; see Mountjoy 1993, p. 82.

178. Palaima 2003.

179. Jones 2002, pp. 358–359, with references; Palaima 2003, p. 200, n. 37.

180. Catling 1964, 1984; Matthäus 1985, pp. 331–334; Hemingway 1996 (but see Catling 1997).

181. Jones 2002.

182. For a full study, see Morris 1990.

183. Murray 1996, pp. 15–18.

184. Bennet 2001, pp. 34–35; see the study in this volume by Dabney, Halstead, and Thomas; Isaakidou et al. 2002.

Also important is the sacrifice of domesticated animals: cattle, pigs, and sheep (and probably other animals documented by recent excavations at the Mycenaean shrine at Ayios Konstantinos on Methana).[185] Their slaughter, preparation, and consumption have a multitude of meanings for the feasting group and its sponsor or sponsors. The animals represent wealth and thus emphasize the special occasion of the feast. Their sacrifice requires expertise—from the manufacture of instruments suitable for killing to knowledge of how to kill, gut, clean, and butcher the animal. Technological skill is also necessary in the preparation—from the manufacture of a variety of vessels and implements to the preparation of the meat by expert cooks, who boil, roast, or grill it, and who use spices and seasonings and a variety of recipes.[186] The animals provide a high level of nutrition for the feasters, and the act of eating them is a sharing of flesh and blood. For this reason the symbolic value of the meat is high, and it is important that this taking of animal life is mediated by ritual, with appropriate respect and offerings to the ancestors and gods. Feasting is therefore often preceded by processions, marking the physical, social, and religious boundaries of the feasting group. It permits all who participate in the feast (and those present but excluded to varying degrees) to prepare themselves to participate and to comprehend the nature, dimensions, and purpose of the feast.

The archaeological record preserves not only generalized information about feasting but also evidence that its practices are interrelated across cultural horizons spanning more than half a millennium. The better part of the evidence comes from the period and culture we designate as Mycenaean, yet it is clear that no understanding of the Mycenaean feast can be gained without attention being given to evidence from the Neopalatial Cretan and Cycladic societies. It is commonplace in Aegean studies that Mycenaean culture is heavily dependent upon and derived from its island predecessors. These archaeologically recognized relationships are not diffusionist "just so" stories, nor are they theories based on models of economic production and exchange, nor iconographically based projections of religious and ideological interaction; instead, they are the result of sustained and intense human social interaction carried out at every level from the personal to the political. Feasting is one of the most ubiquitous and socially productive of these interactions, highly personal and open to infinite cultural variation in the selection of comestibles, their manipulation by preparation and presentation, and customs of their consumption. Feasting can thus be argued to be an appropriate vehicle for many other human activities, especially those that involve production and exchange, all of which depend on human relationships, trust, and sharing.

Feasting is an active, evanescent activity that is continuously transformed as it is performed, and consequently serves many functions in promoting personal, group, economic, ideological, and political aims. Much of what has been presented in this essay corresponds to the documentation in ethnographic studies of feasting in transegalitarian and complex societies,[187] including feasts for promoting group membership and alliances, mobilizing labor, competitive display, and collecting surplus, as well as ritual feasts marking important events in the cycles of the life of a household and community. To advance our understanding of feasting in the pre- and

185. Hamilakis and Konsolaki 2004. They have recovered sheep/goat, goat, cattle, pig, red deer, deer, mouse/rat, rock doves, bird, and fish from rooms A–C in the shrine. Of these, sheep/goat, goat, sheep, and pig predominate in terms of anatomical units represented. Only a few examples (1–3 of each) of mouse/rat, rock dove, bird, and fish were counted. In general on this subject, see Hayden 2001b for a model of the geographic and economic dynamics of animal husbandry and feasting.

186. See Killen 1992, pp. 367–370, on the presence of spices; also McGovern 2003, pp. 262–278.

187. Hayden 2001a, pp. 44–58; Dietler 2001; Junker 2001.

protohistoric Aegean and to identify specific feasts in the archaeological record, archaeologists need to structure their research toward the recovery of the diverse evidence of feasting.[188] Necessary is the proper recovery and analysis of biological remains through sampling and water sieving, as well as the comparative analysis of various lines of recovered evidence—organic and inorganic, stratigraphic and depositional. The most salient evidence is that which was written into the historical record because it was important to the higher orders of society: the preservation of prestige goods, the scribal documentation of chiefly or state activities, and the graphic representation of their sponsored feasting. This rich record bespeaks the importance of feasting to the chiefs and administrators of the Mycenaean polities.

188. See, e.g., the excellent study of the bioarchaeology of feasting at Cahokia by Pauketat et al. (2002).

REFERENCES

Abramovitz, K. 1980. "Frescoes from Ayia Irini, Keos, Parts II–IV," *Hesperia* 49, pp. 57–85.

Adams, W. Y., and E. W. Adams. 1991. *Archaeological Typology and Practical Reality*, New York.

Alt-Ägina IV.3 = I. Kilian-Dirlmeier, *Das mittelbronzezeitliche Schachtgrab von Ägina*, Mainz 1997.

Arnold, B. 1999. "'Drinking the Feast': Alcohol and the Legitimation of Power in Celtic Europe," *CAJ* 9, pp. 71–93.

Asine II = S. Dietz, *Results of the Excavations East of the Acropolis, 1970–1974*, II: *The Middle Helladic Cemetery, the Middle Helladic, and Early Mycenaean Deposits*, Stockholm 1980.

Baines, J., and N. Yoffee. 1998. "Order, Legitimacy, and Wealth in Ancient Egypt and Mesopotamia," in *Archaic States*, ed. G. M. Feinman and J. Marcus, Santa Fe, pp. 199–260.

Becker, C. 1999. "The Middle Neolithic and the Platia Magoula Zarkou: A Review of Current Archaeozoological Research in Thessaly (Greece)," *Anthropozoologica* 30, pp. 3–22.

Bell, C. 1992. *Ritual Theory, Ritual Practice*, New York.

Bennet, J. 1999. "The Meaning of 'Mycenaean': Speculations on Ethnicity in the Aegean Late Bronze Age," *BICS* 43, p. 224 (abstract).

———. 2001. "Agency and Bureaucracy: Thoughts on the Nature and Extent of Administration in Bronze Age Pylos," in *Economy and Politics in the Mycenaean Palace States* (Cambridge Philological Society, Suppl. 27), ed. S. Voutsaki and J. Killen, Cambridge, pp. 25–37.

Bennet, J., and M. Galaty. 1997. "Ancient Greece: Recent Developments in Aegean Archaeology and Regional Studies," *Journal of Archaeological Research* 5, pp. 75–120.

Bennett, E. L., Jr. 1958. *The Mycenae Tablets* II (*TAPS*, n.s. 48), Philadelphia.

———. 1962. "Notes on the Texts in *Mycenae Tablets* II," in *The Mycenae Tablets* III (*TAPS*, n.s. 52), ed. J. Chadwick, Philadelphia, pp. 71–72.

Bennett, E. L., Jr., and J.-P. Olivier. 1973. *The Pylos Tablets Transcribed* 1: *Texts and Notes* (Incunabula graeca 51), Rome.

Benzi, M. 1992. *Rodi e la civiltà micenea*, Rome.

Betancourt, P. P., V. Karageorghis, R. Laffineur, and W.-D. Niemeier, eds. 1999. *Meletemata: Studies in Aegean Archaeology Presented to Malcolm H. Wiener as He Enters His 65th Year* (*Aegaeum* 20), Liège.

Blegen, C. W. 1937. *Prosymna: The Helladic Settlement preceding the Argive Heraeum*, Cambridge.

Borgna, E. 1997. "Some Observations on Deep Bowls and Kraters from the 'Acropoli Mediana' at Phaistos," in *Late Minoan III Pottery: Chronology and Terminology. Acts of a Meeting Held at the Danish Institute at Athens*, ed. E. Hallager and B. P. Hallager, Athens, pp. 273–298.

———. 1999. "Circolazione e uso della ceramica nello scambio cerimoniale tra mondo miceneo palaziale e Cretardominoica: La prospettiva di Festòs nel TM III," in *Επί πόντον πλαζόμενοι: Simposio italiano di studi egei dedicato a Luigi Bernabò Brea e Giovanni Pugliese Carratelli, Roma*, ed. V. La Rosa, D. Palermo, and L. Vagnetti, Rome, pp. 199–205.

Borza, E. N. 1983. "The Symposium at Alexander's Court," in *Ancient Macedonia 3: Papers Read at the Third International Symposium Held at Thessaloniki*, Thessaloniki, pp. 45–55.

Boulotis, C. 1987. "Nochmals zum Prozessionsfresko von Knossos: Palast und Darbringung von Prestige-Objekten," in Hägg and Marinatos 1987, pp. 145–156.

Bourdieu, P. 1980. *The Logic of Practice*, Stanford.

Cain, C. D. 2001. "Dancing in the Dark: Deconstructing a Narrative of Epiphany on the Isopata Ring," *AJA* 105, pp. 27–49.

Cameron, M. A. S. 1964. "An Addition to 'La Parisienne,'" *CretChron* 18, pp. 38–53.

Catling, H. W. 1964. *Cypriot Bronzework in the Mycenaean World*, Oxford.

———. 1984. "Workshop and Heirlooms: Prehistoric Bronze Stands in the East Mediterranean," *RDAC* 1984, pp. 69–91.

———. 1997. "Minoan Metalworking at Palaikastro: Some Questions," *BSA* 92, pp. 51–58.

Cavanagh, W., and C. Mee. 1998. *A Private Place: Death in Prehistoric Greece* (*SIMA* 125), Jonsered.

Cherry, J. F., and J. L. Davis. 1982. "The Cyclades and the Greek Mainland in LC I: The Evidence of Pottery," *AJA* 86, pp. 333–341.

Clark, J., and M. Blake. 1994. "The Power of Prestige: Competitive Generosity and the Emergence of Rank Societies in Lowland Mesoamerica," in *Factional Competition and Political Development in the New World*, ed. E. M. Brumfiel and J. W. Fox, Cambridge, pp. 17–30.

Clarke, M. 2001. "Akha Feasting: An Ethnoarchaeological Perspective," in Dietler and Hayden 2001a, pp. 144–167.

CoMIK = J. Chadwick, L. Godart, J. T. Killen, J. P. Olivier, A. Sacconi, and Y. A. Sakellarakis, *Corpus of Mycenaean Inscriptions from Knossos*, 4 vols., Cambridge 1986–1998.

Corinth XIII = C. W. Blegen, H. Palmer, and R. S. Young, *The North Cemetery*, Princeton 1964.

Davis, E. 1977. *The Vapheio Cups and Aegean Gold and Silver Ware*, New York.

Davis, J. L., and J. Bennet. 1999. "Making Mycenaeans: Warfare, Territorial Expansion, and Representations of the Other in the Pylian Kingdom," in *Polemos: Le contexte guerrier en Égée à l'âge du Bronze. Actes de la 7ᵉ Rencontre égéene internationale, Université de Liège* (*Aegaeum* 19), ed. R. Laffineur, Liège, pp. 105–120.

Demakopoulou, K. 1982. *Το μυκηναϊκό ιερό στο Αμυκλαίο και η ΥΕ ΙΙΙ Γ περίοδος στη Λακωνία*, Athens (privately published).

———. 1990. "The Burial Ritual in the Tholos Tomb at Kokla, Argolis," in *Celebrations of Death and Divinity in the Bronze Age Argolid. Proceedings of the Sixth International Symposium at the Swedish Institute at Athens* (*SkrAth* 4°, 40), ed. R. Hägg and G. C. Nordquist, Stockholm, pp. 113–123.

———. 1993. "Argive Mycenaean Pottery: Evidence from the Necropolis at Kokla (Appendix by R. E. Jones)," in *Wace and Blegen: Pottery as Evidence for Trade in the Aegean Bronze Age, 1939–1989*, ed. C. Zerner, Amsterdam, pp. 57–75.

———. 1997. "Crete and the Argolid in the LM II/LHIIB to IIIA1 Periods: Evidence from Kokla," in *La Crète mycénienne. Actes de la Table ronde internationale organisée par l'École française d'Athènes* (*BCH* Suppl. 30), ed. J. Driessen and A. Farnoux, Athens, pp. 101–112.

Dentzer. J.-M. 1971. "Aux origines de l'iconographie du banquet couché," *RA* 1971, pp. 215–258.

Dickinson, O. T. P. K. 1977. *The Origins of Mycenaean Civilisation* (*SIMA* 49), Göteborg.

Dietler, M., 1990. "Driven by Drink: The Role of Drinking in the Political Economy and the Case of

Early Iron Age France," *JAnthArch* 9, pp. 352–406.

———. 1999. "Rituals of Commensality and the Politics of State Formation in the 'Princely' Societies of Early Iron Age Europe," in *Les princes de la protohistoire et l'émergence de l'état* (*CÉFR* 252), ed. P. Ruby, Rome, pp. 135–152.

———. 2001. "Theorizing the Feast: Rituals of Consumption, Commensal Politics, and Power in African Contexts," in Dietler and Hayden 2001a, pp. 65–114.

Dietler, M., and B. Hayden, eds. 2001a. *Feasts: Archaeological and Ethnographic Perspectives on Food, Politics, and Power*, Washington, D.C.

Dietler, M., and B. Hayden. 2001b. "Digesting the Feast—Good to Eat, Good to Drink, Good to Think: An Introduction," in Dietler and Hayden 2001a, pp. 1–20.

Dietz, S. 1991. *The Argolid at the Transition to the Mycenaean Age*, Copenhagen.

Douglas, M., and C. Isherwood. 1979. *The World of Goods: Towards an Anthropology of Consumption*, New York.

Earle, T. K., and J. E. Ericson. 1977. "Exchange Systems in Archaeological Perspective," in *Exchange Systems in Prehistory*, ed. T. K. Earle and J. E. Ericson, New York, pp. 3–12.

Elias, N. 1978. *The History of Manners*, trans. E. Jephcott, New York.

Erlenmeyer, M.-L., and H. Erlenmeyer. 1956. "Cerviden Darstellungen auf orientalischen und ägäischen Siegel, I," *Orientalia* 25, pp. 149–153.

———. 1957. "Cerviden Darstellungen auf orientalischen und ägäischen Siegel, II," *Orientalia* 26, pp. 321–333.

Evans, A. 1906. *The Prehistoric Tombs of Knossos: The Cemetery of Zafer Papoura, the Royal Tomb of Isopata*, London.

Feinman, G. M. 1998. "Scale and Social Organization: Perspectives on the Archaic State," in *Archaic States*, ed. G. M. Feinman and J. Marcus, Santa Fe, pp. 95–133.

Frödin, O. 1938. *Asine: Results of the Swedish Excavations, 1922–1930*, Stockholm.

Furtwängler, A. 1879. *Mykenische Thongefässe*, Berlin.

Furtwängler, A., and G. Loeschcke. 1886. *Mykenische Vasen: Vorhellenische Thongefässe aus dem Gebiete des Mittelmeeres*, Berlin.

Furumark, A. 1941. *The Mycenaean Pottery: Analysis and Classification*, Stockholm.

Galaty, M. L. 1999a. "Wealth Ceramics, Staple Ceramics: Pots and the Mycenaean Palaces," in *Rethinking Mycenaean Palaces: New Interpretations of an Old Idea*, ed. M. L. Galaty and W. A. Parkinson, Los Angeles, pp. 49–59.

———. 1999b. *Nestor's Wine Cups: Investigating Ceramic Manufacture and Exchange in a Late Bronze Age "Mycenaean" State* (*BAR-IS* 766), Oxford.

Gillis, C. 1991. "Tin in the Aegean Bronze Age," *Hydra* 8, pp. 1–30.

———. 1992. "How I Discovered Gold and Solved the Alchemists' Dream, or Tin-Covered Vessels: Part II," *Hydra* 10, pp. 13–16.

———. 1994. "Binding Evidence: Tin Foil and Organic Binder on Aegean Late Bronze Age Pottery," *OpAth* 20, pp. 57–61.

———. 1996. "Tin at Asine," in *Asine III: Supplementary Studies on the Swedish Excavations, 1922–1930*, ed. R. Hägg, G. C. Nordquist, and B. Wells, Stockholm, pp. 93–100.

———. 1997. "Tin-Covered Late Bronze Age Vessels: Analyses and Social Implications," in *Trade and Production in Premonetary Greece: Production and the Craftsman* (*SIMA-PB* 143), ed. C. Gillis, C. Risberg, and B. Sjöberg, Jonsered, pp. 131–138.

Goody, J. 1982. *Cooking, Cuisine, and Class: A Study in Comparative Sociology*, Cambridge.

Graziadio, G. 1988. "The Chronology of the Graves of Circle B at Mycenae: A New Hypothesis," *AJA* 92, pp. 343–372.

Hägg, R. 1985. "Pictorial Programmes in Minoan Palaces and Villas?" in *L'iconographie minoenne. Actes de la Table ronde d'Athènes* (*BCH* Suppl. 11), ed. P. Darcque and J.-C. Poursat, Athens, pp. 209–217.

———. 1995. "State and Religion in Mycenaean Greece," *Politeia: Society and State in the Aegean Bronze Age. Proceedings of the 5th International Aegean Conference, Heidelberg* (*Aegaeum* 12), ed. R. Laffineur and W.-D. Niemeier, Liège, pp. 387–391.

———. 1996. "The Religion of the Mycenaeans Twenty-Four Years after the 1967 Mycenological Congress in Rome," *Atti e memorie del secondo Congresso internazionale di micenologia, Roma–Napoli 2: Storia* (Incunabula graeca 98), ed. E. De Miro, L. Godart, and A. Sacconi, Rome, pp. 599–612.

Hägg, R., and N. Marinatos, eds. 1987. *The Function of the Minoan Palaces. Proceedings of the Fourth International Symposium at the Swedish Institute in Athens* (*SkrAth* 4°, 35), Stockholm.

Haghia Triada I = P. Militello, *Gli affreschi*, Padua 1998.

Hamilakis, Y. 1998. "Eating the Dead: Mortuary Feasting and the Politics of Memory in the Aegean Bronze Age Societies," *Cemetery and Society in the Aegean Bronze Age* (Sheffield Studies in Aegean Archaeology 1), ed. K. Branigan, Sheffield, pp. 115–132.

———. 1999. "Food Technologies/Technologies of the Body: The Social Context of Wine and Oil Production and Consumption in Bronze Age Crete," *WorldArch* 31, pp. 38–54.

———. 2003. "The Sacred Geography of Hunting: Wild Animals, Social Power, and Gender in Early Farming Societies," in *Zooarchaeology in Greece: Recent Advances* (*BSA* Studies 9), ed. E. Kotjabopoulou, Y. Hamilakis, P. Halstead, C. Gamble, and P. Elefanti, London, pp. 239–247.

Hamilakis, Y., and E. Konsolaki 2004. "Pigs for the Gods: Burnt Animal Sacrifices as Embodied Rituals at a Mycenaean Sanctuary," *OJA* 23, pp. 135–151.

Hayden, B. 1995. "Pathways to Power: Principles for Creating Socioeconomic Inequalities," in *Foundations of Social Inequality*, ed. T. D. Price and G. M. Feinman, New York, pp. 15–86.

———. 2001a. "Fabulous Feasts: A Prolegomenon to the Importance of Feasting," in Dietler and Hayden 2001a, pp. 23–64.

———. 2001b. "The Dynamics of Wealth and Poverty in the Transegalitarian Societies of Southeast Asia," *Antiquity* 75, pp. 571–581.

Hemingway, S. 1996. "Minoan Metalworking in the Postpalatial Period: A Deposit of Metallurgical Debris from Palaikastro," *BSA* 91, pp. 213–252.

Hiller, S. 1996. "Zur Rezeption ägyptischen Motiven in der minoischen Freskenkunst," *Ägypten und Levante* 6, pp. 83–105.

———. 1999. "Egyptian Elements of the Hagia Triada Sarcophagus," in Betancourt et al. 1999, pp. 361–369.

Hodder, I. 1978. *The Spatial Organisation of Culture*, Pittsburgh.

———. 1982. *Symbols in Action: Ethnoarchaeological Studies of Material Culture*, New York.

Immerwahr, S. A. 1966. "The Use of Tin on Mycenaean Vases," *Hesperia* 35, pp. 381–396.

———. 1990. *Aegean Painting in the Bronze Age*, University Park, Penn.

———. 1995. "Death and the Tanagra Larnakes," in *The Ages of Homer: A Tribute to Emily Townsend Vermeule*, ed. J. B. Carter and S. P. Morris, Austin, pp. 109–122.

Isaakidou, V., P. Halstead, J. Davis, and S. Stocker. 2002. "Burnt Animal Sacrifice in Late Bronze Age Greece: New Evidence from the Mycenaean 'Palace of Nestor,' Pylos," *Antiquity* 76, pp. 86–92.

Jellinek, E. M. 1977. "The Symbolism of Drinking: A Culture-Historical Approach," *Journal of Studies on Alcohol* 38, pp. 849–866.

Joffe, A. H. 1998. "Alcohol and Social Complexity in Ancient Western Asia," *CurrAnthr* 39, pp. 297–322.

Jones, M. W. 2002. "Tripods, Triglyphs, and the Origin of the Doric Frieze," *AJA* 106, pp. 353–390.

Junker, L. 2001. "The Evolution of Ritual Feasting Systems in Prehispanic Philippine Chiefdoms," in Dietler and Hayden 2001a, pp. 267–310.

Kanta, A. 1980. *The Late Minoan III Period in Crete: A Survey of Sites, Pottery, and Their Distribution* (*SIMA* 58), Göteborg.

Karageorghis, V. 1957. "A Mycenaean Chalice and a Vase Painter," *BSA* 52, pp. 38–41.

Karo, G. 1930–1933. *Die Schachtgräber von Mykenai*, Munich.

Kilian, K. 1980. "Zur Darstellung eines Wagenrennens aus spätmykenischer Zeit," *AM* 86, pp. 21–31.

———. 1984. "Funktionsanalyse einer Residenz der späten Palastzeit," *ArchKorrBl* 14, pp. 37–48.

———. 1987. "L'architecture des résidences mycéniennes: Origine et extension d'une structure du pouvoir politique pendant l'âge du bronze récent," in *Le système palatial en Orient, en Grèce, et à Rome. Actes du Colloque de Strasbourg*, ed. E. Lévy, Leiden, pp. 203–217.

———. 1988. "The Emergence of Wanax Ideology in the Mycenaean Palaces," *OJA* 7, pp. 291–302.

Kilian-Dirlmeier, I. 1985. "Noch einmal zu den 'Kriegergräbern' von Knossos," *JRGZM* 32, pp. 196–214.

———. 1986. "Beobachtungen zu den Schachtgräbern von Mykenai und zu den Schmuckbeigaben mykenischer Männergräber," *JRGZM* 33, pp. 159–198.

Killen, J. T. 1992. "Observations on the Thebes Sealings," in *Mykenaïka. Actes du IXe Colloque international sur les textes mycéniens et égéens organisé par le Centre de l'antiquité grecque et romaine de la Fondation hellénique des recherches scientifiques et l'École française d'Athènes* (*BCH* Suppl. 25), ed. J.-P. Olivier, Paris, pp. 365–380.

———. 1994. "Thebes Sealings, Knossos Tablets, and Mycenaean State Banquets," *BICS* 39, pp. 67–84.

———. 1998. "The Pylos Ta Tablets Revisited," pp. 421–422, in F. Rougemont and J.-P. Olivier, eds., "Recherches récentes en épigraphie créto-mycénienne," *BCH* 122, pp. 403–443.

Knight, V. J. 2001. "Feasting and the Emergence of Platform Mound Ceremonialism in Eastern North America," in Dietler and Hayden 2001a, pp. 311–333.

Kontorli-Papadopoulou, L. 1996. *Aegean Frescoes with Religious Character* (*SIMA* 127), Göteborg.

Lebessi, A., and P. Muhly. 1987. "The Sanctuary of Hermes and Aphrodite at Syme, Crete," *NatGeogRes* 3:1, pp. 102–112.

———. 1990. "Aspects of Minoan Cult: Sacred Enclosures. The Evidence from the Syme Sanctuary (Crete)," *AA* 1990, pp. 315–336.

Long, C. 1974. *The Ayia Triadha Sarcophagus: A Study of Late Minoan and Mycenaean Funerary Practices and Beliefs* (*SIMA* 41), Göteborg.

Loraux, N. 1981. "La cité comme cuisine et comme partage," *AnnÉconSocCiv* 36, pp. 614–622.

Löwe, W. 1996. *Spätbronzezeitliche Bestattungen auf Kreta* (*BAR-IS* 642), Oxford.

MacGillivray, J. A. 1987. "Pottery Workshops and the Old Palaces in Crete," in Hägg and Marinatos 1987, pp. 273–279.

Marinatos, N. 1993. *Minoan Religion: Ritual, Image, and Symbol*, Columbia, S.C.

Marinatos, S., and M. Hirmer. 1973. *Crete and Mycenae*, New York.

Matthäus, H. 1980. *Die Bronzegefässe der kretisch-mykenischen Kultur* (Prähistorische Bronzefunde 2.1), Munich.

———. 1983. "Minoische Kriegergräber," in *Minoan Society. Proceedings of the Cambridge Colloquium, 1981*, ed. O. Krzyszkowska and L. Nixon, Bristol, pp. 203–215.

———. 1985. *Metallgefässe und Gefässuntersätze der Bronzezeit, der geometrischen und archaischen Periode auf Cypern: Mit einem Anhang der bronzezeitlichen Schwertfunde auf Cypern* (Prähistorische Bronzefunde 2.8), Munich.

McCallum, L. R. 1987a. "Decorative Program in the Mycenaean Palace of Pylos: The Megaron Frescoes" (diss. Univ. of Pennsylvania).

———. 1987b. "Frescoes from the Throne Room at Pylos: A New Interpretation," *AJA* 91, p. 296 (abstract).

McGovern, P. E. 2003. *Ancient Wine: The Search for the Origins of Viniculture*, Princeton.

Melena, J. L. 1997a. "133 Joins and Quasi-Joins of Fragments in the Linear B Tablets from Pylos," *Minos* 29–30 (1994–1995), pp. 271–288.

———. 1997b. "40 Joins and Quasi-Joins of Fragments in the Linear B Tablets from Pylos," *Minos* 31–33 (1996–1997), pp. 159–170.

Moody, J. 1987. "The Minoan Palace as a Prestige Artifact," in Hägg and Marinatos 1987, pp. 235–241.

Moorey, P. R. S. 1980. "Metal Wine Sets in the Ancient Near East," *IrAnt* 15, pp. 181–192.

Morgan, L. 1985. "Idea, Idiom, and Iconography," in *L'iconographie minoenne. Actes de la Table ronde d'Athènes* (*BCH* Suppl. 11), ed. P. Darcque and J.-C. Poursat, Athens, pp. 5–19.

———. 1989. "Ambiguity and Interpretation," in *Fragen und Probleme der Bronzezeitlichen ägäischen Glyptik. Beiträge zum 3. Internationalen Marburger Siegel-Symposium* (*CMS* Beiheft 3), ed. I. Pini, Berlin, pp. 145–162.

———. 1990. "Island Iconography: Thera, Kea, Milos," in *Thera and the Aegean World* III.1, ed. D. A. Hardy, London, pp. 252–266.

———. 1995. "The Wall-Paintings of Ayia Irini, Kea," *BICS* 40, pp. 243–244.

———. 1998. "The Wall Paintings of the North-East Bastion at Ayia Irini, Kea," in *Kea-Kythnos: History and Archaeology* (*Meletemata* 27), ed. L. G. Mendoni and A. Mazarakis Ainian, Athens, pp. 201–210.

Morris, C. E. 1990. "In Pursuit of the White Tusked Boar: Aspects of Hunting in Mycenaean Society," in *Celebrations of Death and Divinity in the Bronze Age Argolid. Proceedings of the Sixth International Symposium at the Swedish Institute at Athens* (*SkrAth* 4°, 40), ed. R. Hägg and G. C. Nordquist, Stockholm, pp. 149–156.

Morris, S. 1989. "A Tale of Two Cities: The Miniature Frescoes from Thera and the Origins of Greek Poetry," *AJA* 93, pp. 511–535.

———. 2000. "From Thera to Scheria: Aegean Art and Narrative," in *The Wall Paintings of Thera: Proceedings of the 1st International Symposium*, ed. S. Sherratt, Athens, pp. 317–331.

Mountjoy, P. A. 1983. "The Ephyraean Goblet Reviewed," *BSA* 78, pp. 265–271.

———. 1986. *Mycenaean Decorated Pottery: A Guide to Identification* (*SIMA* 73), Göteborg.

———. 1993. *Mycenaean Pottery: An Introduction*, Oxford.

———. 1999. *Regional Mycenaean Decorated Pottery*, Rahden.

Murray, O. 1990. "Sympotic History," in *Sympotica: A Symposium on the Symposion*, ed. O. Murray, Oxford, pp. 3–13.

———. 1996. "Hellenistic Royal Symposia," in *Aspects of Hellenistic Kingship*, ed. P. Bilde et al., Aarhus, pp. 15–27.

Mylonas, G. 1973. *Ο Ταφικός Κύκλος Β´ των Μυκηνών*, Athens.

Nordquist, G. C. 1987. *A Middle Helladic Village: Asine in the Argolid*, Uppsala.

Palace of Nestor II = M. Lang, *The Palace of Nestor at Pylos in Western Messenia* II: *The Frescoes*, Princeton 1969.

Palaima, T. G. 1999. "Kn 02–Tn 316," in *Floreant Studia Mycenaea. Akten des X. Internationalen Mykenologischen Colloquiums, Salzburg* (*DenkschrWien* 274), ed. S. Deger-Jalkotzy, S. Hiller, and O. Panagl, Vienna, pp. 437–461.

———. 2003. "The Inscribed Bronze 'Kessel' from Shaft Grave IV and Cretan Heirlooms of the Bronze Artist Named 'Aigeus' *vel. sim.* in the Mycenaean Palatial Period," in *Briciaka: A Tribute to W. C. Brice* (Cretan Studies 9), ed. Y. Duhoux, Amsterdam, pp. 187–201.

Palmer, R. 1994. *Wine in the Mycenaean Palace Economy* (*Aegaeum* 10), Liège.

———. 1995. "Wine and Viticulture in the Linear A and B Texts of the Bronze Age Aegean," in *The Origins and Ancient History of Wine* (Food and Nutrition in History and Anthropology 11), ed. P. E. McGovern, S. J. Fleming, and S. H. Katz, Amsterdam, pp. 269–258.

Panofsky, E. 1939. *Studies in Iconology: Humanistic Themes in the Art of the Renaissance*, New York.

Papadopoulos, T. 1979. *Mycenaean Achaia* (*SIMA* 55), Göteborg.

Pauketat, T. R., L. S. Kelly, G. F. Fritz, N. H. Lopinot, S. Elias, and E. Hargrave. 2002. "The Residues of Feasting and Public Ritual at Early Cahokia," *AmerAnt* 67, pp. 257–279.

Persson, A. W. 1931. *The Royal Tombs at Dendra near Midea*, Lund.

———. 1942. *New Tombs at Dendra near Midea*, Lund.

Piteros, C., J.-P. Olivier, and J. L. Melena. 1990. "Les inscriptions en linéaire B des nodules de Thèbes (1982): La fouille, les documents, les possibilités d'interprétation," *BCH* 114, pp. 103–184.

Platon, N. 1959. "Συμβολή εις την σπουδήν μινωικής της τοιχογραφίας," *ChretChron* 13, pp. 319–345.

———. 1971. *Zakros: The Discovery of a Lost Palace of Ancient Crete*, New York.

Plog, S. 1976. "Measurement of Prehistoric Interaction between Communities," in *The Early Mesoamerican Village*, ed. K. V. Flannery, New York, pp. 255–272.

Popham, M. R. 1973. "Sellopoulo Tomb 4: Some Aspects of the Finds," in *Τα Πεπράγμενα του Γ´ Διεθνούς Κρητολογικού Συνεδρίου*, Athens, pp. 268–273.

Popham, M. R., E. A. Catling, and H. W. Catling. 1974. "Sellopoulo Tombs 3 and 4: Two Late Minoan Graves near Knossos," *BSA* 69, pp. 195–257.

Preston, L. 1999. "Mortuary Practices and the Negotiation of Social Identities at LM II Knossos," *BSA* 94, pp. 131–143.

Rehak, P. 1998. "Aegean Natives in the Theban Tomb Paintings," in *The Aegean and the Orient in the Second Millennium. Proceedings of the 50th Anniversary Symposium, Cincinnati* (*Aegaeum* 18), ed. E. H. Cline and D. Harris-Cline, Liège, pp. 39–51.

———. 2000. "The Isopata Ring and the Question of Narrative in Neopalatial Glyptik," in *Minoisch-mykenische Glyptik: Stil, Ikonographie, Funktion. V. Internationales Siegel-Symposium, Marburg* (*CMS* Beiheft 6), ed. W. Müller, Berlin, pp. 269–276.

Rice, P. M. 1987. *Pottery Analysis: A Sourcebook*, Chicago.

Rutter, J. Forthcoming. "Ceramic Sets in Context: One Dimension of Food Preparation and Consumption in a Minoan Palatial Setting," in *Food, Cuisine, and Society in Prehistoric Greece* (Sheffield Studies in Aegean Archaeology 5), ed. P. Halstead and J. C. Barrett, Sheffield.

Sacconi, A. 1987. "La tavoletta di Pilo Tn 316: Una registrazione di carattere eccezionale?" in *Studies in Mycenaean and Classical Greek Presented to John Chadwick* (*Minos* 20–22), ed. J. T. Killen, J. L. Melena, and J.-P. Olivier, Salamanca, pp. 551–556.

———. 2001. "Les repas sacrés dans les textes mycéniens," in *Potnia: Deities and Religion in the Aegean Bronze Age. Proceedings of the 8th International Aegean Conference, Göteborg* (*Aegaeum* 22), ed. R. Laffineur and R. Hägg, Liège, pp. 467–470.

Säflund, G. 1980. "Sacrificial Banquets in the 'Palace of Nestor,'" *OpAth* 13, pp. 237–246.

Sakellarakis, Y. A. 1970. "Das Kuppelgrab A von Archanes und das kretisch-mykenische Tieropferritual," *PZ* 45, pp. 135–219.

Sakellarakis, Y. A., and E. Sakellarakis. 1991. *Archanes*, Athens.

Sakellariou, A. 1964. *Die minoischen und mykenische Siegel des National Museums in Athen* (*CMS* I), Berlin.

Schmitt Pantel, P. 1990. "Sacrificial Meal and *Symposium*: Two Models of Civic Institutions in the Archaic City?" in *Sympotica: A Symposium on the Symposion*, ed. O. Murray, Oxford, pp. 14–33.

Shaw, M. C. 1972 "The Miniature Frescoes of Tylissos Reconsidered," *AA* 1972, pp. 171–188.

———. 1980. "Painted 'Ikria' at Mycenae?" *AJA* 84, pp. 167–179.

———. 1993. "The Aegean Garden," *AJA* 97, pp. 661–685.

———. 1996. "The Bull-Leaping Fresco from below the Ramp House at Mycenae: A Study in Iconography and Artistic Transmission," *BSA* 9, pp. 167–190.

———. 1997. "Aegean Sponsors and Artists: Reflections of Their Roles in the Patterns of Distribution of Themes and Representational Conventions in Murals," in *TEXNH: Craftsmen, Craftswomen, and Craftsmanship in the Aegean Bronze Age. Proceedings of the 6th International Aegean Conference, Philadelphia* (*Aegaeum* 16), ed. R. Laffineur and P. P. Betancourt, Liège, pp. 481–503.

———. 1999. "A Bronze Age Enigma: The 'U-Shaped' Motif in Aegean Architectural Representations," in Betancourt et al. 1999, pp. 769–779.

Shelmerdine, C. W. 1985. *The Perfume Industry of Mycenaean Pylos* (*SIMA* 34), Göteborg.

Sinopoli, C. M. 1991. *Approaches to Archaeological Ceramics,* New York.

Snyder, L., and E. Andrikou. 2001. "Raw Material for a Helmet? Evidence for Boar's Tusk Harvesting in a Late Helladic Context, Thebes," *AJA* 205, p. 304 (abstract).

Speth, J. 2004. "Boiling vs. Roasting in the Paleolithic: Distinguishing Methods of Cooking Meat and Why It Matters" (paper, Montreal 2004).

Spyropoulos, T. 1973. "Ἀνασκαφή μυκηναϊκῆς Τανάγρας," *Prakt* 1973, pp. 22–25.

Steel, L. 1998. "The Social Impact of Mycenaean Imported Pottery in Cyprus," *BSA* 93, pp. 285–296.

———. 1999. "Wine Kraters and Chariots: The Mycenaean Pictorial Style Reconsidered," in Betancourt et al. 1999, pp. 803–811.

Tiryns II = G. Rodenwaldt, *Die Fresken des Palastes,* Athens 1912.

Turner, V. 1967. *The Forest of Symbols,* Ithaca.

Vandenabeele, F., and J.-P. Olivier. 1979. *Les idéogrammes archéologiques du linéaire B* (*ÉtCrét* 24), Paris.

Ventris, M., and J. Chadwick. 1973. *Documents in Mycenaean Greek,* 2nd ed., Cambridge.

Vermeule, E. 1975. *The Art of the Shaft Graves of Mycenae* (Lectures in Memory of Louise Taft Semple, ser. 3), Cincinnati.

Vermeule, E., and V. Karageorghis. 1982. *Mycenaean Pictorial Vase Painting,* Cambridge, Mass.

Watrous, L. V. 1991. "The Origin and Iconography of the Late Minoan Painted Larnax," *Hesperia* 60, pp. 285–307.

Whallon, R., and J. Brown, eds. 1982. *Essays on Archaeological Typology,* Evanston.

Whitelaw, T. M. 2001. "Reading between the Tablets: Assessing Mycenaean Palatial Involvement in Ceramic Production and Consumption," in *Economy and Politics in the Mycenaean Palace States* (Cambridge Philological Society, Suppl. 27), ed. S. Voutsaki and J. Killen, Cambridge, pp. 51–79.

Wiessner, P. 1983. "Style and Social Information in Kalahari San Projectile Points," *AmerAnt* 48, pp. 253–276.

———. 1989. "Style and Changing Relations between the Individual and Society," in *The Meaning of Things: Material Culture and Symbolic Expression,* ed. I. Hodder, London, pp. 56–63.

———. 2001. "Enga Feasts in a Historical Perspective," in Dietler and Hayden 2001a, pp. 115–143.

Wilkie, N. C. 1992. "The MME Tholos Tomb," in *Excavations at Nichoria in Southwest Greece* II: *The Bronze Age Occupation,* ed. W. A. McDonald and N. C. Wilkie, Minneapolis, pp. 231–344.

Wobst, H. M. 1977. "Stylistic Behavior and Information Exchange," in *For the Director: Research Essays in Honor of James B. Griffin* (Anthropological Papers 6), ed. C. E. Cleland, Ann Arbor, pp. 317–342.

Wright, J. C. 1984. "Changes in Form and Function of the Palace at Pylos," in *Pylos Comes Alive: Industry and Administration in a Mycenaean Palace. Papers of a Symposium,* ed. C. W. Shelmerdine and T. G. Palaima, New York, pp. 19–29.

———. 1987. "Death and Power at Mycenae: Changing Symbols in Mortuary Practice," in *Thanatos: Les coutumes funéraires en Égée à l'âge du Bronze. Actes du Colloque de Liège* (*Aegaeum* 1), ed. R. Laffineur, Liège, pp. 171–184.

———. 1994. "The Spatial Configuration of Belief: The Archaeology of Mycenaean Religion," in *Placing the Gods: Sanctuaries and Sacred Space in Ancient Greece,* ed. S. E. Alcock and R. Osborne, Oxford, pp. 37–78.

———. 1995a. "Empty Cups and Empty Jugs: The Social Role of Wine in Minoan and Mycenaean Societies," in *The Origins and Ancient History of Wine* (Food and Nutrition in History and Anthropology 11), ed. P. E. McGovern, S. J. Fleming, and S. H. Katz, Philadelphia, pp. 287–309.

———. 1995b. "From Chief to King in Mycenaean Greece," in *The Role of the Ruler in the Prehistoric Aegean. Proceedings of a Panel Discussion Presented at the Annual Meeting of the Archaeological Institute of America, New Orleans* (*Aegaeum* 11), ed. P. Rehak, Liège, pp. 63–80.

———. 2001. "Factions and the Origins of Leadership and Identity in Mycenaean Society," *BICS* 45, p. 182 (abstract).

———. Forthcoming a. "Mycenaean Drinking Services and Standards of Etiquette," in *Food, Cuisine, and Society in Prehistoric Greece* (Sheffield Studies in Aegean Archaeology 5), ed. P. Halstead and J. C. Barrett, Sheffield.

———. Forthcoming b. "The Emergence of Leadership and the Origins of Civilisation in the Aegean," in *The Emergence of Civilisation in the Bronze Age Aegean: Retrospect and Prospect* (Sheffield Studies in Aegean Archaeology 6), ed. P. Halstead and J. C. Barrett, Sheffield.

Younger, J. G. 1988. *The Iconography of Late Minoan and Mycenaean Sealstones and Finger Rings,* Bristol.

Zerner, C. W. 1978. "The Beginning of the Middle Helladic Period at Lerna" (diss. Univ. of Cincinnati).

CHAPTER 3

ANIMAL SACRIFICE, ARCHIVES, AND FEASTING AT THE PALACE OF NESTOR

Sharon R. Stocker and Jack L. Davis

ABSTRACT

The contexts of burned faunal assemblages from Blegen's excavations at the Palace of Nestor are examined in this paper. Special attention is given to a deposit of bones found in a corner of room 7 of the Archives Complex. It is argued that these bones, from at least 10 cattle, probably represent the remains of a single episode of burned animal sacrifice and large-scale feasting that occurred shortly before the palace was destroyed. Feasts of this sort are likely to have played a diacritical role in Mycenaean society. The bones may have been brought to room 7 in order to verify to palace authorities that a sacrifice had been completed.

The institution of feasting in Mycenaean palatial society has been a focus of investigations by Aegean prehistorians for more than a decade.[1] Analysis of Linear B texts has demonstrated clearly that revenue received by the palatial administration could be directed toward "the provision of state-organized banquets, whether of a religious or of a secular character."[2] Archaeologists as well as art historians have considered the nature of such events and where they are likely to have been held.[3] In many instances, as Killen has suggested, "state hospitality" no doubt helped "in holding together the fabric of the society."[4] Differential access to food and drink, however, is also likely to have served to define and accentuate differences within that society, through what Dietler has described as the "diacritical" role of feasts.[5]

1. We would like to thank the two *Hesperia* reviewers, Brian Hayden and Jeremy B. Rutter, and John Bennet, Susan G. Cole, Michael Cosmopoulos, Robin Hägg, Yannis Hamilakis, Michael Nelson, Kerill O'Neill, Thomas G. Palaima, Ruth Palmer, Kevin Pluta, Ian Rutherford, and Cynthia W. Shelmerdine for offering comments on this chapter or for responding helpfully to requests for information. We also thank Natalia Vogeikoff-Brogan for facilitating our access to records from the Palace of Nestor excavations that are archived at the American School of Classical Studies at Athens.

2. Killen 1994, p. 70. See also Piteros, Olivier, and Melena 1990, esp. pp. 171–184; Killen 1996, 1998a; Palaima 2000.

3. E.g., McCallum 1987; Shelmer-dine 1998, pp. 84, 87–88; Shelmerdine, forthcoming; Davis and Bennet 1999, pp. 110–111; Whitelaw 2001, p. 58.

4. Killen 1994, p. 70.

5. Dietler (2001, p. 85) writes that a feast "involves the use of differentiated cuisine and styles of consumption as a diacritical symbolic device to naturalize and reify concepts of ranked differences in the status of social orders or classes."

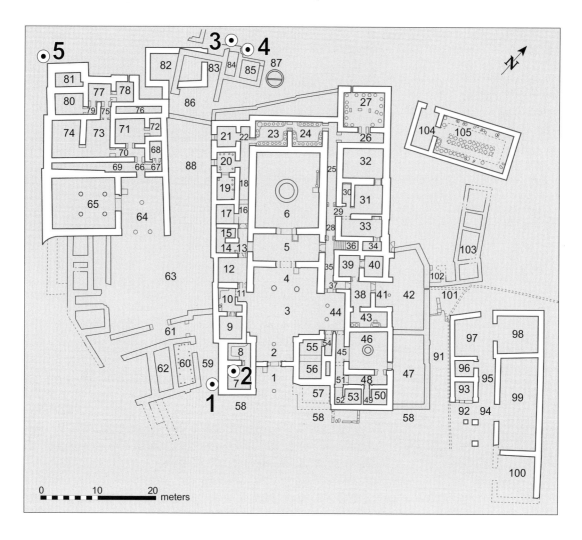

Dietler and Hayden have divided contributions to their recent edited collection, *Feasts: Archaeological and Ethnographic Perspectives on Food, Politics, and Power,* into two parts: papers that consider ethnographical and historical examples of feasting with a view to building frameworks within which archaeological data may be interpreted, and those "that attempt to grapple with the detection of feasting in the material record and to then make plausible inferences about the social life and culture of the people who were producing and participating in those feasts."[6] The present paper falls into the latter category. In it we consider burned faunal remains from Carl Blegen's excavations at the Palace of Nestor at Pylos, newly analyzed by Paul Halstead and Valasia Isaakidou, that promise to shed light on the practice of ritual animal sacrifice and feasting in the Peloponnese at the end of the 13th century B.C. (Fig. 1). In particular we concentrate here on the interpretation of finds from room 7, part of the Archives Complex of the palace. Examination of this room offers us an extraordinary opportunity to integrate information already gleaned from close analysis of the content and context of Linear B texts with the results of study of other artifacts and animal bones that were found in the same room. In so doing we considerably expand remarks and interpretations published elsewhere.[7]

6. Dietler and Hayden 2001, p. 6.

7. Isaakidou et al. 2002; see also Halstead 2003, p. 259. Although in this chapter we start from an analysis of context rather than of faunal remains, we reach several conclusions similar to those of Halstead and Isaakidou (forthcoming); neither colleague should, however, be implicated in any of our more extreme flights of fancy. We are very grateful to Halstead and Isaakidou for sharing their paper with us in advance of its publication and, more generally, for the enjoyable collaboration that we have had with them.

Figure 1 *(opposite)*. **Plan of the Palace of Nestor showing the locations of five groups of burned animal bones. A sixth group was probably from the same general area as groups 3–5.**
R. J. Robertson, after J. C. Wright, based on *Palace of Nestor* I, foldout plan by J. Travlos

Dietler and Hayden observe that it may be possible to recognize the archaeological consequences of particular feasts.[8] We suggest that this is precisely the case at Pylos, where several deposits of faunal remains appear to be the remnants of burned animal sacrifices made on a single occasion and of the consequent distribution of meat to a large number of individuals. The last of these events (represented by finds in room 7) occurred shortly before the final destruction of the Palace of Nestor. We argue that feasts incorporating these practices, among their many other meanings and effects, played a diacritical role within Mycenaean society, and in this regard our paper complements a discussion of hierarchical Mycenaean feasting soon to be published by Lisa Bendall.[9]

ANIMAL BONES FROM THE EXCAVATIONS

In 1997, several members of the Pylos Regional Archaeological Project (PRAP) began to reinventory and publish finds from Blegen's excavations at the Palace of Nestor, now stored in the nearby Archaeological Museum of Hora.[10] One goal of the project was to identify significant groups of archaeological finds left unpublished by Blegen's team. It soon became apparent that there existed a large quantity of well-preserved animal bones (weighing more than 275 kg), most from clearly defined contexts, that had been little studied.[11] The decision was made to embark on a systematic reexamination of all animal bones preserved from Blegen's excavations and of the contexts in which he and his team had discovered them. Toward this end a research team was formed, consisting of Isaakidou, Halstead, and ourselves. Isaakidou and Halstead have been responsible for the analysis of the faunal remains, while we have studied the stratigraphy of the relevant deposits.

In a preliminary inventory made by Halstead and Davis in 1998, Halstead observed that the state of preservation and range of species represented by animal bones from six excavation units from both inside and outside the palace complex were unusual: the bones appeared to have been

8. Dietler and Hayden 2001, pp. 8–9.

9. Bendall, forthcoming. Halstead and Isaakidou (forthcoming) similarly suggest on the basis of the faunal remains in room 7 and elsewhere at Pylos that feasting and animal sacrifice played a significant role in legitimating social distinctions there.

10. This enterprise, called the Hora Apotheke Reorganization Project, has been directed by Stocker, with advice from Davis, Bennet, and Shelmerdine. Research has been conducted under the auspices of the American School of Classical Studies at Athens, in accordance with the terms of a permit granted by the Greek Ministry of Cul-

ture. We are grateful to the late William D. E. Coulson and to James D. Muhly, former directors of the School; to Maria Pilali, administrator of the School; and to the office of the Greek Archaeological Service at Olympia, particularly its director, Xeni Arapoyianni, and Yioryia Hatzi, curator of antiquities. The reorganization of the storerooms and our efforts toward republication of Blegen's finds have been supported by the Institute for Aegean Prehistory and the Louise Taft Semple Fund of the Department of Classics of the University of Cincinnati. We also thank all those who have assisted in reorganizing the second Blegen store-

room, especially Maria Antoniou, Emmett L. Bennett, Hariclia Brecoulaki, Suzanne Hofstra, Julie Hruby, Michael Lane, Sari Miller-Antonio, Lynne Schepartz, Robert Schon, Nick Thompson, and Erin Williams.

11. Some of these bones had been briefly described by Nobis (1993) who, however, did not have access to primary excavation records. Since it was clear to us that the bones that he had examined ranged in date from the end of the Early Bronze Age until the final destruction of the palace in Late Helladic (LH) IIIB, and that he had seen only part of the total collection, a fuller study seemed warranted.

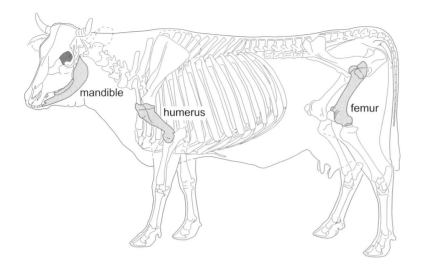

Figure 2. Bovine skeleton showing
bones represented in the deposits of
burned bones. Courtesy V. Isaakidou
and P. Halstead

entirely burned and to consist almost totally of parts of mandibles and leg
joints of cattle (Fig. 2).[12] The six groups of burned bone were studied in
greater detail in September 2000 by Halstead and Isaakidou, who concluded that each is the remnant of a highly structured deposit. The groups
are contaminated by only a few fragments of unburned bone, which clearly
differ from the burned material in terms of their anatomical and/or taxo-
nomic character. The burned material thus seems to have been deposited
with some care, rather than having been discarded with mixed refuse.

It is our contention that these deposits are the end product of ritual
practice, the burned bones probably representing a sacrifice to the gods.
According to Halstead and Isaakidou, all six groups "exhibited a more or
less distinctive degree and type of burning, suggesting derivation from single
burning episodes rather than the collection for disposal of bones burned
independently."[13] Many of the bones bear clear traces of knife marks consistent either with dismembering or filleting, suggesting that they had been
stripped of meat before burning. Deep chop marks or fracture patterns
characteristic of deliberate breakage of the bone, for example in marrow
extraction, were not observed.

Further study confirmed that the burned bone consists almost exclusively of cattle (5–11 head per deposit) with parts of a single red deer in
each of two groups.[14] The bones are highly selective in terms of anatomical

---

12. Halstead 2003, p. 259; Halstead and Isaakidou, forthcoming. The
excavation labels preserved on groups
1–5 record the following information:
1) S2 1954. W Chasm. 10–12.7.54;
2) Room 7 bone: S3 Room of pithos
heap of bones; S3 NW extension;
3) WK4. SW wall E. 17.5.62; 4) WK6.
Fire on top of wall E. p. 161. 7.7.62.
WK354; 5) EBW. 3.6.61. GPA. Σ.
Τμήμα 2, 11. 1.10–1.30. sel. 26. The
label on the sixth group is damaged and
incomplete, but seems to read "PNW"
(see below, n. 17).

13. Halstead and Isaakidou, forthcoming. See also Halstead 2003 and
Isaakidou et al. 2002. Our description
of the bones and their condition is entirely dependent on information provided to us by Halstead and Isaakidou.
Recent discoveries in the Cult Center
at Mycenae and at the Mycenaean
shrine at Ayios Konstantinos on Methana have also been thought to derive
from sacrifices; in addition to references
to these finds in Isaakidou et al. 2002,
see Hamilakis and Konsolaki 2004.
See also Cosmopoulos 2003, pp. 16–18,

regarding evidence for Mycenaean
burned animal sacrifice at Eleusis.
Godart (1999) more generally discusses
the sacrifice of animals, including
cattle, in Linear B texts, while Palaima
(1989) is concerned specifically with
cattle at Pylos.

14. Deer are represented in groups 1
and 6 (Halstead and Isaakidou, forthcoming, table 1; see also above, n. 12,
for the contexts). See Bennet's recent
suggestion (2001, p. 35) that the unique
references to deer in two Cr tablets may
represent "the elite's contribution to

composition, and are composed almost entirely of humerus, femur, and mandible bones (Fig. 2). Many of the cattle seem to have been adult bulls or steers.[15]

In 2001, examination of the excavation contexts of the six deposits of burned bone led us to the conclusion that none could be positively dated earlier than LH IIIA and that all probably belong to contexts dating to LH IIIB.[16] Three, and probably four, of the six deposits of burned bones were found in the northwest part of the site, just outside the Main Building (Fig. 1, groups 3–5), and it seems likely that in each of these places bones from a sacrifice were purposely discarded.[17]

In Classical Greece the selective disposal of bones from a particular sacrifice appears to have been unusual. Németh has reviewed the epigraphical evidence for the treatment of sacrificial waste.[18] Provisions included 1) statutes determining areas of disposal for ashes from the sacrificial altar, dung from animals to be sacrificed, and excrement from the intestines of sacrificed animals; and 2) rules concerning the locations of tanneries that bought the hides of the sacrificed animals. The disposal of bones is not explicitly treated in these texts, however, and archaeological evidence suggests that, more often than not, they were simply swept from the altars and became part of the generalized refuse of a sanctuary.[19]

CONTEXT OF BURNED BONE IN ROOM 7

In contrast to most of the deposits of burned bone mentioned above, one deposit clearly lay on a floor of the Palace of Nestor at the time of its final destruction (Fig. 1, group 2). The faunal remains from this deposit, already recognized by Blegen as the probable remains of sacrifice (see below), were found stored in a wooden box and labeled in a way that left no

feasts from their own special activities." R. Palmer is currently preparing a manuscript on deer in the Cr tablets and in frescoes at Pylos. See also Hamilakis 2003 on the role of hunting in prehistoric Greece.

15. Halstead and Isaakidou, forthcoming. Tablets from Pylos that appear to record sacrificial animals also express a preference for males (see Killen 1994, p. 80). But see Un 6, where only females are recorded. We are grateful to C. Shelmerdine for reminding us of this text.

16. Extensive deposits of animal bones from earlier stages of the palace are preserved, but they are not similar in character to the six groups of burned bone discussed here.

17. Groups 3, 4, and 5 (see above, n. 12) were certainly excavated in these areas. In 2002, comparison of the remains from group 6 with isolated fragments of burned cattle bones from PNW trenches 8/1 and 11, also located in the northwest part of the site, suggested to Halstead and Isaakidou that all derived from the same deposit. It thus appears probable that the bones in the sixth group were found outside the Main Building, in the same general area as groups 3–5. The contexts of these deposits, as well as the nature of the faunal remains from them, will be discussed in greater detail in a future publication coauthored with Isaakidou and Halstead.

In 1954, during excavation of the robbed-out southwest wall of room 7, another deposit of burned bones (group 1) was found. The full label on the container reads "S2 1954. W Chasm. 10–12.7.54 (S2 dug by E. Bennett) to early July: pot in '1939 Trenches, numbered sherds Room 7 (Archives) Chasm.'" A join between a bone in this deposit and one in group 2 was found in September 2002 by Halstead and Isaakidou (we thank them for this information). It is likely that the bones in group 1 had been removed from the floor of room 7 when the southwest wall was robbed in historical times and had been dumped into the trench left after the looting. At present it does not seem that the combination of groups 1 and 2 results in an increase in the minimum number of cattle represented in the deposit in room 7.

18. Németh 1994.

19. E.g., as at Kommos in Crete; see Shaw 2000. At Didyma, intact (but unburned) thigh bones were deposited in special places (Tuchelt 1992). In general, see Hägg 1998 for archaeological evidence for Classical Greek animal sacrifice.

Figure 3. Spearhead and sword in room 7 at the time of excavation. Palace of Nestor Excavations Archive, University of Cincinnati, neg. 52-20: "Spear, Sword, and Tablet no. 10 [= Es 650], from East"

doubt that they had been found in the western corner of room 7.[20] At least 10 head of cattle are represented.[21]

The progress of excavation of room 7 can be reconstructed from the field notebooks. On June 12, 1952, Blegen discovered a deposit of animal bones in room 7 of the Archives Complex (originally known as the "Room of the Pithos," later as the "Annex" to the Archives Room of the palace). He described that day's excavation in trench S3 NW extension (equivalent to the southwest part of room 7) as follows:

> West part of extension to south of it filled with fragments of gigantic pithos. A few tablets under pithos frag[ment]s. Close beside the above mentioned wall several miniature kylikes—1 or 2 intact. Also giant heap of bones apparently animal indicated on Theocharis plan.[22]

Blegen removed the deposit on June 18:

> Start removing heap of bones on W. side of N. Ext. and also the miniature pots and to clear floor, if any, under them.[23]

A spearhead and a sword also lay near the northwest wall of room 7, not far to the northeast of the bones and miniature kylikes. The spearhead is complete; the sword, although shattered when found, is nearly complete and its bronze is well preserved. All of these objects are clearly visible on photographs taken at the time of excavation (Figs. 3, 4).[24] A plan by

20. See n. 12 above for the context indicated on the original excavation label. Group 1 probably belonged to the same deposit; see above, n. 17.

21. Halstead and Isaakidou (forthcoming) suggest that these bones are likely to have been placed in room 7 as a single act of deposition and that they

probably do not represent the gradual accumulation of bones from individually sacrificed animals subsequently burned as a group. They note that their estimate of the minimum number of individual cattle represented in the deposit is likely to be low, given the fragmentary state of the material.

22. CWB 1952, p. 39. The wall near which the miniature kylikes were found is that which divides room 7 from room 8.

23. CWB 1952, p. 57.

24. *Palace of Nestor* I, pp. 94–95, fig. 274, nos. 3 and 4; a drawing of the spearhead is published in Avila 1983, p. 45, no. 99. A fragment of a

Figure 4. Room 7 with bones and pithos, from the north, 1952. Palace of Nestor Excavations Archive, University of Cincinnati, slide 52-65: "Pylos Englianos Annex of Archives Room. Broken Pithos and Bones"

Demetrios Theocharis was not published by Blegen and Rawson, but it and other drawings (Figs. 5, 6) are contained in one of Theocharis's architectural sketchbooks, now preserved in the archives of the American School of Classical Studies at Athens.

In a preliminary report, Blegen suggested that room 7 might be a shrine.[25] In the final publication, however, Blegen and Rawson were more reserved in their judgment:

> On the floor in the south corner of the room on the day of the fire an enormous ribbed pithos evidently stood covered with its lid. A considerable heap of burned animal bones lay in the western corner and close beside them near the northwest wall were found 11 diminutive kylikes, probably votive offerings. What these apparent remains of sacrifices and dedicatory vessels had to do in the tax collector's office raises an unsolved problem.[26]

blade, not from the sword, and possibly part of yet another blade were found in room 7, but their precise findspots cannot be determined. (CWB 1952, p. 28, records a fragment of bronze amid tablets S3-4-7 [Es 644–647], and CWB 1952, p. 38, mentions a "largish piece" of bronze near the bronze sword.) These artifacts are described and illustrated in *Palace of Nestor* I, p. 95, fig. 265, no. 3, and fig. 266, no. 1. A small fragment of silver was also found in the room. For the spearhead and sword, see Hofstra 2000, p. 100. Many small fragments of metal were found in the course of excavations of the palace (Hofstra 2000, pp. 84–86) and it is possible that the scraps of bronze and silver found in room 7 fell into

the room at the time of its destruction.

The black-and-white photographs taken on June 12, 1952, that show the pithos, spearhead, sword, and deposit of bones are numbered P52-18–20. The spearhead, sword, and Linear B tablets are also indicated on a plan drawn by Blegen (CWB 1952, p. 40).

25. Blegen 1953, p. 63.

26. *Palace of Nestor* I, p. 92. The description of the stratigraphy of room 7 published by Blegen and Rawson (*Palace of Nestor* I, pp. 92–95) is entirely supported by the unpublished excavation records. A stratigraphical section by Theocharis (1952 Sketchbooks, American School of Classical Studies at Athens Archives) shows the elevation of the floor of room 7 and the way in which, at its southeastern

side, it ran over the top of an earlier wall of poros blocks; one of these blocks is incised with a double axe sign (*Palace of Nestor* I, pp. 44–45; cf. Nelson 2001, pp. 118–120). Blegen's brief notes document the relative positions in room 7 of the pithos, heap of bones, kylikes, sword, and spearhead. Notebook pages describing the excavation of S3, North Extension and S3, Northwest Extension include CWB 1952, pp. 24, 28, 32, 36, 38–41, 43, 57, 103, and 105. W. A. McDonald appears to have clipped the edge of the deposit of bones in room 7 already in 1939 in his trench I (WAM 1939, pp. 113 and 117, where he describes "just south of room of archives a good many bones extending into east side of trench").

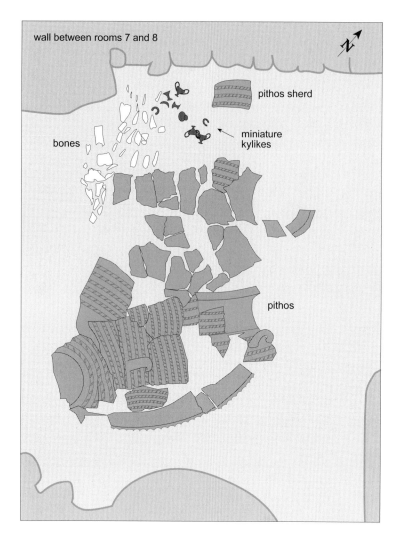

Figure 5. Pithos, miniature kylikes, and bones in room 7. R. J. Robertson, after sketch, not to scale, by D. R. Theocharis. Theocharis 1952 Sketchbooks, American School of Classical Studies at Athens Archives

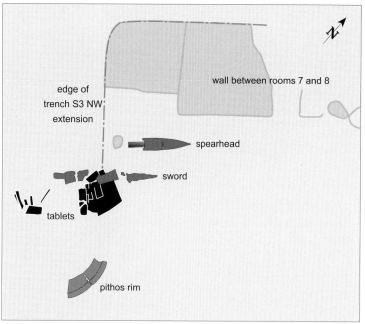

Figure 6. Spearhead and sword in room 7. R. J. Robertson, after sketch, not to scale, by D. R. Theocharis. Theocharis 1952 Sketchbooks, American School of Classical Studies at Athens Archives

Figure 7. Four of the miniature kylikes from room 7 on display in the Hora Museum. Hora Apotheke Reorganization Project Archive, University of Cincinnati

Figure 8. Miniature kylikes in room 7 at the time of excavation, from the north; bones at right. Palace of Nestor Excavations Archive, University of Cincinnati, slide 52-63: "Pylos Annex of Archives Room. Votive Cups"

Study of excavation records and unpublished artifacts permits us to add a few footnotes to Blegen and Rawson's publication. It seems that the only fixed piece of furniture in room 7 was the pithos, which fell with its mouth toward room 8.[27] Other than the pithos and its lid, no ceramic vessels were clearly being used in the room at the time it was destroyed. Some 20–22 miniature kylikes were, however, found in room 7. These include the 11 examples now on display in the Hora Museum (Fig. 7), which Blegen and Rawson specifically say were found near the heap of burned bones (Fig. 8),

27. Pluta (1996–1997, p. 240) has suggested that this pithos could have served as a source of water for forming and reforming tablets. See also Bennet's (2001, p. 27) arguments that at Pylos there may not have

existed documents in any medium other than clay, and that tablets may continually have been recycled (but on the potential difficulties of recycling, see Sjöquist and Åström 1991, pp. 23–24). Blegen and Rawson (*Palace of*

Nestor I, p. 92) thought, on the other hand, that the pithos had been full of oil that, when spilled, fueled the fire in which the Linear B tablets were baked.

Figure 9. A selection of miniature kylikes from room 7 in the store-rooms of the Hora Museum. Hora Apotheke Reorganization Project Archive, University of Cincinnati

as well as those in a container of ceramics labeled "Room 7: Votive Kylikes," now in the storerooms of the museum.[28] It is impossible to establish with precision the findspots within room 7 of this latter group (Fig. 9), which consists of at least nine, and probably 11, miniature kylikes of a style and fabric identical to the 11 examples on display.[29]

ARTIFACTS AND TABLETS IN ROOM 7

It is obvious that all remains in room 7 must be considered in any reconstruction of activities in the room.[30] The key to understanding the presence of burned bones in this room is their spatial association with other artifacts, including Linear B tablets. Pluta has persuasively argued that room 7 was the "office" of the archivist: that he sat there to revise texts and to monitor the flow of tablets that would later be archived in room 8.[31] Tablets appear to have been stored temporarily along the northeast wall of room 7, and more than 200 tablets were in the room at the time of its destruction (Fig. 10).[32]

28. *Palace of Nestor* I, p. 93. In their final publication Blegen and Rawson did not explicitly describe the kylikes in the container, probably because they were fragmentary. In one place (*Palace of Nestor* I, p. 366), they reported that there were 12 miniature kylikes in the room, "eleven of them numbered," while in another place (p. 93), they noted that there were 11 examples. Blegen and Rawson were not entirely consistent in how they reported statistics: in most cases they did not count sherds or fragmentary vessels (but see their description of the contents of room 24; *Palace of Nestor* I, p. 141).

Although they mention (p. 95) that the miniature kylix shape was represented among scattered sherds found in room 7, they do not record the number of sherds or minimum number of vessels.

29. Estimation of the number of vessels seems justified since the excavators do not seem to have discarded any pottery from the deposit that contained the miniature kylikes. In the container there are many fragments from shapes other than miniature kylikes, including larger kylikes of a standard size. There are also very small sherds present, indicating that all of the material was retained. Seven nonjoining handles

of miniature kylix type (i.e., with the handle pressed into place inside the rim) and four straight rim sherds are probably nonjoining fragments of the 9–11 miniature kylikes in the container. Blegen (CWB 1952, p. 29) notes a kylix in the east part of the room; Theocharis, in a 1952 sketchbook, illustrates at least one kylix, perhaps a miniature, in the southeast part of the room.

30. Pluta 1996–1997, p. 247.

31. Pluta 1996–1997, p. 245. A similar scene is depicted in Henry Hankey's well-known drawing; see Chadwick 1976, p. 19, fig. 9.

32. Pluta 1996–1997, pp. 242, 247.

Figure 10. Tablets on the floor of room 7 at the time of excavation.
Palace of Nestor Excavations Archive, University of Cincinnati, slide 52-31: "Pylos Annex from S. Tablets on Floor"

The original position of the tablets in room 7 can be located according to a fine-meshed grid.[33] Several texts appear to be concerned with the provisioning of sacrifices and associated feasts. Palaima has concluded that grid square 52 was "the area for label discards and temporary pre-processing of baskets of tablets brought to the Archives Complex."[34] In this square were found the tablets of the "armor inventory of the Sh series as well as tablets of the Es series that list offerings to Poseidon and key human figures in the Pylos kingdom."[35] Adjacent to these two groups of tablets were the heap of animal bones (concentrated in grid square 51) and the 11 miniature kylikes, spearhead, and sword (grid squares 42, 43, 52, and 53).

Palaima has also observed that grid square 83 at the southern end of room 7 contained a "small and special group of tablets (chiefly and significantly Un 718 and tablets of the Ta series)."[36] Of considerable importance is the fact that Un 718 is a "prospective text" that anticipates offerings that will be made to Poseidon by *e-ke-ra$_2$-wo* (whom Palaima and others believe is the king of Pylos), the military commander, the *da-mo*, and a group called the *wo-ro-ki-jo-ne-jo*.[37] That offerings to Poseidon were in the process of being made when the palace was destroyed is implied by the future tense of the verb "to give." Palaima has concluded that certain texts were retained in this part of room 7 to await "confirmation that the contributions had indeed been made."[38]

33. The grid was originally established by Bennett and Olivier (1976, p. 25, fig. 2), and has recently been adjusted by Pluta (1996–1997, pp. 234–238).

34. Palaima 1995, p. 624, n. 9.

35. Palaima 1995, p. 628.

36. Palaima 1995, p. 624.

37. Killen, however, believes that *wo-ro-ki-jo-ne-jo* is an individual, not a group, and reads the form as a possessive adjective; see Killen 1998b, p. 21,

nn. 7–8. We thank J. Bennet for this reference. On current views concerning the identification of *e-ke-ra$_2$-wo* as the king of Pylos, see Bennet 2001, p. 26, n. 11.

38. Palaima 1995, p. 629.

SACRIFICE, FEASTING, AND ROOM 7

It seems possible that all of the artifacts in room 7, with the exception of the tablets and the pithos and its lid, are remnants of animal sacrifice and ritual dining. The sword could have been involved in the slaughter of sacrificial victims. Knives and swords figure prominently in Aegean Bronze Age iconography of sacrifice, and Killen recently observed that the "axes and swords (or knives) listed [in Ta 716] are attractively interpreted as weapons used to kill sacrificial animals."[39] The spearhead is unexpected, however, since spears, although associated in Bronze Age iconography with hunting and warfare,[40] do not feature in depictions of sacrifice. Might its presence be related to the inclusion of deer remains among the burned bones at Pylos?[41] Support for the idea that the spearhead and sword were ritual instruments comes from the fact that both must have been antiques by the time of the destruction of the Palace of Nestor. Is this an example of religious conservatism? The spearhead is of a Middle Bronze Age type, whereas the sword is of Sandars's type E and probably dates to the 14th century.[42] Hofstra discusses both the spearhead and sword, noting the "oddly archaic form" of the former.[43] Similarly, the coarse red micaceous fabric of the large pithos that stood in room 7 appears to be more characteristic of pottery from levels of the later Middle Bronze Age and early Late Bronze Age than that in use during the final stages of the palace.

Associations of the miniature kylikes with feasting rituals are also likely. Some fragments of wall paintings from the Throne Room (room 6) appear to represent activities associated with drinking. Two tables with two men seated opposite each other are depicted, each man plausibly restored as raising a kylix in a toasting ritual.[44] McCallum restores the Two Men at Table, a bull sacrificed on an altar (19C6), and the Lyre Player and Bird (43H6) in a single outdoor composition that decorated the northeast wall of the Throne Room.[45] Although the hands of the Two Men at Table are not preserved, an association between seated figures and drinking exists in Aegean iconography, e.g., in the Knossos Campstool Fresco, whether or not its fragments are arranged as in Evans's reconstruction.[46] Reexamination of the fresco fragments from the Throne Room in 2002–2003 has shown, however, that fragment 19C6 can no longer be confidently reconstructed as a bull or as any other sacrificial victim.[47]

The precise use of the miniature kylikes in ritual remains unclear. Certainly the diners did not use them at the table as drinking vessels. They are much too small for that. The miniature kylikes could have held only a token amount of liquid (0.009–0.035 l),[48] and we should probably imagine that their content (if any) had symbolic significance.

The attested use of miniature kylikes in the palace is limited to what are arguably ritual contexts in the Throne Room: two were recovered on a plastered table of offerings near the western column of the room, and one lay against the northwest end of the northeast wall of the room.[49] Blegen and Rawson considered the miniature kylix (shape 26) to be local to the southwest Peloponnese.[50] Apart from examples from the palace and in chamber tombs at Volimidia, only a single rim fragment has been recognized in Messenia.[51] Several examples are known, however, from the northeast

39. Killen 1998a, p. 422. For the iconography of sacrifice, see Dietrich 1988, and commentary by N. Marinatos on p. 50 of the same volume; also Marinatos 1986, pp. 22–25.

40. See, e.g., Hofstra 2000, p. 99.

41. Group 1 contained deer bones and is probably from the same deposit as group 2 (see above, nn. 14, 17).

42. Avila 1983, p. 45; Sandars 1963, pp. 132–133.

43. Hofstra 2000, pp. 98–101.

44. See *Palace of Nestor* II, pp. 80–81, frr. 44aH6 and 44bH6.

45. For the Two Men at Table, see McCallum 1987, pp. 90–91, 199; for the bull, pp. 94–95. See also Wright, this volume, p. 43, fig. 13.

46. See Cameron 1964. More generally, see Wright, this volume, for discussion of seated drinking figures in Mycenaean and Minoan iconography.

47. We thank our colleagues H. Brecoulaki, Caroline Zeitoun, and Andreas Karydas for this information.

48. *Palace of Nestor* I, p. 366.

49. *Palace of Nestor* I, pp. 89, 91. Säflund (1980, p. 241) mistakenly cites Blegen and Rawson to the effect that only one miniature was found on the offering table.

50. *Palace of Nestor* I, p. 366.

51. In the settlement at Nichoria; see Shelmerdine 1992, p. 515.

Peloponnese, found in what appear to be ritual contexts.[52] Many complete miniature kylikes were found at the Palace of Nestor itself in the doorway between rooms 18 and 20, and in rooms 20 and 60; these parts of the palace served as repositories of large quantities of plain pottery that may well have been dispensed at feasts.[53] The presence of this shape in association with burned bone in room 7, on the offering table in the Throne Room, and in tombs at Volimidia suggests to us that the miniature kylix was regularly employed in ritual in Messenia and was not a plaything for children, a possibility raised by Blegen and Rawson.[54] Further support for a ritual function may be suggested by traces of burning on the miniature kylikes from the Throne Room, in use at the time of the final destruction of the palace; those from room 7 show similar traces.[55]

Analysis of the Pylos Ta series of tablets suggests that paired dining was a feature of feasting at the Palace of Nestor. Killen has argued that the Ta tablets represent "an audit of the palace's equipment for banqueting, including the consumption of sacrificial animals . . . listed on the occasion of a major feast held to mark the appointment of a new office holder."[56] Palaima agrees that the tablets record banqueting equipment and he has counted the total number of each item in all tablets of the series. Among other objects, 22 seats and 11 tables are recorded, and he imagines 22 individuals present at a feast, seated at these 11 tables in the manner of the representations in the frescoes of the Throne Room.[57] The number of seated banqueters could thus correspond to the number of miniature kylikes found in room 7. If this is not an extraordinary coincidence, two possible conclusions follow: 1) a single miniature kylix was deposited in room 7 on behalf of each of 22 banqueters; and 2) the number 22 could have held special significance at a Mycenaean banquet. Might such a select group of diners have comprised representatives from the principal subcenters of the kingdom of Pylos, perhaps with the addition of several high-ranking officials of the palace itself?[58]

The evidence of the material remains points, however, to the existence of a hierarchy of feasting at Pylos: a more intimate group of seated individuals and a much larger gathering of less privileged attendees.[59] The number of animals represented by the cattle bones in the deposit in room 7

---

52. French 1981, p. 45; Konsolaki-Yannopoulou 2000; Dabney, Halstead, and Thomas, this volume.

53. See Whitelaw 2001, pp. 52–62; we thank J. Hruby for additional information regarding contexts in rooms 18 and 19.

54. *Palace of Nestor* I, p. 366. On the ritual use of larger kylikes, see Säflund 1980.

55. In contrast, the miniature kylikes from rooms 18, 19, 20, and 60, as well as from the "Main Drain" (under corridor 59, just outside room 60), were not burned. We have not succeeded in locating two examples from court 58 in

the palace, reported by Blegen as having been found inside a "stone structure" but not mentioned in the final report. Blegen speculated (CWB 1952, p. 15) that there may have been a shrine in this place.

56. Killen 1998a, p. 421.

57. Palaima 2000, p. 237.

58. There appear to have been ca. 20 higher-order centers in the kingdom. Bennet (2001, p. 32) counts "sixteen or seventeen major centers within the polity other than Pylos itself and Leuktron, possibly the Further Province capital." There is some evidence that the palace was involved in provi-

sioning feasts at these local centers (Bennet 2001, p. 33).

59. On the likely locations for a larger feast in the vicinity of the Palace of Nestor, see Shelmerdine 1998, pp. 84, 88; Davis and Bennet 1999, p. 110; Whitelaw 2001, p. 58. The composition of the wall paintings of the Throne Room suggests that the seated diners ate *al fresco*, rather than inside the palace, but any ritual involving the miniature kylikes may have occurred indoors, since in the Throne Room, as noted above, vessels of this type appear to have been in use at the time of the final destruction of the palace.

implies that 22 banqueters were not the only participants in the sacrifice and associated feasting. The slaughtered animals would have yielded a large quantity of meat, far in excess of the needs of 22 banqueters, and probably enough to supply the entire population of the town around the palace.[60] A Hellenistic inscription from Keos mandated that ca. 1.25 kg of meat be distributed to each male present at a sacrifice[61] and, if distributions at Pylos were on a similar scale, nearly a thousand families could have been provided with meat from the cattle in room 7.[62]

The number of cattle represented in the remains that lay on the floor in room 7 may have been great in comparison to the single bull given to Poseidon in Un 718 by *e-ke-ra₂-wo*, but the existence of other groups of burned bones with the remains of five or more cattle and the Linear B evidence suggest that large-scale sacrifice of bovines was not without precedent at Pylos.[63] Pluta interprets the bones and kylikes in room 7 as "evidence for repeated activity of some sort."[64] It seems unlikely, however, that the bones derive from multiple events of sacrifice at festivals held over several consecutive days, rituals of a type that *are* attested both in Linear B and Hittite texts.[65]

Finally, it needs to be asked why there were artifacts other than tablets in room 7. There is no evidence that burned sacrifices or other rituals were conducted in the room; we can offer no support for Blegen's original hypothesis that room 7 was itself a shrine, nor was the room sufficiently large to have held 22 diners. The miniature kylikes appear to have been transported to room 7 after their ritual use. They do not appear to have been kept there as part of equipment for a banquet, since room 7 was not used

---

60. See also Isaakidou et al. 2002, p. 90, and Halstead and Isaakidou, forthcoming, for the amount of meat likely to have been derived from the sacrifice and the size of the population to which it may have been distributed. Ruschenbusch (1982, p. 180), drawing on Early Modern statistics published by Cipolla (1980, p. 126) and others, estimates an average weight of 200–220 kg per animal. Jameson, on the other hand, quotes an estimate of usable meat provided by adult animals in Dark Age Nichoria that is only half this amount (Jameson 1988, p. 95), and that is the figure employed by Killen (1994, p. 81, n. 53) for Mycenaean times. Even using the lower figure, the sacrifice of 10 cattle would have yielded on the order of 1,000 kg of meat and probably more, since Halstead and Isaakidou (forthcoming) have concluded that the individuals represented in the deposit in room 7 were at the upper end of the size range for cattle at Pylos.

61. *IG* XII v 647; see Ruschenbusch

1982, p. 180, for a discussion of this inscription.

62. Fieldwork sponsored by PRAP has suggested that the minimum size of the community around the Palace of Nestor in LH IIIB was on the order of 12.5 ha (Bennet 1999, p. 13; Davis et al. 1997, pp. 427–430). Carothers and McDonald's (1979, pp. 435–436) regression formula based on examination of populations and areas of modern villages in Messenia yields a population of only 850 individuals, certainly too low an estimate in light of the considerable number of women known to have been resident at the palace (see Chadwick 1988, p. 76; we thank J. Bennet for drawing our attention to this point). Renfrew's (1972, p. 251) estimated settlement density of 300 persons per hectare would yield a population on the order of 3,750 for the settlement at Ano Englianos, but this density figure must be too high. Whitelaw, using a lower density of 200 persons per hectare (and a settlement size

of 15 ha in LH IIIB), estimates the population at ca. 3,000 individuals (Whitelaw 2001, pp. 63–64); a smaller settlement size of 12.5 ha would yield an estimate of 2,500 individuals.

63. See PY Ua 25, where 10 head of cattle (8 males and 2 females) are recorded. Sacconi (2001, p. 469) distinguishes between such "grands banquets d'état" and the "repas typiquement religieux," where daily rations of food in small quantities are distributed to a limited number of individuals participating in a ritual. Hamilakis and Konsolaki (2004, p. 147) note that the burned sacrifices in the Mycenaean shrine at Ayios Konstantinos on Methana may be an example of the latter type of celebration, a case of "empowerment for the few" who may have been provisioned by a palace.

64. Pluta 1996–1997, p. 247.

65. See above, n. 13. Concerning such sacrifices, see Killen 2001; Sacconi 2001; also Ruijgh 2004.

for the storage of ceramics: at least half of the kylikes were piled on the floor in no obvious order, all were burned, and many were broken.

One possible interpretation worth exploring is that the bones, miniature kylikes, and weapons, like the tablets found near them in grid square 52, had recently been brought to room 7. Did the administration of the palace perhaps require physical proof that the rituals in which these objects were involved had been completed? If these artifacts came to room 7 as part of a process of administrative supervision, it may be presumed that, had the palace not been destroyed, the spearhead and sword would have reentered the storerooms of the palace, the bones would have been buried in special deposits like those found to the north and northwest of the palace, and the miniature kylikes would have been otherwise discarded.

A parallel case of administrative supervision might be indicated by tablet Un 718 (the label for which was found in grid square 52) if we accept Palaima's argument that it was being retained in grid square 83 in anticipation of confirmation of contributions, since "major offerings to Poseidon were still in the process of being made at the time that the palace was destroyed."[66] Given the remarkable correspondence between the number of seats recorded in the Ta tablets and the number of miniature kylikes found in room 7, is it possible that both groups of objects were associated with a celebration of the same event, the appointment of the new *da-mo-ko-ro* mentioned in Ta 711?

66. Palaima 1995, p. 629.

REFERENCES

Avila, R. A. J. 1983. *Bronzene Lanzen-und Pfeilspitzen der griechischen Spätbronzezeit* (Prähistorische Bronzefunde 5.1), Munich.

Bendall, L. M. Forthcoming. "Fit for a King? Hierarchy, Exclusion, Aspiration, and Desire in the Social Structure of Mycenaean Banqueting," in *Food, Cuisine, and Society in Prehistoric Greece* (Sheffield Studies in Aegean Archaeology 5), ed. P. Halstead and J. C. Barrett, Sheffield.

Bennet, J. 1999. "Pylos: The Expansion of a Mycenaean Palatial Center," in *Rethinking Mycenaean Palaces: New Interpretations of an Old Idea*, ed. M. L. Galaty and W. A. Parkinson, Los Angeles, pp. 9–18.

———. 2001. "Agency and Bureaucracy: Thoughts on the Nature and Extent of Administration in Bronze Age Pylos," in *Economy and Politics in the Mycenaean Palace States* (Cambridge Philological Society, Suppl. 27), ed. S. Voutsaki and J. Killen, Cambridge, pp. 25–37.

Bennett, E. L., Jr., and J.-P. Olivier. 1976. *The Pylos Tablets Transcribed* 2: *Hands, Concordances, Indices* (Incunabula graeca 59), Rome.

Blegen, C. W. 1953. "The Palace of Nestor Excavations at Pylos, 1952," *AJA* 57, pp. 59–64.

Cameron, M. A. S. 1964. "An Addition to 'La Parisienne,'" *CretChron* 18, pp. 38–53.

Carothers, J., and W. A. McDonald. 1979. "Size and Distribution of the Population in Late Bronze Age Messenia: Some Statistical Approaches," *JFA* 6, pp. 433–454.

Chadwick, J. 1976. *The Mycenaean World*, Cambridge.

———. 1988. "The Women of Pylos," in *Texts, Tablets, and Scribes: Studies in Mycenaean Epigraphy Offered to Emmett L. Bennett, Jr.* (*Minos* Suppl. 10), ed. J.-P. Olivier and T. G. Palaima, Salamanca, pp. 43–93.

Cipolla, C. 1980. *Before the Industrial Revolution: European Society and Economy, 1000–1700*, 2nd ed., New York.

Cosmopoulos, M. B. 2003. "Mycenaean Religion at Eleusis: The Architecture and Stratigraphy of Megaron B," in *Greek Mysteries: The Archaeology and Ritual of Ancient Greek Secret Cults,* ed. M. B. Cosmopoulos, London, pp. 1–24.

CWB 1952 = C. W. Blegen, Pylos Field Notebook, 1952.

Davis, J. L., S. E. Alcock, J. Bennet, Y. G. Lolos, and C. W. Shelmerdine. 1997. "The Pylos Regional Archaeological Project, Part I: Overview and the Archaeological Survey," *Hesperia* 68, pp. 391–494.

Davis, J. L., and J. Bennet. 1999. "Making Mycenaeans: Warfare, Territorial Expansion, and Representations of the Other in the Pylian Kingdom," in *Polemos: Le contexte guerrier en Égée à l'âge du Bronze. Actes de la 7ᵉ Rencontre égéenne internationale, Université de Liège (Aegaeum* 19), ed. R. Laffineur, Liège, pp. 105–120.

Dietler, M. 2001. "Theorizing the Feast: Rituals of Consumption, Commensal Politics, and Power in African Contexts," in *Feasts: Archaeological and Ethnographic Perspectives on Food, Politics, and Power,* ed. M. Dietler and B. Hayden, Washington, D.C., pp. 65–114.

Dietler, M., and B. Hayden. 2001. "Digesting the Feast—Good to Eat, Good to Drink, Good to Think: An Introduction," in *Feasts: Archaeological and Ethnographic Perspectives on Food, Politics, and Power,* ed. M. Dietler and B. Hayden, Washington, D.C., pp. 1–20.

Dietrich, B. C. 1988. "The Instrument of Sacrifice," in *Early Greek Cult Practice. Proceedings of the Fifth International Symposium at the Swedish Institute at Athens (SkrAth* 4°, 38), ed. R. Hägg, N. Marinatos, and G. Nordquist, Stockholm, pp. 35–50.

French, E. 1981. "Cult Places at Mycenae," in *Sanctuaries and Cults in the Aegean Bronze Age,* ed. R. Hägg and N. Marinatos, Stockholm, pp. 41–48.

Godart, L. 1999. "Les sacrifices d'animaux dans les textes mycéniens," in *Floreant Studia Mycenaea. Akten des X. Internationalen Mykenologischen Colloquiums, Salzburg (DenkschrWien* 274), ed. S. Deger-Jalkotzy, S. Hiller, and O. Panagl, Vienna, pp. 249–256.

Hägg, R. 1998. "Osteology and Greek Sacrificial Practice," in *Ancient Greek Cult Practice from the Archaeological Evidence. Proceedings of the Fourth International Seminar on Ancient Greek Cult Organized by the Swedish Institute at Athens (SkrAth* 8°, 15), ed. R. Hägg, Stockholm, pp. 49–56.

Halstead, P. 2003. "Texts and Bones: Contrasting Linear B and Archaeozoological Evidence for Animal Exploitation in Mycenaean Southern Greece," in *Zooarchaeology in Greece: Recent Advances (BSA* Studies 9), ed. E. Kotjabopoulou, Y. Hamilakis, P. Halstead, C. Gamble, and P. Elefanti, pp. 257–261.

Halstead, P., and V. Isaakidou. Forthcoming. "Faunal Evidence for Feasting: Burnt Offerings from the Palace of Nestor at Pylos," in *Food, Cuisine, and Society in Prehistoric Greece* (Sheffield Studies in Aegean Archaeology 5), ed. P. Halstead and J. C. Barrett, Sheffield.

Hamilakis, Y. 2003. "The Sacred Geography of Hunting: Wild Animals, Social Power, and Gender in Early Farming Societies," in *Zooarchaeology in Greece: Recent Advances (BSA* Studies 9), ed. E. Kotjabopoulou, Y. Hamilakis, P. Halstead, C. Gamble, and P. Elefanti, pp. 239–247.

Hamilakis, Y., and E. Konsolaki. 2004. "Pigs for the Gods: Burnt Animal Sacrifices as Embodied Rituals at a Mycenaean Sanctuary," *OJA* 23, pp. 135–151.

Hofstra, S. U. 2000. "Small Things Considered: The Finds from LH IIIB Pylos in Context" (diss. Univ. of Texas at Austin).

Isaakidou, V., P. Halstead, J. Davis, and S. Stocker. 2002. "Burnt Animal Sacrifice in Late Bronze Age Greece: New Evidence from the Mycenaean 'Palace of Nestor,' Pylos," *Antiquity* 76, pp. 86–92.

Jameson, M. H. 1988. "Sacrifice and Animal Husbandry in Classical Greece," in *Pastoral Economies in Classical Antiquity* (Cambridge Philological Society, Suppl. 14), ed. C. R. Whittaker, Cambridge, pp. 87–119.

Killen, J. T. 1994. "Thebes Sealings, Knossos Tablets, and Mycenaean State Banquets," *BICS* 39, pp. 67–84.

———. 1996. "Thebes Sealings and Knossos Tablets," in *Atti e memorie del secondo Congresso internazionale di micenologia, Roma–Napoli* 1: *Filologia* (Incunabula graeca 98), ed. E. De Miro, L. Godart, and A. Sacconi, Rome, pp. 71–82.

———. 1998a. "The Pylos Ta Tablets Revisited," pp. 421–422, in F. Rougemont and J.-P. Olivier, eds., "Recherches récentes en épigraphie créto-mycénienne," *BCH* 122, pp. 403–443.

———. 1998b. "The Role of the State in Wheat and Olive Production in Mycenaean Crete," *Aevum* 72, pp. 19–23.

———. 2001. "Religion at Pylos: The Evidence of the Fn Tablets," in *Potnia: Deities and Religion in the Aegean Bronze Age. Proceedings of the 8th International Aegean Conference, Göteborg (Aegaeum* 22), ed. R. Laffineur and R. Hägg, Liège, pp. 435–443.

Konsolaki-Yannopoulou, E. 2000. "New Evidence for the Practice of Libations in the Aegean Bronze Age," *JPR* 14, pp. 33–34.

Marinatos, N. 1986. *Minoan Sacrificial Ritual: Cult Practice and Symbolism,* Stockholm.

McCallum, L. R. 1987. "Decorative Program in the Mycenaean Palace of Pylos: The Megaron Frescoes" (diss. Univ. of Pennsylvania).

Nelson, M. C. 2001. "The Architecture of Epano Englianos, Greece" (diss. Univ. of Toronto).

Németh, G. 1994. "Μεδ' ὄνθον ἐγβαλἐν: Regulations Concerning Everyday Life in a Greek Sanctuary," in *Ancient Greek Cult Practice from the Epigraphical Evidence. Proceedings of the Second International Seminar on Ancient Greek Cult Organized by the Swedish Institute at Athens (SkrAth* 8°, 13), ed. R. Hägg, Stockholm, pp. 59–64.

Nobis, G. 1993. "Archäozoologische Untersuchungen von Tierresten aus dem 'Palast des Nestor' bei Pylos in Messenien, SW-Peloponnes," *ZfA* 27, pp. 151–173.

Palace of Nestor I = C. W. Blegen and M. Rawson, *The Palace of Nestor at Pylos in Western Messenia* I: *The Buildings and Their Contents,* Princeton 1966.

Palace of Nestor II = M. Lang, *The Palace of Nestor at Pylos in Western Messenia* II: *The Frescoes*, Princeton 1969.

Palaima, T. G. 1989. "Perspectives on the Pylos Oxen Tablets: Textual (and Archaeological) Evidence for the Use and Management of Oxen in Late Bronze Age Messenia (and Crete)," in *Studia Mycenaea (1988)*, ed. T. G. Palaima, C. W. Shelmerdine, and P. H. Ilievski, Skopje, pp. 85–124.

———. 1995. "The Last Days of the Pylos Polity," in *Politeia: Society and State in the Aegean Bronze Age. Proceedings of the 5th International Aegean Conference, Heidelberg* (*Aegaeum* 12), ed. R. Laffineur and W.-D. Niemeier, Liège, pp. 623–633.

———. 2000. "The Pylos Ta Series: From Michael Ventris to the New Millennium," *BICS* 44, pp. 236–237.

Piteros, C., J.-P. Olivier, and J. L. Melena. 1990. "Les inscriptions en linéaire B des nodules de Thèbes (1982): La fouille, les documents, les possibilités d'interprétation," *BCH* 114, pp. 103–184.

Pluta, K. 1996–1997. "A Reconstruction of the Archives Complex at Pylos: A Preliminary Report," *Minos* 31–32, pp. 231–250.

Renfrew, C. 1972. *The Emergence of Civilisation: The Cyclades and the Aegean in the Third Millennium B.C.*, London.

Ruijgh, C. J. 2004. "À propos des nouvelles tablettes de Thèbes, part I: Les trois divinités *ma-ka, o-po-re-i*, et *ko-wa* et les trois subordonnées temporelles dans la série Fq," *Mnemosyne* 57, pp. 1–44.

Ruschenbusch, E. 1982. "Ein Bürgerliste von Koresia und Iulis auf Keos," *ZPE* 48, pp. 175–188.

Sacconi, A. 2001. "Les repas sacrés dans les textes mycéniens," in *Potnia: Deities and Religion in the Aegean Bronze Age. Proceedings of the 8th International Aegean Conference, Göteborg* (*Aegaeum* 22), ed. R. Laffineur and R. Hägg, Liège, pp. 467–470.

Säflund, G. 1980. "Sacrificial Banquets in the 'Palace of Nestor,'" *OpAth* 13, pp. 237–246.

Sandars, N. K. 1963. "Later Aegean Bronze Swords," *AJA* 67, pp. 117–153.

Shaw, J. W. 2000. "Ritual and Development in the Greek Sanctuary," in *Kommos* IV: *The Greek Sanctuary*, ed. J. W. Shaw and M. C. Shaw, Princeton, pp. 699–731.

Shelmerdine, C. W. 1992. "Mycenaean Pottery from the Settlement, Part III: Late Helladic IIIA2–IIIB2 Pottery," in *Excavations at Nichoria in Southwest Greece* II: *The Bronze Age Occupation*, ed. W. A. McDonald and N. C. Wilkie, Minneapolis, pp. 495–517.

———. 1998. "The Palace and Its Operations," in *Sandy Pylos: An Archaeological History from Nestor to Navarino*, ed. J. L. Davis, Austin, pp. 81–96.

———. Forthcoming. "Mycenaean Society," in *Linear B: A Millennium Survey*, ed. Y. Duhoux and A. M. Davies, Louvain.

Sjöquist, K.-E., and P. Åström. 1991. *Knossos: Keepers and Kneaders*, Stockholm.

Tuchelt, K. 1992. "Tieropfer in Didyma: Ein Nachtrag," *AA* 1992, pp. 61–81.

WAM 1939 = W. A. McDonald, Pylos Field Notebook, 1939.

Whitelaw, T. M. 2001. "Reading between the Tablets: Assessing Mycenaean Palatial Involvement in Ceramic Production and Consumption," in *Economy and Politics in the Mycenaean Palace States* (Cambridge Philological Society, Suppl. 27), ed. S. Voutsaki and J. Killen, Cambridge, pp. 51–79.

CHAPTER 4

MYCENAEAN FEASTING ON TSOUNGIZA AT ANCIENT NEMEA

Mary K. Dabney, Paul Halstead, and Patrick Thomas

ABSTRACT

This paper presents a ceremonial feasting deposit from Late Helladic IIIA2 Tsoungiza. The dominance of head and foot bones from at least six cattle suggests on-site butchery, with the possibility that the meat was distributed for consumption elsewhere. The pottery fulfills most of the criteria proposed here for recognizing feasting activities in ceramic assemblages. A ceramic female figure, similar to those from sanctuaries at Phylakopi and Mycenae, ties the feasting to religious rituals. It is suggested that regional feasts contributed to maintaining political and economic alliances within the area around Mycenae.

Ancient Nemea is located in the northeast Peloponnese at the head of the Nemea Valley, outside the Argolid but within two hours walking distance of Mycenae.[1] Excavation of the Bronze Age settlement on the hill of Tsoungiza at Ancient Nemea took place from 1984 to 1986 as part of the Nemea Valley Archaeological Project (NVAP). One of the project goals is to study how the settlement was incorporated into larger social systems during different periods of occupation. After a period of abandonment in the Middle Bronze Age, the site was occupied continuously from the late Middle Helladic (MH) through the Late Helladic (LH) period. The number of structures found in the excavated area of the settlement increased from six during the Early Mycenaean (late MH through LH II) era to 10 in the Late Mycenaean (LH III) era (Fig. 1). Evidence from NVAP's surface survey and from excavations conducted by the University of California at Berkeley in deep trenches underneath the Classical Sanctuary of Zeus in the river valley below Tsoungiza suggests an even greater increase in Late

1. Wright et al. 1990, p. 581, fig. 1. The Nemea Valley Archaeological Project was sponsored by Bryn Mawr College under the auspices of the American School of Classical Studies at Athens and directed by James C. Wright. Funding was provided by the National Endowment for the Human-

ities, the National Geographic Society, the Institute for Aegean Prehistory, and private donors. The final publication of the Late Helladic III settlement by Mary K. Dabney, with studies of ceramics by Patrick Thomas, faunal remains by Paul Halstead, botanical remains by Julie M. Hansen, ground

stone tools by Kathleen Krattenmaker, and chipped stone tools by Anna Karabatsolis, is in preparation.

We wish to thank Brian Hayden, Jeremy B. Rutter, and James C. Wright for their comments and suggestions on this chapter.

78

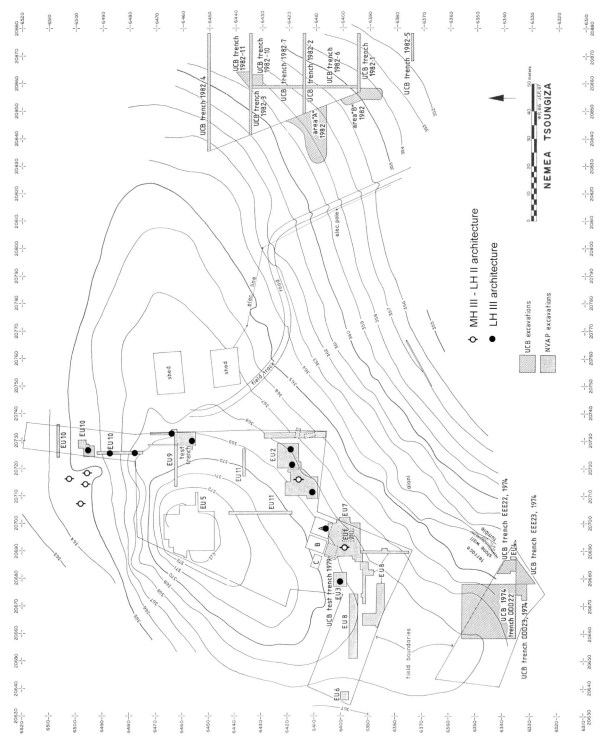

Figure 1. Extent of the Early and Late Mycenaean settlements on Tsoungiza. Contour plan showing trenches and field boundaries, 1986.
W. Payne and J. E. Pfaff

Mycenaean settlement size.[2] Large refuse dumps of Late Mycenaean remains were found throughout the excavated area. One early LH IIIB1 refuse dump contained an estimated 1,400–2,100 vessels representing nearly the full range of ceramic vessel forms known at Mycenae.[3]

What brought about this change to a larger, denser settlement in the LH III period? The answer may lie in the remains of the earliest of these LH III refuse dumps, in excavation unit (EU) 9, the earliest excavated layers of which contained pottery dating to LH IIIA2 (early).[4]

FAUNAL EVIDENCE

The faunal remains from this deposit are distinctive. Cattle make up half of the identified material, with pig, sheep, and goat accounting for most of the remainder, but there are also a few specimens of dog, ass, and red deer. Half of the material exhibited traces of gnawing, indicating that the bone was accessible to scavengers (probably domestic dogs or pigs) either before or after incorporation in the dump. A quarter of the assemblage (including bones of cattle, pig, goat, dog, and ass) bore traces of burning, however, and butchery marks were observed on ca. 4% of the bones (including those of cattle, pig, and dog), leaving no doubt that much or all of the material was butchered and discarded by humans.

In terms of anatomical representation, the remains of pig and sheep/goat include most parts of the carcass; those of dog, ass, and deer are too few for analysis, but remains of cattle are heavily biased toward the head and feet (Table 1). This bias is apparent whether bones are quantified in terms of minimum numbers of anatomical units (MinAU) or minimum numbers of individuals (MNI). Anatomical representation may be shaped by a number of factors, including archaeological retrieval and post-depositional attrition, as well as pre-depositional human behavior. Thus, the absence of such small body parts as the phalanges of pig and sheep/goat might plausibly be attributed to retrieval loss, but the "missing" body parts of cattle are not small and the routine use of sieving at Nemea seems to have ensured fairly complete recovery of identifiable fragments of this large taxon. Similarly, although the assemblage has been extensively gnawed, the missing and scarce body parts include some of the most robust (e.g., distal humerus, distal tibia) as well as the most vulnerable (e.g., proximal humerus).[5] Thus there can be little doubt that the biased anatomical representation of cattle is the result of selective human behavior.

Deposits dominated by head and foot bones of cattle are relatively common in Roman and medieval towns in northwest Europe.[6] Such assemblages are usually interpreted as primary butchery waste discarded by specialist butchers. Because animals are butchered in large numbers, different

2. Cherry, Davis, and Mantzourani 2000, http://classics.uc.edu/NVAP/MycNVAP.html.

3. Thomas 1992, pp. 25–267; Dabney 1997, pp. 469–470.

4. The deposit in EU 9 contains stratigraphic units (SU) 1536, 1540, 1554–1559, 1581–1584, 1588, and 1589 (for the location of EU 9, see Fig. 1). Although some overlap with

LH IIIA1 is possible, the material most convincingly dates to LH IIIA2 (early).

5. Brain 1981, pp. 21–23.

6. E.g., Maltby 1985, p. 55.

TABLE 1. ANATOMICAL REPRESENTATION OF FAUNAL REMAINS IN THE EU 9 DEPOSIT

Anatomical Part	Cattle MinAU	Cattle MNI	Pig MinAU	Pig MNI	Sheep/Goat MinAU	Sheep/Goat MNI
Head						
Horn/Antler	2	1	—	—	2	1
Mandible	3	3	3	3	5	4
Upper Forelimb						
Scapula	1	1	1	1	0	0
Humerus proximal	1	1	3	3	0	0
Humerus distal	0	0	2	2	3	2
Radius proximal	1	1	0	0	1	1
Ulna proximal	0	0	2	2	3	2
Radius distal	0	0	1	1	1	1
Upper Hindlimb						
Pelvis	1	1	1	1	1	1
Femur proximal	0	0	0	0	1	1
Femur distal	1	1	1	1	1	1
Tibia proximal	3	2	1	1	3	3
Tibia distal	2	1	1	1	4	2
Astragalus	1	1	0	0	1	1
Calcaneum	1	1	0	0	0	0
Foot						
Metacarpal proximal	7	5	0	0	0	0
Metacarpal distal	7	4	0	0	0	0
Metatarsal proximal	7	6	0	0	2	2
Metatarsal distal	7	4	0	0	2	2
Phalanx 1	5	2	0	0	0	0
Phalanx 2	1	1	0	0	0	0
Phalanx 3	3	2	0	0	0	0
Total	54	6	16	4	30	5

MinAU = minimum number of anatomical units; *MNI* = minimum number of individuals.

stages of carcass-processing tend to be separated in space and time and, as a result, the waste from different stages tends to be discarded in different contexts. In this case, however, butchery marks and types of fragmentation observed on cattle limb bones suggest that the discarded material does not represent primary butchery waste, but rather carcass parts that had been processed for the extraction of bone marrow. The faunal material thus arguably represents waste from food preparation or consumption, rather than primary butchery.

Segregated discard of particular body parts may also occur for symbolic rather than practical reasons, as is widely illustrated by bone deposits from early historical sanctuary sites in various parts of the Mediterranean.[7] In such sanctuary contexts, the highly symbolic nature of bone deposition is often highlighted by the selection of a particular taxon, age group, body part, or side of body, or by selective treatment (e.g., burning, rapid burial,

7. See references in Isaakidou et al. 2002.

lack of fragmentation). In the present case, the frequency of gnawing indicates that the assemblage as a whole was not accorded immediate burial, and the incidence of gnawing, burning, and old breaks is broadly similar for cattle, pig, and sheep/goat. On the other hand, because experimental data show that most attrition of faunal remains by gnawing takes place within a few hours of discard, burial may have taken place shortly after exposure.[8]

There is no evidence, therefore, other than the selective deposition of heads and feet, that bones of cattle were treated in a distinctive fashion. The age of the cattle represented is varied, including at least one infant, one juvenile, and two adults. Moreover, despite the preponderance of heads and feet, other body parts of cattle are generally underrepresented rather than absent altogether. Although individual body parts display a bias toward left- or right-sided specimens, no consistent pattern of selection was observed. In spite of the association with a possible ceremonial activity (see below), therefore, no faunal evidence suggests that the selective deposition of cattle heads and feet was an act of great symbolic significance. It might be argued that this deposit represents those parts of the carcass not selected for ceremonial treatment, but again the range of body parts missing or underrepresented is too large to offer active support for such an interpretation.

The scale of carcass-processing represented here is difficult to estimate. Surviving and recovered remains of cattle include parts of *at least* six individuals, but this figure is probably an underestimate of the actual number discarded. The excavators estimated that less than half of the dump was excavated. Widespread gnawing is likely to have resulted in some losses, and, even within the head and foot categories, the body parts listed in Table 1 account for only a minority of those expected for six cattle. The duration and number of episodes of deposition are also uncertain, although the condition of the associated ceramics suggests, at most, just a few episodes. Even if only one or two cattle were deposited in each episode, however, a significant quantity of meat would have been involved, which, taken in conjunction with the ceramic evidence, suggests consumption on a large scale. In modern Greece, prior to the introduction of electric refrigerators, cattle were rarely consumed in villages and were normally sold for slaughter in the towns.[9] The scale of meat consumption represented by this deposit is thus certainly consistent with a major feast or series of feasts.

An unresolved question, at this stage, is the fate of the parts of cattle not found in this deposit. As has already been noted, the range of parts missing does not favor destruction in a burned sacrifice,[10] nor does ongoing study of the rest of the LH III faunal assemblage from Tsoungiza indicate deposition elsewhere on the site. A third and intriguing possibility is that the feasts taking place at Tsoungiza involved drinking, sacrifice, and slaughter, followed by some consumption on-site (at least of bone marrow), but that most of the meat from the slaughtered animals was distributed to participants from other settlements for eventual consumption in their own communities. This tentative interpretation would imply that feasting at Nemea had political significance on a regional scale, a possibility further discussed below.

8. Munson and Garniewicz 2003.
9. P. Halstead, unpublished interviews in Macedonia, Epirus, the Peloponnese, the Cyclades, and Crete.
10. Cf. Isaakidou et al. 2002.

CERAMIC EVIDENCE

The identification of ceramic remains resulting from feasting is a difficult task in the absence of a set of vessels or accompanying decorative motifs that are peculiar to that activity. This is true not only for Mycenaean Greece, but for other past cultures as well.[11] Although Stocker and Davis have identified a kind of miniature kylix as an indicator of ritual feasting at Pylos,[12] for the most part Mycenaean feasts seem to have employed pottery that was also employed on an everyday basis. Since Mycenaean settlement deposits are in general dominated by precisely the sorts of serving vessels (such as kylikes) that would presumably be used in feasts, it is useful to attempt to develop criteria to identify ceramic remains from feasting. A combination of characteristics, not ceramic evidence alone, will probably be needed to identify such a deposit. In the case of the material from EU 9, for example, it is important to keep in mind the clear evidence for the butchering of large quantities of meat (see above).

An important preliminary question to ask is whether it is reasonable to expect to find large deposits of ceramics from feasts, since the vessels would retain their utility after the meal was completed, and might continue in use afterward. Deposition of intact vessels and even deliberate destruction of complete vessels are known practices associated with funerary meals,[13] but are not well established in other contexts. Although vessels might be deliberately destroyed during the course of a feast or afterward, as argued below, we need not insist on ritual breakage to suspect that a large feast will leave behind clear ceramic evidence. The presence of large numbers of people and the consumption of wine itself virtually guarantees a number of broken vessels. Moreover, if the participants traveled some distance to take part in the feast and were provided pottery by their host, many would probably discard the vessels before returning home.

As a first step in the development of a model, the sorts of vessels likely to be present in a deposit of ceramics resulting from feasting activities should be considered. It appears sufficiently settled that wine and meat were important components in Mycenaean feasting. The association of the kylix with feasting is agreed upon by virtually all writers; we ought, therefore, to expect that kylikes will compose a large percentage of such a deposit. Further, we can expect that jugs or other pouring vessels for the wine would be present. If ceramic vessels were used for cooking, cooking pots should be present as well, especially if meat was prepared in the form of a stew.[14] If pottery was used for serving meat dishes, an obvious possible form is the Furumark shape (FS 295), a shallow angular bowl (SAB). Although Tournavitou has suggested that the SAB is well designed for serving hot foods,[15] the very large number of such vessels found in room 21, part of the suite of pantries at the palace at Pylos, has been little remarked on. With nearly 1,100 examples from this room alone, it is the second most common shape after the kylix in the pantries and a logical candidate as a serving vessel for meat dishes.[16] Evidence for the function of this vessel as a plate for meat is provided by a recent organic-residue analysis of a SAB from a LH IIIB context at Mycenae that indicated traces of fat.[17]

11. For example, see the discussion concerning Mayan feasting in LeCount 2001, esp. pp. 946–948; see also Blitz 1993 for a study of Mississippian feasting.

12. Stocker and Davis, this volume.

13. See Hamilakis 1998, pp. 119–126, for a review of relevant evidence.

14. Tzedakis and Martlew (1999, pp. 84, 103, 108, 110) have analyzed the organic residue in vessels from Minoan Crete, showing that stews of vegetables, meat, and olive oil were common; similar evidence specifically relating to LH III Thebes, Mycenae, and Midea is also presented (pp. 115–135).

15. Tournavitou 1995, p. 90, fig. 25:4.

16. *Palace of Nestor* I, pp. 129–132.

17. Tzedakis and Martlew 1999, p. 133; the nature of the fat could not, however, be determined. Another possible candidate for a serving vessel is the stemmed bowl (FS 304). This is a shape that first appears in a one-handled form in LH IIIA1 and becomes common in a two-handled form in LH IIIA2.

The ceramics from feasting activities should thus exhibit most of the following criteria:

1. Deviation from the norm in the amount and kind of decoration. If provision of food and drink was the primary purpose served, and the vessels themselves were not valued souvenirs of the feast, elaborate decoration would be unnecessary. A higher-than-usual percentage of unpainted pottery might be found, or painted pots might exhibit a lower-than-usual percentage of patterned examples. The same features could also be observed if the sponsor of the feast wanted to deemphasize social differences and create an atmosphere of equality among the guests.

2. A higher-than-usual percentage of open shapes used to serve food and drink. The kylix should be especially abundant. Based on later practice at Pylos, we might also expect to find substantial numbers of SABs among the open shapes; shallow cups may be present as well, since over 1,000 of them were present in room 21. Dippers and kraters for serving wine are also likely finds.

3. The presence of closed shapes in the form of jugs. Cooking pots of various sorts should be prevalent, especially if meat was prepared in stews.

4. The presence of vessels peculiarly associated with ritual feasting. In the case of Mycenaean Greece, a possible candidate is the miniature kylix with high-swung handles, as argued by Stocker and Davis elsewhere in this volume.

5. A restricted range of vessels. If a deposit is formed primarily from feasting activity, it is likely to exhibit fewer types of vessels than a deposit representing everyday activity, especially in terms of utilitarian vessels employed for processing food or other products.

6. The possible presence of oversized pots for dignitaries or for shared consumption among participants.[18] Both kylikes and unusually large SABs were encountered in the pantries at Pylos. The very few large kylikes present in comparison to kylikes of average size might indicate that sharing occurred only within a select group.[19]

We should now reflect briefly on the process of deposition, beginning with a theoretically ideal situation and then working toward the messier reality likely to confront an excavator. Ideally, a fresh pit would be dug to hold all of the debris from a feast and closed immediately thereafter with a layer of sterile soil. The participants would carefully gather all of the discarded bones and uneaten food and deposit them into the pit; all pots, vessels of other materials, and utensils used, whether broken or unbroken, would be cast in as well. Ceramics from such a deposit would be recognizable archaeologically by very high "mendability" into whole pots, a prevalence of shapes associated with feasting, a lack of shapes associated with other activities, complete chronological homogeneity of shape and decoration, and minimal wear from weathering processes.

18. Blitz (1993) notes in a study of Mississippian feasting that although vessel types from village/nonfeasting contexts were not significantly different from those in presumed feasting contexts associated with the structures on the mounds, pots in use in the latter contexts tended to be larger. Shared consumption would help to reinforce a sense of community.

19. For the SABs, see *Palace of Nestor* I, p. 356; the largest has a rim diameter of 22.5 cm, height of 8 cm, and measured capacity of 1.4 l. Blegen and Rawson (*Palace of Nestor* I, p. 371) also report only six "very large" (type 29h) and six "giant" (type 29i) kylikes from rooms 19 and 20, in contrast to nearly 3,000 other kylikes from the site.

We have no reason, however, to believe that refuse dumps such as those found at Tsoungiza were used exclusively for refuse from large-scale feasts. A realistic model designed to characterize feasting activity needs to take into account the likelihood that two streams of waste might well be flowing into a dump, one derived from feasting and the other from daily use. One can anticipate that the stream of waste from daily activities will in general be more fragmentary, exhibit greater differences in wear, and contain a broader range of the types of vessels in use at the site, not only those associated with eating and drinking. Even if we can develop criteria to distinguish between ceramics from feasting and daily meals, the latter stream of waste may "dilute" the distinctiveness of the waste resulting from feasts. If the feasts are small and infrequent, one can anticipate that their remains in a dump will probably be archaeologically indistinguishable from those of daily meals. In addition, the possibility of a third stream of fill used to cover decaying bones and meat is discussed below.

Distinguishing depositional features from large feasts can be suggested. The first is a general lack of soil matrix between sherds, since substantial quantities of pottery will be deposited at once. In a "dual-use" refuse pit, then, we can anticipate finding substantial areas of densely packed sherds and bones reflective of individual feasts, separated by layers associated with everyday activity, with fewer sherds and more soil matrix. A second feature that can be expected is less general weathering of surfaces, since fewer sherds will be exposed to the effects of weathering if they are dumped in a heap than if they are deposited in other ways.

Obvious disparities and potential difficulties with the model should be considered, along with some reasonable modifications. First, the LH IIIA2 (early) deposit in EU 9 is not composed primarily of whole vessels, although it includes some vessels that are entirely or nearly complete, and it contains substantially more restorable pottery than, for example, a LH IIIB1 deposit excavated in EU 2. Second, the deposit is not chronologically homogeneous: nearly 5% of the sherds belong to earlier periods, a finding that does not appear to be the result of the excavators' cutting into earlier strata. By contrast, fewer than 1% of the sherds in the LH IIIB1 refuse pit in EU 2 belonged to earlier periods.

A rough index of mendable pottery in deposits with broken vessels is the percentage of sherds remaining after mending is complete. After sherds from earlier periods were excluded, the EU 9 deposit, after mending, contained roughly 79% of the initial number of sherds excavated; the EU 2 deposit had 86%. Not only were more joins found in the EU 9 deposit than in the EU 2 deposit, but numerous additional joins could have been made between body sherds in the former deposit had unlimited amounts of time been available. Moreover, only a portion of the EU 9 deposit was recovered, in contrast to the EU 2 deposit, which was completely excavated (the area to the east of EU 9 was private property not purchased for the project). This point has a bearing on any argument about the numbers of relatively whole pots and the amount of faunal material present. The deposit ranged in depth from 0.57 to 1.04 m in a 4×4 m^2 area; the total volume of the deposit was about 13.5 m^3. The percentage of the total deposit excavated is not calculable, but the increasing numbers of sherds found as one moves eastward in successive 1-m-wide strips suggest that a very substantial portion of the deposit lies to the east of the excavated area. The basal levels of EU 9 (SU 1584, 1558, and 1559), which form an area of roughly comparable thickness across the trench, show this clearly: a 4-m-long strip along the E729 grid line running from N459 to N463 contained 699 sherds weighing 8.235 kg; the strip along the E730 grid line, 1,112 sherds weighing 13.616 kg; the strip along E731, 1,215 sherds weighing 14.670 kg; and the strip along E732, 2,297 sherds weighing 22.640 kg. Were the area to the east to be excavated, many more pieces could presumably be joined to those already excavated, since it was not unusual to find pieces from the same pot in the four adjacent units.

That the deposit accumulated in a relatively short period of time and was not built up gradually as the result of daily disposal of rubbish is indicated by several lines of evidence. The excavators noted a number of very dense and thick "lenses" of sherds during the course of excavations; one such lens appears in a section drawing. Little matrix was observed between sherds in these lenses, consistent with dumping large quantities of sherds at once. The deposit in general and the more completely preserved vessels in particular exhibit considerably less surface weathering than the pottery in the EU 2 deposit dating to LH IIIB1, which is consistent with bulk disposal and fairly rapid burial. The EU 9 deposit was excavated in 59 units. Only 15% (9 out of 59) of the units contained heavily worn potsherds and 36% showed light wear; 63% of the units contained large sherds. Of the 37% containing only small to medium-sized sherds, many were from the basal level of the deposit where the sherds were in good condition, but broken into small pieces—almost as though an area had been leveled off and then walked on, breaking the sherds lying on its surface into small fragments. Moreover, the period to which the pottery belongs is a short one, accorded no more than 20–30 years in most absolute chronologies.[20] The deposit was stratified beneath a thin layer of LH IIIA2 (late), so it could not have accumulated over a very long period of time.

Roughly 5% of the sherds belong to earlier periods—an amount somewhat unexpected in a primary disposal context but one consistent with deposition associated with feasting. For symbolic as well as practical reasons, debris from important ceremonies is often destroyed, displayed, or buried rather than merely being left discarded on the ground. A striking Mycenaean example is the series of bone groups from burned sacrifices placed around the Palace of Nestor at Pylos,[21] and such depositional practices were commonplace in later Greek sanctuaries. In this case, refuse from feasting may have been disposed of in the EU 9 pit and then covered with a layer of soil. The great majority of the earlier ceramic material from the pit dates to EH II and III; areas with considerable remains from these periods are immediately at hand to the west and north as a source of fill dirt. A sequence of feasts could thus leave evidence in the form of thick lenses of sherds and bones separated by areas of fill with higher concentrations of earlier sherds, a scenario compatible with the situation in the EU 9 deposit.

In order to assess how well the EU 9 deposit fits the above model for identifying feasting, it is necessary to compare it to other deposits (Table 2). Unfortunately, no settlement deposits from LH IIIA2 (early) have been characterized statistically in a manner comparable to this deposit; few closed settlement deposits of this period have in fact been

20. Wiener 1998.
21. Isaakidou et al. 2002; Stocker and Davis, this volume.

TABLE 2. CERAMIC REMAINS FROM TSOUNGIZA AND RELATED SITES

Site/Sample	Patterned (%)		Linear (%)		Solidly Painted (%)		Unidentifiable (%)		Painted Open vs. Closed Shapes (%)		Painted vs. Unpainted (%)	
Asine, room D, str. 2	Total	10.4	Total	0.5	Total	>80						
N (painted) 884	Open	7.7	Open	0.5			N/A		N/A		Painted	21.3
N (unpainted) 3,271	Closed	2.7	Closed	0.0							Unpainted	78.7
Tsoungiza, EU 9	Total	9.4	Total	21.2	Total	66.8	Total	2.6				
N (painted) 2,160	Open	6.2	Open	12.4	Open	64.2	Open	1.7	Open	84.5	Painted	20.4
N (unpainted) 8,442	Closed	3.2	Closed	8.8	Closed	2.6	Closed	0.9	Closed	15.5	Unpainted	79.6
Tsoungiza, EU 2	Total	24.0	Total	48.3	Total	18.5	Total	9.2				
N (painted) 2,626	Open	18.8	Open	35.0	Open	14.5	Open	7.2	Open	75.5	Painted	14.8
N (unpainted) 15,123	Closed	5.2	Closed	13.3	Closed	4.0	Closed	2.0	Closed	24.5	Unpainted	85.2
Mycenae, Atreus	Total	78.1	Total	21.9								
Bothros	Open	48.0	Open	11.0	N/A		N/A		Open	59.0	N/A	
N (painted) 2,094*	Closed	30.1	Closed	10.9					Closed	41.0		
Mycenae, terrace on	Total	68.4	Total	31.6								
the Atreus ridge	Open	65.0	Open	31.6	N/A		N/A		Open	96.6	N/A	
N (painted) 674	Closed	3.4	Closed	0					Closed	3.4		
Mycenae, terrace below	Total	68.0	Total	32.0								
the House of Shields	Open	54.4	Open	32.0	N/A		N/A		Open	86.4	N/A	
N (painted) 206	Closed	13.6	Closed	0					Closed	13.6		

Percentages are of the total number of painted sherds; N/A = not available or not able to be calculated.

For Tsoungiza, figures reflect numbers after mending and extraction of earlier sherds. In conformity with the Tsoungiza calculations, characteristic handles from Mycenae are counted with the patterned. The "unidentifiable" category includes sherds that had traces of paint, but could not be definitely assigned to the three main categories of patterned, linear, or solidly painted. Unpatterned rims and bases assigned to particular shapes at Mycenae (in published tables) are assumed to have been linear unless explicitly identified as solidly painted.

Percentages were calculated using the following sources: *Asine, room D, stratum 2 (LH IIB–IIIA1):* Frizell 1980, pp. 34–41 (all sherds kept); *Tsoungiza, EU 2 (LH IIIB1):* Thomas 1992, pp. 520–525, figs. 2:1–2:7 (all sherds kept); *Mycenae, Atreus Bothros (LH IIIA1):* French 1964, pp. 260–261 (unpainted and most solidly painted discarded); *Mycenae, terrace on the Atreus ridge (LH IIIA2 [late]):* French 1965, p. 200 (only the "best and most typical pieces kept"); *Mycenae, terrace below the House of Shields (LH IIIA2 [late]):* French 1965, p. 201 (much discarded); *Mycenae, dromos of tomb 505 (LH IIIA2 [late]):* French 1965, p. 202 (at least a third of the originally catalogued sherds lost by the time of analysis; most solidly painted and unpainted sherds appear to have been discarded); *Mycenae, Prehistoric Cemetery,*

identified. In order to have some basis of comparison, however, Table 2 presents statistics for deposits from Asine, Tsoungiza, Mycenae, and Korakou. Usage of these statistics is fraught with difficulties, since at least some sherds (particularly unpainted and solidly painted sherds) from most of the Mycenae deposits were discarded before being analyzed. In addition, because Mycenae was a preeminent site, it is more likely to have remains of feasting activities than a smaller site, and thus using deposits from Mycenae to establish a norm for settlements of all sizes is questionable; deposits from specialized storage areas such as the Petsas House at Mycenae and the so-called Potter's Shop at Zygouries have, for this reason, not been employed. Pottery from Nichoria and Asine is referred to in the following discussion, but it has not generally been quantified in a manner similar to the deposits from Tsoungiza and Mycenae.[22] Although plentiful material is available from Tiryns for LH IIIA2 (late) and LH IIIB1, it too has not been quantified in a readily comparable manner.[23]

22. A statistical breakdown is provided for two admittedly small Nichoria units dating to LH IIIB2: see Shelmerdine 1992, pp. 510–511. Frizell (1980) does quantify LH IIB–IIIA1 strata at Asine, but the frequencies of solidly painted sherds are not explicitly given.

23. See Schönfeld 1988.

TABLE 2—*Continued*

Site/Sample	Patterned (%)		Linear (%)		Solidly Painted (%)		Unidentifiable (%)	Painted Open vs. Closed Shapes (%)		Painted vs. Unpainted (%)	
Mycenae, dromos of	Total	62.3	Total	31.1	Total	6.6					
tomb 505	Open	57.4	Open	24.6	Open	6.6	N/A	Open	88.6	N/A	
N (painted) 61	Closed	4.9	Closed	6.5	Closed	0		Closed	11.4		
Mycenae, Prehistoric	Total	82.2	Total	16.2	Total	1.6					
Cemetery, central	Open	53.7	Open	7.3	Open	1.5	N/A	Open	62.5	N/A	
N (painted) 1,871	Closed	28.5	Closed	8.9	Closed	0.1		Closed	37.5		
Mycenae, room 3	Total	20.5	Total	69.7	Total	9.8					
N (painted) 878	Open	17.3	Open	23.1	Open	8.5	N/A	Open	48.9	Painted	11.1
N (unpainted) ca. 7,000	Closed	3.2	Closed	46.6	Closed	1.3		Closed	51.1	Unpainted	88.9
Mycenae, room 22	Total	25.6	Total	53.5	Total	20.9					
N (painted) 1,240	Open	20.3	Open	23.5	Open	13.5	N/A	Open	57.3	Painted	15.4
N (unpainted) 6,830	Closed	5.3	Closed	30.0	Closed	7.4		Closed	42.7	Unpainted	84.6
Mycenae, Causeway	Total	21.1	Total	74.1	Total	4.8					
N (painted) 825	Open	17.5	Open	33.0	Open	4.4	N/A	Open	54.9	Painted	18.6
N (unpainted) 3,604	Closed	3.6	Closed	41.1	Closed	0.4		Closed	45.1	Unpainted	81.4
Korakou,	Total	21.8	Total	46.9	Total	31.3					
East Alley I–IV	Open	20.2	Open	34.7	Open	N/A	N/A	Open	79.8	N/A	
N (painted) 729**	Closed	1.6	Closed	12.2	Closed	N/A		Closed	20.2		

central (LH IIIB1): French 1966, p. 235 (all unpainted and most linear sherds discarded); *Mycenae, Citadel House, room 3 (LH IIIB1):* Wardle 1969, p. 279 (painted sherds kept; unpainted sherds given a preliminary analysis, but many discarded before final study); *Mycenae, South House, room 22 (LH IIIB1):* Mountjoy 1976, p. 110 (all sherds kept); *Mycenae, Causeway (LH IIIB2):* Wardle 1973, p. 320 (painted sherds kept; unpainted sherds given a preliminary analysis, but many discarded before final study); *Korakou, East Alley I–IV (LH IIIB1):* Rutter 1974, pp. 102–103, fig. 27 (coarse body sherds were discarded; other classes may have been partially discarded).

*Apparently the great majority of the solidly painted sherds were jettisoned before French's study, and so the few remaining have not been taken into account. Those would bring the total number of painted sherds to 2,133.

**In the Korakou East Alley deposit, the number of patterned and linear sherds assigned to LH IIIB is 501; solidly painted sherds present in the preserved collection number 228. Because the solidly painted sherds were not broken down into open or closed shapes, the percentage of open vs. closed shapes is based only on the patterned and linear sherds.

24. By making some assumptions about Frizell's (1980, pp. 34–50) counting procedures, it appears that 11% of the painted sherds from stratum 2 under room D were patterned and fewer than 1% had linear decoration.

As would be expected in any settlement deposit, open shapes are more common in the EU 9 deposit than closed ones. Of the painted pottery, there is a higher percentage of open shapes in the EU 9 deposit than in EU 2 (LH IIIB1): 84.5% vs. 75.5%. In the larger and probably more representative deposits from Mycenae (the Atreus Bothros, Citadel House room 3, South House room 22, and Causeway deposits), the percentage of open painted vessels is typically around 60%. At Korakou, which as a small, nonpalatial site probably offers the best comparison to Tsoungiza, about 80% of the painted sherds are from open shapes.

The unusual nature of the EU 9 deposit is indicated by the low frequency of patterned sherds and sherds with linear decoration, and the high incidence of solidly painted sherds (criterion 1, above). Fewer than 10% of the sherds from the EU 9 deposit bear a pattern, and only 21% have linear decoration. In no other published Mycenaean deposit of LH IIIA–B, with the possible exception of the LH IIB–IIIA1 strata from Asine, does the percentage of painted, patterned sherds fall below 20%.[24] For those deposits where most or all of the painted pottery was saved (Tsoungiza EU 2, Korakou, and Mycenae rooms 3 and 22, and the Causeway deposit), the percentage of patterned pottery typically amounts to 20–25%, and sherds with linear decoration typically comprise half or more of the total painted sherds. Because of the large number of kylikes, roughly 67% of the painted sherds in the EU 9 deposit are solidly painted. It can be argued that, in the absence of settlement groups of comparable date, these percentages relate more to chronology than function, but until additional LH IIIA2 (early) settlements are found, one must work with available evidence.[25]

As the labor-intensive practice of burnishing the surfaces of drinking cups declined during LH IIIA, the application of hard red paint to the surface might have served a similar aesthetic purpose by giving them a shinier, more metallic appearance, and would have lessened the porosity of body walls. One might speculate that the needs of public feasts such as those postulated here demanded greater quantities and more efficient production of drinking vessels, especially if the vessels were broken soon after being used.

The kylix is by far the most common painted shape in EU 9 (criterion 2). Although it is sometimes difficult to distinguish between rims of solidly painted kylikes and those of stemmed bowls, painted kylikes certainly comprise no fewer than 50%, and possibly closer to 55%, of all painted sherds. By contrast, only 7.5% of the LH IIIB1 assemblage in EU 2 is made up of painted kylikes. The bulk of the painted kylikes in EU 9 belong to FS 264, the rounded kylix typical of LH IIIA2, and are solidly painted (Fig. 2); a substantial number of patterned kylikes are present as well, although there are at least 10 solidly painted kylikes for every patterned one.

The kylix is also the form most prevalent among the unpainted sherds: 72% of diagnostic fineware sherds represent various kylix forms, mostly FS 267, the angular kylix, and the rounded kylix in both its deep (FS 264) and shallow (FS 266) variants (Fig. 3). When all unpainted features (e.g., rims, handles, bases) are taken into account, kylikes amount to over 55% of the diagnostic sherds. The percentage of unpainted vessels is less striking when compared to deposits with available statistics for unpainted ware: in the EU 2 deposit, 69% of the fine features belonged to kylix forms and 49.5% of diagnostic sherds; at Mycenae, in the Citadel House, room 3, Wardle notes that unpainted kylikes account for about half the total number of vessels represented in the unpainted pottery; in the South House, room 22, unpainted kylikes account for 62% of all unpainted features.[26]

Another popular open serving vessel present in this deposit is the stemmed bowl, FS 304 (Fig. 4); other than several examples decorated with

25. Although exact numbers are not provided, Martin (1992, p. 488) states that in a pure LH IIIA1 unit at Nichoria, 2% of the sherds were decorated (presumably this figure includes patterned and linear examples), 11% solidly painted, 67% plain ("fine" in terms of terminology employed in characterizing the Tsoungiza deposits), and 20% coarse ("medium-coarse" and "coarse" at Tsoungiza). It is not clear whether these figures are calculated before or after mending. With the data from Tsoungiza aggregated in this fashion, "decorated" sherds would amount to 7.2% of the total deposit, solidly painted to 16.4%, "plain" to 51.4%, and "coarse" to 25%. The prevalence of solidly painted vessels at Nichoria (mostly goblets) may be an indication that this form of decoration is much more common than has been supposed and may continue into LH IIIA2; Shelmerdine (1992, p. 496) notes that solidly painted kylikes and stemmed bowls, taken together, outnumber patterned kylikes in levels she dates to LH IIIA2 (early) by a 3:1 ratio. For Asine, Frizell (1980, pp. 120–121) states only that solidly painted decoration is the most frequent type observed in LH IIB–IIIA1 levels.

26. For the Citadel House, see Wardle 1969, p. 280. For the South House, see Mountjoy 1976, p. 111, table 3.

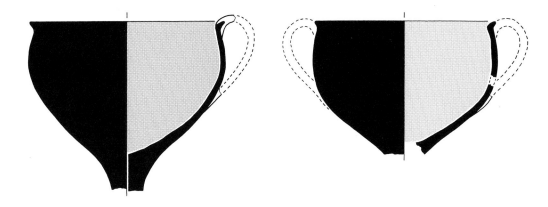

**Figure 2. Solidly painted, rounded
kylikes 1584-2-38** *(left)* **and 1584-2-
90** *(right)***.** Scale 1:3. P. Thomas and
J. E. Pfaff

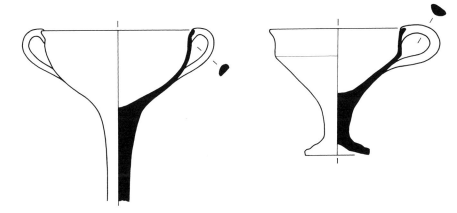

**Figure 3. Unpainted rounded
(shallow) kylix 1588-2-50** *(left)*;
angular kylix 1588-2-25 *(right)*.
Scale 1:3. P. Thomas and J. E. Pfaff

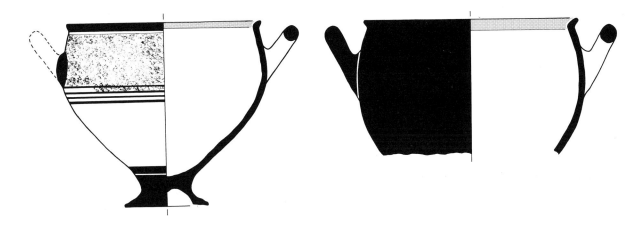

Figure 4. Stemmed bowls 1584-2-18
(left) **and 1588-2-4** *(right)***.** Scale 1:3.
P. Thomas and J. E. Pfaff

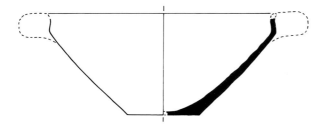

Figure 5. Shallow angular bowl 1584-2-73. Scale 1:3. P. Thomas and J. E. Pfaff

stipple pattern, nearly all of these are solidly painted. They comprise a minimum of 4.6% of the painted sherds, but because of the difficulty in distinguishing between some rims and body sherds of these vessels and those of solidly painted kylikes, the true proportion is probably closer to 10%. The only other open shape among the painted sherds that accounts for more than 2% of the total is a peculiar deep cup (similar to FS 214) with a solidly painted interior.

Of the unpainted pottery, the SAB (FS 295, Fig. 5) accounts for 2.7% of the fine features and 1.1% of all unpainted features; the same percentages apply to the unpainted shallow cup. Dippers make up 2.3% and 0.9% of the unpainted fine features and total unpainted features, respectively. Apart from some conical cups (FS 204), which may have served as lamps, only a small number of open vessels are present. These percentages are comparable to those of the EU 2 deposit. The raw percentages conceal the fact, however, that the remains of the SABs could often be mended into whole profiles or at least very substantial portions of the vessels.

Among closed vessels (criterion 3), large and medium-sized jugs and hydrias are the most common shapes represented in painted and unpainted assemblages in EU 9. Sherds from painted jugs and hydrias make up 4% of all painted sherds (cf. the EU 2 deposit with 9%). At Mycenae, in the Citadel House room 3 deposit, painted jugs comprise 4.9% of the painted sherds; in the South House room 22 deposit, 3.7%. At Korakou, jugs make up roughly 2% of the total painted sherds in the East Alley deposit. Among the unpainted pottery in EU 9, sherds from the jug/hydria make up 15% of all diagnostic sherds, in comparison to 10.5% of all features in the EU 2 deposit. In the South House room 22 deposit at Mycenae, the jug/hydria makes up only 7.5% of the unpainted features; although exact figures are not provided, the percentage in the Citadel House room 3 deposit appears to be even lower.[27] The unpainted jug/hydria may thus be more common in the Tsoungiza EU 9 deposit than is usual.

Cooking vessels of various kinds are present in abundance, including tripod cooking pots, at least three kinds of cooking jar, and two possible cooking lids. In both the EU 2 and EU 9 deposits, cooking vessels make up roughly half of the medium-coarse pottery and a tenth of all unpainted sherds. The latter figure is somewhat more than the 6.6% seen in the South House room 22 deposit at Mycenae.

In terms of the presence of special ritual vessels (criterion 4), this deposit contains a single example of the miniature kylix with high handles (FS 272; Fig. 6) that Stocker and Davis (this volume) connect to ritual feasting at Pylos. The rim diameter is only ca. 8 cm, about half the normal rim diameter of a kylix. This vessel is the only identified example of a

27. Wardle 1969, pp. 280–282; Mountjoy 1976, p. 111.

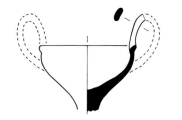

Figure 6. Miniature kylix 1557-2-2.
Scale 1:3. P. Thomas and J. E. Pfaff

miniature kylix at Tsoungiza in LH III levels, and its appearance may represent a link to sacrificial practices and feasting.

The EU 9 deposit includes relatively few medium-coarse and coarse utilitarian vessels (criterion 5). For example, nearly a fifth of the coarse diagnostic sherds from the EU 2 deposit come from vats, tubs, and large basins; because the sherds from these sorts of vessels in EU 9 were in general much smaller and harder to classify than those from the EU 2 deposit, exact percentages are impossible to determine, but comparable vessels appear to account for only 10% of the EU 9 deposit.

Finally, oversized versions of some pots are present (criterion 6). A small number of kylix sherds have rim diameters of more than 20 cm. The FS 295 SABs present in this deposit are on the whole larger than usual. In the EU 2 deposit dating to LH IIIB1, almost all of the SABs have rim diameters that fall between 13 and 16 cm; most of the examples in the EU 9 deposit range from 15 to 18 cm, but a number of examples are considerably larger, with diameters up to 23 cm. The larger specimens are not simply a reflection of their period since the average rim diameter, even in LH IIIA2, ranges from around 15 to 18 cm.

In conclusion, although the partial excavation of the EU 9 deposit and the difficulties in finding comparable data must be considered, the pottery in the EU 9 deposit nevertheless fulfills most of the criteria proposed for recognizing feasting activities in ceramic assemblages.

FEMALE FIGURE AND OTHER EVIDENCE

The presence of a fragmentary ceramic female figure (Figs. 7; 8:a) makes the Tsoungiza deposit stand out as unique. The figure belongs to Elizabeth French's type A, best known from the cult centers at Mycenae and Phylakopi.[28] Only the lower two-thirds was recovered, with attachment scars for the arms on its sides; its restored height is 45 cm. The date of the pottery with which it was deposited confirms a date of LH IIIA for the first appearance of these types of figures, surmised by French from the decoration on figures found in later contexts.[29] A comparable figure, smaller but approximately contemporary, was discovered at Pylos.[30]

At Tsoungiza, no associated architectural context has been identified for the figure. The only excavated structure at the site with LH IIIA2 destruction debris is later (LH IIIA2 [late]) than the EU 9 deposit. This finding is not surprising, considering that the cult centers where similar figures occur were not built until LH IIIA2 and later, when the palatial centers were already established.[31] Although it is possible that the figure was originally housed in a structure that was either not preserved or outside the area excavated,[32] there is no evidence for a built cult center at Tsoungiza.

28. Moore and Taylour 1999, pp. 46–47; French 1985, pp. 214–216, 221.

29. French 1971, pp. 103–105, 109.

30. *Palace of Nestor* III, p. 159, fig. 232:a–c.

31. Wright 1996, p. 61.

32. Wright 1996, pp. 69–70.

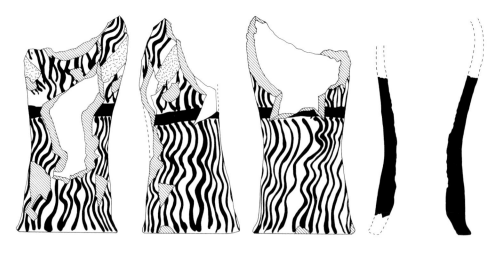

Figure 7. Female figure 1581-2-1.
Scale 1:3. J. E. Pfaff

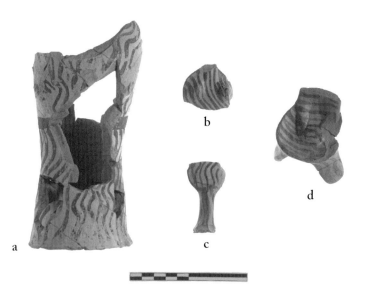

Figure 8. (a) Female figure 1581-2-1;
(b) phi figurine 1581-2-5; (c) phi
figurine 1584-2-1; (d) "breadmaker"
figurine 1559-2-1. Photo T. Dabney

The EU 9 deposit also contained other types of figurines (Fig. 8), including two unusual "breadmaker" figurines, three female figurines, and one bovine figurine. Also found were a ceramic bead, fragments of seven ground stone tools (millstones, handstones, and a whetstone), and one chert and three obsidian retouched chipped stone tools. Plant remains from the deposit are typical of most deposits at Tsoungiza and are not significant because only a few species were found due to poor preservation.[33]

CONCLUSIONS

How are we to understand the social significance of these archaeological remains? The character of the pottery and faunal remains suggests that most of the refuse was deposited shortly after use in a single event or a series of similar specialized events. The predominance of plain vessels used for serving food and drink combined with faunal remains from carcass-processing and the presence of religious display items indicates that this

33. J. M. Hansen (pers. comm.).

event was a feast.[34] The quantity of cattle consumed suggests that there were many participants in the feast, while the consumption of large animals such as adult cattle may indicate that much of the meat (and perhaps drink) for the feast was provided by a single sponsor or, at most, a very restricted number of sponsors.[35] Thus, there are grounds for interpreting the feast(s) at Ancient Nemea in terms of conspicuous generosity by the high-ranking sponsor(s), rather than collectively organized commensality. The large quantity of meat consumed, the small size of the settlement, and the "missing" parts of the cattle also highlight the possibility of a regional feast, involving participants from a number of different settlements. At regional feasts, the elite guests typically take away large portions of food to redistribute in their own villages.[36] The presence of the female figure and other distinctive figurines suggests that this feast was associated with a religious activity. The disposal of the figure along with the remains of feasting may point to a different ceremonial role for this figure than for later figures found in cult centers elsewhere.

The ceremonial feasting deposit described above provides information about the relationship of Ancient Nemea to external social and economic systems. This deposit marks a turning point in the settlement's history, coinciding with the beginning of a period of extensive growth. The person or people who provided the resources for this ceremonial feast created an obligation of reciprocity in those who partook of the feast. The provider(s) not only provided the food and drink but also the containers in which the food and drink were served. This required also acquiring and transporting the vessels from the point of production. Kim Shelton has suggested that the Petsas House at Mycenae, which contained a figure and pottery similar to the material in the Tsoungiza deposit, was a warehouse from which such ceramics were distributed.[37] The feast may have been conducted in such a way that the containers as well as their contents were removed from circulation in the community by their disposal. The disposal of the feasting vessels prevented the participants from reciprocating in kind. The provider(s) would thereby have created a situation entailing reciprocity in other spheres such as consolidation of obligations as trading partners or political allegiance.[38]

By inviting people to partake of the feast, the provider was able to bring affiliated people in the region into a closer social relationship. In studying the use of feasts to mobilize collective labor, Michael Dietler and Ingrid Herbich found that feasts act as a means of converting the raw materials of the feast, agrarian wealth, into social and economic prestige.[39] Providing a feast is a powerful means of expanding political power, one not lost on modern-day politicians and lobbyists. To this one must add the provider's control over a potentially even more significant aspect of social relations, the symbolic belief system as represented by the female figure. The provider's act of introducing and then disposing of the female figure heightens the meaning of the event represented by this deposit. In the context of relations between Ancient Nemea and the closest larger center, Mycenae, the feasting deposit at Tsoungiza might be evidence of the forging of closer social and economic relations that contributed to the growth of the relative importance of both sites within the region during the Mycenaean era.

34. Cf. Hayden 2001, pp. 40–41.
35. These suggestions are based on the assumption that domestic animals were not in communal ownership.
36. B. Hayden (pers. comm.).
37. Shelton 2002.
38. Hayden 2001, pp. 58–59.
39. Dietler and Herbich 2001, p. 252.

The settlement at Tsoungiza was only one of a number of settlements that lay on the northern periphery of Mycenae. Settlements to the east of Tsoungiza at Kleonai and Zygouries, and to the west at Phlious, Ayia Irini, and the settlement associated with the Aidonia cemetery might also have been drawn into Mycenae's social and economic sphere of influence. As Pia de Fidio argues,[40] palace and villages were engaged in a dynamic relationship, not merely one in which the center commanded and the periphery obeyed; within villages themselves, hierarchies emerged. Competition among the elites at these sites could have driven both the practice of feasting and the establishment of public ritual. The rotation of regional feasts involving elites from a number of different centers would have contributed to maintaining regional political and economic alliances.

40. See de Fidio 2001, pp. 23–24.

REFERENCES

Blitz, J. 1993. "Big Pots for Big Shots: Feasting and Storage in a Mississippian Community," *AmerAnt* 58, pp. 80–96.

Brain, C. K. 1981. *The Hunters or the Hunted? An Introduction to African Cave Taphonomy,* Chicago.

Cherry, J. F., J. L. Davis, and E. Mantzourani. 2000. "The Nemea Valley Archaeological Project Archaeological Survey: Internet Edition" (http://classics.uc.edu/NVAP/).

Dabney, M. 1997. "Craft Product Consumption as an Economic Indicator of Site Status in Regional Studies," in *TEXNH: Craftsmen, Craftswomen, and Craftsmanship in the Aegean Bronze Age. Proceedings of the 6th International Aegean Conference, Philadelphia* (*Aegaeum* 16), ed. R. Laffineur and P. P. Betancourt, Liège, pp. 467–471.

de Fidio, P. 2001. "Centralization and Its Limits in the Mycenaean Palatial System," in *Economy and Politics in the Mycenaean Palace States* (Cambridge Philological Society, Suppl. 27), ed. S. Voutsaki and J. Killen, Cambridge, pp. 15–24.

Dietler, M., and I. Herbich. 2001. "Feasts and Labor Mobilization: Dissecting a Fundamental Economic Practice," in *Feasts: Archaeological and Ethnographic Perspectives on Food, Politics, and Power,* ed. M. Dietler and B. Hayden, Washington, D.C., pp. 240–264.

French, E. 1964. "Late Helladic IIIA 1 Pottery from Mycenae," *BSA* 59, pp. 241–261.

———. 1965. "Late Helladic IIIA 2 Pottery from Mycenae," *BSA* 60, pp. 159–202.

———. 1966. "A Group of Late Helladic IIIB 1 Pottery from Mycenae," *BSA* 61, pp. 216–238.

———. 1971. "The Development of Mycenaean Terracotta Figurines," *BSA* 66, pp. 101–187.

———. 1985. "The Figures and Figurines," in C. Renfrew, *The Archaeology of Cult: The Sanctuary at Phylakopi* (*BSA* Suppl. 18), London, pp. 209–280.

Frizell, B. 1980. *An Early Mycenaean Settlement at Asine: The Late Helladic IIB–III A:1 Pottery,* Göteborg.

Hamilakis, Y. 1998. "Eating the Dead: Mortuary Feasting and the Politics of Memory in the Aegean Bronze Age Societies," in *Cemetery and Society in the Aegean Bronze Age* (Sheffield Studies in Aegean Archaeology 1), ed. K. Branigan, Sheffield, pp. 115–132.

Hayden, B. 2001. "Fabulous Feasts: A Prolegomenon to the Importance of Feasting," in *Feasts: Archaeological and Ethnographic Perspectives on Food, Politics, and Power,* ed. M. Dietler and B. Hayden, Washington, D.C., pp. 23–64.

Isaakidou, V., P. Halstead, J. Davis, and S. Stocker. 2002. "Burnt Animal Sacrifice in Late Bronze Age Greece: New Evidence from the Mycenaean 'Palace of Nestor,' Pylos," *Antiquity* 76, pp. 86–92.

LeCount, L. 2001. "Like Water for Chocolate: Feasting and Political Ritual among the Late Classic Maya at Xunantunich, Belize," *American Anthropologist* 103, pp. 935–953.

Maltby, M. 1985. "Patterns in Faunal Assemblage Variability," in *Beyond Domestication in Prehistoric Europe: Investigations in Subsistence Archaeology and Social Complexity,* ed. G. Barker and C. Gamble, New York, pp. 33–74.

Martin, S. L. 1992. "Mycenaean Pottery from the Settlement, Part II: The Late Helladic IIIA1 Pottery," in *Excavations at Nichoria in Southwest Greece* II: *The Bronze Age Occupation,* ed. W. A. McDonald and N. C. Wilkie, Minneapolis, pp. 488–494.

Moore, A. D., and W. D. Taylour. 1999. *Well Built Mycenae* 10: *The Temple Complex,* Oxford.

Mountjoy, P. 1976. "Late Helladic IIIB 1 Pottery Dating the Construction of the South House at Mycenae," *BSA* 71, pp. 77–111.

Munson, P., and R. Garniewicz. 2003. "Age-Mediated Survivorship of Ungulate Mandibles and Teeth in Canid-Ravaged Faunal Assemblages," *JAS* 30, pp. 405–416.

Palace of Nestor I = C. W. Blegen and M. Rawson, *The Palace of Nestor at Pylos in Western Messenia* I: *The Buildings and Their Contents,* Princeton 1966.

Palace of Nestor III = C. W. Blegen, M. Rawson, W. Taylour, and W. P. Donovan, *The Palace of Nestor at Pylos in Western Messenia* III:

Acropolis and Lower Town: Tholoi, Grave Circle, and Chamber Tombs, Discoveries outside the Citadel, Princeton 1973.

Rutter, J. B. 1974. "The Late Helladic IIIB and IIIC Periods at Korakou and Gonia in the Corinthia" (diss. Univ. of Pennsylvania).

Schönfeld, G. 1988. "Bericht zur bemalten mykenischen Keramik: Ausgrabungen in Tiryns 1982/83," *AA* 1988, pp. 153–211.

Shelmerdine, C. W. 1992. "Mycenaean Pottery from the Settlement, Part III: Late Helladic IIIA2–IIIB2 Pottery," in *Excavations at Nichoria in Southwest Greece* II: *The Bronze Age Occupation,* ed. W. A. McDonald and N. C. Wilkie, Minneapolis, pp. 495–517.

Shelton, K. 2002. "The Reopening of Petsas House: The Study of a Ceramic Warehouse and the New Excavations at Mycenae," *AJA* 106, p. 259 (abstract).

Thomas, P. M. 1992. "LH IIIB:1 Pottery from Tsoungiza and Zygouries" (diss. Univ. of North Carolina, Chapel Hill).

Tournavitou, I. 1995. *The "Ivory Houses" at Mycenae* (*BSA* Suppl. 24), London.

Tzedakis, Y., and H. Martlew, eds. 1999. *Minoans and Mycenaeans: Flavours of Their Time,* Athens.

Wardle, K. A. 1969. "A Group of Late Helladic IIIB 1 Pottery from within the Citadel at Mycenae," *BSA* 64, pp. 261–298.

———. 1973. "A Group of Late Helladic IIIB 2 Pottery from within the Citadel at Mycenae: The Causeway Deposit," *BSA* 68, pp. 297–348.

Wiener, M. H. 1998. "The Absolute Chronology of Late Helladic IIIA2," in *Sardinian and Aegean Chronology: Towards the Resolution of Relative and Absolute Dating in the Mediterranean. Proceedings of the International Colloquium "Sardinian Stratigraphy and Mediterranean Chronology," Tufts University* (Studies in Sardinian Archaeology 5), ed. M. S. Balmuth and R. H. Tykot, Oxford, pp. 309–319.

Wright, J. C. 1996. "The Spatial Configuration of Belief: The Archaeology of Mycenaean Religion," in *Placing the Gods: Sanctuaries and Sacred Space in Ancient Greece,* ed. S. E. Alcock and R. Osborne, Oxford, pp. 37–78.

Wright, J. C., J. F. Cherry, J. L. Davis, E. Mantzourani, S. B. Sutton, and R. F. Sutton Jr. 1990. "The Nemea Valley Archaeological Project: A Preliminary Report," *Hesperia* 59, pp. 579–659.

CHAPTER 5

SACRIFICIAL FEASTING IN THE LINEAR B DOCUMENTS

Thomas G. Palaima

ABSTRACT

Linear B tablets and sealings from Thebes, Pylos, and Knossos monitor preparations for communal sacrifice and feasting held at palatial centers and in outlying districts. In this chapter I discuss the nature of the Linear B documents and focus on the fullest archaeological and textual evidence, which comes from Pylos. Translations of the key texts are presented in an appendix. Individuals and groups of varying status were involved in provisioning commensal ceremonies; prominent among the participants were regionally interlinked nobility, the *wanaks* ("king") and the *lāwāgetās* ("leader of the *lāos*"). Commensal ceremonies helped establish a collective identity for inhabitants of palatial territories. Two land-related organizations, the *da-mo (dāmos)* and the *worgioneion ka-ma*, represented different social groups in such unifying ceremonies.

STATE OF THE EVIDENCE

There have been great advances in the study of Linear B documents over the past 25 years.[1] We have a much fuller picture now of feasting rituals within Mycenaean palatial territories. Mycenological advances can be classified as follows: 1) the comparative study of sphragistics (inscribed and uninscribed sealings and their uses);[2] 2) better understanding of Mycenaean technical terminology;[3] and 3) detailed examination of relevant Linear B tablet series.[4] At the same time, Mycenologists have been aware of the need to interpret the inscribed evidence within the context of our increased understanding of palatial architecture and iconography,[5] archival record processing,[6] the material and artifactual record,[7] regional

1. I thank the *Hesperia* referees, and also James C. Wright, for their important critical suggestions and references. On recent advances in the study of Linear B, see Palaima 2003a.

2. Palaima 1987, 1996, 2000a; Piteros, Olivier, and Melena 1990; Killen 1992; Pini 1997.

3. Melena 1983; Killen 1999a; Palaima 2000c.

4. Killen 1994, 1998; Godart 1999; Palaima 2000b; Carter 2003.

5. McCallum 1987; Davis and Bennet 1999, pp. 107–118; Nikoloudis 2001.

6. Palaima 1995a, 2003b; Pluta 1996–1997.

7. Wright 1995a; Shelmerdine 1997; Sacconi 1999; Speciale 1999; Isaakidou et al. 2002.

geography,[8] social power structures,[9] economy and resource management,[10] and anthropological and cross-cultural parallels.[11] As a result, we understand better than ever the significance of centrally organized commensal ceremonies for reinforcing Mycenaean social and political unity and stratification.

The importance of sacrificial feasting ritual in Late Mycenaean palatial society is clearly reflected in the care taken by individuals, whom we conventionally refer to as Mycenaean scribes, in overseeing the preparations for sacrifice and feasting activities.[12] The Linear B feasting data fall mainly into the following categories: first-stage recording of individual contributions of animals for eventual sacrifice and consumption at feasting ceremonies; targeted collection of foodstuffs from various components of the community who would then be symbolically unified and socially positioned by feasting; and inventorying of banqueting paraphernalia, furniture, and instruments of cult.[13]

My purpose here is to discuss the nature of the Linear B data for feasting from various Mycenaean palatial centers and to reconstruct the evidence from Pylos, the site best documented archaeologically and epigraphically. This will make clear how important such unifying ceremonies were and the extent to which they affected individuals and localities, at all levels of the sociopolitical hierarchy, throughout Mycenaean palatial territories.

The key primary texts of importance for discussing sacrificial ritual and feasting ceremony from Thebes, Pylos, and Knossos are presented in English translation in the appendix at the end of this chapter, many translated together for the first time. I translate here those tablets whose contents are vital for a clear understanding of the textual evidence for sacrificial feasting practices. The Pylos Ta tablets, whose many technicalities require major exegesis (see below), and, with one exception, the new tablets from Thebes are not included.[14] The new evidence from Thebes has been subject to very dubious interpretations in the *editio princeps*. Until we reach a clearer consensus on what these texts contain and what their purposes were, and even how many full texts there are, it would be a disservice to incorporate their minimal evidence into discussions of any aspect of Mycenaean culture. One new Thebes tablet, however, has clear and unequivocal relevance to feasting, and I translate and discuss it below.[15]

8. Shelmerdine 1981; Sergent 1994; Bennet 1998b; Davis and Bennet 1999.

9. Rehak 1995; Palaima 1995b; Wright 1995b; Ruijgh 1999; Shelmerdine 1999a.

10. Killen 1985; Morris 1986; Olivier 1996–1997; Lupack 1999, 2002; Halstead 1999, 2002; Palaima 2001.

11. Killen 1994, pp. 70–73; 1999b.

12. Palaima 2003b, pp. 174–177, 188.

13. Other texts may also be related less explicitly to feasting. For example, Bendall (2002, p. 8) reasonably argues from the "general consistency of associations between Fr [oil] tablets and records relating to banquets and festivals" that at least some of the oil recorded as headed out from the palace stores at Pylos to targeted sanctuaries and deities would have been consumed in feasting rituals.

14. I take for granted that readers may look at the standard translations and interpretations of texts, including the Ta series, now 30 to 50 years old, found in Palmer 1963 and Ventris and Chadwick 1973. The meager textual evidence for the provisioning of banquets from the site of Mycenae, which may refer to "vegetarian feasting" of women as attested in the historical Thesmophoria (Detienne and Vernant 1989, pp. 190–191) and perhaps in Homer, is not germane to sacrificial feasting. It is also discussed thoroughly by Carlos Varias Garcia in a forthcoming paper, and is therefore omitted here.

15. See below, p. 120, tablet TH Uo 121. The interpretation of many other of the new Thebes texts as recording ritual offerings of grain and olives to the Earth Mother, Persephone, Zeus of the Fall Harvest, and theriomorphic deities is highly suspect on linguistic and exegetical grounds. See my full reviews (Palaima 2002a, 2003d).

PROBLEMS OF INTERPRETATION

The keys to our current understanding of the textual data are the interpretation of an intentional collection of sealings from Thebes related to the contribution of single animals to a centralized communal sacrifice and feast;[16] the correct identification of the meaning of the term *o–pa* and related terminology for service obligation;[17] and the continuing refinement of the interpretation of the Ta series at Pylos, which deals with furniture, vessels, fire and cooking implements, and tools of sacrifice for a major feasting ceremony.[18] The Linear B tablet evidence is notoriously uneven in its representation of palatial interests from region to region. The sphere of ritual and ceremonial activity is no exception. We are dependent on the hazards of destruction and discovery. For any site, we have but a random selection of records from days, weeks, or months within an annual administrative cycle.[19] We therefore have only a partial view of what must have been fuller documentary oversight of the economic activities that were sufficiently complex and important to warrant inclusion in the internal mnemonic records written in Linear B. The records themselves were kept for subsequent reference by tablet-writers or other palatial officials.[20]

Gaps in our knowledge are glaring and can best be illustrated by examples where our ignorance is almost complete. One case will suffice. The Mycenaean texts provide better documentation for extra-urban sanctuaries and centers of ritual than we have been able to reconstruct from field survey or archaeological excavation.[21] A single tablet such as Pylos Tn 316, which records ceremonial "gift-giving" of sacred heirloom[22] ritual vessels by the palatial center at some time during a specific month of the sacred calendar,[23] specifies at least six well-defined areas where the divine presence of major (e.g., Potnia, Zeus, Hera) and minor (Posidaeia, Iphimedeia, Diwia) deities and even heroes or *daimones* (e.g., the "Thrice-Hero," the "House-Master") could be felt and worshiped. These areas include the general district *pa–ki–ja–ne* and five specific sanctuaries dedicated respectively to Poseidon *(po–si–da–i–jo)*; the deity known as *pe–re–*82 (pe–re–*82–jo)*; Iphimedeia *(i–pe–me–de–ja–<jo>)*; the feminine counterpart of Zeus named Diwia *(di–u–ja–jo)*; and Zeus *(di–wi–jo)*. None of these sanctuaries has yet been located on the ground.

We only know about religious structures or institutions located within such sanctuaries from indirect references within a few tablets. Pylos tablet Jn 829, translated in the appendix below,[24] famously records prospective contributions of recycled "temple" bronze from the 16 principal districts of the two Pylian administrative provinces.[25] The term used here to describe the bronze is *na–wi–jo,* the adjectival form of the unattested noun **na–wo* (literally "place of dwelling" = later Greek *nāos,* canonically translated as "temple"). The term *na–wi–jo* is found nowhere else in the Linear B corpus, even though the contents of Jn 829 imply the ubiquity of such "temples" in all areas of a representative Mycenaean palatial territory. Tn 316 indicates that a single district could have many sanctuaries and undoubtedly "temples." Although the number of such structures must have far exceeded 16, none has been located within the physical geography of Messenia.

16. Piteros, Olivier, and Melena 1990.

17. Killen 1999a.

18. Killen 1998; Speciale 1999; Sacconi 1999; Palaima 2000b; Carter 2003.

19. Bennet (2001, p. 30, fig. 1) provides a good diagram of Mycenaean cycles of administration.

20. Palaima 1995a, 2001.

21. Wright 1994; Hiller 1981.

22. On the probability that the gold kylikes and chalices on Tn 316 are heirlooms, see Vandenabeele and Olivier 1979, pp. 210–216; Palaima 1999, p. 440.

23. Sacconi 1987; Wright 1995a; Palaima 1999.

24. See also Palaima 2001, pp. 157–159.

25. Bennet 1998a, pp. 114–115 and fig. 59. For ways in which textual data and evidence about regional resources are used to locate such sites geographically, see the discussion of Leuktron in Bennet 2002.

Similarly, four tablets of the Thebes Of series (Of 26, 31, 33, 36; not translated here) preserve references to two other structures or institutions within sanctuary areas. These are found in the lexical items *wo-ko-de* and *do-de*. The suffix *-de* is an allative, indicating motion toward the preceding noun forms, which are the ultimate physical destinations of the wool registered on these tablets. The terms **wo-ko* and **do* are connected respectively with later Greek *oikos* and *domos*, both words having in historical Greek the meaning of "house" or house structure. Since the noun form **do* is related to the root **dem*, which means roughly "to build in superimposed layers,"[26] *do-de* must refer to a physical building.

The lesson here is that we should not be disconcerted by the seeming paucity of inscriptional data for commensal ceremonies or the asymmetry of textual evidence from region to region. Nor should we shy away from trying to put together an overall view of feasting practices by assembling data from many sites. This is a valid approach given the relative uniformity of administrative and organizational procedures textually attested in different Mycenaean palatial territories.[27] If we do so, however, we must keep in mind the hyperspecificity of the Linear B documents and constantly be aware that evidence from one territory at one administrative moment may not be *fully* transferable to another territory. We talk about aspects of general Mycenaean culture while always leaving open the strong likelihood that individual sites or regions had their own distinctive variations on the general theme.[28]

PERSONS, PLACES, AND TERMS OF CONTRIBUTION

Commensal ceremonies are meant to unite communities and reinforce power hierarchies by a reciprocal process that combines both generous provisioning by figures close to the center of power or authority and participation in the activities of privileged groups by other individuals. Levels of participation mark status, but the fact of general collective participation symbolizes unity. Mycenaean textual evidence for unification and participation begins with the first-stage recording, mainly on sealings,[29] of the individual animals that will be sacrificed and consumed at communal banquets. The sealings tell us, through the minimal information inscribed on their three facets, about the persons, places, and terms involved in contributing single animals to communal feasts.[30] By understanding the mechanisms of provision, we understand better the significance of Mycenaean feasting ritual.

26. Chantraine 1968–1980, vol. 1, pp. 261–262, s.v. δέμω.

27. Shelmerdine (1999b) describes the elements of variation in administrative practice from site to site. None precludes the combination of data from different stages of record-keeping that we are using here in order to under-stand how commensal ceremonies were organized.

28. Cf. Dabney and Wright 1990.

29. Mycenaean sealings are generally of the type known as two-hole hanging nodules. For the form of nodule and its development from Minoan prototypes, see Hallager 1996, vol. 1, pp. 22–25. For the relation of these nodules to written palatial records and general economic procedures, see Palaima 1987, 2000a, 2000c.

30. Palaima 2000c, pp. 265–269; Piteros, Olivier, and Melena 1990, pp. 112–115, 147–161.

The sealings from Thebes provide our only unambiguous documentation in this regard.[31] A few sealings from other sites might be shown to have some connection to commensal ceremonies.[32] It is not certain, however, that the cloth designated by ideogram *146 on Knossos sealings (e.g., Wm 1714, 1816, 1817, 5860, 8490) and the single livestock registered with the word o-pa on Pylos sealings from the Northeast Workshop (e.g., Wr 1325, 1331) concern sacrificial banquets, as they clearly do on tablet Un 2 from Pylos and on the Wu sealings from Thebes. Thus, we must admit that our secure evidence for first-stage contributions comes from the unique collection of 56 inscribed sealings at Thebes. Forty-seven of these sealings refer by ideogram to the single animals with which the sealings were associated (a 48th animal seems to be partially preserved).[33]

HISTORICAL PARALLELS

We can understand how the Thebes Wu sealings relate to the whole process of ceremonial feasting by looking at parallels both from later Greek history and from other Mycenaean sites. The Thebes sealings were used to certify the contribution of single animals, and in a few cases related supplies such as fodder, which would eventually have been used for sacrifice and consumption. They are therefore preliminary to tablets such as Un 2 and Un 138 from Pylos, on which aggregate foodstuffs, including animals, are recorded. The most conspicuous parallel from the historical period is the annual (with a grand version every fourth year) Panathenaic festival in fifth-century Athens. The purpose of the Panathenaia, especially the quadrennial version, was to reinforce the unity of all members of the community of Athens, "male and female, young and old, rich and poor, citizen and metic alike."[34] By the second half of the fifth century B.C., the sacrifice of hundreds of oxen at the great altar of Athena on the Acropolis and the attendant feasting "came to be regarded as a symbol of the privileged status of the most powerful city in the Aegean world."[35]

The Panathenaia in Periclean Athens had the further purpose of reinforcing the paramountcy of Athens over the members of the Delian League by displaying Athenian power to official visitors from other poleis. It also served to reward, and thereby solidify the loyalty of, officials working for Athenian interests outside the territory of Attica. A scholium to Aristophanes declares: "At the Panathenaia, all Athenian colonies customarily sent a bull to be sacrificed."[36] At the same time, the Panathenaia symbolically unified and rewarded the members of the Athenian community, as did the frequent festivals of animal sacrifice and feasting that took place in every month of the Athenian sacred calendar.[37] Such regularly repeated rituals of communal sacrifice and feasting reminded late-fifth-century Athenian citizens of the benefits and rewards of their imperial power and what they might lose if they did not work hard and cooperatively to maintain their empire.

Given the prevalence of political discord and regional and social factionalism in Athens from the late-seventh-century Cylonian conspiracy

31. Piteros, Olivier, and Melena 1990, pp. 171–184.

32. Cf. the catalogue and analytical index in Palaima 1996, pp. 45–65.

33. Piteros, Olivier, and Melena 1990, p. 174.

34. Neils 1992, pp. 23–24. Simone (1996, p. 23) argues that the Panathenaia was "surely of Bronze Age origin."

35. Shapiro 1996, p. 216.

36. See Ar. Nub. 386 in Dübner [1877] 1969, p. 101; Rutherford 1896–1905, vol. 1, pp. 176–177; Koster 1960, p. 475.

37. Zaidman and Schmitt Pantel 1992, pp. 102–111. Neils (1992, p. 13) estimates that a third of the Athenian year was devoted to festivals involving communal sacrifices and feasting.

through the political revolutions of the last decade of the fifth century, the
need for such unifying ceremonies is easily explained. Zaidman and Schmitt
Pantel write:

> Sacrifice was a powerful ritual moment, present in every festival of
> the Athenian calendar. The number of sacrificial victims, known to
> us through the accounts of the Treasurers of Athene, gives us a
> material measure of the importance of the post-sacrificial feasts. . . .
> The city bore the costs of these sacrifices, either directly or indi-
> rectly. . . . A look down the Athenian monthly calendar shows that,
> with the apparent exception of Maimakterion, not a month passed
> without massive slaughtering of beasts.[38]

We should bear all this in mind as we try to make sense of the poorer
Mycenaean evidence. Similar factors were at play as the elites who controlled the Mycenaean palatial centers tried to assert and maintain their
authority over individuals and communities within their own regions and
to impress elites in potential competitor regions with displays of wealth,
power, munificence, and beneficence. Also, although we cannot precisely
define for the Mycenaean period such important concepts as "citizenship"
and "ethnicity," the Linear B texts amply attest the use of toponymic or
ethnic adjectives to define individuals and groups (cf. *mi-ra-ti-ja* for women
of Miletos or *ko-ri-si-jo* for the men of Korinth, a locality in Bronze Age
Messenia).[39] Texts such as An 610 indicate that the palatial center at Pylos
offered settlement on land to outsiders in exchange for service as "row-
ers."[40] Partaking in central commensal rituals would reinforce a group's
sense of belonging to the community, no matter how the notion of "belonging" was defined.[41]

THE ORGANIZATION OF MYCENAEAN
FEASTS: THE INDIVIDUALS INVOLVED

We can see within the Thebes sealings all the elements of standard organizational control that existed for festivals such as the Panathenaia and
which lay behind both the aggregate or last-stage Linear B texts for feasting (e.g., Pylos tablets Un 2, 138, 718) and records of the centralized
palatial mobilization of resources (e.g., Pylos tablet Jn 829). The Thebes
sealings explicitly record 16 sheep (13 male, two female),[42] 14 goats (six
male, seven female), 10 pigs (six male, two female), two specifically designated "fatted pigs," two cattle (one male, one female), and three indeter-

38. Zaidman and Schmitt Pantel
1992, p. 107.

39. Aura Jorro 1985, pp. 383, 453–
454.

40. Ventris and Chadwick 1973,
pp. 186–187, 431. The categories for
such service are *ki-ti-ta* ("settlers"),
me-ta-ki-ti-ta ("second-stage settlers"),

and *po-si-ke-te-re* ("immigrants").
Cf. Aura Jorro 1985, pp. 367–368,
442–443; 1993, pp. 156–157.

41. Davis and Bennet (1999,
p. 113) speak simply of the process of
"becoming Mycenaean," while carefully outlining the complexity of
belonging to the culture defined by

the Mycenaean palatial system.

42. In some cases, the kind of animal on a sealing can be identified, but
not the gender, resulting in the dis-
crepancy between the total number
of animals and the sum of male and
female animals.

minate yearlings.[43] In addition, a single fragmentary animal ideogram seems to be represented, yielding a total of 48 animals.

This total compares well with the 53 animals recorded, along with other foodstuffs, on Pylos tablet Un 138. There is no reason to press the point by arguing (as have Piteros, Olivier, and Melena)[44] that ideogram *190, which elsewhere seems to refer to something like milk, suet, cheese, or beer, on the Thebes sealings designates an actual animal. This interpretation has been proposed only because five sealings refer to *190 alone and, if *190 were an animal, the numbers of animals on Pylos Un 138 and in the collected Thebes sealings would be equal. But there seems to be nothing ritually important about the number 53, and other feasting texts list other numbers of animals.[45]

We have, then, at least 48 sacrificial animals gathered. Twenty-three different seals were used to impress the 56 nodules from Thebes.[46] In terms of transactional procedures,[47] the number of seals indicates that 23 individuals or institutional entities were involved in making contributions to, or otherwise coordinating preparations for, the single central feasting ceremony with which the Thebes sealings were associated.[48]

In addition, the inscriptions on the three facets of the sealings give a total of eight personal names, each on a single sealing, with two exceptions (each occurring on two sealings). In two cases (both individuals with the ethnic names /Thēbaios/ and /Sameus/), these names occur in the formula: *pa-ro* PERSONAL NAME (dative). This formula, if we extrapolate from Un 138 from Pylos, designates the person who has control over, and responsibility for, the assembled item(s) until the time when they would be transferred to the individuals who directly oversaw their ritual or ceremonial use.

We might imagine that the individuals in the *pa-ro* formula have some form of ritual status, if only for occasions such as the ones with which these documents are associated. When contributions are registered as coming from different components of the whole society, as on Pylos tablet Un 718 (Fig. 1), the individuals into whose charge everything (materials and animals) is given are collectively designated, e.g., *o-wi-de-ta* (plural) = "sheep-flayers" (some kind of sacrificial agents).[49]

On Un 2, where the feasting accompanying the ritual initiation of the king, or *wanaks*, might be assumed to involve all segments of society, an individual with the title *o-pi-te-<u->ke-e-u* ("overseer of *teukhea*") is in

43. Perhaps pigs or cattle, since a goat and a ram are designated as yearlings in sealings Wu 74 and Wu 78 by a phonetic abbreviation, not the stand-alone phonetic ideogram *WE* = YE[AR-LING]. Cf. PY Un 138, where the phonetic ideogram clearly refers to sheep.

44. Piteros, Olivier, and Melena 1990, pp. 163–166, 173.

45. This does not mean that numbers of animals or other paraphernalia in ritual contexts are unimportant. For

example, the association in room 7 of the Archives Complex at Pylos of 20–22 miniature kylikes with burned cattle bones (implying as much as 2,000–2,200 kg of meat) is arguably related to the 22 thrones and stools that are inventoried along with other rich banqueting furniture, vessels, and sacrificial and cooking utensils; see Stocker and Davis, this volume. On the Ta series, see below.

46. Piteros, Olivier, and Melena

1990, pp. 107–112.

47. See Palaima 1987.

48. See Palaima 2000a for how sealings from all sites relate to texts in regard to the overall administrative outreach of the central palatial complexes into their territories. We should note again that our data here come from an administrative collection relating to a single event.

49. For *o-wi-de-ta-i*, see Aura Jorro 1993, p. 258.

Figure 1. Pylos tablet Un 718 (see translation in appendix). H. 19.7, W. 12.7, Th. 1.9 cm. Photographic archives of the Program in Aegean Scripts and Prehistory, University of Texas, Austin. Courtesy Department of Classics, University of Cincinnati.

charge. The title perhaps literally designates him as an official in charge of cooking/feasting paraphernalia.[50] On Un 138 and the Thebes sealings we are operating on the level of individual responsibility. The obligation placed on these individuals to contribute to a commensal sacrificial ceremony was in itself a mark of distinction. Further public honor undoubtedly was accorded to them afterward for successfully performing a conspicuous public obligation for the benefit of so many key figures within the overall community.

Other names on the sealing facets occur in either the nominative (the hypothesis advanced by Piteros, Olivier, and Melena)[51] or the genitive (clearly with *qe-ri-jo-jo* on Wu 58). The genitive would function syntactically as subjective genitive with the transactional term *o-pa*. It is possible, given the need for shorthand brevity on the sealing facets and the known independence of scribes in devising their own notational rules, that some of these presumed nominatives are datives, with the ellipsis of *pa-ro* as in Un 138.5. Alternatively, the nominatives might serve as rubrics and be a shorthand equivalent to the *pa-ro* + dative formula. If this is so, the individuals on the Thebes sealings may also perform the same function as prefestival overseers of the delivered livestock and foodstuffs found in the *pa-ro* formula in the mixed-commodity Un tablets.

50. Killen 1992, p. 376.
51. Piteros, Olivier, and Melena 1990, pp. 155–156.

The best-attested example of such a person is found at Pylos, where an individual named *du-ni-jo* is active within the archives and holds, in one context, the potentially religious title of *du-ma*.[52] But he is not among the four individuals of high social status at Pylos known as "collectors" or the larger number of Pylian "collectors" legitimately identified now by using other criteria.[53] "Collectors" in Mycenaean palatial territories are "aristocratic" individuals who interact with the centers in a full range of economic matters. The same personal names of collectors are found at more than one palatial center, suggesting dynastic links or upper-class cohesion.

At Pylos, the main "collectors" are involved in livestock management. At Knossos, however, at least two collectors (*ko-ma-we* and *a-pi-qo-ta*) are clearly associated in the C(2) series with animals registered for sacrifice. In one case, C(2) 941 + 1016 + *fr.*, the animals are explicitly designated as *sa-pa-ke-te-ri-ja*,[54] literally animals "for ritual slaughter" (from the historically productive root **sphag*).[55] The same root seems to recur in the name of the site that is the best-attested religious area at Pylos: *pa-ki-ja-ne* = *Sphagianes* = "the place of animal slaughter."[56]

The eight named individuals in the closed collection of Thebes Wu sealings may also have a degree of status within the ceremonial/cultic sphere, and they may be of as high a social, political, or economic rank as the "collectors." It is unclear how they relate to the individuals or entities identified by the 23 different seal impressions. Neither group, seal-holders nor those with written personal names, can be identified with the "scribes," insofar as we can understand them from the limited number (10) of tentative palaeographical groupings identified within the sealing inscriptions.[57] From the sphragistic and epigraphical evidence for individuals on the Thebes sealings, however, we can conclude that established procedures were in place to obtain the necessary resources for a sacrificial/feasting event, that these procedures were carefully monitored, and that the fulfillment of obligations in this regard was scrupulously verified. This conclusion in itself argues for regularity in such ritual ceremony.

I have started with the individuals involved in making or overseeing the contributions of sacrificial animals because it is often forgotten that the very mention of an individual by personal name within Linear B palatial records is an indication of significant status. Any clear linkage to the power and prestige of the central palatial authority would have conferred distinction. Involvement in ritual donation for a communal ceremony was certainly a mark of considerable distinction.

Again we may compare the situation in historical Athens, where, among its regular liturgies, the state entrusted the liturgy of *hestiasis*, or "provisioning of a feast," to wealthy individuals in order to give them an arena into which to channel their competitive aggressions and through which to display their sense of public benefaction. In short, *hestiasis* and the ca. 97 liturgies of the regular Athenian calendar year were ways of diffusing *eris* ("strife or political contention") and rewarding good citizens with public honor.[58]

The regional "nobility" who accepted high-ranking but nonetheless subordinate status in the relatively late-forming Mycenaean palatial territories would also have had eristic energies that the central authorities would have wanted to convert into public-spirited projects, particularly feasts.[59]

52. Piteros, Olivier, and Melena 1990, p. 177, n. 321; Lindgren 1973, vol. 1, pp. 43–44; vol. 2, pp. 40–41; Aura Jorro 1985, pp. 195–196.

53. Bennet 1992, pp. 67–69; Olivier 2001.

54. Killen 1994, pp. 73–76.

55. Cf. Chantraine 1968–1980, vol. 4.1, p. 1073, s.v. σφάζω.

56. Aura Jorro 1993, p. 73.

57. Piteros, Olivier, and Melena 1990, pp. 146, 170–171.

58. Zaidman and Schmitt Pantel 1992, p. 95.

59. See Bennet 1998a, pp. 125–127, on the "demotion" of sites, and effectively of their ruling figures, as the palatial site of Ano Englianos became preeminent; and Wright 1995b on the evolution of chiefs into kings.

Such practices are attested in Homer where they are arguably a reminiscence of specific Mycenaean regional practice.[60] The "collectors" as a class even have interstate distinction, if we are to judge by their personal names occurring in connection with important economic activities at more than one palatial site (11 secure cases and 65 or 66 possible cases).[61]

GEOGRAPHICAL IMPLICATIONS

The extent of the "community" involved in the feasting ceremony that lies behind the Thebes sealings is impressive. The three fairly certain toponyms, besides Thebes itself and /Haphaia/, which might be located in the environs of Thebes,[62] are Lamos (located around Mt. Helikon) and Karystos and Amarynthos (located in southern and western Euboia, respectively). These sites contribute to the central communal feast at Thebes. Yet in other textual contexts, at least Amarynthos is the destination of wool coming from the center and again with clear ritual associations.[63] This point raises questions about the role and participation of outlying villages and localities. For example, if a site such as Amarynthos contributes and receives ceremonial materials, to what extent do its citizens or elites share in the central ceremony?

Unfortunately, a definitive answer to such a question is currently beyond the limits of the Linear B data. We can note, however, that, in analogy with imperial Athens, sacrificial animals were transported over long distances. Animals were brought to Mycenaean Thebes across water and from distances well over 50 km away. These contributions imply that these locales bore some form of allegiance to the palatial center at Thebes, or at least acknowledged and respected its power and status.

Similarly, at Pylos, palatially organized communal sacrifice and feasting are monitored on tablets that specifically locate such ceremonies at the regional sites of *ro-u-so* (PY Un 47), *pa-ki-ja-ne* (PY Un 2), and *sa-ra-pe-da* (PY Un 718).[64] Animals for sacrifice and materials for subsequent banqueting are also registered on PY Cn 418, Un 6, Ua 17, and Ua 25, where they are listed in proportional quantities indicative of sacrifice and consumption.[65] At Knossos, livestock designated as "for slaughter" seem to be located at the site of *u-ta-no* (KN X 9191) and perhaps were destined for a site named *a-ka-wi-ja* (KN C(2) 914).[66] In his full analysis of archaeological "deadstock" from Mycenaean palatial centers and of livestock management texts from Knossos and Pylos, Paul Halstead estimates that 1,439 animals at Knossos and 782 at Pylos appear in texts relating to consumption.[67]

60. Cook and Palaima 2001; cf. Killen 1994, p. 80, n. 52. See Sherratt, this volume.

61. Olivier 2001, pp. 155–157. As discussed below, Olivier's (2001, pp. 152–155) identification of *pu₂-ke-qi-ri* in the Pylos Ta series with these high status "international collectors" is important for our understanding of the involvement of this class of individuals in ritual.

62. Piteros, Olivier, and Melena 1990, p. 153, n. 173.

63. Sergent 1994, p. 369. In the Thebes Of series (e.g., Of 25, Of 27) groups of women are identified collectively by adjectival forms of the names of "collectors."

64. See Bendall 2002, p. 9, for the possibility that other localities and sanctuaries might be added to this list.

65. Palaima 1989, pp. 103–110, 119–124; Killen 1994, pp. 79–81; Jameson 1988, pp. 94–100.

66. Killen 1994, pp. 75–78; Aura Jorro 1985, p. 35.

67. Halstead 2002, pp. 152–153, 158–159, 163–165.

THE NATURE OF CEREMONIAL OBLIGATIONS

In addition to ideograms indicating personal names, place-names, and live-stock, the Thebes sealings also have a few entries of what I have called "transactional" terminology.[68] The most significant Theban vocabulary for the purpose of understanding the organized activities leading to feasting ritual are the terms *o-pa*, *a-ko-ra-jo* (cf. *a-ko-ra*), *a-pu-do-ke*, *qe-te-o* (and its neuter plural form *qe-te-a₂*), and *po-ro-e-ko-to*. These terms reflect some of the different mechanisms whereby the central authority mobilized re-sources for commensal ceremonies.

The term *o-pa* occurs on six Thebes sealings (Wu 46, Wu 56, Wu 58, Wu 64, Wu 76, Wu 88). Killen has demonstrated that, in the sphere of animal husbandry, *o-pa* refers to the "finishing" of the animals, that is, bringing them to the expected and satisfactory stage of readiness for their final use.[69] Such *o-pa* work can be performed on already-manufactured items in other areas of production, for example, chariot wheels. The hall-mark of its use in any economic sphere is the customary designation of the individual who performed the *o-pa*, hence the genitive *qe-ri-jo-jo* noted above on Wu 58. Five of the six occurrences of *o-pa* on the Thebes sealings (Wu 46, Wu 56, Wu 58, Wu 76, Wu 88) follow this pattern and three or four of the five also designate that the animal is provided with 30 units of fodder (ideogram *171*),[70] most likely for feeding the animal during the month prior to its eventual ritual slaughter. These five sealings form a coherent record group, since they contain related subject content and are all impressed with the same seal.

The only *o-pa* text that does not contain a personal name designation is Wu 64, which records a yearling *WE*(TALON) and is impressed with a seal found only on this sealing. It is reasonable to hypothesize that the absence of the personal name on Wu 64 is related in some way to the singleton seal impression. Let us assume that the seal impressions on all six *o-pa* sealings—and perhaps on all others as well—somehow designate the individuals or entities that have provided or have taken responsibility for the living animal to which the sealing corresponds. In the case of Wu 64, there would be no ambiguity if the yearling was not, in the end, of proper quality, whether or not the seal-applier was dealing with another party to see to the animal's care. In the case of the remaining five sealings, however, the provider or responsible party (represented by the seal impres-sion) was interacting with five different parties whose *o-pa* work still was in flux, or at risk, because of the time lag of up to 30 days between delivery of the animals and the final event for which the animals were being kept. Thus, he had to designate for those five animals the responsible parties in case a problem occurred or, if all went well, in order to be able to acknowl-edge service performed for him by five people. Even in the preparatory phase before the sacrifice, therefore, we can see a clear community of par-ticipation and a clearly designated hierarchy of responsibility.

The adjectival designation *a-ko-ra-jo* refers to animals that were part of a "collection," as specified by the action noun *a-ko-ra* (cf. later Greek *agora*), the term from which the individuals referred to above as "collec-tors" derive their name. A set of three Theban sealings (Wu 49, Wu 50, and Wu 63), all impressed by the same seal, are inscribed with the word

68. Palaima 2000c.

69. Killen 1999a.

70. Piteros, Olivier, and Melena 1990, pp. 151–152. On Wu 46, Wu 56, and Wu 76, the entry for fodder is preserved. On Wu 88, the third facet has been destroyed and its restoration is conjectural.

qe-te-o and the action noun *a-ko-ra*. The term *qe-te-o* and related forms, as Hutton has convincingly demonstrated,[71] designate the animals here as "to be paid (as part of a religious obligation, penalty or fine)." The animals are also part of collector/collection activity. That these two words can co-exist on the same sealing must mean that the activities inherent in the action noun *a-ko-ra* and the verbal adjective *qe-te-o* can be complementary. The collector, who in this case may be represented by the seal impression, has a herd or herds of livestock that can be described as resulting from "collecting" or as forming a "collection" *(agora),* but he also is responsible for "paying" three animals from his collection as a religious obligation. This is indicated on each of these three sealings by the additional term *qe-te-o*.

The three animals "paid as a religious obligation or penalty" are each a different species: sheep, goat, and pig. The same diversity of species is seen on PY Ua 17 and PY Un 2. Sheep, cattle, and pigs (the canonical *suovetaurilia* combination) occur on PY Ua 25 and Un 6, in both cases with other edible commodities. Of the new Thebes tablets, the proposed "religious" and "ritual" aspects of which must be strongly downplayed,[72] the single fragmentary text Uo 121, a brief and purely mnemonic text without any information except the ideographic entries, fits this pattern of sacrificial animals listed together with foodstuffs.[73]

The two animals that are designated adjectivally as *a-ko-ra-jo* ("associated with collections") are both fatted pigs (Wu 52, Wu 68). The remaining three sealings in this group of five made by the same seal (Wu 53, Wu 70, Wu 72) concern a male cow and two male sheep. The cow (Wu 53) is designated, if the reading is correct, as *qe-te-o,* and one of the two sealings with sheep (Wu 70) gives a personal name. Here again we might think of an ellipsis in the *pa-ro* formula. The individual named *a-e-ri-qo* would then somehow have control of the single sheep connected with this sealing. If the "collector" here is indicated at all, it would be by the seal that has impressed these sealings.

LOCALIZED CEREMONIES AND DEITIES

The Pylos texts, even those of the leaf-shaped Ua series, immediately take us to a much more advanced stage in the preparation for public sacrifice and feasting. The scale of the banqueting provisions is evident from the quantities of animals and foodstuffs listed on the texts. A text such as Un 6 may reflect, in its smaller quantities and in the specification of deities as recipients, more localized ritual ceremonies of sacrifice on a smaller scale (cf. Thebes Uo 121 in this regard). Un 6 lists the allocation of a cow, ewe, boar, and two sows in individual entries to Poseidon and twice to the female deity *pe-re-*82*. In addition, it contains a further entry area recording the kind of collective contribution we have seen on other provisioning texts: cloth, wool, oil, two bulls, two cows, and a missing number of sheep.

The repetition in the entries on lines .3 and .4 of Un 6 most likely indicates two separate "offerings" of this proportional group of sacrificial animals to the deity *pe-re-*82,* perhaps on different days or from different

71. Hutton 1990–1991.
72. Palaima 2002a, 2003d.
73. Aravantinos, Godart, and Sacconi 2001, pp. 40, 306.

sources who were not germane to the record-keeping purposes of the document and are therefore not recorded in the written entries. The order of the entries on Un 6 (Poseidon followed by *pe-re-*82*) parallels the order of sanctuaries listed on the reverse side of Pylos Tn 316, where the sanctuary of *pe-re-*82* immediately follows the entry section for the sanctuary of Poseidon. On this basis we may conjecture that the animals recorded on Un 6 are being donated to sanctuaries in the district of *pa-ki-ja-ne*, where many sacrifices and banquets would have regularly taken place on different occasions. Nonetheless, because the tablet comes from the central palatial archives and because this information is monitored on it, the ceremony does reflect the interests and involvement of the palatial authorities.

On tablet Un 2, a sacrificial and commensal ceremony within the religious territory of *pa-ki-ja-ne* is recorded as taking place on a ceremonial occasion when the *wanaks* is initiated.[74] On Pylos tablet Un 138 (whose numbers of animals, as we noted above, approximate the aggregate totals in the Thebes sealings), the scribe simply noted, most likely for himself or the official with whom he was working,[75] that the feasting provisions were connected with (or perhaps situated at) the site of Pylos. The quantities of provisions are listed as being under the control of two individuals: *du-ni-jo*, whom we have discussed above, and *me-za-wo*. The first, *du-ni-jo*, is in charge of 53 heads of livestock, including three cattle, as well as large amounts of grain, olives (specifically designated as edible), and wine; *me-za-wo* is responsible for a much smaller assemblage of nonanimal foodstuffs. The placement of the entry involving *me-za-wo* at the bottom of the text and the nature of the provisions entrusted to this individual's oversight mirror the placement and nonanimal contributions of the social/land organization known as the *worgioneion ka-ma* on Un 718 (and Er 312). Both appear to be lower-order contributions.

Un 138 gives us a good impression of what a banquet for a thousand or more people would have been like. Such banquets did take place in the environs of the palatial center proper.[76] Still, it is possible—the parallelism of Un 2, Un 47, and Un 718 notwithstanding—that *pu-ro*, which is translated here as a locative "at Pylos," functions like *PU-RO* in Tn 316. It would then indicate the entity that has responsibility to make the "religious payment" designated by the neuter plural form *qe-te-a$_2$*. In this case, the palatial center proper as an institution would be responsible. Pylos in this context would refer to the state in much the same way that *hai Athēnai* in the historical period refers metonymically to the polis of which it was the center.

74. For the timing of this ceremony and its ritual and "historical" implications, see Palaima 1995a, 1995b; for a recent careful review of evidence for the *wanaks*, see Ruijgh 1999. For a brief discussion and analysis of Un 2, see Melena 2001, pp. 71–72.

75. The status of scribes is a topic of much discussion in recent years, particularly whether they can be identified with official titles or individual agents mentioned in the Linear B texts. For the latest review of theories, see Palaima 2003b, pp. 174–177, 187–188.

76. Shelmerdine 1998, pp. 87–88. Cf. Davis and Bennet 1999; Halstead 2002, pp. 178–179; Isaakidou et al. 2002; Stocker and Davis, this volume.

RITUALS OF UNIFICATION AND COLLECTIVE OBLIGATION

Pylos tablet Un 718 (Fig. 1) has been cited since Ventris and Chadwick's 1956 publication as reflecting important social divisions within the palatial territory of Pylos.[77] Because of the types and quantities of items associated with each contributor, the separate sections on the tablet give the impression of being hierarchically arranged. The generally accepted breakdown of the sociopolitical components in this text is: king (*wanaks* or the individual who is the *wanaks*, namely *e-ke-ra₂-wo*), military leader (*ra-wa-ke-ta*), general citizen population/landowners (*da-mo* or the officials who represent the *da-mo*, namely three *te-re-ta*), and a land-tillage or cultic group that allows for the incorporation of non-native residents of Messenia into the unified society (the *worgioneion ka-ma*).[78]

We should note, however, that Un 718 refers explicitly to ceremonial provisioning in honor of Poseidon in a district of Bronze Age Messenia known as *sa-ra-pe-da*, which is not one of the 16 canonical districts or regional centers of palatial Messenia.[79] The scribe (hand 24) of Un 718 and of two related and supporting land series documents (Er 312 and Er 880) was affected in his "dialect spelling" by his interaction with nonpalatial dialect-speakers.[80] One reasonable explanation for this linguistic phenomenon, given the subject matter with which the scribe works, is that the district of *sa-ra-pe-da* (where the feasting event recorded in Un 718 is to take place) is the domain in which this scribe specializes. Of his other texts,[81] Er 312 gives specific details about the relative extent of landholdings for the four contributors on Un 718 (with proportions roughly reflecting the proportions among contributions on Un 718 and with three *telestai* ["service men"] representing the *dāmos*). Er 880 informs us about the nature of the estate of the Mycenaean *wanaks*, whose name is now correctly understood as the outcome of the compound **Egkhes-lauōn* ("he who delights in the spear").[82]

It may be, then, that the locale known as *sa-ra-pe-da* has very strong and special ties to the chief figure of power in the Mycenaean state, and that this scribe is a kind of "royal administrator." It is even possible that *sa-ra-pe-da* may be the place-name for the locality where the sanctuary of Poseidon listed in Tn 316 and implied in Un 6 is located. It would then be a sub-locale of the general district *pa-ki-ja-ne*, which is one of the canonical 16 major districts (cf. Pylos tablets Cn 608, Vn 19, and Vn 20).

77. Ventris and Chadwick 1956, pp. 280–284. For a clear and concise discussion of the social-hierarchical implications of Un 718 and related texts, see Carlier 1984, pp. 54–63. Caution is in order in dealing with the nuances of the term *da-mo* in particular. See below, n. 85, and related discussion.

78. For these categories of contributors, see Carlier 1984, pp. 54–63, esp. p. 54, n. 291, and p. 59; Nikoloudis 2004. Nikoloudis, in her ongoing dissertation work, is exploring how the *ra-wa-ke-ta* functions as the authority figure who integrates "outsiders" into the community. The *worgioneion ka-ma* seems to be an organization that "represents" such outsiders.

79. Aura Jorro (1993, pp. 282–283) lays out the different interpretations proposed for the several occurrences of the term *sa-ra-pe-da*.

80. Palaima 2002b.

81. Not translated here, but see Ventris and Chadwick 1973, pp. 264–269, 451–455.

82. Melena 2001, p. 73.

Un 718 lists nine commodities: wheat, wine, cheese, honey, anointing oil, sheepskin, spelt, and two kinds of sacrificial animals: a single bull, donated significantly by the *wanaks *Egkhes-lauōn,* and male sheep, donated by the *ra-wa-ke-ta* (the military leader)[83] and the *da-mo* (= *dāmos*). All four contributors will give some kind of grain item. All four also will give wine. With their contributions of wine, we can see clearly their status relative to one another, at least insofar as this particular feasting ceremony is concerned: **Egkhes-lauōn,* 86.4 liters; *dāmos,* 57.6 l; *ra-wa-ke-ta,* 19.2 l; *worgioneion ka-ma,* 9.6 l (i.e., a ratio of 9:6:2:1).

As tempting as it is to universalize the evidence of Un 718 with regard to the ranking of powerful figures and social groups in very late palatial Messenia, reasonable caution is in order. Tablet Un 718 is one prospective (notice that the verbal forms here are future) feasting event in a single locality connected with a single deity. The presumed *wanaks* is identified not by his title, but by his personal name, which may have significance in regard to the nature of his obligation here, the resources he will use to meet the obligation, and the terms according to which he and the other contributors participate in this feasting ritual. Moreover, the hypothesis that *sa-ra-pe-da* was located within the district of *pa-ki-ja-ne* and somehow contained the sanctuary of Poseidon mentioned on Tn 316 may not be correct. Accordingly, we have to reckon with the possibility that the particular banqueting ceremony on Un 718 has nothing to do with *pa-ki-ja-ne,* the main religious district in Messenian territory that is always closely associated with the palace at Pylos.

Thus, these four contributors, including the *wanaks* (identified by personal name), could simply be recorded as in the process of discharging a particular regionally based commensal ceremonial obligation, and the quantities of offerings may reflect conditions operating in that locality on this particular occasion.[84] Furthermore, the term *dāmos* has a very specific meaning within the Mycenaean texts. No one has improved on the superb nuancing of its meaning by Lejeune.[85] It makes specific reference to parceled and distributed land and then narrowly to a collective body of local representatives who handle communal land distribution and management. The term does not yet have the semantic value it acquires in certain contexts later in Attic Greek (δῆμος = the citizen body as a whole). In Un 718 it may refer to whatever collective body oversaw land distribution in the area of *sa-ra-pe-da.*

83. See Aura Jorro 1993, pp. 230–231. For other functions of the *ra-wa-ke-ta,* see Nikoloudis's work, above, n. 78.

84. As a parallel, the ceremony on Pylos tablet Tn 316 is focused on female deities, beginning with the Potnia. Thus, Zeus is relegated to the last entry section and Poseidon, the chief male deity in Bronze Age and Homeric Messenia, is not mentioned at all. Given its ritual specificity, Tn 316 does not reflect the general picture of divine worship in Mycenaean palatial Messenia.

85. Lejeune 1972, p. 146. It also is an administrative entity that can have a juridical personality. But it does not mean "people" or "village" as in historical Greek.

CEREMONIAL BANQUETING AT THE PALACE OF NESTOR

The picture of public ceremonial practice that Un 718 presents, cautiously interpreted together with the palatial architecture and iconography, has been thoroughly analyzed in appropriate scholarly contexts elsewhere.[86] Even if Un 718 is locally focused, it would be disingenuous to imagine that its proportions do not give us a rough sense of the power hierarchy of the principal sociopolitical divisions of the region. It is this hierarchy that is reinforced in public commensal ceremonies. The iconographical program of the palatial center and its megaron complex,[87] its stores of banqueting and drinking paraphernalia,[88] and the open-air areas where large numbers of people could gather (e.g., court 63)[89] all argue that some major communal ceremonies of sacrifice and feasting took place in the immediate environs of the palatial center. Hägg summarizes: "processions, libations, and communal feasting are the elements indicated by the iconography and archaeological finds [of the central megaron complex of the Palace of Nestor]."[90]

Tablets of the Pylos Ta series are now thought to record the furniture and sacrificial and banqueting paraphernalia associated with such a ceremony.[91] A full discussion of the palaeographical, archival, text pragmatic, and linguistic details of each of the 13 individual texts is required to understand the full meaning of the set. Such a treatment, which is in progress, would require a separate small monograph and is beyond the scope and purpose of this chapter. Certain salient points, however, can be made here.

The Ta series was discovered in a single location within the central archives at Pylos. These tablets are clearly associated with Pylos Un 718, not certainly in terms of final file-grouping, but at least in terms of subject matter and internal record-keeping chronology.[92] The Ta tablets are among the last records to have been entered into the administrative processing stage within the central archives. The mutual isolation of Un 718 and the Ta tablets in grid 83 of room 7 within the Archives Complex is significant. They were separated from other inscribed tablets, in an area to the left upon entering room 7 from portico 1.[93] Their location suggests that the

86. Palaima 1995a, 1995b. See in general McCallum 1987; Rehak 1995; and now Davis and Bennet 1999; Nikoloudis 2001, pp. 14–21.

87. McCallum 1987; Killen 1998; Palaima 1995b, 2000b; Shelmerdine 1999a, pp. 20–21; Speciale 1999.

88. The storage in the Palace of Nestor of ceramics such as kylikes for use in feasting rituals is conveniently summarized in Galaty 1999, pp. 50–51: 1,100 kylix fragments from halls 64 and 65, and 2,853 kylikes from room 19.

89. Davis and Bennet 1999, pp. 110–111.

90. Hägg 1996, p. 607.

91. Killen 1998; Palaima 2000b; see now Carter 2003 for a better comparative understanding of the exact nature of the inventorying process involved here. For the Ta series in general, see Ventris and Chadwick 1973, pp. 332–348, 497–502.

92. Palaima 1995a, 2003b; Pluta 1996–1997.

93. Palaima and Wright (1985) argued, based on the flow of traffic through the Palace of Nestor and the distribution of Linear B tablets, that there were full doors into both rooms 7 and 8 of the Archives in the final architectural phase of the palace. This hypothesis gains further support now that we know about the importance of feasting activities in court 63 as well as possibly outside in court 58. There would have been considerable traffic between these outer courts and room 7, and into room 8 from court 3, the pantries in rooms 9–10, and the megaron complex directly.

tablets had just arrived or at least been placed together in a special area for handy access to their information. The prospective nature of Un 718 also supports our conjecture that these texts are relevant to events in the last days of the Palace of Nestor.

In order to understand the administrative and archaeological significance of the Ta set, it is important to recall that, like all other Linear B tablets, they are economic accounting documents. The most important pieces of information entered in documents of account are the numbers. In over 50 years of Mycenological scholarship, only Gallavotti has attempted to work out the specific numbers of different kinds of objects in the entire set of tablets and to consider whether these numbers had any significance for our understanding of the purpose of the set and how the different numbers of items might relate one to the other.[94] Here we shall be especially concerned with thrones, sitting stools, and tables, since their relative numbers provide evidence for the number of individuals who would have been accorded privileged positions, in this case for seating and dining, at the commensal event with which the Ta series was associated. The identification and numbers of the implements used for sacrifice are probably also ceremonially significant.

The record-keeping assignments of the "scribe" (hand 2) of the Ta series are among the most important of the many that can be attributed to identifiable scribes at Pylos or elsewhere.[95] In addition to the Ta series, this individual was responsible for the principal surviving taxation records for the nine and seven provincial districts of the palatial territory controlled by Pylos (Ma series); a major set of bronze allotment records (Jn series); the record, discussed above, that deals with the recycling and transfer of bronze between the "religious" sphere and the "secular" sphere for the purpose of military weapon manufacture (Jn 829); and records of perfumed oil distributions (Fr series).[96]

The Ta tablets of hand 2 also pertain to the affairs of the most elevated level of the Mycenaean sociopolitical hierarchy. In the Ta set, he was "inventorying" about 60 objects in all:[97] 33 separate pieces of elaborate furniture, ca. 20 vases or receptacles (ewers, shallow pans, tripods, closed jars, and *di-pa* vases, all metallic versions and some clearly heirlooms: e.g., *di-pa, pi-je-ra, qe-ra-na, qe-to, ti-ri-po*),[98] two portable hearths with their accompanying fire-related utensils, two sacrificial knives (first correctly

94. Gallavotti 1972; all of the other scholarly treatments of this series either leave particular tablets or lines out of discussion, do not consider the aggregate numbers, or do not attempt to reach reasoned solutions about the numbers in specific problematical entries. For example, Palmer (1957), in arguing that the Ta series is a "tomb inventory," omits all mention of tablet Ta 716 and deals only

with the remaining 12 tablets.

95. Palaima 1988, pp. 66–68, 188–189.

96. Perfumed oil is distributed to major deities (*ma-te-re te-i-ja* ["divine mother"], *te-o-i* ["the gods"], *po-ti-ni-ja* ["Lady," twice], *po-ti-ni-ja a-si-wi-ja* ["Lady of Asia"], *u-po-jo po-ti-ni-ja* ["Lady of the sacrificial post," interpreting **u-po* according to Sucharski and Witczak 1996, pp. 9–10]); to the

main religious district of Bronze Age Messenia (*pa-ki-ja-ni-jo-i, pa-ki-ja-na-de*), and to the *wanaks* (king) of Pylos himself (*wa-na-ka-te*, three times).

97. The best illustrations of the ideographically represented items are found in Bennett and Olivier 1973, p. 230. See also Ventris 1955.

98. Cf. Vandenabeele and Olivier 1979, pp. 221–241; Palaima 2003c.

identified by Hiller in 1971),[99] two sacrificial stunning axes,[100] and two ceremonial bridles.[101]

Ta 711 is the header text for the series and it declares first the context for the recording of this inspection inventory: "Thus observed *pu₂-ke-qi-ri* in inspection when the *wanaks* appointed *au-ke-wa* as *da-mo-ko-ro*."[102] Whether the inventoried items were used for a feasting ceremony on the occasion of this royal "appointment" or the temporal clause signals that the individual named *au-ke-wa* now assumes responsibility for the maintenance of these sacrificial and feasting items in his new position as *da-mo-ko-ro* is impossible for us to decide. Fortunately, it is not crucial for our understanding that the items entered in the Ta tablets make up a list of paraphernalia for a commensal ceremony. Given the presence of metal vessels that were heirlooms, their damage from use over time, and the ornate and costly embellishments and inlay on the items of furniture, we may posit that this set of equipment was repeatedly used on banqueting occasions.[103]

STATUS OF ELITES

The inspector *pu₂-ke-qi-ri* is among the expanded list of "international" collector names, a repertory of personal names of politically and economically elite individuals who are attested in documents from more than one Mycenaean palatial territory and hint at aristocratic or dynastic associations among elites in different regions.[104] The elevated economic interests of the collectors—a *pu₂-ke-qi-ri* has a group of female cloth workers under his control at the site of Thebes (Of 27)—and the attested involvement of collectors in the provision of sacrificial animals at Knossos, perhaps implicit in the Thebes sealings, furnish a reasonable explanation for why *pu₂-ke-qi-ri* would be in charge of inventorying this feasting equipment at Pylos. Imagine the resources and organization needed to acquire the precious materials and to mobilize specialized craftspeople to produce and maintain a single nine-footed table composed of stone with ebony support

99. Hiller 1971, pp. 82–83, an identification ignored in the general and specialized literature, e.g., Vandenabeele and Olivier 1979, pp. 47–49.

100. Speciale 1999, pp. 294–296; Nikoloudis 2001, pp. 21, 31, fig. 6.

101. Del Freo (1990, p. 315) argues convincingly that the *pa-sa-ro* listed nonideographically on Ta 716 (see below, Fig. 2), along with the sacrificial knives and stunning axes, are "chains." We can refine this now with our better understanding of the feasting context of the Ta series. A gloss in Hesychius tells us that ψαλόν is a "kind of bridle." This is a direct reference to the bridle bit that restrains an animal. Cf. Chantraine 1968–1980, vol. 4.2, p. 1285, s.v. ψαλόν.

The ψάλιον in its normal use is the ring or chain that passes under the chin of an animal and helps to restrain it. The use of the word to mean "chain" generically is poetical. On Pylos Ta 716 we have a pair of gold-leaf–covered (i.e., ritual) bridle chains. These go together with the two heirloom Minoan stunning axes *(wa-o)* and the two sacrificial knives *(qi-si-pe-e)* to make up two sets of ritual slaughtering implements for the sacrifice of the animals.

102. Ventris and Chadwick 1973, pp. 335–336, 497.

103. Palaima 2003c. The collection of documents from the Pylos archives gives us a strong impression of selective and partial monitoring of different spheres of activity. Thus, in the series dealing with women and children and their rations, we find references to very few of the major districts where work of interest to the central palatial authorities must have been taking place. If we reason by analogy, we would conclude that "inventories" of paraphernalia for other ceremonies were not kept after they had served their ephemeral purposes.

104. Killen 1979, pp. 176–179; Olivier 2001, pp. 139–141, 151–152, 155.

elements and ivory inlaid decorative elements (Ta 713.1) or a throne made primarily of rock crystal "inlaid" with blue-glass paste, emerald-color paste, and gold and having a back support "inlaid" with gold figures of men and date palm trees (Ta 714.1–.2).[105]

The *wanaks* and an official (the *da-mo-ko-ro*) connected with the interests of the *dāmos* organizations are also part of the motivation for compiling this inventory. The scribe begins the actual process of inventorying by listing *qe-ra-na* (ewers) that are designated as "pertaining to the *wanasseus*," i.e., the official who has to do with the affairs of the *wanassa*, or "queen."[106] The "collector" involved in this feasting occasion, *pu₂-ke-qi-ri*, and his attendant scribe next turn their attentions to Cretan heirloom tripods. They are able to distinguish them by the style of the master tripod-makers (*o-pi-ke-wi-ri-je-u* and *ai-ke-u* or **34-ke-u*) who originally manufactured them. This ability is yet another indication of the rank and cultural attainments of *pu₂-ke-qi-ri*, as he operates on the palatial level of society connected with this luxurious paraphernalia.[107]

POSITIONING, PARTICIPATION, AND PARAPHERNALIA

The megaron fresco program at Pylos shows paired figures seated at tables and engaged in ritual drinking (and perhaps feasting),[108] making it worthwhile to consider the Ta furniture assemblage in terms of elite seating and table arrangements for a related feasting ceremony.[109] It can be demonstrated that the Ta inventory itemizes 11 tables *(to-pe-za)*, six thrones *(to-no)*, and 16 stools *(ta-ra-nu-we)*,[110] all made of costly wood or stone and exquisitely constructed in combination with precious inlay materials and figural decorations. The numbers here may not be haphazard. There are 22 pieces of furniture for seating and 11 tables,[111] which would allow for the kind of pairing observed in the iconographical record (albeit on "campstools"). Three sets of matched throne and stool ensembles are identified (Ta 708.2–.3, Ta 707.1–.3). We move into the realm of pure speculation when we propose reasons behind these numbers, for example that the six thrones may reflect distinguished positions at the banquet for six authority figures as reflected in Un 718 and its related tablets: one throne for the *wanaks*, one for the *ra-wa-ke-ta*, three for the three *telestai* representing the *da-mo*, and one for a representative of the *worgioneion ka-ma*.

105. The exact technical meaning of the term *a-ja-me-no/-na*, interpreted as "inlaid" because it clearly refers to a technique of using precious substances as decorative elements in furniture, has not been determined. The throne itself is described as *we-a₂-re-jo* ("made of rock crystal"). Four other thrones are made from a variety of ebony.

106. Aura Jorro 1993, p. 403.

107. Palaima 2003c.

108. Wright 1995b. See also Wright, this volume, p. 43, fig. 13, and his cautions about representations of feasting in the Pylos frescoes.

109. We should stress again that the megaron proper was *not* the location of large-scale feasting of the kind implied by the Un tablets.

110. Vandenabeele and Olivier 1979, pp. 161–176; the *ta-ra-nu-we* (cf. later Greek *thrānos* ["rower's

bench"]) are particularly suitable for sitting on. The thrones and tables are not represented ideographically and therefore are unfortunately not treated in Vandenabeele and Olivier 1979.

111. See Isaakidou et al. 2002; and Stocker and Davis, this volume, for discussion of the roughly corresponding number of miniature ritual kylikes discovered together with the remains of burned cattle bones (see above, n. 45).

Figure 2. Pylos tablet Ta 716. H. 3.3, W. 14.8, Th. 1.4 cm. Photographic archives of the Program in Aegean Scripts and Prehistory, University of Texas, Austin. Courtesy Department of Classics, University of Cincinnati.

The paraphernalia itemized in the Ta set cover the needs of all stages of a commensal ceremony. As noted above, Ta 716 (Fig. 2) lists two ceremonial gold bridle rings and chains by which key animals would have been ritually led to the point of sacrifice, two stunning axes to be used in their slaughtering ritual, and two sharp sacrificial knives to slit the throats of the animals.[112] Equipment for preparing and maintaining the necessary fire is included. Portable hearths and tripods were used for the preparation of food; "burned-away legs" on one example indicate that it was used in cooking.[113] Containers for holding food provisions and for ceremonial and practical pouring appear, as do the luxurious thrones, stools, and tables at which the privileged participants would have been seated. Elite ceremonial items are emphasized, while more mundane items such as drinking cups are missing. We learn of these from texts such as Pylos Tn 316, the archaeological record of the Pylos pantries, and the gold and silver versions favored in elite burials.[114] The larger community of participants presumably used clay kylikes of the sort stored in the palatial pantries.[115]

CONCLUSION

The Mycenaean textual evidence takes us through the process of preparing for and conducting a commensal ceremony. Combining this evidence to form a general Mycenaean composite is, as mentioned at the outset, a reasonable procedure, given the uniformity of administrative and organizational practices and structures textually attested in different palatial territories. The Linear B tablets and sealings record the contribution of sacrificial animals and banqueting consumables, the paraphernalia and furniture that would be used at the banquet, and the implements of sacrifice. They specify the places sending animals destined for sacrifice and feasting. They tell us who was responsible for providing or overseeing materials, individually and collectively, and what elements of society would have been brought together, unified, and ranked according to status in sacrificial and banqueting ceremonies. They give us a picture of the geographical range involved in the provisioning and participating stages for such ceremonies and of where they took place in the territorial landscape. They hint at how such ceremonies fit in with activities at sanctuaries and cult locales in the formal religious sphere. They demonstrate the privileging of the elite class of individuals known as "collectors." In the Pylos Ta series, we see how one such collector saw to the interests of the *wanaks, wanassa,* and other important figures or segments of Pylian society. The tablets and sealings provide an economic subtext for all aspects of feasting ceremony. As is fitting for Linear B records, however, they leave us with more problems to explore.

112. See above, nn. 99–101. Cf. Lesy 1987, pp. 126–130, for the use of such a ritual knife, called a *halef,* by Orthodox Jewish ritual slaughterers, or *shochets.*

113. These portable hearths, of course, would not have been used for the large-scale roasting of the sacrificial animals listed on the Un tablets.

114. Vandenabeele and Olivier 1979, pp. 207–216.

115. See above, n. 88.

APPENDIX

TRANSLATED TEXTS

The following conventions are used in presenting the translations of pertinent sealings and tablets from Thebes, Pylos, and Knossos:

[= broken to right
] = broken to left
? = doubtful reading or interpretation[116]

Facets of sealings are indicated by small Greek letters. Ruled lines of tablets are indicated by Arabic numerals, and unruled lines by small Roman letters. Capital Roman letters indicate lines that are only partially demarcated by rule lines. Ideograms are indicated by small capital letters. The raised letters m, f, and x refer to an animal's gender (male, female, indeterminate, respectively). Liters are abbreviated as "l" only when space will not permit the word to be given in full.

Mycenaean words are given in their original form when the interpretation is in doubt; possibilities or the semantic category of the words are given in parentheses or footnotes, or they are discussed above in the text of this chapter. I use italics, even when they are not required by Mycenological editing conventions, to highlight elements of the translation that are of particular importance for discussion.

The term F-PIG refers to "fatted pig." I subscribe to the proposal of R. Palmer that the traditional identifications of the ideograms HORDEUM as "barley" and GRANUM as "wheat" are probably to be reversed.[117] In the texts below I have made this change.

REPRESENTATIVE SEALINGS FROM THEBES

The first five *o-pa* sealings listed below all bear an impression from the same seal. The term *o-pa* means that the animals have been brought into a condition suitable for sacrifice.[118]

TH Wu 46   .α GOAT[f]
            .β of *Praus*, *o-pa* work
            .γ *cyperus*-fodder 30

116. Readings of single signs that are virtually certain based on textual parallelism have been restored.
117. Palmer 1992.
118. See n. 69 above, with related text.

TH Wu 56   .α   GOAT^m
                  .β1 *Ophelestās*
                  .β2 *o-pa* work
                  .γ   *cyperus*-fodder 30

TH Wu 58   .α   PIG
                  .βa *o-pa* work
                  .βb of *Therios*
                  .γ   (at) Amarynthos

Line .βb was written (and thus read) before .βa.

TH Wu 76   .α   CATTLE^f
                  .β1 a-e-ri-qo (a personal name)
                  .β2 *second line of facet left blank*
                  .γ   *o-pa* work   *cyperus*-fodder 30

TH Wu 88   .α   GOAT^x
                  .β   *Lamios* , *o-pa* work
                  .γ   *facet missing*

The following related sealing bears an impression from a different seal:

TH Wu 64   .α   YEARLING
                  .β   *o-pa* work
                  .γ   *line left blank*

The following three sealings form a set, each bearing the impression of the
same seal. They are the only sealings at Thebes with the terms *a-ko-ra*
("collection") and *qe-te-o* ("to be paid," most likely as a religious fine or
exaction).

TH Wu 49   .α   SHEEP^m
                  .β   qe-te-o
                  .γ   a-ko-ra

TH Wu 50   .α   GOAT^f
                  .β   qe-te-o
                  .γ   a-ko-ra

TH Wu 63   .α   PIG^f
                  .β   qe-te-o
                  .γ   a-ko-ra

The following sealings all bear the same seal impression. Two (Wu 52 and
68) also have the adjective *a-ko-ra-jo* ("pertaining to an *a-ko-ra* or collection") inscribed on them.

TH Wu 52   .α   F-PIG
                  .β   a-ko-ra-jo
                  .γ   *line left blank*

TH Wu 53	.α	CATTLE^m (reading tentative)
	.β	qe-te-o?
	.γ	i-ri-ja

TH Wu 68	.α	F-PIG
	.β	a-ko-ra-jo
	.γ	*line left blank*

TH Wu 70	.α	SHEEP^m
	.β–γ.1	a-e-ri-qo (a personal name)
	.2	*line left blank*

TH Wu 72	.α	SHEEP^m
	.β	*line left blank*
	.γ	*line left blank*

The following three sealings come from a group of seven sharing the same seal impression. These three are the only sealings from Thebes with the neuter plural form of the verbal adjective *qe-te-o*: *qe-te-a$_2$*. They also are the only sealings with the allative form of the place-name Thebes: *te-qa-de* = "to Thebes."

The term *qe-te-a$_2$* is best explained as a neuter plural that was used because the scribe focused on the aggregate group of animals and did not differentiate this transactional term according to the gender of the individual animals connected with each sealing. The entry "to Thebes" suggests that the sealings were made and inscribed somewhere removed from the palatial center in anticipation of the delivery of the animals to the center.

TH Wu 51	.α	PIG^m
	.β	te-qa-de
	.γ	qe-te-a$_2$

TH Wu 65	.α	SHEEP^f
	.β	te-qa-de
	.γ	qe-te-a$_2$

TH Wu 96	.α	PIG^f
	.β	te-qa-de
	.γ	qe-te-a$_2$

Among these seven sealings is also the only sealing with the verbal transactional term *a-pu-do-ke* ("he has paid in"). The sealing is one of two in this set that refers to the inscrutable commodity *190*.

TH Wu 89	.α	*190*
	.β	a-pu-do-ke
	.γ	*line left blank*

PERTINENT TABLET FROM THEBES

The tablet presented here was found in a different archaeological context than the sealings.

TH Uo 121   .a   SHEEPSKIN 1   WINE 9.6 liters[
           .b   SHEEP 1   GOAT 1 *190[

PERTINENT TABLETS FROM PYLOS

PY Jn 829

.1   thus will give the ko-re-te-re, and du-ma-te,[119]
.2   and po-ro-ko-re-te-re, and key-bearers, and "fig-supervisors," and "digging supervisors"
.3   temple bronze as points for light javelins and spears

.4	at pi-*82	ko-re-te	BRONZE 2 kg	po-ro-ko-re-te	BRONZE 0.75 kg
.5	at me-ta-pa	ko-re-te	BRONZE 2 kg	po-ro-ko-re-te	BRONZE 0.75 kg
.6	at pe-to-no	ko-re-te	BRONZE 2 kg	po-ro-ko-re-te	BRONZE 0.75 kg
.7	at pa-ki-ja-ne	ko-re-te	BRONZE 2 kg	po-ro-ko-re-te	BRONZE 0.75 kg
.8	at a-pu₂	ko-re-te	BRONZE 2 kg	po-ro-ko-re-te	BRONZE 0.75 kg
.9	at a-ke-re-wa	ko-re-te	BRONZE 2 kg	po-ro-ko-re-te	BRONZE 0.75 kg
.10	at ro-u-so	ko-re-te	BRONZE 2 kg	po-ro-ko-re-te	BRONZE 0.75 kg
.11	at ka-ra-do-ro	ko-re-te	BRONZE 2 kg	po-ro-ko-re-te	BRONZE 0.75 kg
.12	at ri-]jo	ko-re-te	BRONZE 2 kg	po-ro-ko-re-te	BRONZE 0.75 kg
.13	at ti-mi-to-a-ko	ko-re-te	BRONZE 2 kg	po-ro-ko-re-te	BRONZE 0.75 kg
.14	at ra-]wa-ra-ta₂	ko-re-te	BRONZE 2.75 kg	po-ro-ko-re-te	BRONZE 0.75 kg
.15	at sa-]ma-ra	ko-re-te	BRONZE 3.75 kg	po-ro-ko-re-te	0.75 kg
.16	at a-si-ja-ti-ja	ko-re-te	BRONZE 2 kg	po-ro-ko-re-te	0.75 kg
.17	at e-ra-te-re-wa	ko-re-te	BRONZE 2 kg	po-ro-ko-re-te	0.75 kg
.18	at za-ma-e-wi-ja	ko-re-te	BRONZE 3.75? kg	po-ro-ko-re-te	0.75 kg
.19	at e-ro	ko-re-te	BRONZE 3.75? kg	po-ro-ko-re-te	0.75 kg

PY Tn 316

Front:

.1   Within [the month] of Plowistos? (or Phlowistos? or Prowistos?)[120]
.2   performs a holy ritual[121] at *Sphagianes,* and brings gifts and leads
.3   PYLOS *po-re-na* to *Potnia* GOLD KYLIX 1   WOMAN 1
.4   to *Manassa*   GOLD BOWL 1   WOMAN 1   to *Posidaeia* GOLD BOWL 1   WOMAN 1
.5   to *Thrice-Hero* GOLD CHALICE 1   to *House-Master* GOLD KYLIX 1

119. The term *du-ma-te* ("masters") is the plural of *du-ma,* which is used as a title of *du-ni-jo,* who is found in the *pa-ro* formula on Un 138. The contrast here (Palaima 2001) seems to be between "secular" palatially appointed *ko-re-te-re* (singular *ko-re-te*) and *po-ro-ko-re-te-re* (singular *po-ro-ko-re-te*) and the officials who would interface with them in providing "temple" bronze,

namely the *du-ma-te,* the "key-bearers" (known from other contexts to be religious officials), and agricultural officials related to the holdings of beneficial plots in sacred areas.

120. Given other occurrences of this word in the "recipient" slot of oil offering texts, it is most reasonable to interpret it as the name of a deity, linked alternatively with "sailing" or

"flowering" or "knowing." See Aura Jorro 1993, pp. 150–151; Weilhartner 2002.

121. Hereafter abbreviated **phr.** The word thus translated may also simply refer to ritual "sending." For a full up-to-date interpretation and review of other scholarly theories on Tn 316, see Palaima 1999.

.6		*narrow line left blank*
.7		*line left blank*
.8		*line left blank*
.9	PYLOS	*line left blank*
.10		*line left blank*

Remaining portion of this side of tablet without rule lines

Reverse:

v.1		**phr** at the *sanctuary of Poseidon* and the town leads
v.2		and brings gifts and leads *po-re-na*
v.3a	PYLOS	*a* [122]
v.3		GOLD KYLIX 1 WOMAN 2 to *Bowia*[123] and X of *Komawentei-*
v.4		**phr** at the *sanctuary of pe-re-*82* and at the *sanctuary of Iphimedeia* and at the *sanctuary of Diwia*
v.5		and brings gifts and leads *po-re-na* to *pe-re-*82* GOLD BOWL 1 WOMAN 1
v.6		PYLOS to *Iphimedeia* GOLD BOWL 1 to *Diwia* GOLD BOWL 1 WOMAN 1
v.7		to *Hermes Areias* GOLD CHALICE 1 MAN 1
v.8		**phr** at the *sanctuary of Zeus* and brings gifts and leads *po-re-na*
v.9		to *Zeus* GOLD BOWL 1 MAN 1 to *Hera* GOLD BOWL 1 WOMAN 1
v.10		PYLOS to *Drimios the son of Zeus* GOLD BOWL 1
v.11		*line left blank*
v.12		*narrow line left blank*
v.13		*line left blank*
v.14		*line left blank*
v.15	PYLOS	*line left blank*
v.16		*line left blank*

Remaining portion of this side of tablet without rule lines

PY Ua 17

.1   ]   163.2 liters   WINE 1,371.2 liters
.2   ]   7 SHEEP[f] 7   YE(ARLING) 17   GOAT[m] 31   PIG[f] 20

Bottom edge:]14   [
Reverse:]30?[   ]67.2 liters? [   ] 41.6 liters

PY Ua 25

.1   F-PIG 3   CATTLE[f] 2   CATTLE[m] 8
.2   SHEEP[m] 67

Reverse: WHEAT 2,864 liters

122. The single sign on line v.3a completes the spelling of the name of the divinity: "The Lady of the Tresses," a suitable name for a female deity in the sanctuary of Poseidon. Given the occurrence of a "collector" known as *ko-ma-we*, it is also possible that *ko-ma-we-te-ja* here designates a woman as "woman of *ko-ma-we*."

123. "The Cattle-ish Lady," also a suitable name for a female deity in the sanctuary of Poseidon.

PY Un 2

.1 at *Sphagianes* at the initiation of the *wanaks*
.2 *a-pi-e-ke*,[124] the *teukhea*-overseer[125]
.3 WHEAT 1,574.4 liters   CYPERUS+PA 14.4 liters   owed 8 liters
.4 SPELT 115.2 l   OLIVES 307.2 l   *132* 19.2 l   *ME* 9.6 l[126]
.5 FIGS 96 liters   CATTLE 1   SHEEP^m 26   SHEEP^f 6   GOAT^m 2
      GOAT^f 2
.6 F-PIG 1?   PIG^f 6   WINE 585.6 liters   CLOTH 2

PY Un 6

Front:

.0   *fragmentary above*
.1 to Posei[don]   CATTLE^f[ ]   SHEEP^f[ ]   PIG-BOAR 1   PIG^f 2
.2   *narrow line left blank*
.3 to *pe-re-*82*   CATTLE^f 1   SHEEP^f 1   PIG-BOAR 1   PIG^f 2
.4 to *pe-re-*82*   CATTLE^f 1   SHEEP^f 1   PIG-BOAR 1   PIG^f 2
.5   *narrow line left blank*
.6 CLOTH 37   CLOTH ?+*WE* [   ]   WOOL 5
.7 ANOINTING OIL 12.8 liters[
.8 CATTLE^m 2   CATTLE^f 2   SHEEP^x? [

Reverse:

Top portion unruled

v.1] priestess (dative?)   CLOTH+TE? [
v.2 ke]y-bearer (dative?)   CLOTH+TE [

PY Un 47

.1   at *Lousos* the territory of *Lousos* [
.2 FIGS 91.2 liters   *i*[
.3 CYPERUS+O 328 liters   WINE [
.4 WHEAT 3,952 liters   *ka*[127]
.5 SHEEP^m 13   SHEEP^f 8   YEARLING[

PY Un 138

.1 at Pylos , qe-te-a$_2$, pa-ro , *du-ni-jo*
.2 WHEAT 1,776 liters   food OLIVES 420.8 liters
.3 WINE 374.4 liters   SHEEP^m 15   YEARLING 8   SHEEP^f 1
      GOAT^m 13   PIG 12
.4 F-PIG 1   CATTLE^f 1   CATTLE^m 2
.5 *me-za-wo-ni*[128]   WHEAT 462.4 liters   fruit OLIVES 672 liters

124. The term *a-pi-e-ke* is a compound verb, the root of which means "send" or "dedicate" or "hold."

125. The term *teukhea* as an element of the compound either means "equipment" in the general sense of paraphernalia, or military equipment, i.e., "weapons," most likely the former. Killen (1992, p. 376) connects this title, and the word from which it is formed, with cooking vessels or dining service.

126. *ME* is measured in liquid measure and probably stands for *me-ri*, or "honey."

127. Perhaps a reference to *ka-pa* olives, i.e., olives that have just been harvested.

128. A personal name in the dative to be interpreted with an ellipsis of *pa-ro*.

PY Un 718 (Fig. 1)

.1 at *sa-ra-pe-da* donation(s) to Poseidon
.2 to the sheep-flayers a donation of such an amount *Egkhes-lauōn*
.3 will contribute BARLEY 384 liters   WINE 86.4 liters   CATTLE^m 1
.4 cheese CHEESE 10 units   sheepskin HIDE 1
.5 of honey 4.8 liters
.6   *line left blank*
.7 thus also the *dāmos*   BARLEY 192 liters   WINE 57.6 liters
.8 SHEEP^m 2   CHEESE 5 units   anointing oil ANOINTING OIL 3.2 l   HIDE 1
.9 and so much the *lāwāgetās* will contribute
.10 SHEEP^m 2   flour   SPELT 57.6 liters
.11 WINE 19.2 liters thus also the *worgioneion ka-ma*
.12 BARLEY 57.6 liters   WINE 9.6 liters   CHEESE 5 units   honey[
.13   [   ] of honey? 9.6 liters

PERTINENT TABLETS FROM KNOSSOS

KN C(2) 913

.1 pa-ro , *e-te-wa-no* (personal name) , *a₃* GOAT^m 1 [
.2 pa-ro *ko-ma-we-te* (personal name) GOAT^m 1 pa[

KN C(2) 941 + 1016 + *fr.*

.A   SHEEP^m 8[
.B pa-ro / *a-pi-qo-ta* (personal name) , for slaughter SHEEP^f 10[

REFERENCES

Aravantinos, V. L., L. Godart, and
    A. Sacconi. 2001. *Thèbes: Fouilles de
    la Cadmée* 1: *Les tablettes en linéaire
    B de la Odos Pelopidou, édition et com-
    mentaire,* Pisa.

Aura Jorro, F. 1985. *Diccionario micé-
    nico* 1, Madrid.

———. 1993. *Diccionario micénico* 2,
    Madrid.

Bendall, L. M. 2002. "A Time for
    Offerings: Dedications of Perfumed
    Oil at Pylian Festivals," in Bennet
    and Driessen 2002, pp. 1–9.

Bennet, J. 1992. "Collectors or Owners?"
    in Olivier 1992, pp. 65–101.

———. 1998a. "The Linear B Archives
    and the Kingdom of Nestor," in
    Davis 1998, pp. 111–133.

———. 1998b. "The PRAP Survey's
    Contribution," in Davis 1998,
    pp. 134–138.

———. 2001. "Agency and Bureau-
    cracy: Thoughts on the Nature and
    Extent of Administration in Bronze
    Age Pylos," in *Economy and Politics
    in the Mycenaean Palace States*
    (Cambridge Philological Society,
    Suppl. 27), ed. S. Voutsaki and
    J. Killen, Cambridge, pp. 25–37.

———. 2002. "*Re-u-ko-to-ro za-we-te:*
    Leuktron as a Secondary Capital in
    the Pylos Kingdom?" in Bennet and
    Driessen 2002, pp. 11–30.

Bennet, J., and J. Driessen, eds. 2002.
    *A-NA-QO-TA: Studies Presented to
    J. T. Killen (Minos 33–34),* Sala-
    manca.

Bennett, E. L., Jr., and J.-P. Olivier.
    1973. *The Pylos Tablets Transcribed* 1:
    Text and Notes (Incunabula graeca
    51), Rome.

Carlier, P. 1984. *La royauté en Grèce
    avant Alexandre,* Strasbourg.

Carter, A. L. 2003. "Ancient Invento-
    ries: A Comparative Study of Tem-
    ple Inventories from Athens and
    Delos and the Linear B Inventories
    from Pylos and Knossos" (M.A.
    thesis, Univ. of Texas, Austin).

Chantraine, P. 1968–1980. *Diction-
    naire étymologique de la langue
    grecque: Histoire des mots,* 4 vols.,
    Paris.

Cook, E., and T. G. Palaima. 2001.
    "Sacrifice and Society in the *Odys-
    sey*" (paper, San Diego 2001).

Dabney, M. K., and J. C. Wright. 1990.
    "Mortuary Customs, Palatial Soci-
    ety, and State Formation in the
    Aegean Area: A Comparative
    Study," in *Celebrations of Death and
    Divinity in the Bronze Age Argolid.
    Proceedings of the Sixth International
    Symposium at the Swedish Institute at
    Athens (SkrAth 4°, 40),* ed. R. Hägg
    and G. C. Nordquist, Stockholm,
    pp. 45–53.

Davies, A. M., and Y. Duhoux, eds.
    1985. *Linear B: A 1984 Survey,*
    Louvain.

Davis, J. L., ed. 1998. *Sandy Pylos: An
    Archaeological History from Nestor to
    Navarino,* Austin.

Davis, J. L., and J. Bennet. 1999. "Mak-
    ing Mycenaeans: Warfare, Territori-
    al Expansion, and Representations
    of the Other in the Pylian King-
    dom," in *Polemos: Le contexte guerrier
    en Égée à l'âge du Bronze. Actes de la
    7ᵉ Rencontre égéenne internationale,
    Université de Liège (Aegaeum 19),*
    ed. R. Laffineur, Liège, pp. 105–120.

Deger-Jalkotzy, S., S. Hiller, and
    O. Panagl, eds. 1999. *Floreant Studia
    Mycenaea. Akten des X. Internatio-
    nalen Mykenologischen Colloquiums,
    Salzburg (DenkschrWien 274),*
    Vienna.

Del Freo, M. 1990. "Miceneo *a-pi to-
    ni-jo* e la serie Ta di Pilo," *SMEA*
    28, pp. 287–331.

Detienne, M., and J.-P. Vernant. 1989.
    *The Cuisine of Sacrifice among the
    Greeks,* trans. P. Wissing, Chicago.

Dübner, F. [1877] 1969. *Scholia Graeca
    in Aristophanem,* repr. Hildesheim.

Galaty, M. L. 1999. "Wealth Ceramics,
    Staple Ceramics: Pots and the
    Mycenaean Palaces," in Galaty and
    Parkinson 1999, pp. 49–59.

Galaty, M. L., and W. A. Parkinson,
    eds. 1999. *Rethinking Mycenaean
    Palaces: New Interpretations of an
    Old Idea,* Los Angeles.

Gallavotti, C. 1972. "Note omeriche e
    micenee III: La sala delle cerimonie
    nel palazzo di Nestore," *SMEA* 15,
    pp. 24–32.

Godart, L. 1999. "Les sacrifices d'ani-
    maux dans les textes mycéniens," in
    Deger-Jalkotzy, Hiller, and Panagl
    1999, pp. 249–256.

Hägg, R. 1996. "The Religion of the
    Mycenaeans Twenty-Four Years
    after the 1967 Mycenological Con-
    gress in Rome," *Atti e memorie del
    secondo Congresso internazionale di
    micenologia, Roma–Napoli* 2: *Storia*
    (Incunabula graeca 98), ed. E. De
    Miro, L. Godart, and A. Sacconi,
    Rome, pp. 599–612.

Hallager, E. 1996. *The Minoan Roun-
    del and Other Sealed Documents in the
    Neopalatial Linear A Administration
    (Aegaeum 14),* 2 vols., Liège.

Halstead, P. 1999. "Towards a Model
    of Mycenaean Palatial Mobiliza-
    tion," in Galaty and Parkinson 1999,
    pp. 35–41.

———. 2002. "Texts, Bones, and
    Herders: Approaches to Animal
    Husbandry in Late Bronze Age
    Greece," in Bennet and Driessen
    2002, pp. 149–189.

Hiller, S. 1971. "Beinhaltet die Ta-Serie
    ein Kultinventar?" *Eirene* 9, pp. 69–86.

———. 1981. "Mykenische Heilig-
    tümer: Das Zeugnis der Linear B-
    Texte," in *Sanctuaries and Cults in
    the Aegean Bronze Age. Proceedings
    of the First International Symposium
    at the Swedish Institute in Athens
    (SkrAth 4°, 28),* ed. R. Hägg and
    N. Marinatos, Stockholm, pp. 95–
    126.

Hutton, W. F. 1990–1991. "The Mean-
    ing of the Word *qe-te-o* in Linear B,"
    Minos 25–26, pp. 105–131.

Isaakidou, V., P. Halstead, J. Davis, and
    S. Stocker. 2002. "Burnt Animal
    Sacrifice in Late Bronze Age
    Greece: New Evidence from the
    Mycenaean 'Palace of Nestor,'
    Pylos," *Antiquity* 76, pp. 86–92.

Jameson, M. H. 1988. "Sacrifice and
    Animal Husbandry in Classical
    Greece," in *Pastoral Economies in
    Classical Antiquity* (Cambridge
    Philological Society, Suppl. 14),
    ed. C. R. Whittaker, Cambridge,
    pp. 87–119.

Killen, J. T. 1979. "The Knossos Ld(1)
    Tablets," in *Colloquium Mycenaeum.
    Actes du sixième Colloque internatio-
    nal sur les textes mycéniens et égéens
    tenu à Chaumont sur Neuchâtel,*
    ed. E. Risch and H. Mühlestein,
    Neuchâtel, pp. 151–181.

————. 1985. "The Linear B Tablets and the Mycenaean Economy," in Davies and Duhoux 1985, pp. 241–305.

————. 1992. "Observations on the Thebes Sealings," in Olivier 1992, pp. 365–380.

————. 1994. "Thebes Sealings, Knossos Tablets, and Mycenaean State Banquets," *BICS* 39, pp. 67–84.

————. 1998. "The Pylos Ta Tablets Revisited," pp. 421–422, in F. Rougemont and J.-P. Olivier, eds., "Recherches récentes en épigraphie créto-mycénienne," *BCH* 122, pp. 403–443.

————. 1999a. "Mycenaean *o-pa*," in Deger-Jalkotzy, Hiller, and Panagl 1999, pp. 325–341.

————. 1999b. "Critique: A View from the Tablets," in Galaty and Parkinson 1999, pp. 87–90.

Koster, W. J. W. 1960. *Scholia in Aristophanem* 4: *Jo. Tzetzae Commentarii in Aristophanem* 2: *In Nubes,* Groningen.

La Rosa, V., D. Palermo, and L. Vagnetti, eds. 1999. Ἐπί πόντον πλαζόμενοι: *Simposio italiano di studi egei dedicato a Luigi Bernabò Brea e Giovanni Pugliese Carratelli, Roma,* Rome.

Lejeune, M. 1972. "Le *damos* dans la société mycénienne," in *Mémoires de philologie mycénienne* 3 (Incunabula graeca 99), Rome, pp. 137–154.

Lesy, M. 1987. *The Forbidden Zone,* New York.

Lindgren, M. 1973. *The People of Pylos: Prosopographical and Methodological Studies in the Pylos Archives,* 2 vols., Uppsala.

Lupack, S. 1999. "Palaces, Sanctuaries, and Workshops," in Galaty and Parkinson 1999, pp. 25–34.

————. 2002. "The Role of the Religious Sector in the Economy of Late Bronze Age Mycenaean Greece" (diss. Univ. of Texas, Austin).

McCallum, L. R. 1987. "Decorative Program in the Mycenaean Palace at Pylos: The Megaron Frescoes" (diss. Univ. of Pennsylvania).

Melena, J. L. 1983. "Further Thoughts on Mycenaean *o-pa*," in *Res Mycenaeae: Akten des VII. Internationalen Mykenologischen Colloquiums, Nuremberg,* ed. A. Heubeck and G. Neumann, Göttingen, pp. 258–286.

————. 2001. *Textos griegos micénicos comentados,* Vitoria-Gasteiz.

Morris, H. J. 1986. "An Economic Model of the Late Mycenaean Kingdom of Pylos" (diss. Univ. of Minnesota).

Neils, J., ed. 1992. *Goddess and Polis: The Panathenaic Festival in Ancient Athens,* Princeton.

Nikoloudis, S. 2001. "Animal Sacrifice in the Mycenaean World," *JPR* 15, pp. 11–31.

————. 2004. "Food and Drink for Poseidon and the Internal Ordering of PY Un 718" (paper, San Francisco 2004).

Olivier, J.-P., ed. 1992. *Mykenaïka: Actes du IXe Colloque international sur les textes mycéniens et égéens organisé par le Centre de l'antiquité grecque et romaine de la Fondation hellénique des recherches scientifiques et l'École française d'Athènes* (*BCH* Suppl. 25), Athens.

————. 1996–1997. "El comercio micénico desde la documentación epigráfica," *Minos* 31–32, pp. 275–292.

————. 2001. "'Les collecteurs': Leur distribution spatiale et temporelle," in *Economy and Politics in the Mycenaean Palace States* (Cambridge Philological Society, Suppl. 27), ed. S. Voutsaki and J. Killen, Cambridge, pp. 139–157.

Palaima, T. G. 1987. "Mycenaean Seals and Sealings in Their Economic and Administrative Contexts," in *Tractata Mycenaea. Proceedings of the Eighth International Colloquium on Mycenaean Studies, Ohrid,* ed. P. H. Ilievski and L. Crepajac, Skopje, pp. 249–266.

————. 1988. *The Scribes of Pylos* (Incunabula graeca 87), Rome.

————. 1989. "Perspectives on the Pylos Oxen Tablets: Textual (and Archaeological) Evidence for the Use and Management of Oxen in Late Bronze Age Messenia (and Crete)," in *Studia Mycenaea (1988),* ed. T. G. Palaima, C. W. Shelmerdine, and P. H. Ilievski, Skopje, pp. 85–124.

————. 1995a. "The Last Days of the Pylos Polity," in *Politeia: Society and State in the Aegean Bronze Age. Proceedings of the 5th International Aegean Conference, Heidelberg* (*Aegaeum*

12), ed. R. Laffineur and W.-D. Niemeier, Liège, pp. 623–633.

————. 1995b. "The Nature of the Mycenaean Wanax: Non-Indo-European Origins and Priestly Functions," in Rehak 1995, pp. 119–139.

————. 1996. "Sealings as Links in an Administrative Chain," in *Administration in Ancient Societies. Proceedings of Session 218 of the 13th International Congress of Anthropological and Ethnological Sciences, Mexico City,* ed. P. Ferioli, E. Fiandra, and G. G. Fissore, Turin, pp. 37–66.

————. 1999. "Kn02–Tn 316," in Deger-Jalkotzy, Hiller, and Panagl 1999, pp. 437–461.

————. 2000a. "The Palaeography of Mycenaean Inscribed Sealings from Thebes and Pylos, Their Place within the Mycenaean Administrative System, and Their Links with the Extra-Palatial Sphere," in *Minoisch-mykenische Glyptik: Stil, Ikonographie, Funktion. V. Internationales Siegel-Symposium, Marburg* (*CMS* Beiheft 6), ed. W. Müller, Berlin, pp. 219–238.

————. 2000b. "The Pylos Ta Series: From Michael Ventris to the New Millennium," *BICS* 44, pp. 236–237.

————. 2000c. "Transactional Vocabulary in Linear B Tablet and Sealing Administration," in *Administrative Documents in the Aegean and Their Near Eastern Counterparts,* ed. M. Perna, Turin, pp. 261–276.

————. 2001. "The Modalities of Economic Control at Pylos," *Ktema* 26, pp. 151–159.

————. 2002a. Rev. of Aravantinos, Godart, and Sacconi 2001, in *Minos* 35–36, pp. 475–486.

————. 2002b. "Special vs. Normal Mycenaean: Hand 24 and Writing in the Service of the King?" in Bennet and Driessen 2002, pp. 205–221.

————. 2003a. "Archaeology and Text: Decipherment, Translation, and Interpretation," in *Theory and Practice in Mediterranean Archaeology: Old World and New World Perspectives,* ed. J. K. Papadopoulos and R. M. Leventhal, Los Angeles, pp. 45–73.

————. 2003b. "'Archives' and 'Scribes' and Information Hierarchy in Mycenaean Greek Linear B Records," in *Ancient Archives and Archival Traditions: Concepts of Record-Keeping in the Ancient World,* ed. M. Brosius, Oxford, pp. 153–194.

———. 2003c. "The Inscribed Bronze 'Kessel' from Shaft Grave IV and Cretan Heirlooms of the Bronze Age Artist Named 'Aigeus' *vel sim.* in the Mycenaean Palatial Period," in *Briciaka: A Tribute to W. C. Brice* (Cretan Studies 9), ed. Y. Duhoux, Amsterdam, pp. 187–201.

———. 2003d. Rev. of Aravantinos, Godart, and Sacconi 2001, in *AJA* 107, pp. 113–115.

Palaima, T. G., and J. C. Wright. 1985. "Ins and Outs of the Archives Rooms at Pylos: Form and Function in a Mycenaean Palace," *AJA* 89, pp. 251–262.

Palmer, L. R. 1957. "A Mycenaean Tomb Inventory," *Minos* 5, pp. 58–92.

———. 1963. *The Interpretation of Mycenaean Greek Texts,* Oxford.

Palmer, R. 1992. "Wheat and Barley in Mycenaean Society," in Olivier 1992, pp. 475–497.

Pini, I., ed. 1997. *Die Tonplomben aus dem Nestorpalast von Pylos,* Mainz.

Piteros, C., J.-P. Olivier, and J. L. Melena. 1990. "Les inscriptions en linéaire B des nodules de Thèbes (1982): La fouille, les documents, les possibilités d'interprétation," *BCH* 104, pp. 103–184.

Pluta, K. 1996–1997. "A Reconstruction of the Archives Complex at Pylos: A Preliminary Report," *Minos* 31–32, pp. 231–250.

Rehak, P., ed. 1995. *The Role of the Ruler in the Prehistoric Aegean. Proceedings of a Panel Discussion Presented at the Annual Meeting of the Archaeological Institute of America, New Orleans* (*Aegaeum* 11), Liège.

Ruijgh, C. J. 1999. "ϝάναξ et ses dérivés dans les texts mycéniens," in Deger-Jalkotzy, Hiller, and Panagl 1999, pp. 523–535.

Rutherford, W. G., ed. 1896–1905. *Scholia Aristophanica: Being Such Comments Adscript to the Text of Aristophanes as Have Been Preserved in the Codex Ravennas,* 3 vols., London.

Sacconi, A. 1987. "La tavoletta di Pilo Tn 316: Una registrazione di carattere eccezionale?" in *Studies in Mycenaean and Classical Greek Presented to John Chadwick* (*Minos* 20–22), ed. J. T. Killen, J. L. Melena, and J.-P. Olivier, Salamanca, pp. 551–556.

———. 1999. "La tavoletta PY Ta 716 e le armi di rappresentanza nel mondo egeo," in La Rosa, Palermo, and Vagnetti 1999, pp. 285–289.

Sergent, B. 1994. "Les petits nodules et la grande Béotie (première partie)," *RÉA* 96, pp. 365–384.

Shapiro, H. A. 1996. "Democracy and Imperialism: The Panathenaia in the Age of Pericles," in *Worshipping Athena: Panathenaia and Parthenon*, ed. J. Neils, Madison, pp. 215–225.

Shelmerdine, C. W. 1981. "Nichoria in Context: A Major Town in the Pylos Kingdom," *AJA* 85, pp. 319–324.

———. 1997. "Review of Aegean Prehistory VI: The Palatial Bronze Age of the Southern and Central Greek Mainland," *AJA* 101, pp. 537–585.

———. 1998. "The Palace and Its Operations," in Davis 1998, pp. 81–96.

———. 1999a. "Administration in the Mycenaean Palaces: Where's the Chief?" in Galaty and Parkinson 1999, pp. 19–24.

———. 1999b. "A Comparative Look at Mycenaean Administration(s)," in Deger-Jalkotzy, Hiller, and Panagl 1999, pp. 555–576.

Simone, E. 1996. "Theseus and Athenian Festivals," in *Worshipping Athena: Panathenaia and Parthenon,* ed. J. Neils, Madison, pp. 9–26.

Speciale, M. S. 1999. "La tavoletta PY Ta 716 e i sacrifici di animali," in La Rosa, Palermo, and Vagnetti 1999, pp. 291–297.

Sucharski, R. A., and K. T. Witczak. 1996. "*U-po-jo-po-ti-ni-ja* and the Cult of Baetyls," *ZivaAnt* 46, pp. 5–12.

Vandenabeele, F., and J.-P. Olivier. 1979. *Les idéogrammes archéologiques du linéaire B* (*ÉtCrét* 24), Paris.

Ventris, M. 1955. "Mycenaean Furniture on the Pylos Tablets," *Eranos* 53, pp. 3–4, 109–124.

Ventris, M., and J. Chadwick. 1956. *Documents in Mycenaean Greek,* Cambridge.

———. 1973. *Documents in Mycenaean Greek,* 2nd ed., Cambridge.

Weilhartner, J. 2002. "Überlegungen zu dem mykenischen Begriff *po-ro-wi-to-jo* auf PY Tn 316," *Kadmos* 41, pp. 155–161.

Wright, J. C. 1994. "The Spatial Configuration of Belief: The Archaeology of Mycenaean Religion," in *Placing the Gods: Sanctuaries and Sacred Space in Ancient Greece,* ed. S. E. Alcock and R. Osborne, Oxford, pp. 37–78.

———. 1995a. "Empty Cups and Empty Jugs: The Social Role of Wine in Minoan and Mycenaean Societies," in *The Origins and Ancient History of Wine* (Food and Nutrition in History and Anthropology 11), ed. P. E. McGovern, S. J. Fleming, and S. H. Katz, Philadelphia, pp. 287–309.

———. 1995b. "From Chief to King in Mycenaean Greece," in Rehak 1995, pp. 63–80.

Zaidman, L. B., and P. Schmitt Pantel. 1992. *Religion in the Ancient Greek City,* trans. P. Cartledge, Cambridge.

CHAPTER 6

AEGEAN FEASTING:
A MINOAN PERSPECTIVE

Elisabetta Borgna

ABSTRACT

This survey of feasting in Bronze Age Crete reveals that feasts could be either exclusive elite celebrations or unrestricted occasions in which social identity rather than power was most important. In contrast, Mycenaean feasting on the Greek mainland seems to have arisen from elite customs aimed at exclusion. A comparison of the evidence for Late Minoan IIIC feasting at Phaistos and convivial practices on the mainland indicates new Mycenaean components to Cretan feasting, suggesting that the earlier pattern had shifted and that Cretan feasts had similarly become elite instruments of competition and negotiation for authority.

The purpose of this chapter is to investigate the archaeological evidence for convivial practices in Bronze Age Crete and to compare it with the material indications of feasting on the mainland of Greece.[1] Through comparison of Mycenaean evidence and two large LM IIIB–C pottery assemblages at Phaistos, I point out discrepancies as well as reciprocal contributions in traditions of Minoan and Mycenaean feasting. I suggest that the evidence from Phaistos demonstrates that communal drinking and feasts in LM IIIB–C Crete were celebrated to facilitate social communication and promote ideological strategies and political activities.

In the following study, I take into account the role that pottery plays in the investigation and recognition of social patterns in feasting. In ceramic

1. I would like to thank Sharon Stocker and James Wright for inviting me to participate in the colloquium on Mycenaean feasts held at the Annual Meeting of the Archaeological Institute of America in Philadelphia in 2002. Funding from the Institute for Aegean Prehistory enabled me to attend. I am particularly indebted to Wright for invaluable comments and suggestions. I also wish to thank Filippo Carinci for reading and commenting on the text,

and the *Hesperia* referees, Brian Hayden and Jeremy Rutter, who drew my attention to important points. The drawings for this chapter are by Giuliano Merlatti and Orazio Pulvirenti and belong to the archive of the Scuola Archeologica Italiana di Atene; I thank the director of the Italian School, Emanuele Greco, for permitting their publication. All photographs are by the author. I am profoundly grateful to Vincenzo La Rosa, director of the

Italian excavations at Ayia Triada and Phaistos, who involved me in the study of Late Minoan (LM) III Phaistos.

The periods of Minoan Crete referred to throughout this chapter are as follows: Prepalatial (Early Minoan [EM] I–Middle Minoan [MM] IA); Protopalatial (MM IB–IIB); Neopalatial (MM IIIA–LM IB); Monopalatial (LM II–IIIA1); Final Palatial (LM IIIA2–IIIB [early]); and Postpalatial (LM IIIB [late]–C).

studies, the application of ethnographically observed patterns of the deployment of decorative styles provides sociofunctional explanations of pottery usage. Variability among these patterns provides a key to understanding strategies of social communication and ideological and political manipulation of the occasions and places of social exchange.[2] According to one model, two modes of decorative variability point to two different social dynamics.[3] The first, qualitative variability (i.e., variability by alternation of the decorative elements and substitution or variation of secondary motifs and ornamental details), is employed to negotiate cultural and social identity within the context of balanced confrontations among equal social components; the second, additive or vertical variability (i.e., by accumulation and redundancy of decorative elements), expresses social competition aimed at establishing vertical relationships and hierarchical order.

FEASTING AT LM IIIC PHAISTOS

As I have discussed elsewhere, qualitative variability (substitution) at Phaistos was used for the decoration of LM IIIB and IIIB–C vessels in a symbolic style that asserts social divisions on a horizontal level, while quantitative variability (accumulation) marked the local expressions of the LM IIIC elaborate style, which was more generally associated with elite settlements and included many examples of pictorial pottery.[4] This latter style, in particular, might be explained as a kind of "elite" or "iconographic" style according to definitions applied in anthropological studies, by which decorative components are encoded with elite ideological and political messages.[5] The exclusive association of the most elaborate symbolic and iconographic styles with ceramics reserved for drinking (and possibly also for religious offerings) supports the hypothesis that highly competitive feasts were celebrated as occasions of conspicuous consumption and served to promote the ideological strategies of dominant groups during the last phases of Minoan civilization.

At Phaistos I have identified two sites where communal wine consumption and ritual meals took place, the summit of the Acropoli Mediana and the Casa a ovest del Piazzale I at its southern foot (Fig. 1).[6] The Acropoli Mediana is the settlement's highest and most visible site; toward the end of LM III it was used for convivial ceremonies.[7] The large number of kraters and deep bowls found in this area (see, e.g., Figs. 2, 4, 5:1, 3–5) indicates events with open, communal participation.[8] The many kraters accompanying the even more numerous deep bowls may make it possible to identify sets of vessels corresponding to independent units of distribution and consumption, which could have been used in a sequence of ongoing ceremonies from the end of LM IIIB until the middle of LM IIIC. The variability in fabric and morphology of the pottery (indicating different production units) may suggest that the participants in the feasts came from different residential sites around Phaistos.

The elaborate decoration of this pottery (Figs. 2, 4, 5:1) may be a form of highly competitive display indicating that ceramics were important for the negotiation of status. The presence of female and animal figurines

Figure 1 (opposite). Plan of the western court of the palace at Phaistos, with Mycenaean remains indicated by hatchmarks in the area of A (Casa a ovest del Piazzale I), B, and C. After Levi 1976, pl. 2

2. See, e.g., Wiessner 1983, 1984, 1989; Graves 1994; Hantman and Plog 1984. For Archaic Greek pottery, see Morgan 1991; Morgan and Whitelaw 1991; and see in general Plog 1980, 1995; Conkey and Hastorf 1990. See also Borgna 1999b, and forthcoming.

3. Pollock 1983.

4. Borgna 2003a, pp. 23–27, 354–357; and forthcoming.

5. For the definition of symbolic and iconographic styles, see Plog 1995.

6. Borgna 1997a, 1999b, 2000, 2003a, and forthcoming.

7. Borgna 1997b, 1999a, 2003a, pp. 357–371.

8. Open, fine, decorated vessels for consumption make up 80% of the assemblage; the 214 deep bowls and 70 kraters constitute our best sample of these shapes for the LM IIIC period.

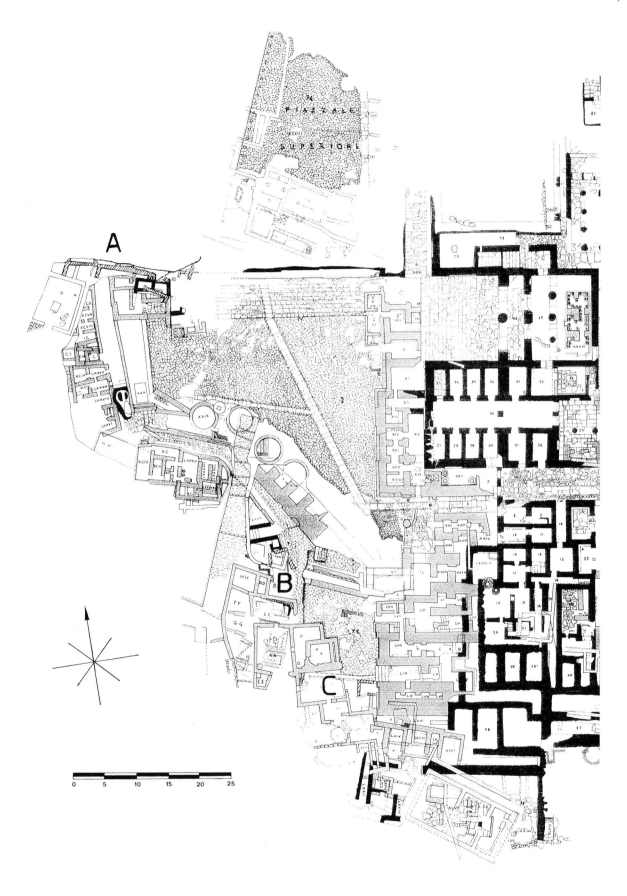

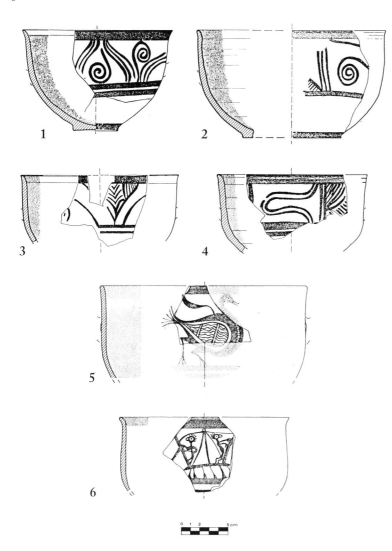

Figure 2. Deep bowls (1–4) and stemmed bowls (5, 6) from the Acropoli Mediana

on the Acropoli Mediana (Figs. 3, 5:2), together with the style of the pottery (Fig. 5:3–5), is evidence of Mycenaean influence. Both the krater and the deep bowl are dependent on Mycenaean functional models and are signs of a substantial "Mycenaeanization" of the local material culture, perhaps as a result of a strategic and selective adoption of mainland elements by the Cretan elite to claim social authority and status.[9]

A similar abundance of decorated deep bowls and fine dinnerware (Figs. 6–8) and a plenitude of kitchen wares (Fig. 9) distinguish the Casa a ovest I.[10] Ashes and coals, broken kraters, and a table or bench mark an occupation level in one room and represent evidence of a possible ceremonial rite. A bronze knife and two bronze sickles (Figs. 10, 11) from the building might be interpreted, together with other evidence such as a bronze bowl and a ceramic stand with elaborate pictorial decoration (Fig. 12), as symbolic artifacts suited to the celebration of banquets. Other finds, such

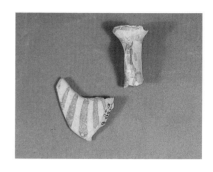

Figure 3. Figurine from the Acropoli Mediana

9. For "Mycenaeanization" at Phaistos, see Borgna 1997b. Cf. Clark and Blake 1994; Wright, forthcoming.

10. Laviosa 1973; Borgna 1997a, 2000, 2001.

Figure 4 *(top)*. Kraters (1–3) from the Acropoli Mediana

Figure 5 *(bottom)*. Krater (1), figurine (2), and deep bowls (3–5) from the Acropoli Mediana

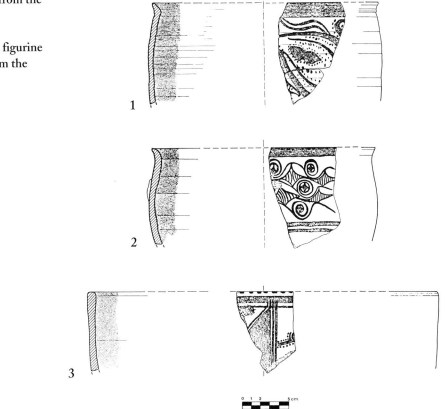

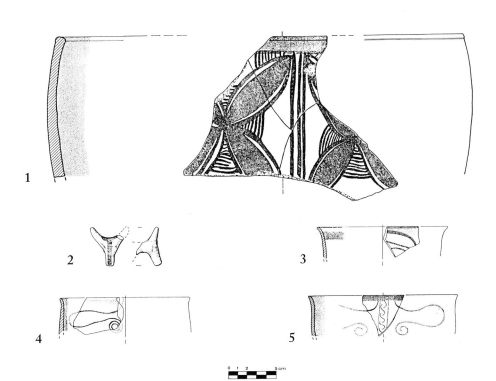

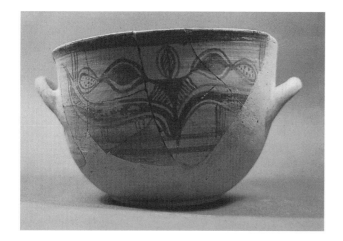

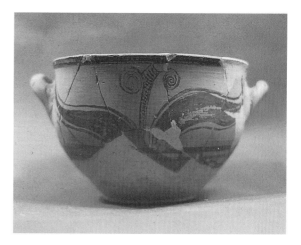

Figure 6 *(top)*. Deep bowls from the
Casa a ovest del Piazzale I

Figure 7 *(middle)*. Krater fragments
from the Casa a ovest del Piazzale I

Figure 8 *(bottom)*. Pithoid jar from
the Casa a ovest del Piazzale I

Figure 9. Cooking jar from the Casa
a ovest del Piazzale I

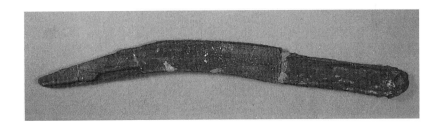

Figure 10. Bronze knife from the
Casa a ovest del Piazzale I

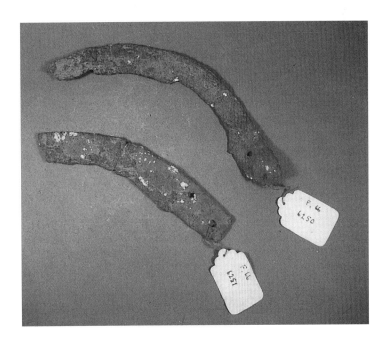

Figure 11. Bronze sickles from the
Casa a ovest del Piazzale I

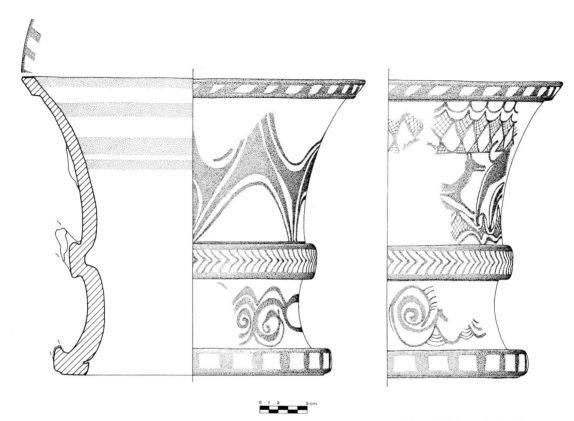

Figure 12. Stand with figurative decoration from the Casa a ovest del Piazzale I

as large storage vessels, unpainted and coarse pottery, weights, and spindle whorls, seem to point not so much to a ritual site as to a domestic structure. The storage and production activities reflect the important economic role of the building, or *oikos*, which may have been an elite dwelling devoted to the control and manipulation of farm produce during the LM IIIC and possibly Subminoan periods.

In an earlier paper on the Acropoli Mediana and the Casa a ovest del Piazzale I, I suggested that the two types of ceremony were related to separate spheres of social exchange, dependent on distinct social roles and with different political implications.[11] The one, on the Acropoli Mediana, I interpreted as a kind of public banquet, less exclusive and more open to heterogeneous social components in comparison with that of the Casa a ovest, but at the same time having the function of creating hierarchical relationships and dependencies. The other, in the Casa a ovest, I interpreted as a more restricted rite, aimed at strengthening elite social ties and maintaining economic and possibly political authority.

A thorough investigation will perhaps permit us to distinguish definitively between the functions that these two feasting sites had within the social organization of Phaistos, which I have suggested was a simple form of chiefdom toward the end of the second millennium B.C.[12] In the attempt to find a connection between the two ritual occasions—which in the end might be the archaeological poles of a unique event, albeit separated within the settlement—I first limit myself to underlining features that seem exclusive to either occasion and may help to distinguish feasting patterns according to anthropological classifications.

11. Borgna, forthcoming.
12. See Borgna 2003a, pp. 370–371; 2003b, pp. 159–164.

The depositional pattern of the Acropoli assemblage suggests that community assembly and consumption were among the major activities pursued, as well as cleaning up, without any manifest emphasis upon indoor/outdoor separation.[13] In the Casa a ovest, elaborate preparation and possibly restricted indoor ritual activity, together with the storage of food and serving vessels, are especially apparent. From the very large number of individual drinking and eating vessels—too many for a gathering indoors—we can infer the occurrence of outdoor assemblies, possibly in some kind of court or open space. The importance of sharing at the Acropoli might therefore stand in opposition to the hoarding and distributing practices in the Casa a ovest, indicating different functions and meanings for the ritual occasions.

The Acropoli deposit spans a period from the end of LM IIIB into LM IIIC, the period when population begins to be concentrated at Phaistos. This period was a highly critical one for social life in Crete, following shifts in settlement, political disruption, and dispersal of population. We might explain the Acropoli as one of a few Cretan places where aggregation and social cohesion around new settlements and eminent individuals occurred. Such individuals, by assuming Mycenaean social habits and behavior, were to become the main leaders within LM IIIC society.[14] Moreover, the Acropoli assemblage can be compared with LM IIIB pottery assemblages from a few Cretan caves, which are characterized primarily by the association of serving and sometimes storage vessels, including in particular deep bowls and kraters.[15] On the basis of these considerations, the convivial gatherings on the Acropoli Mediana could be interpreted as "celebratory feasts," performed in order to encourage social bonding[16] and as devices for aggregating dispersed populations or for reaffirming social distance in concentrated populations.[17] Possibly regional in scope, these feasts might therefore be considered part of the class of "entrepreneurial" or "empowering feasts," as defined by Dietler.[18]

The meals prepared and consumed at the Casa a ovest, on the other hand, are better described as "competitive feasts," probably celebrating events directly linked with economic goals and serving a more particular function as redistributive devices.[19] The feasts might also have involved two types of ritual celebration, each with a special role. Ritual furniture found inside, such as the pictorial stand (Fig. 12), some kraters, and the bronzes, might be the archaeological remains of a rite of hosting and gift-giving among equal social components or between groups that initiated and maintained alliances, especially for access to resources or to exchange partners.[20] The high number of stored and discarded individual serving vessels might point, however, to a more open, outdoor participation, central to redistribution or patron-role feasts, in which retainers and commoners participated.[21]

It is necessary to defer a detailed discussion on the functions and significance of the Phaistian feasts to a more advanced stage of research at the site. Nonetheless, since we are able to highlight the presence of several Mycenaean cultural elements of feasting, I concentrate in the remainder of this chapter on the relationship between Minoan and Mycenaean banqueting practices.

13. Cf. Goody 1982, pp. 47–48.

14. See Borgna 2003b.

15. For the Mamelouko cave, see Kanta 1980, pp. 228–229; for the Lilianou cave, Kanta 1971; see also Koumarospilia (Kanta 1980, p. 231) and the Idaean cave (Vasilakis 1990, pp. 130–134).

16. Hayden 1996, p. 135.

17. DeBoer 2001, p. 215.

18. Dietler 1996, pp. 92–96; 2001, pp. 76–80.

19. Cf. Dietler 1996, p. 97. "Empowering" and "patron-role" feasts can be expressions of the same "consumption politics" within the same "consumption community" (for terminology, see Dietler 2001, pp. 76–85, 93–94; Hayden 2001, p. 58).

20. See Perodie 2001, esp. p. 210. For the role of exchange in Postpalatial Crete, see Borgna 2003b.

21. Hayden 1996, p. 129; Dietler 2001, pp. 82–85; cf. also Junker 2001, p. 271. On the practice of discarding vessels used on ritual occasions within the domestic area, see Junker 2001, p. 285.

FEASTING IN MINOAN AND MYCENAEAN CONTEXTS

In a previous paper, I suggested that drinking activities in relevant socio-political contexts constituted a contribution from mainland Greece to Cretan culture, where ritual meals and large communal gatherings for cult ceremonies and festivals were already well rooted in local tradition.[22] In a Cretan context the exclusive nature of Mycenaean banqueting practices was possibly modified, the ceremonies becoming less exclusive and more a means of social control in contexts outside of the palaces.

Consumption of wine cannot be ascribed exclusively to Mycenaean influence, however; several authors claim it was a long-established social custom in Crete and an ideological instrument of emerging elites from Prepalatial times.[23] The transfer of the banquet from the palatial court into the urban context could be explained more as the result of the political collapse of palatial societies and the ensuing instability of political systems across the Aegean than as a specific Cretan innovation.[24] The widespread and uniform diffusion of such assemblages as deep bowls and kraters—possibly constituting a drinking set—suggests this. As mentioned above, some LM IIIB pottery groups from caves, which include deep bowls, cups, one or more kraters, and sometimes stirrup jars (together with some roughly contemporary grave assemblages),[25] might be related to the diffusion throughout Postpalatial Crete of a ritual of aggregation consisting mostly of convivial practices.

To refine this argument and clarify the differences between Minoan and Mycenaean practices, I next summarize the evidence for banqueting in Crete and on the mainland in terms of feasting places and occasions, requisites of participation, the nature and function of feasts, and different strategies of the elite.

VARIETY OF FEASTING PLACES AND OCCASIONS

From the Early Minoan period onward, it is possible to recognize a considerable variety of banqueting occasions and convivial ceremonies. These events include funerary celebrations, purely religious ceremonies, and ritual activities relevant to the establishment of social relationships in Cretan communities—as the well-known evidence from Myrtos and the new discoveries at Prepalatial Knossos suggest.[26] The places devoted to such celebrations were often expressly prepared, as indicated by the paved areas and enclosures in the Prepalatial cemeteries, thus demonstrating that social practices concerning the manipulation and, presumably, consumption

22. Borgna 1997a, pp. 210–211; cf. Borgna 2003a, pp. 369–370. On the Mycenaean "symposium" see, e.g., Wright 1995a, 1995b, forthcoming; Carter 1997.

23. E.g., Rehak and Younger 2001, pp. 430, 437, 439; Hamilakis 1996, 1999; cf. Deliyanni 2000.

24. For the end of the palatial phase at Pylos, see Sherratt 2001, p. 229; cf. Davis and Bennet 1999, p. 110. On the complete remodeling of the palace architecture, possibly also for ritual purposes, see Wright 1984.

25. See above, n. 15, for specific

caves, and below, n. 104, on grave assemblages.

26. For Myrtos, see Carinci and D'Agata 1989–1990, pp. 223–224; Gesell 1985, p. 114, no. 89; for Knossos, see Wilson and Day 2000; Day and Wilson 2002.

of food belonged to a structured and complex communal ideology. Formal areas within cemeteries dating from later Prepalatial and Protopalatial times are often associated with material assemblages remarkable for the huge number of serving and consuming vessels, especially conical cups.[27] The conical cups were generally not deposited inside the graves, which, as several have argued, may indicate that these ritual areas served as communal shrines and constituted a physical setting for communal ritual activities aimed at maintaining social stability and cohesion.[28] A similar function can be ascribed to peak sanctuaries (the main ritual foci for the aggregation of rural population), where communal rites, including consumption, would have shifted at the beginning of Minoan palatial civilization.[29]

The number of locations used for banqueting increased during the Protopalatial and Neopalatial periods. Palaces were provided with several banqueting rooms and structures, each potentially suited to different ritual and social functions. Cultic installations were located in the western wings of the palaces, focusing in particular on small rooms opening on the western court, such as the well-known sanctuary at Phaistos, which was equipped with cooking and serving utensils.[30] Huge banqueting halls with elaborate architectural elements were usually located in the northern wings of the palaces, and were provided with ceramic kitchen and dinnerware.[31] These finds, together with other evidence, make clear that activities of manipulation and consumption were at the palaces' expense and were subject to highly structured ritual codes, possibly including the institution of tribute to support the organization of feasts.[32]

Several foci of ritual celebration are detectable within single architectural compounds, as, for example, in the supposed Neopalatial palaces at Chania and Galatas. Impressive concentrations of pottery suited for dining and drinking have been found in association with several structures in Chania, notably the West Court and the Great Hall. Many conical cups were brought to light in the West Court, while ceremonies in the Great Hall, with a platform for a lustral basin, were perhaps characterized by restricted attendance.[33] The cultic complex of Daskaloyannis Street, including pits and drains filled with bones, ash, pots, and conical cups, supplements our picture.[34] At the newly discovered palace at Galatas, important indications of ritual consumption were found in several rooms of the building, including the east wing with the "Cooking Place," columnar hall, pillar hall, and room 22 in the west wing.[35] Outside the palaces—at extra-urban sanctuaries and religious sites such as caves and peak sanctuaries—

27. See below, n. 62.

28. Branigan 1970b, pp. 98, 132–138 (regarding also the possible transfer of ritual communal activity from the cemeteries to the western courts of the palaces); Branigan 1970a, p. 94; 1993, pp. 76–78 (the author suggests here a limited phenomenon with a restricted attendance); 1998b, pp. 19–21. See in general Walberg 1987, pp. 56–57; Soles 1992, pp. 237–

238; Hamilakis 1998, pp. 119–120.

29. Peatfield 1987. For a recent discussion of peak sanctuaries, see Haggis 1999.

30. Gesell 1985, pp. 120–124, no. 102; Carinci and D'Agata 1989–1990, pp. 228–229; Watrous 2001, p. 202. For an explanation of the similar structural layout in the southwestern wing of the palace, see Carinci, forthcoming.

31. Graham 1961; 1987, pp. 125–

128; for Zakros, see Platon 1971, pp. 203–209; in general, Cultraro 2001, pp. 178–187.

32. See Marinatos 1986, pp. 37–39. For tribute (in Mesopotamia), see Schmandt-Besserat 2001.

33. Andreadaki-Vlasaki 2002, p. 162.

34. Andreadaki-Vlasaki 1997b, pp. 566–571; 2002, pp. 160–161.

35. Rethemiotakis 2002, pp. 58–59.

evidence is clear that ritual meals were an inherent part of common religious belief and practice.[36]

A marked political dimension may be detected in Neopalatial aristocratic dwellings. Bronze sheet-metal vessels suitable for the consumption of food and drink by elites were often deposited in hoards or treasuries,[37] and assemblages of pottery were sometimes discarded together with ashes, food, and the remains of offerings.[38] In the Neopalatial period in particular, plentiful amounts of tableware or conical cups began to appear in several extrapalatial settlement contexts, such as the possibly elite dwellings at Petras and Galatas.[39] At the same time, certain small rooms in Neopalatial villas may have served as locations for the celebration of *andreia* for a limited number of participants.[40] Such evidence supports the view that in palatial Crete banqueting practices consisted of an articulated series of events in terms of location, function, and purpose; moreover, it would seem to imply that in Neopalatial times in particular, elite ideology of consumption was materialized according to a common and codified architectonic language. Household urban shrines (at Pseira, for example) provide a further variety of such evidence.[41]

A brief consideration of the ceramic evidence reinforces this view, for it brings to our attention a number of different pottery assemblages, all suited to preparation and consumption activities, but each possibly used according to particular conditions. Though the published reports do not permit one to single out well-defined sets of vessels used exclusively on specific ritual occasions and in specific architectural and social frameworks, general trends relevant to the social use of certain vessels and to the functional composition of tableware can be raised.

Fine Kamares cups, jugs, and other pouring vessels are characteristic of aristocratic assemblages in the official halls and residential rooms of the palaces.[42] More particularly, at the end of the Prepalatial period at Knossos, the footed goblet and the angular bridge-spouted jar were commonly associated with one another,[43] replaced in the Protopalatial period by the straight-sided cup and the bridge-spouted jar. In the Protopalatial period, the patterns used for the decoration of such pairs of vessels permit one to recognize the introduction of true drinking sets,[44] which may have been

36. See Carinci and D'Agata 1989–1990, pp. 226–228, for MM I; Watrous 2001, pp. 193–196, for MM I–II evidence at Mount Juktas and Atsipades; Rehak and Younger 2001, pp. 433–434, with references, for Neopalatial settings in particular. For Kato Syme, see Kanta 1991, p. 482; Lebessi and Muhly 1990; Rehak and Younger 2001, p. 434. For caves, see Tyree 2001, esp. pp. 45–46.

37. *PM* II.2, pp. 627–659; Georgiou 1979; cf. Mochlos: Soles and Davaras 1996, pp. 192–193, pl. 54.

38. For evidence from Tylissos, Nirou Chani, and Sklavokambos, see Platon 1947, p. 636; Wiener 1984,

pp. 20–21; Gesell 1985, p. 135, no. 125, for Tylissos, house A; cf. Graham 1975, pp. 143–144; Marinatos 1986, pp. 37–39. See Gesell 1985, p. 31, no. 100; p. 118, no. 94, for evidence of ritual activity at Palaikastro involving ashes, animal bones, and cups; in general, Rehak and Younger 2001, p. 439.

39. Rupp and Tsipopoulou 1999, pp. 730–731; Rethemiotakis 2002, pp. 60–61 (buildings 1 and 3).

40. Koehl 1997; Carter 1997, pp. 86–89; Rehak and Younger 2001, pp. 401–402; cf. Betancourt and Marinatos 1997, p. 96, for Nirou Chani, room 12.

41. Betancourt 2001. For the "independent sanctuary" at Rousses, Chondros Viannou, with burned deposits and more than 400 conical cups (MM III–LM IA), see Platon 1962, pp. 145–146; Gesell 1985, p. 134, no. 122.

42. For Phaistos and Mallia, see Graham 1961. For Phaistos in particular, see the specialized sets and the evidence of burned bones from rooms LIII–LV, LXII: Levi 1976, pp. 91–110, and below, n. 49. In general, Day and Wilson 1998; Momigliano 2000, pp. 101–102.

43. MacGillivray 1998, p. 94.

44. MacGillivray 1987, pp. 273–276.

instruments of limited and exclusive convivial practices where hosts and guests were intended to be individually identified. In contrast, in the Prepalatial period, sets of drinking vessels (pouring vessels with matching cups) are not detectable.[45] This pattern might be an indication of completely different social strategies in convivial practices, which originally aimed at communal involvement rather than at restricted social exchange. In addition, cups, goblets, conical cups, and juglets—mostly unpainted or decorated with extremely simple, linear patterns that are often roughly executed—are common in the palaces as well as in sanctuaries and cultic installations, including tomb annexes, and may have been used during communal ritual meetings where attendance was unrestricted.[46]

Although plain juglets and conical cups are ubiquitous in the MM period, it is nonetheless possible to recognize a selective occurrence of this pottery in deposits characterized by huge numbers of vessels and associated with architectural and topographic settings suited to housing many people and central to activities involving intense social exchange, such as public meeting and administration. In room 25 of the palace at Phaistos, well known for its administrative documents, many conical cups and more than 400 juglets *(boccaletti)* were brought to light;[47] moreover, a large number of juglets, conical cups, bowls, bridge-spouted jars, and small storage jars *(stamnoi)*—mostly coarse and plain or painted with simple decorations— come from a deposit associated with the central court and belonging to the earliest phase of the palace.[48] In contrast, pottery assemblages consisting mostly of fine Kamares vessels come from inner residential or ceremonial rooms of the palace. Without excluding conical cups and juglets, these assemblages are made up mainly of cups and bridge-spouted jars, together with a range of shapes (e.g., large bowls and kraters or fruitstands) that characterize elite convivial occasions.[49] A similar opposition can be detected in funerary assemblages in which bridge-spouted jars and cups, as well as miniature storage jars, appear to have been included as customary belongings of the dead, while impressive numbers of pouring vessels such as juglets and pitchers *(oinochoai)*, together with conical cups, are primarily associated with annexes and ritual places outside the tombs, as exemplified by the funerary complex at Kamilari.[50]

In Neopalatial times, while deposits consisting of tens or hundreds of conical cups occur frequently in different settings and contexts,[51] elite consumption can perhaps be identified by the occurrence of pairs of identical vessels or finely decorated dinner sets (continuing a tradition that started with MM Kamares ware).[52] Pairs of vessels may have been used in

45. Momigliano 2000, p. 101.

46. See below. For large attendance at palatial Petras involving the use of conical cups, see Rupp and Tsipopoulou 1999.

47. Levi 1976, pp. 394–397; Carinci 1997, p. 321.

48. Levi 1976, pp. 271–274.

49. For exclusive sets at Phaistos, see, e.g., room LVII: Levi 1976, pp. 91–96; 524–535; cf. Carinci 1997.

50. Levi 1961–1962; Levi 1976, p. 725. For the ritual use of conical cups on the altar in the Recinto delle offerte, see Levi 1976, p. 740.

51. Cf. the Neopalatial tombs at Poros: Lebessi 1967; Dimopoulou-Rethemiotaki 1992, pp. 528–529; Dimopoulou 1999, p. 29. Cf. Alberti 2001 for the simpler furniture of some Protopalatial tombs.

52. For pairs of vessels, Rehak and

Younger 2001, p. 414. For sets, see, e.g., the group from Gypsades consisting of a jar, dish, and two cups, all decorated with reed patterns: *PM* II.2, pp. 549–550. Cf. the chalice/rhyton, two rhyton cups, jug, and cups from the LM IA Acropolis House at Knossos: Catling, Catling, and Smyth 1979, p. 45, fig. 31; see also Rutter, forthcoming, for Neopalatial Kommos.

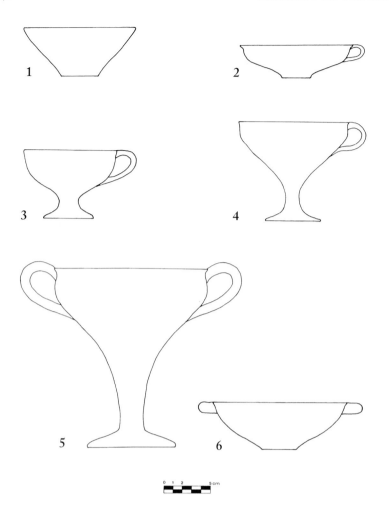

Figure 13. Common LM III fine
unpainted shapes: 1) conical cup;
2) shallow cup; 3) champagne cup;
4) low-stemmed goblet; 5) loop-
handled kylix; 6) shallow bowl.
After Hallager 1997a, p. 408, figs. A:2, 6, 8,
B:5; p. 409, fig. C:2, 3

rituals of hospitality to enhance reciprocal personal bonds. In addition,
some vessels may have been suited almost exclusively to ritual activities
involving liquids, like "communion cups," which are found in the thousands in sanctuaries such as Kato Syme, but rarely in settlements or tombs.[53]

In the Monopalatial, Final Palatial, and Postpalatial periods, differentiated sets of vessels may indicate similar multidimensional aspects of banqueting. In LM III, however, convivial occasions were possibly mobilized
by elite ideologies and attended by limited and exclusive sectors of the
population; this is suggested by the presence of so-called champagne cups
(Fig. 13:3), which probably served the same purpose as conical cups. During LM III we see an overlap in the use of these two shapes in purely
religious contexts, and champagne cups seem to have played the same roles
as conical cups in earlier times.[54] The two vessels, however, are not exclu-

53. Kanta 1991, p. 482; cf. Lebessi
1975, pp. 193–194, pls. 197, 198;
1986, p. 354, pl. 237. This evidence
stands in opposition to the record
on the mainland, which shows that
the same ceramic shapes, especially
kylikes, were used on many different

celebratory occasions, both secular and
cultic.
54. See, e.g., the champagne cups on
the altar in the Shrine of the Double
Axes at Knossos: *PM* II.1, pp. 335–
338; cf. other evidence from a shrine
detected by Popham (1970, p. 191). For

similarity of ritual and depositional
mode, compare the champagne cup
found inside a krater at LM III Milatos
(below, n. 104) with the conical cup
found inside a cooking pot at LM I
Poros (Lebessi 1967, p. 200).

sive; rather they are placed together within the same deposits, in particular within LM III tombs—further evidence of their similar and possibly complementary functions.[55] The champagne cups show special attention to manufacture and surface treatment, which may be indications that they imitate metal forms. Considered in conjunction with the shape of the bowl and the distinctive stemmed foot, such care may be interpreted as having highly symbolic significance. On this basis, we may infer that offering and consumption were included within the elite sphere of social exchange on religious occasions as well. The more selective mode of deposition of champagne cups, with a less-widespread distribution than that of conical cups and discard patterns that never involve such high numbers of vessels, suggests that, although plainware (Fig. 13) was used in similar ritual settings in LM III, it also had more selective social purposes than in earlier times, possibly as a consequence of the impact of Mycenaean social behavior on the islanders.

On the basis of our current state of knowledge and available publications, banqueting practices on mainland Greece appear not to have entailed as rich a variety of equipment or as elaborate a series of structures as is found on Crete.[56] The origins of convivial practices on the mainland appear to have been rooted in the private sphere of elite social values, which emphasized generosity and hospitality in the framework of direct, reciprocal transactions. That these transactions never involved large groups is suggested by the occurrence of pairs of identical serving vessels in both settlements and wealthy tombs toward the end of the Middle Helladic (MH) period.[57] With particular regard to funerary assemblages, the distribution of the earliest evidence matches the geography of the emerging Mycenaean palatial societies and reveals a purely sociopolitical dimension.[58] MH banquets served mainly as an assertion of vertical differentiation and as a materialization of the ideology of a limited segment of society.[59] Only in Late Helladic (LH) III did different settings for the banquets—both funerary and domestic—emerge. The archaeological record permits one to infer that, although the nature of the feasts was generally homogeneous and

55. Conical cups were placed in LM II–IIIA tombs, but they occur as isolated examples in comparison with earlier assemblages (Popham, Catling, and Catling 1974, p. 209, for Sellopoulo; Baxévani-Kouzioni and Markoulaki 1996, p. 653, figs. 14, 15; Platon 1957, p. 622, fig. 3, and Kanta 1980, pp. 58–68, for Episkopi, tomb B, with six examples; Halbherr 1901, pl. 11, and Kanta 1980, pp. 75–76, for Erganos). The champagne cup is typical of LM IIIA2–IIIB grave goods, and in turn appears singly or in small concentrations (cf. Andreadaki-Vlasaki 1997a, p. 500, for Chania; Tzedakis 1988 for Armenoi). Both types of vessel occur in assemblages dated late in Final

Palatial or early in Postpalatial times, such as at Phoinikia (Kanta 1980, pp. 24–25) and Gournes (Chatzidakis 1918, p. 75, fig. 19; pp. 83–85, fig. 32: tomb 5); for both vessel types in settlement deposits, possibly attesting ritual activities, see Ayia Triada, "strato VII, saggio III" (below, n. 105). On the appearance of champagne cups, see in general Betancourt 1985, p. 164; *Kommos* III, p. 132 ("goblet"); on the decrease of conical cups in LM IIIA coinciding with an increase of champagne cups, see Rehak and Younger 2001, p. 446. Champagne cups are one of the few LM III vessel shapes devoid of decoration (cf. Hallager 1997b, p. 23), apart from other apparently

Mycenaean-influenced vessels, such as goblets, kylikes, and shallow bowls (see Fig. 13:4–6). For the possible dependence on metal models, see Popham 1969, p. 301. On limited attendance on ritual occasions in LM III, see also Hamilakis 1998, pp. 125–126.

56. For differences in kitchenwares and cooking practices of the Minoans and Mycenaeans, see Borgna 1997a.

57. Nordquist 1999; 2002, esp. p. 132; see Wright, this volume, pp. 19, 21–23, tables 1–5.

58. See below, n. 72.

59. Cf. Cavanagh 1998, p. 111. For ideological materialization, see Demarrais, Castillo, and Earle 1996.

derived ultimately from the sponsoring activity of palatial authorities, the performances could have had different purposes and been promoted to facilitate communal participation on religious occasions.[60]

REQUISITES OF PARTICIPATION

Analysis of the Minoan evidence suggests that the manipulation, offering, and consumption of food and drink supported not only strategies of exclusion by the elite, but also substantial rites of aggregation and cohesion. In EM I, the vessel probably used for ritual drinking was the large chalice, whose shape suggests that it functioned directly as a communal drinking vessel rather than as a mixing or serving vessel.[61] As mentioned above, huge numbers of individual vessels imply large social gatherings from late Prepalatial into Neopalatial times. In the EM–MM Phourni cemetery at Archanes, more than 300 vessels, mostly conical cups, have been found in association with the paved area near the terrace in front of building 6 and near tholos B. From building 4 (LM IA), which has been interpreted as a workshop for wine production, 250 conical cups were brought to light.[62] At Ayia Triada, impressive numbers of conical cups, jugs, and plates come from recent excavations in the annexes (the so-called *camerette*) south of tholos A (MM I).[63]

At the beginning of the MM period, several deposits of many fine cups together with serving vessels in the palatial centers point to the importance of communal consumption, as do huge assemblages of conical cups—found in palatial clusters such as at Petras and Galatas and extra-palatial centers such as Nirou Chani—in later periods.[64] The LM Mansion at Kastelli Pediada has been interpreted as a focal place for libation and dining on the basis of large amounts of pottery.[65] Even when the quantity is insufficient to infer communal participation on a large scale, form, manufacturing technique, and surface treatment of the conical cups—extremely simple and highly standardized[66]—seem to underplay individual identity in favor of group affiliation (or exclusion), and to promote social solidarity and foster a sense of community.[67]

Pottery used for ritual meals at cultic feasts, such as at MM and LM Kato Syme, consists mostly of simple undecorated domestic ware. Kamares

60. Wright, forthcoming. The well-known evidence of Tsoungiza, for example, has been connected with the emergence of the palaces: Wright 1994, pp. 69–70. For palatial contexts in LH III, consider the discussion on the occurrence of large festivals involving offerings to the gods and distribution of goods: Piteros, Olivier, and Melena 1990; Killen 1994; Hägg 1995; Sacconi 2001. On Tsoungiza and other occasions of public feasting in Mycenaean palace societies, see the chapter by Dabney, Halstead, and Thomas, and other contributions to this volume.

61. Cf. Wilson and Day 2000, esp. p. 28. For the ceremonial function of the chalice, see also Haggis 1997, p. 298.

62. Sakellarakis and Sakellaraki 1972; Sakellarakis and Sapouna-Sakellaraki 1997, pp. 227–229, 396 (cf. also for building 17); Soles 1992, p. 145.

63. For the new data I thank Filippo Carinci, who is studying the pottery. See also La Rosa 2001, p. 224; for the context, Cultraro 2000. Cf. the huge number of conical cups detected in the context of ritual smashing in the cemetery of Drapanias Kisamou: *AR* 2000–2001, pp. 140–141.

64. Rethemiotakis 2002. For MM IA deposits at Knossos, see Momigliano 1991, esp. pp. 155 (Upper East Well), 176 (north quarter of the city), 220 (house B); also *PM* I, pp. 186–188, figs. 135, 136 (deposit under the West Court). For Galatas, see also Rethemiotakis 1999a, 1999b.

65. Rethemiotakis 1997.

66. Gillis 1990; Wiener 1984; Knappett 1999. For recent considerations on typological variabilities, see also Van de Moortel 2001, pp. 47–50, 60–68.

67. Cf. also Hamilakis 2002, pp. 196–197.

and other prestigious decorative styles occur rarely, which may mean that the prevailing ideology emphasized the community rather than individuality. Elaborate modes of discard of vessels and feasting remains (e.g., the rows of 200 ordered, upside-down conical cups in the pillar room of house B at Gypsades)[68] make it clear that ritual actions were encoded in a strict liturgy. Knowledge and control of these ritual practices were probably sources of power and authority, in contrast to single performances, which seldom constituted an important arena for social and political competition.[69]

The restricted access to banquets detected in some contexts, such as Prepalatial tombs and Neopalatial dwellings, has been explained by several scholars as the attempt by emerging elites to manipulate instruments of social power and political legitimization by favoring exclusion and selective affiliation.[70] This evidence, however, reflects secondary strategies aimed at mobilizing practices that originally focused on the sanction of unity and community belonging. As an example, the wide diffusion in EM IIB of the low-footed goblet or eggcup, a vessel suited to individual use in contrast with the earlier chalice,[71] might be viewed as a later attempt by elites to emphasize personal roles within the established ideology of ceremonial consumption.

Mainland Greece provides evidence for a different pattern. To the best of my knowledge, the earliest certain banqueting finds appear in the most complex MH tombs, mainly dating toward the end of the period, and are fully integrated into the framework of highly competitive struggles for political authority. The exclusive and restricted nature of Early Mycenaean feasts is best illustrated by tumuli in the Argolid and by shaft grave enclosures, as well as by examples of later tholoi and wealthy chamber tombs.[72] The occurrence of precious metal vessels suited to drinking appears to confirm that Mycenaean convivial habits favored exclusion rather than cohesion.[73] Restricted attendance at feasts sanctioned bonds with powerful ancestors, legitimized power, and strengthened ties among equals.[74]

Funerary evidence suggests a similar trend in Crete, and indicates Mycenaean influence in LM III. Such influence is particularly manifest in the funerary enclosure of Archanes, the burial place of a group of people who were separated from the rest of the community and shared common modes of aristocratic ritual consumption.[75] Toasting and ritual smashing of vessels at the tombs may also be connected with Mycenaean customs, as

68. Hogarth 1899–1900, p. 76; *PM* II.2, p. 548, fig. 348; Wiener 1984, p. 20. Cf. also Knossos, Southwest Pillar Crypt (*PM* IV.1, p. 3; Gesell 1985, p. 92, no. 39); Sklavokampos, room 8 (Marinatos 1939–1941, p. 74; Gesell 1985, p. 135, no. 123); Archanes (Sakellarakis and Sapouna-Sakellaraki 1997, pp. 227–228).

69. Cf. Moody 1987, p. 240.

70. For Prepalatial tombs, see Branigan 1993, p. 78; for Neopalatial elites, Hamilakis 1999; Moody 1987; cf. also Wilson and Day 1999, esp. p. 43; Wilson and Day 2000, p. 62.

71. Wilson and Day 1999; 2000, p. 28; cf. Day and Wilson 2002, pp. 151–152. For the chalice, see above, n. 61.

72. See, e.g., the funerary evidence at Mycenae, Prosymna, Asine, Dendra, Argos, Kokla, and Menidi: cf. Demakopoulou 1990; Kontorli-Papadopoulou 1995, pp. 118–120; Cavanagh 1998, pp. 106–107; Hamilakis 1998, pp. 119–120; Cavanagh and Mee 1998, pp. 111–112; Wright, forthcoming. For MH rites, see Nordquist 1990; cf. Kilian-Dirlmeier 1995, pp. 49–52; *Alt-Ägina* IV.3, pp. 120–122; Voutsaki

1998, p. 44. In general on the shaft graves: Dickinson 1977 (e.g., pp. 43, 47); Kilian-Dirlmeier 1986; Graziadio 1988, p. 346; 1991, p. 405; cf. Cavanagh and Mee 1998, pp. 50–51.

73. For detailed discussion of metal vessels, see Wright, this volume.

74. Cf. Dabney and Wright 1990.

75. Kallitsaki 1997; in general on the problem of warrior graves and tombs with bronzes in Crete, see Matthäus 1983; Kilian-Dirlmeier 1985; Haskell 1989, pp. 102–106; for further bibliography, see Löwe 1996.

several groups of broken kylikes near LH/LM III tombs indicate.[76] Such practices could be a sign of the celebration of communal banquets or drinking at funerals. To confirm such a hypothesis we should be able to identify ceramic sets that are separate from the personal furniture of the dead and were used for preparation and consumption of funeral meals or drinks. Notwithstanding the ambiguous state of documentation and publication of Mycenaean funerary assemblages, it is notable that the number of vessels reported from Mycenaean tombs is never as large as that of vessels detected in the EM, MM, and LM cemeteries of Crete. The most remarkable deposit, chamber tomb 13 at Dendra, consists of 200 sherds belonging to 40 goblets, which pales in comparison with the hundreds of vessels recorded from some Cretan assemblages.[77] Furthermore, the little Mycenaean evidence that can be considered reliable as an indication of communal rites practiced near tombs comes from inside single funerary complexes and tombs, that is, in the dromoi and near the *stomia* of the tholoi and inside the tumuli and funerary enclosures.[78] Such installations, whether or not they served to celebrate convivial feasts, do not appear to have been intended for a gathering of the whole community; rather, by promoting exclusion, they would have stressed links and solidarity among the few attendees who were close to the families and the households of the eminent dead.

The attendance of commoners at elite celebrations, which is also reasonably supposed to have been encouraged by the dominant ideology, may have been channeled toward other behaviors and practices. When we consider both the importance of processions, as recently detected in the Mycenaean religious performances, and the setting of important Mycenaean funerary and celebratory monuments, we might propose that interaction between elites and commoners in order to sponsor elite activities and enterprises could have taken place during funerary processions as well.[79] Only within the framework of the sponsorship and organization of the LH III palaces did mainland feasts become instruments of social control by promoting inclusive ideological strategies and behavior, including possibly open participation and the direct involvement of commoners.[80]

76. In Crete, see, e.g., Kamilari: Novaro 1999, p. 151, n. 7; p. 157, figs. 1, 2; Poros: Lebessi 1967, p. 204, pl. 181; Armenoi: Tzedakis 1988, p. 513; Hamilakis 1998, p. 122; Gournes: Chatzidakis 1918, pp. 75–77, figs. 19, 21. In the cases of Armenoi and Gournes, we have a thorough picture of the ritual meal, which seems to have been not only symbolically represented, but actually consumed, as the articulation of vessel shapes and other remains indicate.

77. See Åström 1977, p. 72; cf. the evidence recorded at Mycenae by Wace (1932, p. 131; p. 38 for Kalkani, tomb 544; and p. 35 for tomb 523, with a

niche excavated near the *stomion*). For the Early Mycenaean period, see Cavanagh and Mee 1998, p. 55; cf. Åström 1987, p. 215; Wilkie 1987; and summary in *AR* 1981–1983, p. 26, for Kokla.

78. Cavanagh and Mee 1998, p. 54, for evidence of burned layers and ashes near the *stomia* of tholoi; cf. also p. 72; Protonotariou-Deilaki 1990, p. 82, for Kazarma; Persson 1942, pp. 56–59, for tombs 9–10 at Dendra. For special structures, see Protonotariou-Deilaki 1990, p. 82 (Argos A and C), and recently Hielte-Stavropoulou 2001.

79. See now Vikatou 2001. On the

lack of large meeting places in Mycenaean urban settings, see Cavanagh 2001; for the limited space within religious buildings, cf. Albers 2001, pp. 136–138. See in particular Hägg 2001, on processions, and Wright 1987, on the setting of Mycenaean funerary monuments.

80. Official communal ceremonies could have remained restricted and exclusive, however, as seems to be indicated by selected ritual instruments, including a few miniature vessels, in association with evidence for communal banqueting at Pylos: Isaakidou et al. 2002, p. 90.

NATURE AND FUNCTION OF FEASTING

In the Minoan world the same ideological strategy, aimed at strengthening solidarity and reducing members to anonymous, faceless participants, underlined the huge distance of the community from the center of power. For example, at Ayia Triada stone chalices appear to have been used in the rooms belonging to the Quartiere signorile di nord-ovest, where, according to Robert Koehl, the rites of the *andreion* were performed, while hundreds of conical cups, which were probably involved in the same rites of ritual consumption, were found in the nearby storeroom.[81] The technical and morphological standardization of these vessels, devoid of stylistic elaboration, and the difference in the raw material between the chalices and the cups are clear signs of the unlikelihood of interaction between elites, at the focal center of the rite, and the public, which may have watched or participated but only as anonymous actors. A similar inference can be drawn at Mallia, house Za, where the furniture of ceremonial hall 5, together with finds from the nearby storerooms, permits one to associate a single stone rhyton with hundreds of conical cups.[82]

In Minoan ritual, the distance between the common populace and the elites was metaphorically expressed in iconographic representations such as the genii and the enthroned deity (which appear, for example, on the well-known ring from Tiryns).[83] Among examples of this iconographic type that show serving and pouring activities, the Kamilari clay model best illustrates these activities as tasks of subordinates or nonhuman beings, excluded from social exchange.[84] It is clear that although elite/nonelite interaction during the ritual performances was minimal, the center derived its authority from the community by asserting its unity and cohesion.

In contrast to practices associated with Minoan feasts, service and distribution in Mycenaean feasts had a completely different status. Originally the activities were restricted to the elite stratum, and even though feasting seems to have expanded to include most, if not all, of the population, the "symposiastic" structure of the feast continued to be central to its practice. In such a setting, the central person, as a kind of *primus inter pares*, interacted dramatically with the participants by appointing rights of attendance and status.

The Mycenaean krater, the most meaningful symbol of drink distribution, is a monumental version—again a kind of *primus inter pares*—of the individual drinking vessel, as the typological development of its form during LH III clearly indicates. In the earliest LH III phases, when the drinking set is dominated by goblets and kylikes, the stemmed krater with vertical handles, similar to a large goblet, is the vessel used for holding and distributing wine. From late LH IIIB onward, as the kylix is gradually replaced by the deep bowl, the krater, now plain and with horizontal handles, is transformed into a huge bowl as well.[85] Another important vessel used for distribution is the dipper,[86] a typical Mycenaean form also found in LM III contexts. Formerly in Crete, the dipper had appeared exclusively as coarse kitchenware and may have been used only for cooking.[87] The importance of distribution in the Mycenaean banquet seems therefore to express the need of the sponsors to assert their authority by demonstrating a

81. Halbherr, Stefani, and Banti 1980, pp. 63, 84–85, 112, figs. 32, 33. For the interpretation as an *andreion*, see Koehl 1997 and above, n. 40. For the possible cultic role of Magazzino 15 (with two central pillars), see Militello 2001, p. 161.

82. Demargne and Gallet de Santerre 1953, pp. 69–72.

83. Sakellariou 1964, pp. 202–203, no. 179 (see also Wright, this volume, p. 45, fig. 16). For the relevance to wine-drinking rituals, cf. Rehak and Younger 2001, p. 430.

84. Levi 1961–1962; Novaro 1999; Lefèvre-Novaro 2001.

85. See Furumark shapes (FS) 9 and 255 for LH IIIA (e.g., Mountjoy 1986, pp. 60, 65, figs. 70, 75) and FS 281, 284, and 305 for IIIB (Mountjoy 1986, pp. 116–119, figs. 142, 143, 146).

86. Mountjoy 1986, pp. 87, 116 (FS 236).

87. See, e.g., Borgna 1997a, p. 197, fig. 7 (LM III).

power of attraction throughout the process of negotiating identity and status within a selected group of participants.

Bell-kraters were not as widely imitated in LM Crete, nor as often imported, as kylikes, goblets, and bowls. At the Unexplored Mansion at Knossos, for instance, kraters are not represented.[88] In contrast, the amphoroid krater, clearly distinguished from individual drinking vessels by its shape, asserts a distance between the host and the commoners and therefore would have been accepted in the LM III assemblages.

In the Minoan world, from the EM period onward, preparation and manipulation were apparently more relevant activities than consumption in the ideology of communal feasts, as the huge variety of kitchen instruments and the elaboration of pouring vessels, with great emphasis on spouts, demonstrate.[89] Mobilization of labor for storing and processing of food was much more important than consumption in the Cretan ideology of power relationships.[90] The stylistic elaboration and regulation of Mycenaean kylikes and drinking vessels, in contrast, suggest that consumption was subject to ritual codes and constituted an important social arena for the negotiation of power and status.[91]

When the Cretan elites, in the transformative LM social framework, began to acquire and emphasize habits of conspicuous consumption in competitive relationships among emerging groups, they devoted much more care than previously to stylistic elaboration of drinking sets, often decorated according to the dynamics of group identity and affiliation.[92] For this purpose, Cretan elites borrowed from the Mycenaean world vessels such as the kylix, goblet, bowl, and krater in order to emphasize the moment of consumption. From LM II onward, the pottery used in commensal politics and convivial ceremonies is finely executed and generally decorated, thereby revealing the strategies of elite groups.

From the evidence reviewed here, the differences between Minoan and Mycenaean feasting practices confirm what has long been known from other fields of research, namely, that the social structure of Cretan communities was different from that of mainland communities from the Early Bronze Age onward. In Crete, banqueting seems to have represented roles and values peculiar to the political strategies of so-called corporate societies or group-oriented chiefdoms.[93] Power was structured and controlled within the limits set by the prevailing corporate cognitive code, which considered individuals as anonymous, and embodied principles of community solidarity and unity. Open communal occasions that emphasized these principles, however, were only one type of Minoan feast; other, more exclusive, elite celebrations emphasized different strategies of social control. In terms of the manipulation of food and drink, Cretan society emerges as a very complex civilization, provided with a variety of banqueting practices that were multidimensional and largely dependent on communal ideologies, and thus subject to structured behavior and rules. By contrast, banqueting in the Mycenaean world was originally a powerful competitive instrument, one peculiar to small-scale network communities and enhanced by exclusionary power strategies. According to a recent dual-processual theory of social evolution, the political actors of exclusionary polities developed a political system around their monopoly of sources of power based

88. Popham 1984. For the Mycenaean origin of the Ephyrean goblet, conical bowl, kylix, and krater, see Niemeier 1985, pp. 195–197; Betancourt 1985, p. 154; Popham 1988, p. 222; Haskell 1997, p. 188. French (1997) argues that the Cretans imported the social function of the goblet and not merely the shape.

89. Cf. Borgna 1997a, p. 205.

90. Consider the important relationships between ritual activity and storage as detected in Minoan architecture: Hitchcock 2000, pp. 145–156.

91. Cf. Dabney 1997.

92. See above, n. 52; for the stylistic elaboration of drinking vessels from LM I onward, see the documentation in Betancourt 1985, p. 149, and passim.

93. Blanton et al. 1996; Feinman 2000. For group-oriented chiefdoms, cf. Renfrew 1974; Drennan 1991, p. 284, in particular for the trajectory from group-oriented chiefdoms to early states. For relevant ideological strategies, see also Haggis 1999, pp. 78, 81; for recent discussion on corporate societies and Minoan Crete, see Schoep 2002; Hamilakis 2002.

on a network of exchange relations, in which the individual dimension never faded. In this kind of network strategy, feasts occur frequently and constitute an active and dynamic means of social exclusion and attainment of power.[94]

LH/LM III ELITE STRATEGIES

In LH IIIA–B Greece, banquets and feasts, though not completely restricted to the palaces, were primarily regulated, sponsored, and organized by the central authorities. As a powerful instrument for status negotiation, banqueting may have been mobilized by the palatial elites and, for the local population, could have been limited mainly to the private sphere of funerals, where social bonds were reproduced in a highly symbolic and idealized manner and would not affect the concrete balance of power relationships.[95] In LH IIIB, the central phase of the Mycenaean palatial age, feasts were dramatically controlled and perhaps even opposed by the central authorities in the funerary sphere as well, as emerges from a brief survey of grave goods.[96]

Notwithstanding the imbalance of documentation, intriguing differences between mainland Greek and Cretan mortuary practices during LH/LM III can be pointed out. Generally speaking, apart from the rich drinking and serving metalware found in wealthy Early Mycenaean tombs, grave goods that may be less ambiguously interpreted as direct belongings of the dead do not have a clear connection with feasts or banquets: the goods include primarily closed vessels, with only a few isolated goblets or kylikes, while the krater is seldom found. Representation of the dead as a host or officiator of banquets on a large scale seems to have been exclusively channeled through the disposal of precious metal vessels into selected early LH III tombs. Metalware assemblages, including a wide range of articulated shapes and functions suited to preparing, cooking, serving, mixing, and distributing, constitute the best evidence for detecting ritualized conviviality in the Mycenaean world,[97] and within the tombs they establish a direct link with the palatial furniture for official feasts, as corroborated by Linear B documents.[98] As confirmation, the rare deposits of

94. Blanton et al. 1996; cf. Galaty and Parkinson 1999. It is possible that competitive feasts, at the transition from the MH period to the Mycenaean world, were expressions of "entrepreneurial" or "empowering" activities (Dietler 1996, pp. 92–96; 2001, pp. 76–77). Although feasts on the mainland possibly developed into more complex forms of banqueting according to diacritical patterns of conviviality, they never reached the elite level of banqueting of Minoan Crete. On the occurrence of highly competitive feasts and general alliance-building activities within societies provided with network

strategies of political power, see Junker 2001, p. 282.

95. The shift of energy investment from secular architecture (the megaron) to burial monuments (the large tholos) at Nichoria at the beginning of the palatial age may be considered a relevant indication; see Shelmerdine 1999, p. 559, and references.

96. See Voutsaki 1995, p. 59; 1999, pp. 112–113; Cavanagh and Mee 1998, p. 126. For funerals as places where "rank and status are actively contested," see Parker Pearson 2002, pp. 84–85. It seems to be meaningful that the architectural structures for possible commu-

nal celebrations of single families and *oikoi*, such as altars (above, n. 78), date almost exclusively to the Early Mycenaean period.

97. Matthäus 1980, pp. 17–53; cf. Darcque 1987, pp. 198–200.

98. See, e.g., the Ta tablets, recently discussed by Killen (1998) and Palaima (2000); also Speciale 1999. Cf. Ventris and Chadwick 1956, pp. 332–346, esp. pp. 325–326. We may suppose that similar rich assemblages were placed in some LH IIIA2–IIIB wealthy tombs as well, such as the tholoi at Mycenae.

pottery recognizable as drinking sets within early LH III tombs generally consist of plain unpainted or "tinned" fine vessels, intended to imitate metalware and usually placed together within special settings of the tombs, such as shafts or niches, as are metal vessels.[99] In the Mycenaean world the palatial ideology seems therefore to have mobilized communal feasting activities by channeling convivial practices through manners and expressions peculiar to "diacritical" palatial feasts.[100]

The shifting of social practices such as banqueting from the secular arena of settlements to the private sphere of funerals—itself evidence of Mycenaean influence—is responsible for the emergence of wealthy and warrior graves with bronzes in the Mycenaean, or Monopalatial, period at Knossos and, slightly later, at Phaistos, Archanes, Rethymnon, and Chania.[101] This shift may represent an attempt to restrict convivial practices to a certain social component. The considerable decrease in wine consumption in LM III Crete is explained by Yannis Hamilakis as an outcome of the strict control and centralization of the Mycenaean administration.[102] Indeed, convivial practices and ritual meals are attested at an official level by remains of sacrifices and in depictions, in particular in frescoes, such as those from Ayia Triada—highlighting the lyre player together with the representation of stags—and possibly at Archanes.[103] In contrast to the Mycenaean evidence, in some less distinguished, advanced LM III graves, drinking activities are represented not by metalware assemblages but by elaborate, decorated ceramic dinner sets, including kraters, goblets, kylikes, deep bowls, cups, and dippers—vessel shapes that are also found in contemporary settlements.[104] From such evidence, banqueting can be inferred to have been more widely practiced and less strictly controlled than on the mainland, and definitely independent of a diacritical pattern of exclusivity.

In Cretan communities, in effect, even in the Monopalatial phase, and especially in LM IIIA2–B, it is quite probable that habits of commensal politics were never completely limited to the private sphere of funerary feasts, and banquets continued to be celebrated in aristocratic and secular dwellings. Several sites provide evidence in support of this hypothesis. At Ayia Triada, the ritualization of convivial practices could have served to stress important secular events as well, such as the foundation of imposing

99. Cf. the ceramic assemblage from shaft II of tomb 10 at Dendra: Persson 1942, p. 59 (see also Wright, this volume, p. 25, fig. 5). In Crete, cf. Zapher Papoura, pit-graves 66 and 67 (Evans 1906, pp. 71–74). For metal sets in Crete, see in particular the Tomb of the Tripod Hearth and the Chieftain's Grave at Zapher Papoura (Evans 1906, pp. 34–35, 51–59).

100. Dietler 1996, esp. p. 106.

101. For Phaistos and Kalyvia: Savignoni 1904; *Creta antica*, pp. 136–137; Archanes: Kallitsaki 1997; Rethymnon: Markoulaki and Baxévani-

Kouzioni 1997 (Pangalochori); Papadopoulou 1997 (Armenoi); Chania: Andreadaki-Vlasaki 1997a. For warrior graves, see above, n. 75.

102. Hamilakis 1999, esp. p. 48.

103. For the frescoes, recently published from the settlement, see *Haghia Triada* I, pp. 283–308. Although of uncertain provenance, the evidence relevant to sacrifice and feasting could belong to the megaron; in this case, it would fit the palatial etiquette of ritual consumption and would be related to the ideological expressions of palatial elites. A good comparison is

the Campstool Fresco from Knossos: Cameron 1987; Immerwahr 1990, pp. 84, 176, Kn no. 26; Wright 1995a. For the sarcophagus, La Rosa 1999; for sacrifice at Archanes, Sakellarakis 1970; for literature on the subject, Borgna 1999b, p. 201.

104. Cf. Tzedakis 1988, p. 513 (Armenoi, but evidence mainly from dromoi); Phoinikia: Kanta 1980, pp. 24–25; Gournes, tomb 2: Chatzidakis 1918, pp. 76–77 (dromos); Stylos: Kanta 1980, p. 235; Milatos: Evans 1906, pp. 93–98; Kanta 1980, pp. 125–126, figs. 52, 53.

buildings.[105] A further example is a ceramic assemblage consisting of a kylix, stemmed conical bowl or small krater, champagne cup, small jug, two shallow cups, and many conical cups found in room D 1 at Chondros Viannou; the room had a central pillar and was possibly a banqueting hall.[106] In room II 2 of Quartier Nu at Mallia, sets of kylikes, champagne cups, and *kalathoi* were found, together with a stirrup jar, amphora, and krater; in a pit deposit from the same area were fragments belonging to kylikes, champagne cups, deep bowls, cups, a stirrup jar, other jars, and cooking pots mixed with ashes and coals, as well as bronze items such as a double-axe, possibly used for sacrifice.[107] Such evidence might be related to ritual celebrations outside the control of the central authority, as is clearer in the case of the LM IIIB–C assemblages at Phaistos.

From the record outlined above, a complex pattern of feasting and ceremonial authority, in multiple locations and with multiple purposes, is seen not only in the earlier palatial periods, but also in Final Palatial Crete. This pattern may be explained as a mark of local heritage, though the intrinsic nature and purposes of elite banquets would have been, at that time, deeply modified by Mycenaean interaction. The secular use of competitive feasts within extrapalatial social practices might already have gained force in Crete in LM II–IIIA1, thanks to both the strong Mycenaean influence and the stability and power of Cretan elites, while only after the collapse of central powers did banqueting become (possibly throughout the Aegean) a widespread occasion for ideological and political mobilization and struggle, important in creating power relationships in the new political arena of unstable systems.

CONCLUSIONS

Feasting activities in Minoan Crete were more suited than those of mainland Greece to facilitating community solidarity through widespread attendance. At the same time, toward the end of the Late Bronze Age, outside palatial contexts they became—earlier and more easily than on the mainland, where political banquets were mainly a matter of palatial control—strategic instruments of political dialogue in the hands of different aristocratic groups with common symbols and ideologies. The elite dwellings and settlements would have already borrowed from the mainland the language of commensal competitive politics during the Mycenaean domination of Crete beginning early in LM II–IIIA, when the practices

105. In the trench cut for the foundation of the stoa ("saggio III, strato VII"), a deposit of tableware together with bones and burned remains was found that was interpreted by the excavators as the remains of a meal consumed by the builders (La Rosa 1980, pp. 337–338, fig. 47; 1986, pp. 53–55, fig. 5). For evidence of a pottery deposit in association with

building foundations from the transition between the Protopalatial and Neopalatial periods, see La Rosa 1980, pp. 302–306, figs. 10–12.

106. Platon 1997, pp. 362–363, 370–371.

107. Farnoux 1990; Driessen and Farnoux 1992, 1994; Farnoux 1997, p. 267.

of conspicuous consumption of wine and food gradually became a power-ful means of competition and exclusion outside the control of the palatial authorities.[108]

In LM IIIC Phaistos, as discussed above, we can attribute to the local cultural tradition the multidimensional and multipurpose occurrence of feasting as well as the important role played by food processing on ritual occasions. Nonetheless, we can also perceive a strong Mycenaean cultural component at work in highly competitive convivial occasions, the function of which was to create hierarchical relationships and dependencies and legitimize the status quo.

The complex variety in place, nature, and function of Cretan convivial ceremonies seems detectable even in Postpalatial and Dark Age Crete. As emerges from the framework proposed by Alexander Mazarakis Ainian,[109] the layout of several Subminoan and Protogeometric settlements points to a complex variety of independent religious and secular buildings, as at Kavousi, Karphi, and possibly Kephala Vasilikis and Chalasmenos, where these changes are already apparent in LM IIIC.[110] Ritual equipment, in-cluding artifacts connected with feasting, appears to differ according to cultic or political and social functions,[111] thus demonstrating that ceremo-nial performances and display were encoded in a structured and shared ideology. Furthermore, within some settlements ceremonial evidence de-rives from several houses, possibly belonging to different, albeit equal, emerging social groups. A multicentered pattern of political authority is suggested by the topographically marginal location of some aristocratic buildings, which had to contend with other buildings for a central social position—illustrated, for example, by the Geometric house at Phaistos, recently interpreted as a kind of *andreion*.[112] The framework of Dark Age settlements on the mainland is completely different and much simpler, as demonstrated by the case of Nichoria. There, a single major building, pos-sibly having both religious and political functions, rose above the other undifferentiated houses at the beginning of the Dark Age period and gradu-ally increased in importance and authority.[113]

On the subject of banquets the Homeric world offers fruitful com-parisons to the Cretan evidence. Different types of banquets existed in discrete spheres of social exchange and served distinct strategies of power mobilization, involving both the maintenance of the status quo and com-petition for definition of status.[114] Comparison with the Homeric world is valid if we consider that Postpalatial and Dark Age societies, on the one hand, and Homeric society, on the other, are all characterized by social groups founded on aggregations of male warriors, and supporting domi-

108. For the importance of local elites in Late Bronze Age Crete, see, e.g., Shelmerdine 1999, p. 564. For the mobilization of power by local elites in Neopalatial Crete, cf. Christakis 1999.

109. Mazarakis Ainian 1997.

110. For Kavousi and Karphi in particular, see Mazarakis Ainian 1997, pp. 208–210, 218–220; Nowicki 2000,

pp. 97–99, 157–164; on Vronda, Kavousi, see also Day 1997. On the cultic complex at Kephala Vasilikis, including an articulated cluster of rooms, each related to different func-tions, see Eliopoulos 1998; on Chalas-menos, see Tsipopoulou 2001.

111. In general, see Rehak and Younger 2001, pp. 460–461.

112. Mazarakis Ainian 1997, pp. 228–229, 273; cf. Cucuzza 1998; 2000, pp. 298–303.

113. Mazarakis Ainian 1997, p. 74; Coulson 1983, p. 18; McDonald and Coulson 1983, p. 328.

114. See esp. van Wees 1995; Raaflaub 1997, p. 643; Sherratt, this volume.

nant individuals.[115] These individuals, the "big men" or chiefs, employed the practice of holding communal banquets as a means of attracting consent, maintaining cohesion, forming alliances, or striving for dominance among equal individuals or *oikoi*. At Phaistos, as I stated above, only increased field research will determine whether the banquets held on the summit of the Acropoli Mediana and in the multiroomed building of the Casa a ovest del Piazzale I represented expressions of confrontation and competition among homogeneous social elements or, by serving different social and political purposes, were signs of an articulated system within a structured and complex community such as we find later in the Homeric world.

In a number of Cretan settlements dating to the transition between the Bronze Age and the Iron Age, evidence for similar feasting practices has been recognized underneath later temples and sanctuaries as well as public and political buildings. On the one hand, the evidence from LM III Prinias makes it especially clear that the sites occupied by Archaic temples had sometimes been, in LM III, open areas devoted to activities of ritual consumption.[116] The Acropoli Mediana at Phaistos could be relevant in this regard, particularly given hints of the existence of an Archaic temple on the top of the hill.[117] On the other hand, rulers' dwellings in Dark Age and Geometric Crete may have carried on roles and functions of previous buildings, including the custom of communal feasting. The so-called aristocratic *andreion* of Geometric Phaistos could be a direct successor of the elite LM IIIC buildings or *oikoi* located in the nearby area, such as the Casa a ovest.

In closing, I stress again the importance of using pottery style to monitor social and ideological relationships within the framework of use and circulation of drinking vessels for ritual consumption. On the basis of the stylistic elaboration of ceramic sets, it is possible to follow the political development of Cretan societies to the end of the Bronze Age and into the beginning of the Iron Age. The stylistic display and decoration of LM IIIC vessels suitable for distribution (kraters) and individual consumption (deep bowls) reflect the openness of the communities and the strong interaction between givers and receivers within the social arena of feasts, in which intense social and ideological exchanges took place in order to create and modify social relationships. In later contexts, and more clearly during the Middle Protogeometric period, stylistic limitation and exclusion especially affected the minor vessels used for individual consumption. Thus deep bowls and cups are now completely coated or dipped, while the huge kraters, symbols of central distribution, are highly decorated.[118] Such transformation of the drinking sets could be a consequence of both a major change in feasting habits—no longer involving competition in order to attract and recruit followers and retainers—and a political transition toward more fixed and structured social organizations.[119]

115. Rowlands 1980, p. 21; Mazarakis Ainian 1997, pp. 358–372; Donlan and Thomas 1993; Donlan 1985, 1989, 1994, 1997a, 1997b.

116. Pernier 1914, pp. 25–29, 73, fig. 40 (top left); Mazarakis Ainian 1997, pp. 224–226, esp. p. 226; on recent research, Palermo 1999. For deposits with ashes, animal bones, and pottery, see the recent evidence from refuge settlements such as Pefki Kastellopoulo and Arvi Fortetsa: Nowicki 1994, pp. 250–253; Nowicki 1996, p. 264; 2000, p. 239.

117. La Rosa 1997.

118. For instance at Knossos, North Cemetery: Coldstream and Catling 1996, vol. 1, pp. 7–8, 239–253 (tombs E, F), 285; vol. 2, pp. 368, 378; cf. Popham 1992 for Subminoan finds. For Protogeometric "crockery for a funerary symposium," including a decorated krater and monochrome skyphoi: Coldstream 2002, pp. 215–216, pls. 13 (6.13), 14 (6.16–18). For the meaningful shift at Protogeometric Kavousi, see Gesell, Day, and Coulson 1995. See also D'Agata 1999, pp. 197–204, for monochrome deep bowls in settlement assemblages from LM IIIC (late) onward.

119. Cf., e.g., Mazarakis Ainian 1997, p. 358.

REFERENCES

Albers, G. 2001. "Rethinking Mycenaean Sanctuaries," in Laffineur and
Hägg 2001, pp. 131–141.

Alberti, L. 2001. "Costumi funerari
mediominoici a Cnosso: La necropoli di Mavro Spileo," *SMEA* 43,
pp. 163–187.

Alt-Ägina IV.3 = I. Kilian-Dirlmeier,
*Das mittelbronzezeitliche Schachtgrab
von Ägina,* Mainz 1997.

Andreadaki-Vlasaki, M. 1997a. "La
nécropole du Minoen Récent III de
la ville de La Canée," in Driessen
and Farnoux 1997, pp. 487–509.

———. 1997b. "Πόλη Χανιών: Οικό-
πεδο Ν. Κανιαμού," *ArchDelt* 47,
Β΄2 (1992), pp. 566–574.

———. 2002. "Are We Approaching
the Minoan Palace of Khania?" in
Driessen, Schoep, and Laffineur
2002, pp. 157–166.

Åström, P. 1977. *The Cuirass Tomb
and Other Finds at Dendra* 1: *The
Chamber Tombs* (*SIMA* 4), Göteborg.

———. 1987. "Intentional Destruction
of Grave Goods," in Laffineur 1987,
pp. 213–217.

Baxévani-Kouzioni, K., and S. Markoulaki. 1996. "Une tombe à chambre
MR III à Pankalochori (nome de
Réthymnon)," *BCH* 120, pp. 641–
703.

Betancourt, P. P. 1985. *The History of
Minoan Pottery,* Princeton.

———. 2001. "The Household Shrine
in the House of the Rhyta at
Pseira," in Laffineur and Hägg
2001, pp. 145–149.

Betancourt, P. P., V. Karageorghis,
R. Laffineur, and W.-D. Niemeier,
eds. 1999. *Meletemata: Studies in
Aegean Archaeology Presented to
Malcolm H. Wiener as He Enters His
65th Year* (*Aegaeum* 20), Liège.

Betancourt, P. P., and N. Marinatos.
1997. "The Minoan Villa," in
*The Function of the "Minoan
Villa." Proceedings of the Eighth
International Symposium at the
Swedish Institute at Athens* (*SkrAth*
4°, 35), ed. R. Hägg, Stockholm,
pp. 91–98.

Blanton, R. E., G. M. Feinman, S. A.
Kowalewski, and P. N. Peregrine.

1996. "A Dual-Processual Theory
for the Evolution of Mesoamerican
Civilization," *CurrAnthr* 37, pp. 1–14.

Borgna, E. 1997a. "Kitchen-Ware from
LM IIIC Phaistos: Cooking Traditions and Ritual Activities in LBA
Cretan Societies," *SMEA* 39,
pp. 189–217.

———. 1997b. "Some Observations
on Deep Bowls and Kraters from
the 'Acropoli Mediana' at Phaistos,"
in Hallager and Hallager 1997,
pp. 273–298.

———. 1999a. "Central Crete and
the Mycenaeans at the Close of the
Late Bronze Age: The Evidence of
the 'Acropoli Mediana' at Phaistos,"
in *Η περιφέρεια του μυκηναικού
κόσμου. Α΄ Διεθνές Διεπιστημονικό
Συμπόσιο, Λαμία,* Lamia, pp. 353–
370.

———. 1999b. "Circolazione e uso
della ceramica nello scambio cerimoniale tra mondo miceneo palaziale e Creta tardominoica: La prospettiva di Festòs nel TM III," in
La Rosa, Palermo, and Vagnetti
1999, pp. 199–205.

———. 2000. "Food Preparation and
Ritual Activity in LM IIIC Crete,"
in *Πεπραγμένα Η΄ Διεθνούς Κρητολογικού Συνεδρίου,* Herakleion,
pp. 147–159.

———. 2001. "Il periodo TM IIIB/C:
La Casa a ovest del Piazzale I," in
*I cento anni dello scavo di Festòs:
Giornate Lincee,* Rome, pp. 273–298.

———. 2003a. *Il complesso di ceramica
TM III dell'Acropoli Mediana di
Festòs (scavi 1955)* (Studi di archeo-
logia cretese 3), Catania.

———. 2003b. "Settlement Patterns,
Exchange Systems, and Sources of
Power in Crete at the End of the
Late Bronze Age," *SMEA* 45,
pp. 153–183.

———. Forthcoming. "Social Meanings of Drink and Food Consumption at LM IIIC Phaistos," in Halstead and Barrett, forthcoming.

Branigan, K. 1970a. *The Foundations of
Palatial Crete in the Early Bronze
Age,* New York.

———. 1970b. *The Tombs of Mesara: A
Study of Funerary Architecture and*

Ritual in Southern Crete, 2800–1700 B.C., London.

———. 1993. *Dancing with Death: Life and Death in Southern Crete, c. 3000–2000 B.C.*, Amsterdam.

———, ed. 1998a. *Cemetery and Society in the Aegean Bronze Age* (Sheffield Studies in Aegean Archaeology 1), Sheffield.

———. 1998b. "The Nearness of You: Proximity and Distance in Early Minoan Funerary Behaviour," in Branigan 1998a, pp. 13–26.

Cameron, M. A. S. 1987. "The 'Palatial' Thematic System in the Knossos Murals: Last Notes on Knossos Frescoes," in Hägg and Marinatos 1987, pp. 321–328.

Carinci, F. M. 1997. "Pottery Workshops at Phaestos and Haghia Triada in the Protopalatial Period," in Laffineur and Betancourt 1997, pp. 317–322.

———. Forthcoming. "Circulation Patterns and Functions of the South West Wing of the First Palace at Phaistos," in *Θ΄ Διεθνές Κρητολογικό Συνέδριο*, Herakleion.

Carinci, F. M., and A.-L. D'Agata. 1989–1990. "Aspetti dell'attività cultuale a Creta nel III e nel II millennio," *ScAnt* 3–4, pp. 221–242.

Carter, J. B. 1997. "*Thyasos* and *Marzeah*: Ancestor Cult in the Age of Homer," in *New Light on a Dark Age: Exploring the Culture of Geometric Greece*, ed. S. Langdon, Columbia, Mo., pp. 72–112.

Catling, E. A., H. W. Catling, and D. Smyth. 1979. "Knossos 1975: Middle Minoan III and Late Minoan I Houses by the Acropolis," *BSA* 74, pp. 1–80.

Cavanagh, W. 1998. "Innovation, Conservatism, and Variation in Mycenaean Funerary Ritual," in Branigan 1998a, pp. 103–114.

———. 2001. "Empty Space? Courts and Squares in Mycenaean Towns," in *Urbanism in the Aegean Bronze Age* (Sheffield Studies in Aegean Archaeology 4), ed. K. Branigan, Sheffield, pp. 119–134.

Cavanagh, W., and C. Mee. 1998. *A Private Place: Death in Prehistoric Greece* (*SIMA* 125), Jonsered.

Chatzidakis, Y. 1918. "Μινωικοί τάφοι εν Κρήτη," *ArchDelt* 4, pp. 45–87.

Christakis, K. S. 1999. "Pithoi and Food Storage in Neopalatial Crete: A Domestic Perspective," *WorldArch* 31, pp. 1–20.

Clark, J., and M. Blake. 1994. "The Power of Prestige: Competitive Generosity and the Emergence of Rank Societies in Lowland Mesoamerica," in *Factional Competition and Political Development in the New World*, ed. E. M. Brumfiel and J. W. Fox, Cambridge, pp. 17–30.

Coldstream, J. N. 2002. "Knossos: Geometric Tombs Excavated by D. G. Hogarth," *BSA* 97, pp. 201–216.

Coldstream, J. N., and H. W. Catling, eds. 1996. *Knossos North Cemetery: Early Greek Tombs* (*BSA* Suppl. 28), 4 vols., London.

Conkey, M. W., and C. A. Hastorf, eds. 1990. *The Uses of Style in Archaeology*, Cambridge.

Coulson, W. D. E. 1983. "The Architecture," in *Excavations at Nichoria in Southwest Greece* III: *Dark Age and Byzantine Occupation*, ed. W. A. McDonald, W. D. E. Coulson, and J. Rosser, Minneapolis, pp. 9–60.

Creta antica = *Creta antica: Cento anni d'archeologia italiana, 1884–1984* (Exhibition Catalogue, Church of Ayios Markos, Herakleion), Rome 1984.

Cucuzza, N. 1998. "Geometric Phaistos: A Survey," in *Post-Minoan Crete. Proceedings of the First Colloquium on Post-Minoan Crete Held by the British School at Athens and the Institute of Archaeology, University College London*, ed. W. G. Cavanagh and M. Curtis, London, pp. 62–68.

———. 2000. "Funzione dei vani nel quartiere geometrico di Festòs," in *Πεπραγμένα Η΄ Διεθνούς Κρητολογικού Συνεδρίου*, Herakleion, pp. 295–307.

Cultraro, M. 2000. "La brocchetta dei vivi per la sete dei morti: Riconsiderazione delle camerette a sud della grande tholos di Haghia Triada," in *Πεπραγμένα Η΄ Διεθνούς Κρητολογικού Συνεδρίου*, Herakleion, pp. 309–326.

———. 2001. *L'anello di Minosse:*

Archeologia della regalità nell'Egeo minoico, Milan.

Dabney, M. K. 1997. "Craft Product Consumption as an Economic Indicator of Site Status in Regional Studies," in Laffineur and Betancourt 1997, pp. 467–471.

Dabney, M. K., and J. C. Wright. 1990. "Mortuary Customs, Palatial Society, and State Formation in the Aegean Area: A Comparative Study," in Hägg and Nordquist 1990, pp. 45–53.

D'Agata, A.-L. 1999. "Defining a Pattern of Continuity during the Dark Age in Central-Western Crete: Ceramic Evidence from the Settlement of Thronos/Kephala (Ancient Sybrita)," *SMEA* 41, pp. 181–218.

Darcque, P. 1987. "Les tholoi et l'organisation socio-politique du monde mycénien," in Laffineur 1987, pp. 185–205.

Davis, J. L., and J. Bennet. 1999. "Making Mycenaeans: Warfare, Territorial Expansion, and Representations of the Other in the Pylian Kingdom," in *Polemos: Le contexte guerrier en Égée à l'âge du Bronze. Actes de la 7ᵉ Rencontre égéenne internationale, Université de Liège* (*Aegaeum* 19), ed. R. Laffineur, Liège, pp. 105–120.

Day, L. P. 1997. "The Late Minoan IIIC Period at Vronda, Kavousi," in Driessen and Farnoux 1997, pp. 391–406.

Day, P. M., and D. E. Wilson. 1998. "Consuming Power: Kamares Ware in Protopalatial Knossos," *Antiquity* 72, pp. 350–358.

———. 2002. "Landscape of Memory, Craft, and Power in Prepalatial and Protopalatial Knossos," in *Labyrinth Revisited: Rethinking "Minoan" Archaeology*, ed. Y. Hamilakis, Oxford, pp. 143–166.

DeBoer, W. R. 2001. "The Big Drink: Feast and Forum in the Upper Amazon," in Dietler and Hayden 2001, pp. 215–239.

Deliyanni, E. E. 2000. "Το κρασί στη μινωική Κρήτη," in *Πεπραγμένα Η΄ Διεθνούς Κρητολογικού Συνεδρίου*, Herakleion, pp. 355–371.

Demakopoulou, K. 1990. "The Burial Ritual in the Tholos Tomb at Kokla,

Argolis," in Hägg and Nordquist 1990, pp. 113–123.

Demargne, P., and H. Gallet de Santerre. 1953. *Fouilles exécutées à Mallia: Explorations des maisons et quartiers d'habitation* 1: *1921–1948*, Paris.

Demarrais, E., L. J. Castillo, and T. Earle. 1996. "Ideology, Materialization, and Power Strategies," *CurrAnthr* 31, pp. 15–31.

Dickinson, O. T. P. K. 1977. *The Origins of Mycenaean Civilisation* (*SIMA* 49), Göteborg.

Dietler, M. 1996. "Feasts and Commensal Politics in the Political Economy: Food, Power, and Status in Prehistoric Europe," in *Food and the Status Quest: An Interdisciplinary Perspective*, ed. P. Wiessner and W. Schiefenhövel, Providence, pp. 87–125.

———. 2001. "Theorizing the Feast: Rituals of Consumption, Commensal Politics, and Power in African Contexts," in Dietler and Hayden 2001, pp. 65–114.

Dietler, M., and B. Hayden, eds. 2001. *Feasts: Archaeological and Ethnographic Perspectives on Food, Politics, and Power*, Washington, D.C.

Dimopoulou, N. 1999. "The Neopalatial Cemetery of the Knossian Harbour-Town at Poros: Mortuary Behaviour and Social Ranking," in *Eliten in der Bronzezeit*, pp. 27–36.

Dimopoulou-Rethemiotaki, N. 1992. "Πόρος: 14ο Δημοτικό Σχολείο," *ArchDelt* 42, B'2 (1987), pp. 528–531.

Donlan, W. 1985. "The Social Groups of Dark Age Greece," *CQ* 80, pp. 293–308.

———. 1989. "The Pre-State Community in Greece," *SymbOslo* 64, pp. 5–29.

———. 1994. "Chief and Followers in Pre-State Greece," in *From Political Economy to Anthropology: Situating Economic Life in Past Societies*, ed. C. A. M. Duncan and D. W. Tandy, Montreal, pp. 34–51.

———. 1997a. "The Homeric Economy," in *A New Companion to Homer*, ed. I. Morris and B. Powell, Leiden, pp. 649–667.

———. 1997b. "The Relationship of Power in the Pre-State and Early State Polities," in *The Development of the Polis in Archaic Greece*, ed. L. G. Mitchell and P. J. Rhodes, London, pp. 39–48.

Donlan, W., and C. G. Thomas. 1993. "The Village Community of Ancient Greece: Neolithic, Bronze, and Dark Ages," *SMEA* 31, pp. 61–71.

Drennan, R. 1991. "Pre-Hispanic Chiefdom Trajectories in Mesoamerica, Central America, and Northern South America," in *Chiefdoms: Power, Economy, and Ideology*, ed. T. Earle, Cambridge, pp. 263–287.

Driessen, J., and A. Farnoux. 1992. "Malia: Quartier Nu," in "Rapports sur les travaux de l'École française d'Athènes en 1991," *BCH* 116, pp. 733–742.

———. 1994. "Mycenaeans at Malia?" *Aegean Archaeology* 1, pp. 54–64.

———, eds. 1997. *La Crète mycénienne: Actes de la Table Ronde internationale organisée par l'École française d'Athènes* (*BCH* Suppl. 30), Athens.

Driessen, J., I. Schoep, and R. Laffineur, eds. 2002. *Monuments of Minos: Rethinking the Minoan Palaces. Proceedings of the International Workshop "Crete of the Hundred Palaces," Louvain* (*Aegaeum* 23), Liège.

Eliopoulos, T. 1998. "A Preliminary Report on the Discovery of a Temple Complex of the Dark Ages at Kephala Vasilikis," in *Eastern Mediterranean: Cyprus, Dodecanese, Crete, 16th–6th Cent. B.C. Proceedings of the International Symposium, Rethymnon*, ed. V. Karageorghis and N. Stampolidis, Athens, pp. 301–313.

Eliten in der Bronzezeit = Eliten in der Bronzezeit: Ergebnisse zweier Kolloquien in Mainz und Athen, Mainz 1999.

Evans, A. 1906. *The Prehistoric Tombs of Knossos: The Cemetery of Zafer Papoura, the Royal Tomb of Isopata*, London.

Farnoux, A. 1990. "Malia: Nord de l'Atelier de Sceaux," in "Rapports sur les travaux de l'École française d'Athènes en 1989," *BCH* 114, pp. 912–919.

———. 1997. "Quartier Gamma at Malia Reconsidered," in Hallager and Hallager 1997, pp. 259–272.

Feinman, G. M. 2000. "Corporate/Network: New Perspectives on Models of Political Action and the Puebloan Southwest," in *Social Theory in Archaeology*, ed. M. B. Schiffer, Salt Lake City, pp. 31–51.

French, E. B. 1997. "Ephyrean Goblets at Knossos: The Chicken or the Egg," in Driessen and Farnoux 1997, pp. 149–152.

Galaty, M. L., and W. A. Parkinson. 1999. "Putting Mycenaean Palaces in Their Place: An Introduction," in *Rethinking Mycenaean Palaces: New Interpretations of an Old Idea*, ed. M. L. Galaty and W. A. Parkinson, Los Angeles, pp. 1–8.

Georgiou, H. 1979. *The Late Minoan I Destruction of Crete: Metal Groups and Stratigraphic Considerations*, Los Angeles.

Gesell, G. C. 1985. *Town, Palace, and House Cult in Minoan Crete*, Göteborg.

Gesell, G. C., L. P. Day, and W. D. E. Coulson. 1995. "Excavations at Kavousi, Crete, 1989 and 1990," *Hesperia* 64, pp. 67–120.

Gillis, C. 1990. *Minoan Conical Cups: Form, Function, and Significance*, Göteborg.

Goody, J. 1982. *Cooking, Cuisine, and Class: A Study in Comparative Sociology*, Cambridge.

Graham, J. W. 1961. "The Minoan Banquet Hall: A Study of the Blocks North of the Central Court at Phaistos and Mallia," *AJA* 65, pp. 165–172.

———. 1975. "The Banquet Hall of the Little Palace," *AJA* 79, pp. 141–144.

———. 1987. *The Palaces of Crete*, 3rd ed., Princeton.

Graves, M. W. 1994. "Kalinga Social and Material Culture Boundaries: A Case of Spatial Convergence," in *Kalinga Ethnoarchaeology: Expanding Archaeological Method and Theory*, ed. W. A. Longacre and J. M. Skibo, Washington, D.C., pp. 13–49.

Graziadio, G. 1988. "The Chronology of the Graves of Circle B at

Mycenae: A New Hypothesis," *AJA* 92, pp. 343–372.

———. 1991. "The Process of Social Stratification at Mycenae in the Shaft Grave Period: A Comparative Examination of the Evidence," *AJA* 95, pp. 403–440.

Hägg, R. 1995. "State and Religion in Mycenaean Greece," in Laffineur and Niemeier 1995, pp. 387–391.

———. 2001. "Religious Processions in Mycenaean Greece," in *Contributions to the Archaeology and History of the Bronze and Iron Ages in the Eastern Mediterranean: Studies in Honour of Paul Åström*, ed. P. M. Fischer, Vienna, pp. 143–147.

Hägg, R., and N. Marinatos, eds. 1987. *The Function of the Minoan Palaces. Proceedings of the Fourth International Symposium at the Swedish Institute in Athens* (*SkrAth* 4°, 35), Stockholm.

Hägg, R., and G. C. Nordquist, eds. 1990. *Celebrations of Death and Divinity in the Bronze Age Argolid. Proceedings of the Sixth International Symposium at the Swedish Institute at Athens* (*SkrAth* 4°, 40), Stockholm.

Haggis, D. C. 1997. "The Typology of the Early Minoan I Chalice and the Cultural Implications of Form and Style in Early Bronze Age Ceramics," in Laffineur and Betancourt 1997, pp. 291–299.

———. 1999. "Staple Finance, Peak Sanctuaries, and Economic Complexity in Late Prepalatial Crete," in *From Minoan Farmers to Roman Traders: Sidelights on the Economy of Ancient Crete*, ed. A. Chaniotis, Stuttgart, pp. 53–85.

Haghia Triada I = P. Militello, *Gli affreschi*, Padua 1998.

Halbherr, F. 1901. "Cretan Expedition XI. Three Cretan Necropoleis: Report on the Researches at Erganos, Panaghia, and Courtes," *AJA* 5, pp. 259–293.

Halbherr, F., E. Stefani, and L. Banti. 1980. "Haghia Triada nel periodo tardopalaziale," *ASAtene* 55 (1977), pp. 9–296.

Hallager, B. P. 1997a. "LM III Pottery Shapes and Their Nomenclature," in Hallager and Hallager 1997, pp. 407–417.

———. 1997b. "Terminology—The Late Minoan Goblet, Kylix, and Footed Cup," in Hallager and Hallager 1997, pp. 15–47.

Hallager, E., and B. P. Hallager, eds. 1997. *Late Minoan III Pottery: Chronology and Terminology. Acts of a Meeting Held at the Danish Institute at Athens*, Athens.

Halstead, P., and J. C. Barrett, eds. Forthcoming. *Food, Cuisine, and Society in Prehistoric Greece* (Sheffield Studies in Aegean Archaeology 5), Sheffield.

Hamilakis, Y. 1996. "Wine, Oil, and the Dialectics of Power in Bronze Age Crete: A Review of the Evidence," *OJA* 15, pp. 1–32.

———. 1998. "Eating the Dead: Mortuary Feasting and the Politics of Memory in the Aegean Bronze Age Societies," in Branigan 1998a, pp. 115–132.

———. 1999. "Food Technologies/ Technologies of the Body: The Social Context of Wine and Oil Production and Consumption in Bronze Age Crete," *WorldArch* 31, pp. 38–54.

———. 2002. "Too Many Chiefs? Factional Competition in Neopalatial Crete," in Driessen, Schoep, and Laffineur 2002, pp. 179–199.

Hantman, J. L., and S. Plog. 1984. "The Relationship of Stylistic Similarity to Patterns of Material Exchange," in *Contexts for Prehistoric Exchange*, ed. J. E. Ericson and T. K. Earle, New York, pp. 237–263.

Haskell, H. W. 1989. "LM III Knossos: Evidence beyond the Palace," *SMEA* 27, pp. 81–110.

———. 1997. "Mycenaeans at Knossos: Patterns in the Evidence," in Driessen and Farnoux 1997, pp. 187–193.

Hayden, B. 1996. "Feasting in Prehistoric and Traditional Societies," in *Food and the Status Quest: An Interdisciplinary Perspective*, ed. P. Wiessner and W. Schiefenhövel, Providence, pp. 127–146.

———. 2001. "Fabulous Feasts: A Prolegomenon to the Importance of Feasting," in Dietler and Hayden 2001, pp. 23–64.

Hielte-Stavropoulou, M. 2001. "The Horseshoe-Shaped and Other Structures and Installations for Performing Rituals in Funeral Contexts in Middle Helladic and Early Mycenaean Times," in Laffineur and Hägg 2001, pp. 103–111.

Hitchcock, L. 2000. *Minoan Architecture: A Contextual Analysis*, Jonsered.

Hogarth, D. G. 1899–1900. "Knossos II: Early Town and Cemeteries," *BSA* 6, pp. 70–85.

Immerwahr, S. A. 1990. *Aegean Painting in the Bronze Age*, University Park, Pa.

Isaakidou, V., P. Halstead, J. Davis, and S. Stocker. 2002. "Burnt Animal Sacrifice in Late Bronze Age Greece: New Evidence from the Mycenaean 'Palace of Nestor,' Pylos," *Antiquity* 76, pp. 86–92.

Junker, L. L. 2001. "The Evolution of Ritual Feasting Systems in Prehispanic Philippine Chiefdoms," in Dietler and Hayden 2001, pp. 267–310.

Kallitsaki, H. 1997. "The Mycenaean Burial Enclosure in Phourni, Archanes," in Driessen and Farnoux 1997, pp. 213–227.

Kanta, A. 1971. "Το σπήλαιο του Λιλιανού," *CretChron* 23, pp. 425–439.

———. 1980. *The Late Minoan III Period in Crete: A Survey of Sites, Pottery, and Their Distribution* (*SIMA* 58), Göteborg.

———. 1991. "Cult, Continuity, and the Evidence of Pottery at the Sanctuary of Syme Viannou, Crete," in *La transizione dal Miceneo all'alto arcaismo: Dal palazzo alla città. Atti del Convegno Internazionale, Roma*, ed. D. Musti et al., Rome, pp. 479–505.

Kilian-Dirlmeier, I. 1985. "Noch einmal zu den 'Kriegergräbern' von Knossos," *JRGZM* 32, pp. 196–214.

———. 1986. "Beobachtungen zu den Schachtgräbern von Mykenai und zu den Schmuckbeigaben mykenischer Männergräber," *JRGZM* 33, pp. 159–198.

———. 1995. "Reiche Gräber der mittelhelladischen Zeit," in Laffineur and Niemeier 1995, pp. 49–54.

Killen, J. T. 1994. "Thebes Sealings, Knossos Tablets, and Mycenaean

State Banquets," *BICS* 39, pp. 67–84.

———. 1998. "The Pylos Ta Tablets Revisited," pp. 421–422, in F. Rougemont and J.-P. Olivier, eds., "Recherches récentes en épigraphie créto-mycénienne," *BCH* 122, pp. 403–443.

Knappett, C. 1999. "Can't Live without Them—Producing and Consuming Minoan Conical Cups," in Betancourt et al. 1999, pp. 415–419.

Koehl, R. 1997. "The Villas at Ayia Triada and Nirou Chani and the Origin of the Cretan *andreion*," in *The Function of the "Minoan Villa." Proceedings of the Eighth International Symposium at the Swedish Institute at Athens* (*SkrAth* 4°, 35), ed. R. Hägg, Stockholm, pp. 137–149.

Kommos III = L. V. Watrous, *The Late Bronze Age Pottery*, Princeton 1992.

Kontorli-Papadopoulou, L. 1995. "Mycenaean Tholos Tombs: Some Thoughts on Burial Customs and Rites," in *Klados: Essays in Honour of J. N. Coldstream*, ed. C. Morris, London, pp. 111–122.

Laffineur, R., ed. 1987. *Thanatos: Les coutumes funéraires en Égée à l'âge du Bronze. Actes du Colloque de Liège* (*Aegaeum* 1), Liège.

Laffineur, R., and P. P. Betancourt, eds. 1997. *TEXNH: Craftsmen, Craftswomen, and Craftsmanship in the Aegean Bronze Age. Proceedings of the 6th International Aegean Conference, Philadelphia* (*Aegaeum* 16), Liège.

Laffineur, R., and R. Hägg, eds. 2001. *Potnia: Deities and Religion in the Aegean Bronze Age. Proceedings of the 8th International Aegean Conference, Göteborg* (*Aegaeum* 22), Liège.

Laffineur, R., and W.-D. Niemeier, eds. 1995. *Politeia: Society and State in the Aegean Bronze Age. Proceedings of the 5th International Aegean Conference, Heidelberg* (*Aegaeum* 12), Liège.

La Rosa, V. 1980. "La ripresa dei lavori ad Haghia Triada: Relazione preliminare sui saggi del 1977," *ASAtene* 55 (1977), pp. 297–342.

———. 1986. "Haghia Triada II: Relazione preliminare sui saggi del 1978 e 1979," *ASAtene* 57–58 (1979–1980), pp. 49–164.

———. 1997. "Per la Festòs di età arcaica," in *Studi in memoria di Lucia Guerrini*, ed. M. G. Picozzi and F. Carinci, Rome, pp. 63–87.

———. 1999. "Nuovi dati sulla tomba del sarcofago dipinto di Haghia Triada," in La Rosa, Palermo, and Vagnetti 1999, pp. 177–188.

———. 2001. "Minoan Baetyls: Between Funerary Rituals and Epiphanies," in Laffineur and Hägg 2001, pp. 221–227.

La Rosa, V., D. Palermo, and L. Vagnetti, eds. 1999. Επί πόντον πλαζόμενοι: Simposio italiano di studi egei dedicato a Luigi Bernabò Brea e Giovanni Pugliese Carratelli, Roma, Rome.

Laviosa, C. 1973. "La casa TM III a Festòs: Osservazioni sull'architettura cretese in età micenea," in *Antichità cretesi: Studi in onore di Doro Levi* 1 (*CronCatania* 12), Catania, pp. 79–88.

Lebessi, A. 1967. "Ανασκαφή τάφου εις Πόρον Ηρακλείου," *Prakt* 1967, pp. 195–209.

———. 1975. "Ιερόν Ερμού και Αφροδίτης εις Σύμην Βιάννου," *Prakt* (1973), pp. 188–199.

———. 1986. "Ιερό του Ερμή και της Αφροδίτης στη Σύμη Βιάννου," *Prakt* (1983), pp. 348–366.

Lebessi, A., and P. Muhly. 1990. "Aspects of Minoan Cult: Sacred Enclosures. The Evidence from the Syme Sanctuary (Crete)," *AA* 1990, pp. 315–336.

Lefèvre-Novaro, D. 2001. "Un nouvel examen des modèles réduits trouvés dans la grande tombe de Kamilari," in Laffineur and Hägg 2001, pp. 89–98.

Levi, D. 1961–1962. "La tomba a tholos di Kamilari presso Festòs," *ASAtene* 39–40, pp. 7–148.

———. 1976. *Festòs e la civiltà minoica* 1, Rome.

Löwe, W. 1996. *Spätbronzezeitliche Bestattungen auf Kreta* (*BAR-IS* 642), Oxford.

MacGillivray, J. A. 1987. "Pottery Workshops and the Old Palaces in Crete," in Hägg and Marinatos 1987, pp. 273–279.

———. 1998. *Knossos: Pottery Groups of the Old Palace Period* (*BSA* Studies 5), London.

Marinatos, N. 1986. *Minoan Sacrificial Ritual: Cult Practice and Symbolism*, Stockholm.

Marinatos, S. 1939–1941. "Το μινωικόν μέγαρον Σκλαβοκάμπου," *ArchEph* 1939–1941, pp. 69–96.

Markoulaki, S., and K. Baxévani-Kouzioni. 1997. "Une tombe à chambre du MR IIIA à Pangalochori, Réthymnon," in Driessen and Farnoux 1997, pp. 293–295.

Matthäus, H. 1980. *Die Bronzegefässe der kretisch-mykenischen Kultur* (Prähistorische Bronzefunde 2.1), Munich.

———. 1983. "Minoische Kriegergräber," in *Minoan Society. Proceedings of the Cambridge Colloquium, 1981*, ed. O. Krzyszkowska and L. Nixon, Bristol, pp. 203–215.

Mazarakis Ainian, A. 1997. *From Rulers' Dwellings to Temples: Architecture, Religion, and Society in Early Iron Age Greece (1100–700 B.C.)*, Jonsered.

McDonald, W. A., and W. D. E. Coulson. 1983. "The Dark Age at Nichoria: A Perspective," in *Excavations at Nichoria in Southwest Greece* III: *Dark Age and Byzantine Occupation*, ed. W. A. McDonald, W. D. E. Coulson, and J. Rosser, Minneapolis, pp. 316–329.

Militello, P. 2001. "Archeologia, iconografia, e culti ad Haghia Triada in età TM IB," in Laffineur and Hägg 2001, pp. 159–168.

Momigliano, N. 1991. "MM IA Pottery from Evans' Excavations at Knossos: A Reassessment," *BSA* 86, pp. 149–271.

———. 2000. "Knossos 1902, 1905: The Prepalatial and Protopalatial Deposits from the Room of the Jars in the Royal Pottery Stores," *BSA* 95, pp. 65–105.

Moody, J. 1987. "The Minoan Palace as a Prestige Artifact," in Hägg and Marinatos 1987, pp. 235–241.

Morgan, C. 1991. "Ethnicity and Early Greek States," *PCPS* 37, pp. 131–163.

Morgan, C., and T. Whitelaw. 1991. "Pots and Politics: Ceramic Evidence for the Rise of the Argive State," *AJA* 95, pp. 79–108.

Mountjoy, P. A. 1986. *Mycenaean Decorated Pottery: A Guide to Identification* (*SIMA* 73), Göteborg.

Niemeier, W.-D. 1985. *Die Palaststilkeramik von Knossos: Stil, Chronologie, und historischer Kontext*, Berlin.

Nordquist, G. C. 1990. "Middle Helladic Burial Rites: Some Speculations," in Hägg and Nordquist 1990, pp. 35–41.

———. 1999. "Pairing of Pots in the Middle Helladic Period," in Betancourt et al. 1999, pp. 569–573.

———. 2002. "Pots, Prestige, and People: Symbolic Action in Middle Helladic Burials," *OpAth* 27, pp. 119–135.

Novaro, D. 1999. "I modellini fittili della tomba di Kamilari: Il problema cronologico," in La Rosa, Palermo, and Vagnetti 1999, pp. 151–161.

Nowicki, K. 1994. "A Dark Age Refuge Centre near Pefki, East Crete," *BSA* 89, pp. 235–268.

———. 1996. "Arvi Fortetsa and Loutraki Kandiloro: Two Refuge Settlements in Crete," *BSA* 91, pp. 253–285.

———. 2000. *Defensible Sites in Crete, c. 1200–800 B.C. (Late Minoan IIIB/IIIC through Early Geometric)* (*Aegaeum* 21), Liège.

Palaima, T. G. 2000. "The Pylos Ta Series: From Michael Ventris to the New Millennium," *BICS* 44, pp. 236–237.

Palermo, D. 1999. "Il deposito votivo sul margine orientale della Patela di Prinias," in La Rosa, Palermo, and Vagnetti 1999, pp. 207–213.

Papadopoulou, E. 1997. "Une tombe à tholos 'intra muros': Le cas du cimitière MR d'Armenoi," in Driessen and Farnoux 1997, pp. 319–340.

Parker Pearson, M. 2002, *The Archaeology of Death and Burial*, 2nd ed., College Station, Tex.

Peatfield, A. 1987. "Palace and Peak: The Political and Religious Relationship between Palaces and Peak Sanctuaries," in Hägg and Marinatos 1987, pp. 89–93.

Pernier, L. 1914. "Templi arcaici sulla patela di Prinias in Creta: Contributi allo studio dell'arte dedalica," *ASAtene* 1, pp. 18–111.

Perodie, J. R. 2001. "Feasting for Prosperity: A Study of Southern Northwest Coast Feasting," in Dietler and Hayden 2001, pp. 185–214.

Persson, A. W. 1942. *New Tombs at Dendra near Midea*, Lund.

Piteros, C., J.-P. Olivier, and J. L. Melena. 1990. "Les inscriptions en linéaire B des nodules de Thèbes (1982): La fouille, les documents, les possibilités d'interprétation," *BCH* 114, pp. 103–184.

Platon, L. 1997. "Caractère, morphologie et datation de la bourgade postpalatiale de Képhali Chondrou Viannou," in Driessen and Farnoux 1997, pp. 357–373.

Platon, N. 1947. "Ἡ ἀρχαιολογική κίνησις ἐν Κρήτῃ κατά τα ἔτη 1941–1947," in "Χρονικά," *CretChron* 1, pp. 631–640.

———. 1957. "Ἀνασκαφή ΥΜ ΙΙΙ λαξευτῶν τάφων εἰς τὴν περιοχήν Ἐπισκοπῆς καὶ Σταμνίων Πεδιάδος Ἡρακλείου," *Prakt* (1952), pp. 619–630.

———. 1962. "Ἀνασκαφή Χόνδρου Βιάννου," *Prakt* (1957), pp. 136–147.

———. 1971. *Zakros: The Discovery of a Lost Palace of Ancient Crete*, New York.

Plog, S. 1980. *Stylistic Variation in Prehistoric Ceramics: Design Analysis in the American Southwest*, Cambridge.

———. 1995. "Approaches to Style: Complements and Contrasts," in *Style, Society, and Person: Archaeological and Ethnological Perspectives*, ed. C. Carr and J. E. Neitzel, London, pp. 369–386.

Pollock, S. 1983. "Style and Information: An Analysis of Susiana Ceramics," *JAnthArch* 2, pp. 190–234.

Popham, M. R. 1969. "The Late Minoan Goblet and Kylix," *BSA* 64, pp. 299–304.

———. 1970. "A Late Minoan Shrine at Knossos," *BSA* 65, pp. 191–194.

———, ed. 1984. *The Minoan Unexplored Mansion at Knossos* (*BSA* Suppl. 17), London.

———. 1988. "The Historical Implications of the Linear B Archive at Knossos Dating to Either ca. 1400 B.C. or 1200 B.C.," *Cretan Studies* 1, pp. 217–227.

———. 1992. "Subminoan Pottery," in *Knossos from Greek City to Roman Colony: Excavations at the Unexplored Mansion* II, ed. L. H. Sackett, (*BSA* Suppl. 21), London, pp. 59–66.

Popham, M. R., E. A. Catling, and H. W. Catling. 1974. "Sellopoulo Tombs 3 and 4: Two Late Minoan Graves near Knossos," *BSA* 69, pp. 195–257.

Protonotariou-Deilaki, E. 1990. "Burial Customs and Funerary Rites in the Prehistoric Argolid," in Hägg and Nordquist 1990, pp. 69–83.

Raaflaub, K. A. 1997. "Homeric Society," in *A New Companion to Homer*, ed. I. Morris and B. Powell, Leiden, pp. 624–648.

Rehak, P., and J. G. Younger. 2001. "Neopalatial, Final Palatial, and Postpalatial Crete," in *Aegean Prehistory: A Review* (*AJA* Suppl. 1), ed. T. Cullen, Boston, pp. 383–465.

Renfrew, C. 1974. "Beyond a Subsistence Economy: The Evolution of Social Organization in Prehistoric Europe," in *Reconstructing Complex Societies: An Archaeological Colloquium* (*BASOR* Suppl. 20), ed. C. B. Moore, Cambridge, Mass., pp. 69–95.

Rethemiotakis, G. 1997. "Τὸ μινωικὸ 'κεντρικό κτίριο' στο Καστέλλι Πεδιάδας," *ArchDelt* 47 (1992), pp. 29–64.

———. 1999a. "The Hearths of the Minoan Palace at Galatas," in Betancourt et al. 1999, pp. 721–728.

———. 1999b. "Social Rank and Political Power: The Evidence from the Minoan Palace at Galatas," in *Eliten in der Bronzezeit*, pp. 19–26.

———. 2002. "Evidence on Social and Economic Changes at Galatas and Pediada in the New-Palace Period," in Driessen, Schoep, and Laffineur 2002, pp. 55–69.

Rowlands, M. J. 1980. "Kinship, Alliance, and Exchange in the European Bronze Age," in *The British*

Later Bronze Age (*BAR-IS* 83), ed. J. Barrett and R. Bradley, Oxford, pp. 15–55.

Rupp, D. W., and M. Tsipopoulou. 1999. "Conical Cup Concentrations at Neopalatial Petras: A Case for a Ritualized Reception Ceremony with Token Hospitality," in Betancourt et al. 1999, pp. 729–733.

Rutter, J. Forthcoming. "Ceramic Sets in Context: One Dimension of Food Preparation and Consumption in a Minoan Palatial Setting," in Halstead and Barrett, forthcoming.

Sacconi, A. 2001. "Les repas sacrés dans les textes mycéniens," in Laffineur and Hägg 2001, pp. 467–470.

Sakellarakis, Y. A. 1970. "Das Kuppelgrab A von Archanes und das kretisch-mykenische Tieropferritual," *PZ* 45, pp. 135–219.

Sakellarakis, Y. A., and E. Sakellaraki. 1972. "Ἀποθέτης κεραμεικῆς τῆς τελευταίας φάσεως τῶν προανακτορικῶν χρόνων εἰς Ἀρχάνας," in "Χρονικά," *ArchEph* 1972, pp. 1–11.

Sakellarakis, Y., and E. Sapouna-Sakellaraki. 1997. *Archanes: Minoan Crete in a New Light*, Athens.

Sakellariou, A. 1964. *Die minoischen und mykenischen Siegel des National Museums in Athen* (*CMS* I), Berlin.

Savignoni, L. 1904. "Scavi e scoperte nelle necropoli di Phaestos," *MonAnt* 14, pp. 501–666.

Schmandt-Besserat, D. 2001. "Feasting in the Ancient Near East," in Dietler and Hayden 2001, pp. 391–403.

Schoep, I. 2002. "Social and Political Organization on Crete in the Proto-Palatial Period: The Case of Middle Minoan II Malia," *JMA* 15, pp. 101–132.

Shelmerdine, C. W. 1999. "A Comparative Look at Mycenaean Administration(s)," in *Floreant Studia Mycenaea. Akten des X. Internationalen Mykenologischen Colloquiums, Salzburg* (*DenkschrWien* 274), ed. S. Deger-Jalkotzy, S. Hiller, and O. Panagl, Vienna, pp. 555–576.

Sherratt, S. 2001. "Potemkin Palaces and Route-Based Economies," in *Economy and Politics in the Mycenaean Palace States* (Cambridge Philological Society, Suppl. 27),

ed. S. Voutsaki and J. Killen, Cambridge, pp. 214–238.

Soles, J. S. 1992. *The Prepalatial Cemeteries at Mochlos and Gournia and the House Tombs of Bronze Age Crete* (*Hesperia* Suppl. 24), Princeton.

Soles, J. S., and C. Davaras. 1996. "Excavations at Mochlos, 1992–1993," *Hesperia* 65, pp. 175–230.

Speciale, M. S. 1999. "La tavoletta PY Ta 716 e i sacrifici di animali," in La Rosa, Palermo, and Vagnetti 1999, pp. 291–297.

Tsipopoulou, M. 2001. "A New Late Minoan IIIC Shrine at Halasmenos, East Crete," in Laffineur and Hägg 2001, pp. 99–101.

Tyree, E. L. 2001. "Diachronic Changes in Minoan Cave Cult," in Laffineur and Hägg 2001, pp. 39–50.

Tzedakis, Y. 1988. "Ἀρμένοι," *ArchDelt* 35, B'2 (1980), pp. 512–517.

Van de Moortel, A. 2001. "The Area around the Kiln and the Pottery from the Kiln Dump," in J. W. Shaw, A. Van de Moortel, P. M. Day, and V. Kilikoglou, *A LM IA Ceramic Kiln in South-Central Crete: Function and Pottery Production* (*Hesperia* Suppl. 30), Princeton, pp. 25–110.

van Wees, H. 1995. "Princes at Dinner: Social Event and Social Structure in Homer," in *Homeric Questions: Essays in Philology, Ancient History, and Archaeology, Including the Papers of a Conference Organized by the Netherlands Institute at Athens*, ed. J. P. Crielaard, Amsterdam, pp. 147–182.

Vasilakis, A. 1990. "Μινωική κεραμεική ἀπό τό Ἰδαίον Ἄντρον," in Πεπραγμένα τοῦ ΣΤ' Διεθνοῦς Κρητολογικοῦ Συνεδρίου, Α'1, Chania, pp. 125–134.

Ventris, M., and J. Chadwick. 1956. *Documents in Mycenaean Greek*, Cambridge.

Vikatou, O. 2001. "Σκηνή πρόθεσης ἀπό τό μυκηναικό νεκροταφείο τῆς Ἀγίας Τριάδας," in *Forschungen in der Peloponnes. Akten des Symposions anlässlich der Feier "100 Jahre Österreichisches Archäologi-*

sches Institut Athen," Athen, ed. V. Mitsopoulos-Leon, Athens, pp. 273–284.

Voutsaki, S. 1995. "Social and Political Processes in the Mycenaean Argolid: The Evidence from the Mortuary Practices," in Laffineur and Niemeier 1995, pp. 55–66.

———. 1998. "Mortuary Evidence, Symbolic Meanings, and Social Change: A Comparison between Messenia and the Argolid in the Mycenaean Period," in Branigan 1998a, pp. 41–58.

———. 1999. "Mortuary Display, Prestige, and Identity in the Shaft Grave Era," in *Eliten in der Bronzezeit*, pp. 103–117.

Wace, A. J. B. 1932. *Chamber Tombs at Mycenae* (Archaeologica 82), Oxford.

Walberg, G. 1987. "Early Cretan Tombs: The Pottery," in Laffineur 1987, pp. 53–60.

Watrous, L. V. 2001. "Crete from Earliest Prehistory through the Palatial Period," in *Aegean Prehistory: A Review* (*AJA* Suppl. 1), ed. T. Cullen, Boston, pp. 157–223.

Wiener, M. H. 1984, "Crete and the Cyclades in LM I: The Tale of the Conical Cups," in *The Minoan Thalassocracy: Myth and Reality. Proceedings of the Third International Symposium at the Swedish Institute in Athens* (*SkrAth* 4°, 32), ed. R. Hägg and N. Marinatos, Stockholm, pp. 17–26.

Wiessner, P. 1983. "Style and Social Information in Kalahari San Projectile Points," *AmerAnt* 48, pp. 253–276.

———. 1984. "Reconsidering the Behavioural Basis for Style: A Case Study among the Kalahari San," *JAnthArch* 3, pp. 190–234.

———. 1989. "Style and Changing Relations between the Individual and Society," in *The Meanings of Things: Material Culture and Symbolic Expression*, ed. I. Hodder, London, pp. 56–63.

Wilkie, N. 1987. "Burial Customs at Nichoria: The MME Tholos," in Laffineur 1987, pp. 127–135.

Wilson, D. E., and P. M. Day. 1999. "EM IIB Ware Groups at Knossos:

The 1907–1908 South Front Tests," *BSA* 94, pp. 1–62.

———. 2000. "EM I Chronology and Social Practice: Pottery from the Early Palace Tests at Knossos," *BSA* 95, pp. 21–63.

Wright, J. C. 1984. "Changes in Form and Function of the Palace at Pylos," in *Pylos Comes Alive: Industry and Administration in a Mycenaean Palace. Papers of a Symposium,* ed. C. W. Shelmerdine and T. G. Palaima, New York, pp. 19–29.

———. 1987. "Death and Power at Mycenae: Changing Symbols in Mortuary Practice," in Laffineur 1987, pp. 171–184.

———. 1994. "The Spatial Configuration of Belief: The Archaeology of Mycenaean Religion," in *Placing the Gods: Sanctuaries and Sacred Space in Ancient Greece,* ed. S. E. Alcock and R. Osborne, Oxford, pp. 37–78.

———. 1995a. "Empty Cups and Empty Jugs: The Social Role of Wine in Minoan and Mycenaean Societies," in *The Origins and Ancient History of Wine* (Food and Nutrition in History and Anthropology 11), ed. P. E. McGovern, S. J. Fleming, and S. H. Katz, Philadelphia, pp. 287–309.

———. 1995b. "From Chief to King in Mycenaean Greece," in *The Role of the Ruler in the Prehistoric Aegean. Proceedings of a Panel Discussion Presented at the Annual Meeting of the Archaeological Institute of America, New Orleans (Aegaeum 11),* ed. P. Rehak, Liège, pp. 63–80.

———. Forthcoming. "Mycenaean Drinking Services and Standards of Etiquette," in Halstead and Barrett, forthcoming.

CHAPTER 7

A Goodly Feast ... A Cup of Mellow Wine: Feasting in Bronze Age Cyprus

Louise Steel

ABSTRACT

Recent studies have focused on the consumption of food and drink in antiquity, specifically employing anthropological perspectives to examine the social aspects of these activities. In light of these studies, I review in this chapter the evidence for feasting as a group activity in Cyprus during the third and second millennia B.C. and argue that the practice of feasting was used to reinforce group ties. The main focus is the impact of Mycenaean customs on indigenous Cypriot feasting practices between the 14th and 12th centuries B.C.

THE ANTHROPOLOGY OF FOOD AND DRINK

The consumption of food and drink represents more than the biological act of meeting necessary subsistence requirements, since it is also a culturally constructed social act.[1] Components of human diet are essentially anthropogenic; they are culturally transformed from their raw state into a transient element of material culture prior to consumption. Moreover, food and drink are symbolically charged because they represent embodied material culture, produced specifically to be ingested into the human body.[2] Indeed, Hamilakis comments that "humans as social entities make themselves through the consumption of food and drink."[3] Dining and drinking are the focus of social interaction both within the immediate household context and throughout the wider community.[4] The consumption of food and drink is used in the construction of social identities, shared experiences of consumption resulting in a corporate sense of identity.[5]

The social connotations of diet are culturally specific and are constructed according to modes of preparation, service, and consumption.

1. I am grateful to the Institute for Aegean Prehistory for funding my visit to the 103rd Annual Meeting of the Archaeological Institute of America, held in Philadelphia in January 2002, where an early version of this paper was presented. Particular thanks are due to James C. Wright for inviting me to take part in this very enjoyable and productive symposium on Mycenaean feasting, and to the *Hesperia* reviewers, Jeremy B. Rutter and Brian Hayden, for their helpful and informative comments and suggestions.

2. Dietler 2001, p. 72.
3. Hamilakis 1998, p. 116.
4. Hastorf 1991, p. 134.
5. Hamilakis 1998, p. 116.

Within these social codes we see the construction of food taboos: the definition of certain foods as clean or unclean, edible or inedible. Concepts of distinctive food tastes, accepted combinations of dietary elements in the construction of cuisines, and required modes of preparation and consumption are incorporated into concepts of ethnicity.[6] As a corollary, the associated paraphernalia used in the preparation, serving, and consumption of food and drink are also culturally specific. Similarly, the locations where these activities take place are defined within strict cultural norms, with food preparation areas frequently distinct from areas for dining and for the disposal of the debris of feasting. Even within certain social contexts these vary according to the context of consumption: distinctions in diet and eating habits may refer to internal cultural boundaries by reflecting gender differences, age distinctions, and social status. Special foods, different modes of preparation, and utensils might be used for religious ceremonies including rites of passage, religious festivals, and burial rites.[7]

Although diet is closely interwoven with expressions of cultural identity, it is an arena that is susceptible to modification as a result of outside influence. This is particularly apparent in the changing patterns of social dining in the Greek and Roman world brought about by increasing social and economic contact.[8] In archaeological contexts, changes in dietary practices, and thus the appearance of novel elements in the ceramic repertoire, are frequently attributed to the arrival of new population groups. One of the most frequently cited examples is the change in the Canaanite ceramic repertoire at the beginning of the Iron Age with the introduction of the Philistine Bichrome style, especially new forms such as the side-spouted strainer jug and the deep bowl or skyphos.[9] Changes in dietary practices and food preparation are further illustrated by the appearance of new types of cooking pot.[10] Alternative causal factors, however, should also be considered, in particular, the role of imported exotic commodities and esoteric knowledge in the construction of political and ideological power.[11] One such example is elite appropriation of imported, and thus exotic, alcoholic beverages and associated drinking equipment for use in exclusive high-status feasts.[12] This is exemplified by the spread of the symposium, and of the custom of dining in a reclining position, from the Near East to the Greek world during the Archaic period, and the dissemination of Greek and Phoenician drinking equipment and concepts of the Homeric banquet to central Italy.[13] Similarly, in Old Kingdom Egypt the elite used wine and drinking equipment imported from the southern Levant in exclusive diacritical drinking ceremonies.[14]

A clear distinction can be drawn between everyday consumption of staples within a household context and the larger ceremonial gatherings and ritual feasts that mark special occasions and define social relations. Feasts stand out from normal consumption practices by virtue of their location, the quantity and possibly the choice of food and drink consumed, and the associated paraphernalia, i.e., not only the dining services but also the dress and ornamentation of the participants.[15] Typically feasts might include luxury foodstuffs that were distinct from the staples consumed in everyday diet. While it might be prohibitive to rear livestock for consump-

6. Dietler 2001, p. 89.

7. James 1996, p. 80; Lindsay 2001, pp. 67–77.

8. See Dunbabin 2001.

9. Side-spouted jug: Dothan 1982, pp. 132–155, figs. 21–31, pls. 46–62; skyphos: Dothan 1982, pp. 98–102, figs. 3–7, pls. 2–7.

10. Killebrew 1999.

11. Helms (1988) has clearly demonstrated how knowledge of geographically distant places and foreign customs and consumption of exotica come under the domain of religious specialists and elites.

12. Dietler 1990, p. 386.

13. Joffe 1998, p. 307 (and references). See also Carter 1995 for a discussion of the possible spread of Levantine dining practices to the Aegean world as early as the Minoan-Mycenaean palatial period in the second millennium B.C.

14. Joffe 1998, p. 302.

15. Dietler 2001, p. 89.

tion of meat as a staple, numerous ethnographic studies have illustrated the prestige value of large livestock such as goats and, in particular, cattle, especially males with impressive coats and horns.[16] The consumption of meat within a feasting context is therefore something special, a highly symbolic display of wealth and status. Feasts might also be differentiated by the use of exotic foods, or foods with psychoactive properties, such as alcoholic beverages. The symbolic importance of alcoholic drinks derives in part from their peculiar mood-enhancing properties and from the process of manufacture, "a quasi-magical transformation of food into a substance that, in turn, transforms human consciousness."[17] Alcohol serves to construct "an ideal world" and is particularly appropriate for ceremonial consumption and the forging of alliances.[18] In terms of embodied material culture, therefore, alcohol occupies a privileged place, and its production and consumption are closely controlled.[19]

Feasts are major arenas for public display. They are visual pageants, occasions for music, dancing, recitation of epics, and shared consumption of the fruits of labor. The social and political functions of feasting are closely intertwined. Hospitality is used to establish and maintain social relations and to forge alliances, and feasts are frequently venues for the exchange of gifts.[20] Different modes of feasting are described in the ethnographic literature. At the basic level, food is shared within the household and with close kin. Some feasts incorporate the wider community. Not only do these feasts create shared sentiments of identity and belonging, but they are also occasions for social competition. Regular and lavish hospitality allows the host to accrue prestige and standing (symbolic capital) within a community. In effect, the enhancement of the host's standing within the community will "buy" influence over decisions made by the community. Hospitality may be reciprocal, with different individuals hosting feasts on a variety of occasions. Prestige and social standing are renegotiated in a continuous cycle of feasting—the so-called entrepreneurial, or empowering, feasts.[21] Such feasts might be used to create and maintain alliances within the community at different levels. Empowering, or work-party, feasts might also be used to mobilize labor. In effect a host will be able to mobilize a work force to complete a project, in return for which he or she provides food and drink. The more generous the reputation of the host, the greater the symbolic capital, and the more effective the work-party feast will be.[22]

Patron-role feasts are hosted by a single individual who asserts and maintains his elevated social position within the community, while the guests symbolically acknowledge their subordinate role through acceptance of the patron's hospitality. Effectively, patron-role feasts are used to proclaim and legitimize asymmetrical, hierarchical power systems.[23] Frequently, tribute of food and drink will be used to supply patron-role feasts. In the context of communal feasts, symbolic expression lies in the quantities of food and drink provided. In contrast to inclusive communal feasts, patron-role feasts allow hospitality to be manipulated to demonstrate exclusivity, such as social ranking, and also to facilitate alliance formation and demonstrate membership in social or political groupings (as illustrated by, e.g., the *marzeah* of Near Eastern sources and by the Greek symposium).[24]

16. Croft 1991, p. 74; Keswani 1994, pp. 257–260.

17. Dietler 2001, p. 73.

18. Sherratt 1997, pp. 388–392; Joffe 1998, p. 298.

19. Joffe (1998, pp. 298–304) notes such control for both ancient Egypt and Mesopotamia (and also for modern societies).

20. This can be seen, for example, in Early Dynastic Mesopotamia. Schmandt-Besserat (2001) argues that the palace banquets were major occasions for the presentation of offerings to the king and the gods, and indeed that these feasts played a central role in the palatial redistribution economy.

21. Dietler 1996, pp. 92–96; 2001, pp. 76–82.

22. Dietler 1996, pp. 93–95.

23. Dietler 1996, p. 97; 2001, pp. 82–85.

24. Carter 1995, p. 300, n. 54, p. 305.

Diacritical feasts are used as symbols of exclusive membership. These feasts are characterized by distinctive cuisine (exotic foods or complicated modes of preparation) and elaborate dining sets, and frequently make reference to specialized knowledge of external, exotic social practices as a means of demonstrating their exclusivity.[25] These elements of diacritical feasts make up a distinctive package of practices that are readily identifiable in the archaeological record. The symbolic force of the diacritical feast lies in its manipulation of an exclusive style that is closely guarded by the elite, through their privileged access to limited supplies of exotica. Even so, these practices are open to emulation on the part of groups aspiring to an elevated social status and we might expect a degree of fluidity in the choice of symbolic, ideological referents used by the elite.[26]

The development of increasingly sophisticated scientific techniques and the application of anthropological models to archaeological material have enhanced current interest in ancient diet and dining practices.[27] There are, however, numerous problems involved in exploring patterns of food consumption in the past, notably the distinction between staple consumption and feasting in an archaeological context.[28] In the Bronze Age Aegean and the ancient Near East, archaeological material is supplemented by textual sources and a rich corpus of representational material.[29] In the absence of detailed iconography and written documents, however, the only source of evidence available for analysis is the archaeological record. This includes concentrations of the debris of food and drink together with specialized apparatus for their service and consumption, patterns of differential disposal of faunal remains, and possibly the identification of specialized locations for these activities.

In the following discussion, I examine the evidence for feasting in Cyprus during the third and second millennia b.c. Given the limited textual and iconographic data available, emphasis is on the archaeological remains, which range in date from the Chalcolithic period through the Late Bronze Age.[30] The time span allows us to identify indigenous, intrinsically Cypriot aspects of consumption and to assess the extent to which changing practices are a result of internal social transformations rather than external influence.

25. Dietler 2001, pp. 85–86; see also Helms 1988 for a discussion of elite control of esoteric knowledge and the exotic.

26. Dietler 2001, pp. 86–88.

27. New techniques for studying archaeozoological and archaeobotanical assemblages include residue analysis of pottery and isotope analysis of human bones; see Tzedakis and Martlew 1999. Of particular interest to the discussion of exclusive, diacritical feasts is the evidence gleaned from the skeletal remains in the two grave circles at Mycenae. Stable isotope analysis indicates that the high-status males from these grave circles had privileged access to marine foods and consumed more of these than either the women buried in the grave circles or the adults (of indeterminate sex) buried in the LH I–II chamber tombs at Mycenae (Tzedakis and Martlew 1999, pp. 222–223, 226–227, 230–231).

28. Dietler 1996, pp. 98–99; 2001, p. 89.

29. For Aegean iconography, see Carter 1995; Rehak 1995; Wright, this volume. For Aegean textual data, see Palmer 1994; Palaima, this volume. Schmandt-Besserat (2001, pp. 391–395), for example, has explored the context and pattern of Sumerian feasting with reference to images of banqueting in glyptic art and on the Royal Standard of Ur; she also discusses (pp. 397–401) early mythological and economic texts.

30. The chronological and cultural distinction between the Early and Middle Cypriot periods (Early and Middle Bronze Age) has yet to be clearly defined. For the purposes of this chapter I refer to the two periods collectively as the "prehistoric Bronze Age," following Knapp 1990, p. 154. This time period is distinct from the subsequent Late Cypriot (LC) period, or Late Bronze Age (LBA) in terms of material culture, settlement pattern, and socioeconomic organization.

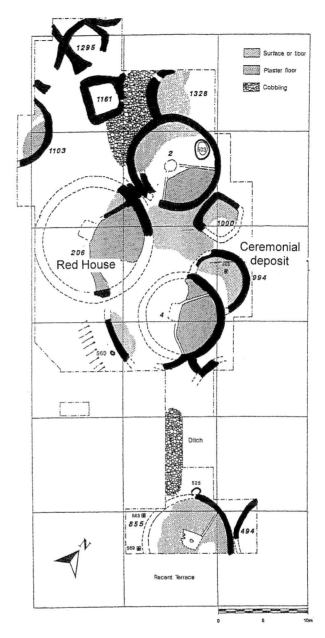

Figure 1. Plan of the ceremonial area at Kissonerga-Mosphilia. After Peltenburg et al. 1998, fig. 31

CHALCOLITHIC AND PREHISTORIC BRONZE AGE

Recently Peltenburg has suggested that evidence for communal feasting on Cyprus can be identified as early as the Middle Chalcolithic period, specifically in specialized structures within the spatially discrete ceremonial area at Kissonerga-Mosphilia (Fig. 1).[31] This area provided an arena for the performance of ritual in the open air, as well as a series of architecturally distinctive and functionally specialized houses of symbolic significance, most notably the so-called Red House. A large number of bowls (Fig. 2) were found in this structure, including vessels used for display in serving food, suggestive of ceremonial competitive feasting.[32]

The dietary components, and in particular the beverages, of these feasts have not been identified. There is no evidence for the introduction

31. Peltenburg 2001, pp. 129–133.
32. Bolger 1998, pp. 125–126; Peltenburg 1998, p. 248.

Figure 2. Decorated Red-on-White ware bowls from Kissonerga-Mosphilia. After Peltenburg et al. 1998, figs. 63, 64

of orchard husbandry to Cyprus prior to the Bronze Age, and any alcoholic beverage probably would not have been made from grapes. Similarly, cattle husbandry was only introduced to the island during the Early Bronze Age, and faunal assemblages suggest that caprines and fallow deer were the main meat components of the Cypriot diet in the Chalcolithic period. Presumably meat was not a staple but was restricted to specialized consumption in feasting contexts.[33] An unexpectedly high ratio of adult males to females among the caprines is represented in the faunal assemblages of Chalcolithic settlements. If herds were being bred for either their meat potential or milk products, a higher ratio of females might be expected. Wool production, on the other hand, should result in an equal ratio of males and females. The faunal assemblage, however, implies a rather uneconomical breeding strategy, with the maintenance of herds of goats with full-grown males. It is likely that adult male goats were desirable as a symbolic statement of social status, wealth, and prestige, and valued for their horns and coats.[34]

Major social, economic, and cultural transformations in Cyprus at the beginning of the Late Chalcolithic period foreshadow the developments of the subsequent Bronze Age.[35] These are particularly evident in the ceremonial or ritual arena, indicating a major shift in the underlying ideological system. Most notably, Cyprus was beginning to emerge from cultural isolation and to come in contact with populations of southwest Anatolia. One of the most marked changes is evident in pottery production—in particular, the introduction of bowls and flasks in a new monochrome style (Fig. 3).[36] These vessels include specialized containers for a new liquid commodity; the concentration of spouted flasks in building 7 at Lemba-Lakkous, associated with a complex of basins and grinding equipment, is very suggestive of beer production.[37] The development of some form of patron/elite control of food production is illustrated by the large-

33. See discussion in Keswani 1994.
34. Croft 1991, p. 74.
35. See, e.g., Peltenburg et al. 1998.
36. Bolger 1994, p. 13; 1998, p. 120.
37. Peltenburg et al. 1985, pp. 121–122, 328; Keswani 1994, pp. 266–267.

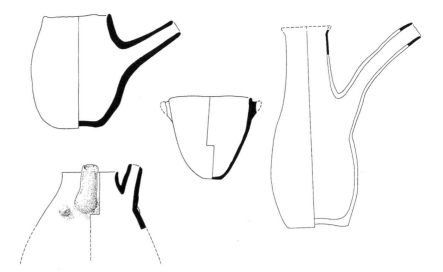

Figure 3. Late Chalcolithic monochrome feasting equipment from Kissonerga-Mosphilia. After Peltenburg et al. 1998, fig. 71

38. Peltenburg 1998, p. 252.

39. Peltenburg 1998, p. 253.

40. Dietler 1996, pp. 92–97 (empowering feasts are here referred to as entrepreneurial feasts); 2001, pp. 76–85. See discussion above.

41. Manning 1993, pp. 44–48.

42. Manning 1993, p. 45; Keswani 1994, pp. 270–271; Herscher 1997, pp. 31–34.

43. Keswani 1994, p. 270, table 4; Herscher 1997, pp. 31–32.

scale storage facilities in the Pithos House at Kissonerga-Mosphilia.[38] The faunal assemblage recovered from this building, with a high incidence of deer bone *(Dama mesopotamica),* is atypical of the Late Chalcolithic period. Peltenburg suggests that hunting had become a high-status activity in this period, controlled by the occupants of the Pithos House.[39] Alternatively, this building may have been associated specifically with communal feasting. Deer was not a staple dietary element but might have been consumed as part of a ceremonial ritual. On the basis of available archaeological evidence, Chalcolithic feasting appears to have been conducted at a communal level. There is no clear evidence for exclusivity in location, consumption, or paraphernalia. Instead, these early feasting patterns comply with the criteria put forward for empowering and patron-role feasts.[40]

Certainly by the beginning of the Bronze Age, ceremonial drinking and group feasting formed an important element of Cypriot social practice. During this period Cyprus was characterized by small farming communities located in inland villages. The apparent social and cultural isolation that characterized the earlier prehistory of the island continued, with very little evidence for external contact. Internally there is little clear evidence for social stratification. Even so, Manning has interpreted funerary ritual as the major arena for display by an emergent elite.[41] He argues that this display is illustrated by conspicuous consumption of new metal artifacts (especially weapons) and the development of elaborate burial rituals, which incorporated a major feasting element. He emphasizes the appearance of a range of vessels specifically associated with storing, pouring, and serving liquids (Fig. 4), and the development of a number of elaborate multipiece vessels with exaggerated spouts. These, he suggests, were intended for the ceremonial consumption of exotic alcoholic drinks as part of an elite funerary feast that accentuated membership in the exclusive group being buried in these tombs.[42]

Further evidence for ceremonial feasting is indicated by the presence of quantities of cattle and caprine bones in funerary contexts. This pattern is particularly evident at Vounous, where large joints of meat were found in jars and basins, and also at Lapithos-Vrysi tou Barba.[43] The association

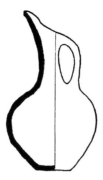

Figure 4. Philia Red Polished
jugs with cutaway spouts from
Khrysiliou-Ammos tomb 1.
After Bolger 1983, p. 64, fig. 3:1, 2

between cattle and ritual contexts—indicative of prestige display, sacrifice, and high-status feasting—is further illustrated by the well-known Vounous model and other rare representational ceramic models that were deposited in a small number of tombs and portray bucrania. Similarly, bovine protomes on bowls and spouted jugs denote the symbolic significance and ceremonial consumption of cattle.[44] Hunting continued to have prestigious connotations in the prehistoric Bronze Age, and deer commonly adorn Red Polished drinking vessels.[45] The consumption of food and drink within the context of funerary ritual is symbolically charged and enhances sensory participation on the part of the mourners. Funerary ritual appears to play a central role in the development of feasting practices in Bronze Age Cyprus. The close relationship between death and the consumption of food and drink is similarly apparent in the contemporary Aegean.[46]

The equipment and major dietary components of this feasting (cattle and possibly also alcoholic beverages such as wine) were introduced to the island from Anatolia. Rather than explaining these changes in the context of diffusion of population, it is preferable to view them in terms of the transferal of esoteric knowledge of exotic drinking customs and the novel use of external referents in the expression of identity and status. A similar phenomenon is evident in the contemporary southern Aegean, with the predominance of Anatolian drinking and pouring shapes among the ceramic repertoire of the Kastri group.[47] There is, however, a significant distinction in the nature and scale of contacts between Anatolia and Cyprus, on the one hand, and Anatolia and the southern Aegean, on the other. The pervasiveness of the "Anatolian" components in Cyprus, which involved extensive consumption of meat and display of bucrania, resulted in a major impact on the material culture, social organization, and economy of the island. In contrast, the Anatolian component of the Kastri material is more limited and is, in effect, represented by a discrete drinking set. Although there is evidence for the development of exclusive feasting activities on Cyprus during the prehistoric Bronze Age (including privileged access to symbolically charged representational material, sacrifice, consumption and display of cattle as part of funerary ceremonies, and possibly control over the consumption of novel alcoholic beverages), the difference between exclusive and communal feasting activities is indistinct, implying that the social boundaries defined by these feasting patterns were fluid.

44. Morris 1985, pp. 190–200, pls. 219–222; Keswani 1994, pp. 268, 270–271.

45. Morris 1985, pp. 185–189, pls. 215, 216.

46. Hamilakis 1998.

47. Broodbank 2000, pp. 310–313. Broodbank (p. 311) suggests that the mimicking of Anatolian culture as represented by the Kastri group is part of a wider phenomenon of increasing infiltration of exotic materials, technologies, and ideas into the Aegean.

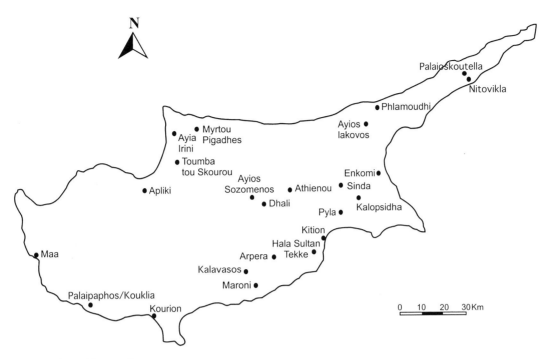

Figure 5. Map of Late Bronze Age Cyprus. D. Druce

LATE BRONZE AGE

Cyprus is characterized during the Late Bronze Age by considerable societal and economic changes, most notably increasing social complexity, the establishment of important urban centers along the southern coast (Fig. 5), and the integration of the island into the extensive trading networks of the eastern Mediterranean (possibly as a major diplomatic player). The syncretic nature of Late Cypriot (LC) society is clearly illustrated by the use of external referents in the construction of elite identities. Aegeanizing and orientalizing prestige goods are common in the elite burials of the coastal urban centers.[48] A particularly intriguing axis of cultural and economic interaction existed between Mycenaean Greece, Ugarit, and Cyprus. This is especially evident in the ivory-working school of the 13th century, but is also reflected in the importation of Mycenaean pottery to Cyprus and Ugarit, which occurs at a larger scale than elsewhere in the eastern Mediterranean.[49]

The Cypriot agricultural base continued with very little change from the earlier Bronze Age. The dietary staples were cereals (wheat and barley) and lentils. There is also unequivocal evidence for the introduction of orchard husbandry to Cyprus at this time, specifically the cultivation of

48. Keswani 1989a, pp. 58–59.

49. On the ivory-carving school, see Hood [1978] 1988, pp. 130–131, fig. 122. For discussion of the trade in Mycenaean pottery, see Sherratt 1999. For large-scale importation of Myce-naean pottery to Ugarit, see most recently Yon, Karageorghis, and Hirschfeld 2000; van Wijngaarden 2002, pp. 37–73. For Mycenaean pottery in Cyprus, see van Wijngaarden 2002, pp. 125–202; Steel, forthcoming.

olives and grapes.[50] Given the evidence for wine production and consumption in the contemporary Aegean, and the long history of wine production in the Levant, it seems likely that wine was also produced in Cyprus, although this has not yet been confirmed through residue analyses of LC pottery.[51]

Archaeozoological remains indicate that sheep, goat, cattle, and pig were all bred,[52] although it is unclear to what extent meat products were incorporated within the LC diet as staples. Based on the profile of bones recovered from two wells at Kouklia-Evreti, Halstead argues that while sheep and cattle were raised for their secondary products (wool and traction power), goat was primarily raised for meat.[53] Even so, consumption of sheep and cattle was strictly controlled. Indeed, the continuing symbolic importance of cattle in LBA Cyprus is indicated by the totemic use and public display of bucrania, usually in sanctuaries but also to mark the limits of the settlement at Morphou.[54] Deer, which had played an important role in Cypriot subsistence practices from the Neolithic, are rare in LC contexts (although deer bones have been found at Myrtou-Pigadhes, Kouklia-Evreti, and Maa-Palaiokastro),[55] and they played only a very limited role in LC cuisine. Croft notes that very few animal bones littered the settlement contexts at Kalavasos, illustrative of formalized disposal practices[56] and possibly strict control over the distribution and consumption of meat products. This pattern indicates a degree of control more typical for luxury commodities used in feasting than for everyday staples.

A closer look at two LBA deposits interpreted as feasting debris, at Kalavasos and Kouklia, provides further information. A rich deposit of animal bones and seeds was found in a possible latrine (A173) in the administrative building X at Kalavasos-Ayios Dhimitrios (Fig. 6). Seed remains of lentil, fig, grape, and olive were found in association with bones of sheep or goat, apparently derived from joints of meat, together with game bird and fish bones.[57] The fill also contained a large number of restorable vessels, with an unusually high incidence of Mycenaean imports.[58] Open vessels, such as cups and bowls, were predominant. For the most part these were complete or intact, suggesting rapid accumulation of the ceramics. The context (the elite, administrative quarter of the site) and the composition of the environmental remains and ceramic assemblage imply that elite feasting took place within the settlement at Kalavasos. The sym-

50. At Kalavasos-Ayios Dhimitrios, for example, domesticated grape pips were found in building I, associated with a sunken pithos, and in buildings III, VIII, and IX; olive was found in buildings VIII, X, and especially in building IX (Hansen 1989, pp. 82–92). Olive is also reported at Hala Sultan Tekke (Hjelmqvist 1979) and Apliki (Helbaek 1962), and domesticated grape at Kalopsidha (Helbaek 1966) and Hala Sultan Tekke (Hjelmqvist 1979). Hamilakis (1996; 1999, p. 45) questions whether the olive had culinary value in the Bronze Age Aegean, arguing that its primary use was to manufacture the luxury perfumed oils that were so prized in Aegean palatial society and that these played an important role in rituals of competitive consumption and gift exchange. This argument might be extended to LBA Cyprus, where there is substantive evidence for oil production, in particular at Kalavasos-Ayios Dhimitrios (Hansen 1989, p. 89; Keswani 1992).

51. Joffe 1998; Tzedakis and Martlew 1999, pp. 142–179.

52. Halstead 1977; Croft 1989; Larje 1992.

53. Halstead 1977, pp. 265–268.

54. Reese 1990, pp. 390–391; Webb 1999, pp. 251–252.

55. Zeuner and Cornwall 1957, pp. 97–98; Halstead 1977, p. 267; Croft 1988.

56. Croft 1989, p. 70.

57. South 1988, p. 227; South and Russell 1993, pp. 304–306.

58. South and Russell 1993, p. 306.

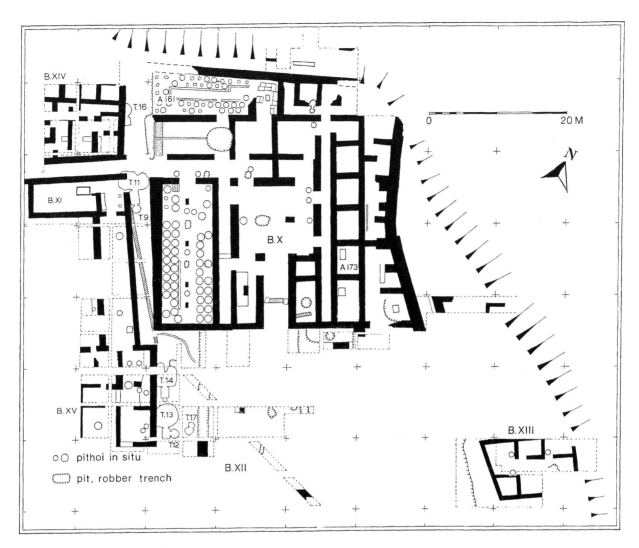

Figure 6. Plan of Kalavasos-Ayios Dhimitrios, northeast area, showing location of A173. After South and Todd 1997, p. 73, fig. 1

bolic force for this LC feast derives from the "architectonically distinguished setting" and the use of exotic dining equipment; the feasting debris evidently embodies "exclusive and unequal commensal circles."[59]

Clear differentiation between the debris of everyday consumption and the disposal of the remnants of feasting is illustrated by the composition of two wells, TE III and TE VIII, excavated at Kouklia-Evreti. The composition of the fill of TE VIII is typical of settlement debris accumulated over a long period of time.[60] The bones, for example, are extremely fragmentary. In contrast, the bones from TE III were well preserved and, in some cases, articulated, implying the rapid accumulation of material from a single event prior to deposition.[61] This interpretation is substantiated by the preservation of the associated pottery, which included pieces from restorable vessels distributed throughout the deposit.[62] The character of the fill of TE III is suggestive of debris from a single feasting event, as has been proposed for A173 at Kalavasos. Halstead argues that the rapid accumulation of bones indicates large-scale consumption of meat, and represents either the debris from dining or a communal (nonexclusive) festival.[63] The profiles of the deposits of TE III at Kouklia and A173 at

59. Dietler 2001, pp. 85–86.
60. Based on the range of animals consumed and deposited in TE VIII, I would, nonetheless, argue that the deposit comprises the debris of elite dining, although not necessarily from a single exclusive diacritical feast.
61. Halstead 1977, pp. 269–270.
62. Halstead 1977, p. 271.
63. Halstead 1977, p. 271.

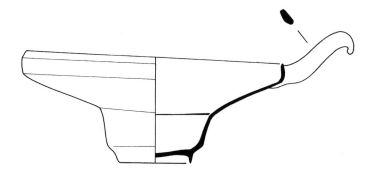

Figure 7. Base Ring II carinated cup.
After Mee and Steel 1998, no. 66, pl. 11

Kalavasos are strikingly similar, suggesting culturally constructed methods of disposing of feasting debris in LBA Cyprus. Formalized deposition of such debris is also indicated by the accumulation of fineware ceramics in wells at Hala Sultan Tekke and Palaipaphos.[64]

At Kouklia, the proximity of the two wells to a sanctuary places the feasting and dining events associated with the deposits within a specialized, liminal context. Moreover, the range of animals deposited is not typical of LC faunal assemblages: large quantities of fallow deer were found in both wells. The elite connotations of deer, already evident in the Late Chalcolithic period, apparently persisted into the Late Bronze Age. Hunting was an elite pastime, and while deer no longer played an important role in daily diet, they had immense symbolic significance in exclusive feasts. Cattle are also plentiful in both deposits. The many horns in TE III[65] suggest that symbolic consumption and display of animal wealth played an important role in LC feasting. Worked astragali from the deposit may indicate that gaming or fortune-telling took place.[66] The combination of cattle and deer bones has also been identified in a well at Kalavasos (A26),[67] an atypical finding for the site that suggests specialized patterns of consumption similar to those proposed for the Kouklia wells.

The practice of feasting is further implied by the range of ceramics used in specific contexts. No clear evidence points to specific structures having been used as dining rooms or feasting halls. Nevertheless, the repeated combination of specific ceramic forms in a variety of contexts is suggestive of communal drinking practices. The LC drinking set comprised kraters, jugs and tankards for serving liquids, and bowls. Although no direct evidence substantiates an association with alcoholic beverages, the repeated combinations of these forms imply the social importance of the consumption of certain liquids.

Alcoholic beverages are an important element in social display and competitive feasting.[68] It is entirely plausible that wine (which had a long history of consumption in the Near East) was the preferred beverage in Cyprus, and also that the dissemination of this beverage was strictly controlled by certain elements of LC society. Initially the indigenous finewares (Base Ring and White Slip) were used both for serving and consumption of liquids. By the 14th and 13th centuries, however, there is considerable evidence from both settlement and funerary contexts for the incorporation of Mycenaean forms into the Cypriot drinking set.[69] The impact of Mycenaean drinking vessels is rather erratic and there was a marked tendency to favor the indigenous Base Ring cups (Fig. 7). These

64. Öbrink 1979; Maier 1997, p. 101.

65. Halstead 1977, p. 270.

66. In this context we should note the importance of astragali in LC sanctuaries and tomb groups. See Halstead 1977, p. 271; Webb 1999, p. 250; South 2000, p. 355.

67. Croft 1989, p. 70.

68. Joffe 1998, p. 298; Dietler 2001, pp. 73–74.

69. Steel 1998, pp. 291–292.

Figure 8. Mycenaean pictorial krater from Enkomi. Courtesy Cyprus Museum, Nicosia

cups are particularly common in sanctuary contexts, where it has been argued that they might have been used for pouring libations.[70] They were the preferred Cypriot drinking cup and the shape would have been particularly suited for drinking wine, as the sediment would settle in the central cavity, leaving a clear liquid at the top.[71] Even so, there is a concentration of Mycenaean drinking vessels (including kylikes, cups, and bowls) in A173 at Kalavasos and in the wells at Kouklia that probably derive from elite feasting events.[72] In most contexts the choice of drinking vessel remained idiosyncratic and an element of personal choice, at least until the later 13th century, when Mycenaean shallow bowls and local imitations gradually became predominant.

The Mycenaean krater (Fig. 8) had an enormous impact on the Cypriot ceramic repertoire, and presumably also on the practice of competitive feasting/drinking.[73] The open krater, amphoroid krater, and bell krater were all imported. Occasionally they are found in settlement contexts, as in well deposits at Hala Sultan Tekke.[74] For the most part, however, they occur in funerary contexts, and they were certainly a prerequisite element for inclusion in high-status burials in the coastal urban centers. This pattern might seem to suggest that the Mycenaean krater had little impact on activities within the settlement, but use-wear analysis indicates that these vessels were used over a lengthy period before they were deposited in tombs.[75]

The limited occurrence of Mycenaean kraters within the settlement reflects their prestigious connotations. Rather than serving as items of everyday use, the kraters were carefully curated and used only on specific occasions, such as ceremonial feasts. The krater formed the centerpiece of the LC drinking set. It was primarily intended for display, hence the preference for kraters with elaborate pictorial decoration, especially chariot scenes referring to elite lifestyles. These objects were deliberately removed from circulation and deposited in tombs as elements of elite funerary

70. Vaughan 1991, p. 124.

71. Russell 1986, p. 66.

72. Kalavasos: South and Russell 1993, p. 306; Kouklia: Maier 1983, pp. 229–230; 1997, pp. 93–95.

73. Steel 1998, p. 293.

74. Öbrink 1979, p. 54, fig. 138.

75. Keswani 1989b, p. 562.

Figure 9. WPWM III pottery from Kouklia: skyphoi *(top)* **and shallow bowls.** After Maier 1973, pp. 70, 74, figs. 2, 7; Kling 1989, p. 161, fig. 20:1a, c

display, further enhancing their prestigious status. Although jugs (either local wares or Mycenaean imports) are also found, it appears that the more common Cypriot practice was to serve the wine or other liquid directly from the krater. Bowls have been found inside kraters at Enkomi (Swedish Expedition tombs 6 and 18) and Kalavasos.[76] Although Mycenaean pottery is the preferred tableware for LC competitive feasting, it appears that the Cypriot elite did not emulate the cultural practices and feasting paraphernalia of the Mycenaean palatial elite, who preferred drinking equipment of gold or silver.[77] Instead, the Cypriots used Mycenaean imports according to local practices and taste, and appear to have been referencing Ugaritic patterns of wine consumption.[78] The Cypriot elite thus invested the krater with the symbolic connotations of belonging to an exclusive commensal group with esoteric knowledge of foreign patterns of consumption.[79] They also strictly limited the circulation of the Mycenaean krater to elite display and consumption; this exclusivity is likewise evident in the pictorial decoration of the kraters.[80]

The greatest impact of Mycenaean drinking equipment on the Cypriot assemblage was during the later 13th and 12th centuries B.C. The prevalence of locally produced "Mycenaean-style" (White Painted Wheelmade [WPWM] III) pottery in LC IIC–IIIA contexts—skyphoi, shallow bowls, and kraters—is striking and it is noteworthy that the primary "Mycenaeanizing" forms are those associated with dining (Fig. 9).[81] Although this phenomenon has traditionally been attributed to demic diffusion, recent studies have emphasized change in local pottery production and style.[82]

76. South and Todd 1997, p. 73.

77. See Wright, this volume.

78. This is inferred from the high incidence of Mycenaean kraters and drinking vessels recovered from both settlement and funerary contexts at Ugarit; cf. Yon, Karageorghis, and Hirschfeld 2000, pp. 12–15. The representation on a Ugaritic vessel of Yarim

approaching El clearly illustrates the Ugaritic mode of consumption (Courtois 1969, p. 111, fig. 13). A krater is placed on a tripod or table in front of the seated god, El, who is drinking from a kylix-shaped vessel. Yarim is holding a dipper jug, possibly for serving the beverage contained in the krater or for pouring a libation to El.

79. Helms 1988; Dietler 2001, p. 86.

80. Steel 1998, pp. 292–294; 1999, p. 808; Yon, Karageorghis, and Hirschfeld 2000, pp. 12–13.

81. Cadogan 1991, p. 170; Sherratt 1991, p. 192.

82. See, e.g., Sherratt 1991 (and references).

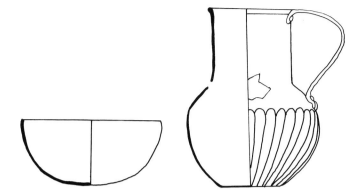

Figure 10. Metal drinking set from Hala Sultan Tekke tomb 23. After Niklasson 1983, pp. 204–205, figs. 489, 490

It appears that the WPWM III drinking sets illustrate a shift in style, and emulation of the previously exclusive Mycenaean forms. In contrast to the restricted distribution of imported Mycenaean kraters apparent in LC IIA–B, the WPWM III dining sets occur widely, suggesting that they were readily available in antiquity, and that a shift in the symbolic style used for diacritical feasting had taken place.[83] Mycenaean dinner services fell out of favor with the Cypriot elite and from LC IIC to LC IIIA, the new prestigious form was the metal drinking set (e.g., Fig. 10).[84]

Much of the evidence for LC drinking sets derives from funerary assemblages and sanctuaries. Certainly, the provision of drinking sets was essential for LC tomb groups but it is unclear whether they were used for funerary feasts or intended as equipment for the deceased. The ceramic vessels from LC tombs are largely intact, however, implying that they were funerary offerings to the deceased rather than the debris of funerary feasts in their honor or objects for communing with the ancestors. Food was deposited in tomb groups[85] and there is some evidence that animal sacrifice and feasting on the part of the mourners was an integral element of funerary ritual—an embodied practice within a liminal location defining relations between the mourners, the deceased, and the ancestors.[86] Animal bones and sherds were recovered from areas of intense burning overlying the sealed chambers of tombs I and II at Morphou-Toumba tou Skourou. Tumuli at Korovia-Palaioskoutella covered complexes of basins and pits containing splinters of animal bone in a matrix of sticky soil and ash, apparently the residue of libations (of wine or oil?) and animal sacrifice.[87]

In sanctuary contexts open forms predominate, but their associated activities remain elusive. The shape most generally associated with LC

83. Dietler 1996, p. 98; 2001, p. 86.

84. Keswani 1989a, p. 65. The bronze drinking sets that became the preferred drinking equipment during the 13th and 12th centuries on Cyprus reflect southern Levantine and Egyptian influence. This is clearly seen by comparing the equipment deposited in Hala Sultan Tekke tomb 23 (Niklasson 1983, pp. 204–205, figs. 488–490) with that found in the burials at Deir el-Balah (Dothan 1979, pp. 66–69, figs. 148–151).

85. At Kalavasos, for example, sheep/goat, bird, and fish bone have been identified. See Croft 1989, pp. 70–71; South 2000, pp. 352, 361.

86. See the discussion on mortuary feasting and embodiment in Hamilakis 1998, pp. 115–119.

87. Webb 1992, pp. 92–93.

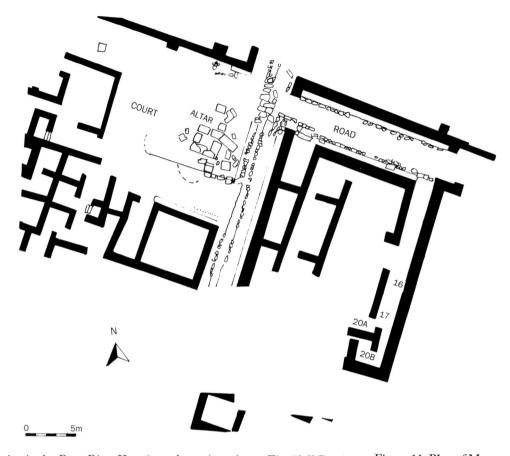

N

0   5m

cult practice is the Base Ring II carinated cup (see above, Fig. 7).[88] Possibly these cups were used in the performance of cult, such as feasting by the worshippers and offering of libations to the deities. Mycenaean bowls are more unusual, but occur in small quantities. For example, a concentration of Mycenaean pottery in the courtyard area of the sanctuary at Myrtou-Pigadhes in front of the altar (Fig. 11) included 12 open forms: deep bowls (Furumark shapes [FS] 284–285), shallow bowls (FS 296), cups (FS 220), a kylix (FS 256–259), and possibly two bell kraters (FS 281).[89] These may be interpreted as the residue of ceremonial activity incorporating consumption and display. Other elements of the Mycenaean drinking set were found in small quantities in the subsidiary rooms, but these were greatly outnumbered by the indigenous forms, in particular the Base Ring carinated cup. In everyday patterns of dining and ritual consumption within sanctuaries, the preferred drinking vessel was the indigenous Base Ring cup. Although kraters are not found in large numbers they are present in most ritual deposits[90] and Webb argues that they were used as cult equipment,

Figure 11. Plan of Myrtou-Pigadhes.
After Taylor 1957, p. 11, fig. 7

88. Webb 1999, pp. 189–192. See, e.g., the large number of Base Ring cups from the sanctuary at Myrtou-Pigadhes (Catling 1957, pp. 36–38, fig. 18). This form continued to be the ritual vessel of choice into the earliest phase of the Cypriot Iron Age, even after Base Ring ware ceased to be produced, as is amply illustrated by the

finds from the Sanctuary of the Ingot God at Enkomi. The typical Base Ring carinated cup is found in large quantities in the 11th-century deposits at the site, but made in a plain, coarseware fabric. See, e.g., Courtois 1971, pp. 254–256, figs. 93, 94:a–c, e–i, l–m, 95:b–d. A similar phenomenon is also evident at Kouklia (Jones and

Catling 1986, p. 595).
89. Catling 1957, pp. 42–48, fig. 20.
90. In addition to the two bell kraters reported at Myrtou-Pigadhes, there were four possible amphoroid kraters (FS 53–55); Catling 1957, pp. 42–44, fig. 20.

for example in libation ceremonies.[91] Given the prevalence of drinking equipment and the common occurrence of kraters in LC sanctuaries, it seems reasonable to interpret these assemblages as the material correlates of ritual/ceremonial feasting on the part of a religious hierarchy. Certainly, the range of pottery replicates the drinking equipment found in other contexts in LBA Cyprus. Moreover, the intoxicating properties of an alcoholic beverage like wine would have been appropriate for consumption in a ritual context.[92] The pottery, therefore, is indicative of a ceremonial, cultic context for the consumption of alcohol.

Further evidence for dining within a cultic context is furnished by the faunal assemblages from the sanctuaries. Animal bones are found in all cult assemblages. In most sanctuaries juvenile cattle *(Bos taurus)* are predominant, with smaller quantities of bird and fish bone,[93] but large quantities of deer *(Dama mesopotamica)* were recovered at Myrtou-Pigadhes.[94] The prevalence of certain bones—the skulls, horns (or antler), and long bones—illustrates the consumption of the primary meat-bearing parts of the animal within a religious context and also indicates that the animals were butchered away from the sanctuary. The long bones are possibly the debris of a sacrificial practice such as ritual feasting. At Myrtou-Pigadhes they are found in rooms 16, 17, and 20, together with a number of scapulas.[95] The associated pottery is appropriate to the presentation, service, and consumption of food and drink: Plain White offering stands, Base Ring carinated cups, bowls in a variety of wares, and jugs. The importance of dining as an element of religious ritual can be paralleled by similar activity in other cultural contexts, such as Late Bronze Age Crete, and Archaic and Classical Greece.[96] The accumulation of skulls, deer antler, and goat horns in the courtyard at Myrtou-Pigadhes, close to the altar,[97] more plausibly relates to symbolic display and is an integral element of Cypriot cult practices, possibly introduced during the prehistoric Bronze Age.[98] This form of display is not paralleled in sanctuaries in the contemporary Aegean.[99]

CONCLUSIONS

Communal feasting practices in Cyprus have a long pedigree, possibly stretching back into the Chalcolithic period, but were certainly established by the prehistoric Bronze Age. Salient characteristics of these feasting practices include symbolic consumption of meat—primarily beef, but also sheep and goat, and possibly deer—and the introduction of exotic alcoholic beverages. By the LC period, hierarchical divisions in society are defined through patterns of exclusive, diacritical feasting. These are marked by distinctive and exclusive locations for consumption, differential access to certain dietary products (cattle and deer), possibly strict control over consumption of wine, and certainly privileged access to exotic dining sets (Mycenaean kraters), which reference esoteric knowledge of Ugaritic dining practices. LC feasting activity is largely inferred from the ceramic assemblages found in tombs and sanctuaries, but the remains of diacritical feasts are also evident in certain settlement contexts, illustrating formalized patterns of the disposal of the debris of feasting.

91. Webb 1999, p. 197. Webb also notes the occurrence of a krater among a group of libation vessels on an Aegeanizing cylinder from Idalion.

92. Joffe 1998, p. 298; Dietler 2001, p. 73.

93. Webb 1999, pp. 250–252.

94. Zeuner and Cornwall 1957, pp. 97–98.

95. Zeuner and Cornwall 1957, p. 99. Similar debris from ceremonial feasting has been identified in the Mycenaean palace at Pylos: a concentration of burned bones (primarily long bones) associated with a number of miniature cups and kylikes found in room 7 (Isaakidou et al. 2002; Stocker and Davis, this volume).

96. Bergquist 1988; Lebessi and Muhly 1990, p. 327; Bookidis 1993.

97. Zeuner and Cornwall 1957, p. 97.

98. See discussion above.

99. J. B. Rutter (pers. comm.).

REFERENCES

Barlow, J. A., D. R. Bolger, and B. Kling, eds. 1991. *Cypriot Ceramics: Reading the Prehistoric Record,* Philadelphia.

Bergquist, B. 1988. "The Archaeology of Sacrifice: Minoan-Mycenaean versus Greek," in *Early Greek Cult Practice. Proceedings of the Fifth International Symposium at the Swedish Institute at Athens* (*SkrAth* 4°, 38), ed. R. Hägg, N. Marinatos, and G. C. Nordquist, Stockholm, pp. 21–34.

Bolger, D. R. 1983. "Khrysiliou-Ammos, Nicosia-Ayia Paraskevi, and the Philia Culture of Cyprus," *RDAC* 1983, pp. 60–73.

———. 1994. "Engendering Cypriot Archaeology: Female Roles and Statuses before the Bronze Age," *OpAth* 20, pp. 9–17.

———. 1998. "The Pottery," in Peltenburg et al. 1998, pp. 93–147.

Bookidis, N. 1993. "Ritual Dining at Corinth," in *Greek Sanctuaries: New Approaches,* ed. N. Marinatos and R. Hägg, London, pp. 45–61.

Broodbank, C. 2000. *An Island Archaeology of the Cyclades,* Cambridge.

Cadogan, G. 1991. "Cypriot Bronze Age Pottery and the Aegean," in Barlow, Bolger, and Kling 1991, pp. 169–171.

Carter, J. B. 1995. "Ancestor Cult and the Occasion of Homeric Performance," in *The Ages of Homer: A Tribute to Emily Vermeule,* ed. J. B. Carter and S. P. Morris, Austin, pp. 285–312.

Catling, H. W. 1957. "The Bronze Age Pottery," in Taylor 1957, pp. 26–59.

Courtois, J.-C. 1969. "La maison du prêtre aux modèles de poumon et de foies d'Ugarit," in *Ugaritica 6: Publié à l'occasion de la XXXe campagne de fouilles à Ras Shamra (1968),* ed. C. F.-A. Schaeffer, Paris, pp. 91–119.

———. 1971. "Le sanctuaire du dieu au lingot d'Enkomi-Alasia (Chypre)," in *Alasia 1,* ed. C. F.-A. Schaeffer, Paris, pp. 151–362.

Croft, P. 1988. "Animal Remains from Maa-Palaeokastro," in V. Karageorghis and M. Demas, *Excavations at Maa-Palaeokastro, 1979–1986,* Nicosia, pp. 449–457.

———. 1989. "Animal Bones," in A. K. South, P. Russell, and P. S. Keswani, *Vasilikos Valley Project 3: Kalavasos-Ayios Dhimitrios* II: *Ceramics, Objects, Tombs, Specialist Studies* (*SIMA* 71.3), Göteborg, pp. 70–72.

———. 1991. "Man and Beast in Chalcolithic Cyprus," *BASOR* 282–283, pp. 63–79.

Dietler, M. 1990. "Driven by Drink: The Role of Drinking in the Political Economy and the Case of Early Iron Age France," *JAnthArch* 9, pp. 352–406.

———. 1996. "Feasts and Commensal Politics in the Political Economy: Food, Power, and Status in Prehistoric Europe," in *Food and the Status Quest: An Interdisciplinary Perspective,* ed. P. Wiessner and W. Schiefenhövel, Providence, pp. 87–125.

———. 2001. "Theorizing the Feast: Rituals of Consumption, Commensal Politics, and Power in African Contexts," in *Feasts: Archaeological and Ethnographic Perspectives on Food, Politics, and Power,* ed. M. Dietler and B. Hayden, Washington, D.C., pp. 65–114.

Dothan, T. 1979. *Excavations at the Cemetery of Deir el-Balah* (*Qedem* 10), Jerusalem.

———. 1982. *The Philistines and Their Material Culture,* Jerusalem.

Dunbabin, K. 2001. "*Ut Graeco more biberetur:* Greeks and Romans on the Dining Couch," in *Meals in a Social Context: Aspects of the Communal Meal in the Hellenistic and Roman World,* 2nd ed., ed. I. Nielsen and H. S. Nielsen, Aarhus, pp. 81–101.

Halstead, P. 1977. "A Preliminary Report on the Faunal Remains from Late Bronze Age Kouklia, Paphos," *RDAC* 1977, pp. 261–275.

Hamilakis, Y. 1996. "Wine, Oil, and the Dialectics of Power in Bronze Age Crete: A Review of the Evidence," *OJA* 15, pp. 1–32.

———. 1998. "Eating the Dead: Mortuary Feasting and the Politics of Memory in the Aegean Bronze Age Societies," in *Cemetery and Society in the Aegean Bronze Age* (Sheffield Studies in Aegean Archaeology 1), ed. K. Branigan, Sheffield, pp. 115–132.

———. 1999. "Food Technologies/Technologies of the Body: The Social Context of Wine and Oil Production and Consumption in Bronze Age Crete," *WorldArch* 31, pp. 38–54.

Hansen, J. 1989. "Botanical Remains," in A. K. South, P. Russell, and P. S. Keswani, *Vasilikos Valley Project 3: Kalavasos-Ayios Dhimitrios* II: *Ceramics, Objects, Tombs, Specialist Studies* (*SIMA* 71.3), Göteborg, pp. 82–93.

Hastorf, C. A. 1991. "Gender, Space, and Food in Prehistory," in *Engendering Archaeology: Women and Prehistory,* ed. J. M. Gero and M. W. Conkey, Oxford, pp. 132–159.

Helbaek, H. 1962. "Late Cypriote Vegetable Diet at Apliki," *OpAth* 4, pp. 171–186.

———. 1966. "What Farming Produced at Cypriote Kalopsidha," in P. Åström, *Excavations at Kalopsidha and Ayios Iakovos in Cyprus* (*SIMA* 2), Lund, pp. 115–126.

Helms, M. W. 1988. *Ulysses' Sail: An Ethnographic Odyssey of Power, Knowledge, and Geographical Distance,* Princeton.

Herscher, E. 1997. "Representational Relief on Early and Middle Cypriot Pottery," in *Four Thousand Years of Images on Cypriote Pottery. Proceedings of the Third International Conference of Cypriote Studies, Nicosia,* ed. V. Karageorghis, R. Laffineur, and F. Vandenabeele, Brussels, pp. 25–36.

Hjelmqvist, H. 1979. "Some Economic Plants and Weeds from the Bronze Age of Cyprus," in U. Öbrink, *Hala Sultan Tekke 5: Excavations in Area 22, 1971–1973 and 1975–1978* (*SIMA* 45.5), Göteborg, pp. 110–133.

Hood, S. [1978] 1988. *The Arts in Prehistoric Greece,* repr. Harmondsworth.

Isaakidou, V., P. Halstead, J. Davis, and S. Stocker. 2002. "Burnt Animal Sacrifice in Late Bronze Age

Greece: New Evidence from the
Mycenaean 'Palace of Nestor,'
Pylos," *Antiquity* 76, pp. 86–92.

James, A. 1996. "Cooking the Books:
Global or Local Identities in Contemporary British Food Cultures,"
in *Cross-Cultural Consumption:
Global Markets, Local Realities,*
ed. D. Howes, London, pp. 77–92.

Joffe, A. H. 1998. "Alcohol and Social
Complexity in Ancient Western
Asia," *CurrAnthr* 39, pp. 297–322.

Jones, R. E., and H. W. Catling. 1986.
"Cyprus 2500–500 B.C.: The Aegean
and the Near East, 1500–1050 B.C.,"
in R. E. Jones, *Greek and Cypriot
Pottery: A Review of Scientific Studies*
(Fitch Laboratory Occasional
Paper 1), Athens, pp. 523–625.

Keswani, P. S. 1989a. "Dimensions of
Social Hierarchy in Late Bronze
Age Cyprus: An Analysis of the
Mortuary Data from Enkomi,"
JMA 2, pp. 49–86.

———. 1989b. "Mortuary Ritual and
Social Hierarchy in Bronze Age
Cyprus" (diss. Univ. of Michigan).

———. 1992. "Gas Chromatography
Analyses of Pithoi from Kalavasos-
Ayios Dhimitrios: A Preliminary
Report," pp. 141–146, in A. K.
South, "Kalavasos-Ayios Dhimitrios
1991," *RDAC* 1992, pp. 133–146.

———. 1994. "The Social Context of
Animal Husbandry in Early
Agricultural Societies: Ethno-
graphic Insights and an Archaeo-
logical Example from Cyprus,"
JAnthArch 13, pp. 255–277.

Killebrew, A. E. 1999. "Late Bronze
and Iron I Cooking Pots in Canaan:
A Typological, Technological, and
Functional Study," in *Archaeology,
History, and Culture in Palestine and
the Near East: Essays in Memory of
Albert E. Glock,* ed. T. Kapitan,
Atlanta, pp. 83–126.

Kling, B. 1989. "Local Cypriot Features
in the Ceramics of the Late Cypriot
IIIA Period," in *Early Society in
Cyprus,* ed. E. J. Peltenburg, Edinburgh, pp. 160–170.

Knapp, A. B. 1990. "Production, Location, and Integration in Bronze Age
Cyprus," *CurrAnthr* 31, pp. 147–
176.

Larje, R. 1992. "The Bones from the
Bronze Age Fortress of Nitovikla,

Cyprus," in G. Hult, *Nitovikla
Reconsidered,* Stockholm, pp. 166–
175.

Lebessi, A., and P. Muhly. 1990.
"Aspects of Minoan Cult: Sacred
Enclosures. The Evidence from the
Syme Sanctuary (Crete)," *AA* 1990,
pp. 315–336.

Lindsay, H. 2001. "Eating with the
Dead: The Roman Funerary Banquet," in *Meals in a Social Context:
Aspects of the Communal Meal in
the Hellenistic and Roman World,*
2nd ed., ed. I. Nielsen and H. S.
Nielsen, Aarhus, pp. 67–80.

Maier, F. G. 1973. "Evidence for Mycenaean Settlement at Old Paphos,"
in *Acts of the International Archaeological Symposium "The Mycenaeans
in the Eastern Mediterranean,"* Nicosia, pp. 68–78.

———. 1983. "New Evidence for the
Early History of Palaepaphos," *BSA*
78, pp. 229–233.

———. 1997. "The Mycenaean Pottery
of Palaipaphos Reconsidered," in
*Proceedings of the International Ar-
chaeological Conference "Cyprus and
the Aegean in Antiquity, from the Prehistoric Period to the 7th Century A.D.,"*
Nicosia, pp. 93–102.

Manning, S. W. 1993. "Prestige, Distinction, and Competition: The
Anatomy of Socioeconomic Complexity in 4th–2nd Millennium
B.C.E. Cyprus," *BASOR* 292, pp. 35–
58.

Mee, C., and L. Steel. 1998. *The Cyp-
riote Collections in the University of
Liverpool and the Williamson Art
Gallery and Museum* (Corpus of
Cypriote Antiquities 17; *SIMA*
20.17), Jonsered.

Morris, D. 1985. *The Art of Ancient
Cyprus, with a Check-List of the
Author's Collection,* Oxford.

Niklasson, K. 1983. "A Shaft-Grave
of the Late Cypriote III Period,"
in P. Åström, E. Åström, A. Hatziantoniou, K. Niklasson, and
U. Öbrink, *Hala Sultan Tekke* 8:
Excavations 1971–79 (*SIMA* 45.8),
Göteborg, pp. 169–213.

Öbrink, U. 1979. *Hala Sultan Tekke* 6:
A Sherd Deposit in Area 22 (*SIMA*
45.6), Göteborg.

Palmer, R. 1994. *Wine in the Mycenaean
Palace Economy* (*Aegaeum* 10), Liège.

Peltenburg, E. J. 1998. "The Character
and Evolution of Settlements at
Kissonerga," in Peltenburg et al.
1998, pp. 233–260.

———. 2001. "A Ceremonial Model:
Contexts for a Prehistoric Building
Model from Kissonerga, Cyprus,"
in *"Maquettes architecturales" de
l'antiquité: Regards croisés (Proche-
Orient, Egypte, Chypre, bassin égéen
et Grèce, du néolithique à l'époque
hellénistique),* ed. B. Muller, Paris,
pp. 123–141.

Peltenburg, E. J., et al. 1985. *Lemba
Archaeological Project 1: Excavations
at Lemba Lakkous, 1976–1983*
(*SIMA* 70.1), Jonsered.

———. 1998. *Lemba Archaeological
Project 2.1A: Excavations at Kisso-
nerga-Mosphilia, 1979–1992*
(*SIMA* 70.2), Jonsered.

Reese, D. S. 1990. "The Human and
Animal Bones," in E. D. T. Vermeule and F. Z. Wolsky, *Toumba tou
Skourou: A Bronze Age Potters' Quarter on Morphou Bay in Cyprus,* Cambridge, Mass., pp. 388–392.

Rehak, P. 1995. "Enthroned Figures in
Aegean Art and the Function of
the Mycenaean Megaron," in *The
Role of the Ruler in the Prehistoric
Aegean. Proceedings of a Panel Discussion Presented at the Annual Meeting of the Archaeological Institute of
America, New Orleans* (*Aegaeum* 11),
ed. P. Rehak, Liège, pp. 95–117.

Russell, P. J. 1986. "The Pottery from the
Late Cypriot IIC Settlement at Kalavasos-Ayios Dhimitrios, Cyprus: The
1979–1984 Excavation Seasons"
(diss. Univ. of Pennsylvania).

Schmandt-Besserat, D. 2001. "Feasting
in the Ancient Near East," in *Feasts:
Archaeological and Ethnographic Perspectives on Food, Politics, and Power,*
ed. M. Dietler and B. Hayden,
Washington, D.C., pp. 391–403.

Sherratt, A. 1997. "Cups That Cheered:
The Introduction of Alcohol to Pre-
historic Europe," in *Economy and
Society in Prehistoric Europe: Chang-
ing Perspectives,* ed. A. Sherratt,
Edinburgh, pp. 376–402.

Sherratt, E. S. 1991. "Cypriot Pottery
of Aegean Type in LC II–III: Problems of Classification, Chronology,
and Interpretation," in Barlow, Bolger, and Kling 1991, pp. 185–198.

Sherratt, S. 1999. "*E pur si muove:* Pots, Markets, and Values in the Second Millennium Mediterranean," in *The Complex Past of Pottery: Production, Circulation, and Consumption of Mycenaean and Greek Pottery (Sixteenth to Early Fifth Centuries B.C.),* ed. J. P. Crielaard, V. Stissi, and G. J. van Wijngaarden, Amsterdam, pp. 163–211.

South, A. K. 1988. "Kalavasos-Ayios Dhimitrios 1987: An Important Ceramic Group from Building X," *RDAC* 1988, pp. 223–228.

———. 2000. "Late Bronze Age Burials at Kalavasos-Ayios Dhimitrios," in Πρακτικά του Τρίτου Διεθνούς Κυπρολογικού Συνεδρίου Α΄: Αρχαίον τμήμα, Nicosia, pp. 345–364.

South, A. K., and P. Russell. 1993. "Mycenaean Pottery and Social Hierarchy at Kalavasos-Ayios Dhimitrios, Cyprus," in *Proceedings of the International Conference "Wace and Blegen: Pottery as Evidence for Trade in the Aegean Bronze Age, 1939–1989,"* ed. C. Zerner, Amsterdam, pp. 303–310.

South, A. K., and I. A. Todd. 1997. "Vasilikos Valley and the Aegean from the Neolithic to the Late Bronze Age," in *Proceedings of the International Archaeological Conference "Cyprus and the Aegean in Antiquity, from the Prehistoric Period to the 7th Century A.D.,"* Nicosia, pp. 71–76.

Steel, L. 1998. "The Social Impact of Mycenaean Imported Pottery in Cyprus," *BSA* 93, pp. 285–296.

———. 1999. "Wine Kraters and Chariots: The Mycenaean Pictorial Style Reconsidered," in *Meletemata: Studies in Aegean Archaeology Presented to Malcolm H. Wiener as He Enters His 65th Year (Aegaeum* 20), ed. P. P. Betancourt, V. Karageorghis, R. Laffineur, and W.-D. Niemeier, Liège, pp. 803–811.

———. Forthcoming. "A Reappraisal of the Distribution, Context, and Function of Mycenaean Pottery in Cyprus," in *La céramique mycénienne entre l'Égée et le Levant,* ed. J. Balensi et al., Lyon.

Taylor, J. du Plat. 1957. *Myrtou-Pigadhes: A Late Bronze Age Sanctuary in Cyprus,* Oxford.

Tzedakis, Y., and H. Martlew, eds. 1999. *Minoans and Mycenaeans: Flavours of Their Time,* Athens.

van Wijngaarden, G. J. 2002. *Use and Appreciation of Mycenaean Pottery in the Levant, Cyprus, and Italy (ca. 1600–1200 B.C.),* Amsterdam.

Vaughan, S. 1991. "Material and Technical Classification of Base Ring Ware: A New Fabric Typology," in Barlow, Bolger, and Kling 1991, pp. 119–130.

Webb, J. M. 1992. "Funerary Ideology in Bronze Age Cyprus—Toward the Recognition and Analysis of Cypriote Ritual Data," in *Studies in Honour of Vassos Karageorghis,* ed. G. C. Ioannides, Nicosia, pp. 87–99.

———. 1999. *Ritual Architecture, Iconography, and Practice in the Late Cypriot Bronze Age (SIMA-PB* 75), Jonsered.

Yon, M., V. Karageorghis, and N. Hirschfeld. 2000. *Céramiques mycéniennes (Ras Shamra-Ougarit* 13), Paris.

Zeuner, F. E., and I. W. Cornwall. 1957. "The Animal Remains and Soil Samples," in Taylor 1957, pp. 97–102.

CHAPTER 8

FEASTING IN HOMERIC EPIC

Susan Sherratt

ABSTRACT

Feasting plays a central role in the Homeric epics. The elements of Homeric feasting—values, practices, vocabulary, and equipment—offer interesting comparisons to the archaeological record. These comparisons allow us to detect the possible contribution of different chronological periods to what appears to be a cumulative, composite picture of around 700 B.C. Homeric drinking practices are of particular interest in relation to the history of drinking in the Aegean. By analyzing social and ideological attitudes to drinking in the epics in light of the archaeological record, we gain insight into both the prehistory of the epics and the prehistory of drinking itself.

THE HOMERIC FEAST

There is an impressive amount of what may generally be understood as feasting in the Homeric epics.[1] Feasting appears as arguably the single most frequent activity in the *Odyssey* and, apart from fighting, also in the *Iliad*. It is clearly not only an activity of Homeric heroes, but also one that helps demonstrate that they are indeed heroes. Thus, it seems, they are shown doing it at every opportunity, to the extent that much sense of realism is sometimes lost—just as a small child will invariably picture a king wearing a crown, no matter how unsuitable the circumstances. In *Iliad* 9, for instance, Odysseus participates in two full-scale feasts in quick succession in the course of a single night: first in Agamemnon's shelter (*Il.* 9.89–92), and almost immediately afterward in the shelter of Achilles (9.199–222). Later in the same night, on their return from their spying mission, he and Diomedes sit down to dine, drink, and pour a libation again (10.576–579). A similar sequence occurs in *Odyssey* 15–16. First, Telemachos and his companions, upon arriving at Ithaca early in the morning, prepare their meal and eat and drink their fill together (15.500–502). As soon as Telemachos has finished making the customary after-dinner speech, he sets off for the swineherd Eumaios's yard. No sooner has he arrived there than he sits down to another repast of roasted meat, bread, and wine (16.46–55). Later, in *Odyssey* 20, two full-scale feasts appear to

1. My thanks to John Bennet, Peter Haarer, and Andrew Sherratt for coming to my rescue on various points of ignorance or uncertainty, and for supplying a number of much needed references; to the *Hesperia* reviewers for further helpful comments and suggestions; and to James Wright for his invaluable assistance in providing Figure 1. Translations of the *Iliad* and *Odyssey* are based on those by R. Lattimore (Chicago 1961; New York 1968).

run into one another, with a disconcertingly abrupt change of scene: one held by the suitors in Odysseus's palace, complete with the slaughter and cooking of animals (20.248–256), and the other, apparently including the same people, held in the grove of Apollo, seemingly before the first has even got into its stride (20.276–280).

To a modern-minded reader of the epics, all this stopping to eat and drink can seem tedious. It interrupts the flow of the story (especially in the *Odyssey*) and distracts us from the plot, particularly since it often takes up a large number of lines and tends to be couched in repetitive, predictable language. Indeed, feasting scenes are among the most regularly formulaic in layout and vocabulary in the epics, ranking alongside other genre scenes such as arming.[2] Even when they are condensed into only a few lines they often preserve this character, frequently appearing as reduced versions of the more fully described scenes, using a selection of the stock lines, phrases, and vocabulary that regularly occur in the lengthier accounts as a *pars pro toto* shorthand to suggest the whole. In this way, at least some of the distinctive features of the fully described Homeric feast (meat-eating, wine-drinking, and inclusion of the gods by a ritual "sacrifice" and libation) are usually explicitly present or implied. Even breakfast (ἄριστον) can be seen to be a feast (see, e.g., *Il.* 24.123–125, where the element of feasting is suggested by the hallowing ["sacrificing" in the literal sense of the word] and consumption of a sheep). Thus, as described, Homeric feasting takes place as a matter of course every day, whenever named heroes and their companions prepare and eat a meal together, whenever they arrive somewhere and hospitality is offered and before they depart, before and at the conclusion of every heroic enterprise, and whenever they want to win the gods to their side. Feasting is ubiquitous and constant—it is what Homeric heroes do in company at every opportunity.

Within this framework, however, there are a number of variations, particularly of emphasis, designed to suit particular contexts. At one end of the spectrum are feasts whose primary stated purpose is to propitiate gods (such as the feast associated with Nestor's sacrifice of a cow to Athena in *Odyssey* 3), for which the bulk of the description is devoted to the elaborate ritual surrounding the slaughter, dismembering, and cooking of the animal. At the other end are primarily secular feasts where this ritual aspect is either omitted from the description or reduced to the odd word or line— just enough to suggest that the animal is still hallowed ("sacrificed") before slaughter, and that the gods received their share of the meat and the wine by burning and libation, even if this is no less perfunctory than a grace said automatically before meals. In terms of practice, however, no very clear dividing line exists between these two types of feast, and the differences lie principally in the amount of detail in which the elements of the feast, from slaughter to consumption, are described. When they are not described (or not in detail), we are given no reason to believe that there is any substantial difference in the basic methods and procedures involved. Thus, Eumaios's feasts for Odysseus in *Odyssey* 14.72–114 and 14.414–456 are, to all intents and purposes, secular feasts, yet most of the elements contained are also standard elements of more overtly god-centered sacrificial feasts, such as that to Athena in *Odyssey* 3 or that to Apollo in *Iliad* 1. In this respect,

2. Kirk 1962, p. 167.

Homeric feasting forms a continuum, from the fully detailed step-by-step account of the slaughter, cooking, and eating of the meat, and the mixing, libation, and drinking of the wine, which together may take up several dozen lines, to the quick two-line drink and libation before bed.

Indeed, despite the importance accorded in the epics to propitiating the gods explicitly by means of animal sacrifice, there is much in the nature of divine inclusion in the Homeric feast—including the explicitly sacrificial feast—that seems curiously ambivalent in this respect. As G. S. Kirk has pointed out, after the sacrifice, Homeric heroes get down to the secular business of meat-eating with almost indecent speed, and with almost no ritual transition from the sacrifice itself except for the treatment of the "divine portion."[3] Ultimately, the gods are seen less as remote recipients of sacrifice than as straightforward (if unseen) coparticipants in the feast, alongside and more or less equal to mortal heroes (as, we are told, they actually were in the past [*Od.* 7.201]).

From a practical point of view, this approach has certain advantages for human feasters, since it removes any clear distinction between sacrifice and feasting, to the extent that sacrifice to a god in most cases appears as little more than a good excuse for yet another party,[4] just as, conversely, all feasting is assured of divine sanction by the simple means of giving the gods their token share of food or wine. It is particularly convenient that, because the gods have ichor rather than blood in their veins (*Il.* 5.341–342),[5] they do not actually eat mortal meat, and are therefore content with the smell of fat burning around extracted bones (which would not be eaten anyway), leaving most of the more edible portions for their mortal cofeasters. Exceptionally, only in *Odyssey* 14.435–436 is a portion of the cooked meat set aside unburned for Hermes and the nymphs—an arguably less sophisticated approach that finds numerous correlates in folk practices such as the bowl of milk left overnight for the pixies or the mince pie laid out for Santa Claus. The fact that gods particularly appreciate hecatombs—which, if taken literally, ought to mean a hundred oxen killed, cooked, and eaten at

---

3. Kirk 1981, p. 70.

4. The Greek verb ἱερεύω (lit. "make holy"), which we translate as "sacrifice," does not in itself suggest the connotations of self-denial that we associate with the English word. On the contrary, in its Homeric use it sometimes carries positive implications of self-indulgence: cf., e.g., *Od.* 17.535–536, where ἱερεύοντες, as uttered by Penelope, clearly has no more meaning than "slaughtering for consumption." The exceptions to the almost complete identification of sacrifice with feasting (and vice versa) in the epics are the sacrifices associated with the pledging of the oaths concerning the duel between Menelaos and Paris in *Il.* 3 and with the swearing of fidelity between Agamemnon and Achilles in *Il.* 19.190,

250–268, where the meat is either not eaten at all or not eaten on the spot.

5. On the introduction of the concept of ichor, see Kirk 1990, p. 104; Lorimer 1950, p. 466, n. 3. On the development of divine physiology and diet in general and its possible part in the differentiation of the Olympian gods from their oriental relatives, see Kirk 1990, pp. 1–14. When the gods on Olympos feast, they may drink nectar rather than wine, but they do so with the same equipment and often are described in much the same language as mortal heroes in their earthly houses (*Il.* 1.493–611).

The idea (cf. Kirk 1990, pp. 10–14) that a sanitized view of the Olympian gods who feed primarily on their own special food and drink and secondarily

on the fragrance of burning fat or evaporated wine (cf., e.g., *Il.* 1.462–463 = *Od.* 3.459–460) may be the culmination of a long process of theological development is borne out by the difficulty of accommodating the ubiquitous practice of libation within this view. Pouring libations onto the ground hardly seems compatible with the idea of the essence of the wine rising upward to its recipients. While it is almost certainly too simplistic to see this as a holdover from a pre-Olympian age characterized by the worship of predominantly chthonic deities, it nevertheless underlines the mix of sometimes apparently anomalous notions and practices that together make up Homeric views of and attitudes toward the gods.

once—seems as good an excuse as any for the kind of very large-scale communal feasting implied by the sacrifice to Poseidon in *Odyssey* 3. The other useful side of this, of course, is that joining in the feast also brings obligations, both for mortals (*Il.* 4.343–346, 18.546) and for deities (*Il.* 4.45–46).

From another point of view, we can probably distinguish two main types of feast, differentiated on organizational grounds. One is the feast provided by a host at his own expense for his companions or guests, as when, for instance, Agamemnon and Achilles prepare feasts in their shelters at Troy (*Il.* 9.89–92); when the hospitality of the feast is offered to the wandering Odysseus by Alkinoos, Circe, or Eumaios (*Il.* 9.199–222); or when Alkinoos provides a feast for all after the assembly of the Phaeacians (*Od.* 8.39).[6] Another is the communal feast to which each contributes his share, such as the "bring a bottle" party held in Menelaos's palace in honor of his daughter's marriage during Telemachos's visit (*Od.* 4.621–624), the community feast in honor of Poseidon arranged by Nestor in which each of the settlements surrounding Pylos contributes nine bulls (*Od.* 3.4–67), or Penelope's account of the proper feasting behavior of would-be suitors (*Od.* 18.277–279). The outdoor feasts of Odysseus and his companions, for which they catch their own food and share the provisions they have brought or acquired collectively, probably also fall into this category (cf., e.g., *Od.* 10.155–184).[7] While it goes without saying that feasting (as almost everything else) in the epics is mainly the province of heroes and gods, enough ambiguity exists in both categories to suggest that virtually everyone can join in at some time or other (cf. *Od.* 15.373–379). In an ideal world, shepherds have plenty of meat (*Od.* 4.87–88), and even reapers share in the royal ox-roast portrayed on Achilles' shield.[8] At any rate, the two clear categories of the hosted and communal feasts stand in blatant contrast to the travesty of the suitors' feasting day in and day out on Ithaca, at the absent Odysseus's expense and against his son's will, and to the reckless action of Odysseus's companions in killing and eating the cattle of Apollo in defiance of an express ban (*Od.* 11.108–117, 12.264–419). The suitors, for good measure, also violate the code associated with feasting in other ways—by mistreating the servants in Odysseus's palace, and by their churlish treatment of Odysseus in disguise as a suppliant beggar. Similarly, other acclaimed villains such as Aigisthos and even Herakles pervert the ethics of the feast by murdering their guests at table (*Od.* 11.409–415, 21.26–30; cf. also 9.478–479).

The ingredients of a Homeric feast are typically meat, cereal (probably implicitly, as well as explicitly, in the form of bread),[9] and wine, with the emphasis above all on the consumption of meat in the form of domestic cattle, sheep, goats, and pigs and—on occasion, with divine assistance—hunted game, such as mountain goats (*Od.* 9.155) or a deer (*Od.* 10.156–177). This emphasis on meat can be seen as at least partly an epic ideal (it is extremely unlikely that any members of a Homeric or pre-Homeric audience, however exalted, dined on meat with the regularity that Homer's heroes do—though, as we shall see, there may have been times when it was relatively widely eaten within certain sectors of Aegean society). In the epics, meat in the form of flocks and herds is a regular index of an

6. See also *Od.* 1.374–375, where Telemachos suggests that the suitors take turns in giving feasts in their own households, eating up their own possessions.

7. A possible third category, of which we may catch a rare and elusive glimpse, is the public subscription feast with which Odysseus, disguised as the Cretan Aithon, claims to have entertained himself at Knossos (*Od.* 19.194–198)—in other words, a contributory feast in which the contributors themselves possibly do not take part. There is also a curious passage in *Il.* 17.249–250, where Agamemnon and Menelaos are said to drink "at the expense of the people" (δήμια πίνουσιν). The existence of this third category, however, is extremely shadowy in the epics.

8. *Il.* 18.560, where πάλυνον probably implies that the barley is scattered on the ox.

9. Usually σῖτος, presumably in a secondary sense of bread made from grain (since it is sometimes referred to as piled up in baskets: *Od.* 1.147), but also on occasion ἄρτον (e.g., *Od.* 17.343, 18.120).

individual's worth—his own personal property—even though others may look after the animals on his behalf.[10] Ideally, it derives from specially fattened animals that take time and expense to produce. Thus, although it is a renewable resource, it cannot be renewed quickly—hence the despair with which Telemachos contemplates the suitors' reckless dissipation of the herds and flocks that represent the tangible wealth of his paternal inheritance.[11] The implication of this is that meat can be eaten on a regular basis only by a wealthy elite (though even then not every day, let alone at every meal), and by others mainly as a result of the former's beneficence on certain regulated occasions. Indeed, this is what is implied by the "excuse" of divine encouragement, or at least divine involvement in epic feasts. Not only does this involvement sanction the improbably constant meat-eating activities of named heroes, but it provides opportunities for festivals at which meat may be eaten by very large gatherings of people. The observation or belief that meat gives strength and courage (even if sometimes false courage: *Il.* 8.229–232) merely adds to its desirable qualities.

Lest we should think the heroic diet monotonous, however, the presence of many other "things to eat" (εἴδατα πολλά) is frequently, though obscurely, signaled—at least where feasts in a domestic setting are concerned—by the following repeated lines:

σῖτον δ' αἰδοίη ταμίη παρέθηκε φέρουσα,
εἴδατα πόλλ' ἐπιθεῖσα, χαριζομένη παρεόντων

A modest housekeeper brought in and set down bread [or cereal food],
adding many other things to eat, giving freely of what was in store.
Od. 1.139–140, also 4.55–56, 7.175–176, 10.371–372, 15.138–139, 17.94–95

What these things might be we are not told, but black puddings (*Od.* 20.25–26), cheeses, fish and other seafood, onions, leeks, olives, honey, and various types of fruit including apples, pears, pomegranates, and figs are all mentioned at various points in the epics (often in similes) and might have been assumed by Homeric audiences to be potentially included among

---

10. Odysseus, for instance, owned 12 herds of cattle, and equal numbers of flocks of sheep and goats and herds of pigs pastured by his own herdsmen outside Ithaca (*Od.* 14.100–102), a situation that finds broad analogies in the Linear B texts, where the palaces appear to have interests in livestock spread over very wide areas (Killen 1994; Chadwick 1976, pp. 127–132; Piteros, Olivier, and Melena 1990). For the transport by boat of animals destined for feasting, see *Od.* 20.187; cf. Piteros, Olivier, and Melena 1990, pp. 116–133, for the transport of livestock for similar purposes from Karystos and Amarynthos on Euboia to Thebes.

11. Cf. *Od.* 14.13–20, where 600 pigs have been reduced to 360 by the suitors' depredations. In this connection, a particularly striking feature of the *Iliad* is the silence about how and where the Achaean heroes obtained the vast numbers of animals they appear to have sacrificed and consumed at Troy (cf., e.g., *Il.* 7.465–466), which suggests that, in general, the epic tradition did not include much consideration of the problems involved in servicing a large collective Achaean army. Indeed, only the Trojans and their allies seem to recognize food supplies as a potential problem, as when Hector mentions

how he wears down his people by providing gifts and food for the allies (*Il.* 17.225–226), or when Pandaros explains to Aineias that he did not bring his chariot horses to Troy because of the difficulties of feeding them appropriately in a situation where too many fighters were gathered in one place away from home (*Il.* 5.202–204). By contrast, however, we are told quite explicitly whence and how the Achaeans at Troy obtained their wine (*Il.* 9.71–72); and, as we shall see, the movement of wine as gifts or in commercial transactions figures frequently in the epics.

them.[12] The importance of (sea) salt is also indicated on several occasions (e.g., *Il.* 9.215; *Od.* 17.455, 23.270).

We are given several descriptions of the process of slaughtering, though it is not clear that the detailed variations have any systematic significance except insofar as they may be appropriate for different types of animals (themselves appropriate for different gods). Only once are the horns of a cow gilded (*Od.* 3.437–438; though cf. also *Il.* 10.294), which not only signals a very special occasion presided over by an ancient and venerable hero, but seems to mark this particular act of slaughter more firmly as representative of institutionalized sacrifice with a feast tacked on (as public sacrifice often appears to be in historical Greece), and less as a customary prelude to a hearty feast. The animals (if more than one) may be arranged in a circle, or (if one) the participants may arrange themselves in a circle around the animal. At this point, the hairs of the head may be cut off and thrown in the fire, and barley is scattered.[13] The implement used to cut the throat of the victim may be an axe or a knife, and the blood may be collected (and perhaps used to make the black puddings).

The standard method of cooking, whenever we hear anything about it, is the barbecue, which real heroes are clearly expected to accomplish for themselves rather than leave to underlings (*Il.* 19.316–317; cf. *Od.* 15.321–324; and contrast the behavior of the suitors, *Od.* 4.681–683).[14] After slaughtering and skinning, the meat is cut up and put on spits (ὀβελοί) and roasted over a fire, then lifted off and either distributed directly or placed on boards for subsequent distribution. In contexts where sacrifice to the gods is emphasized, this is preceded by descriptions of the thigh bones being cut out, wrapped in fat with token strips of flesh laid over them, marinated with wine libations, and burned on a σχίζη (a splinter of peeled wood, *Il.* 2.425). It is at this point, also, that the innards, which cook much more quickly than the flesh, are eaten, like the *kokoretsi* that precedes the meat at a modern Greek sheep roast. On at least one occasion, the divine portions are simply thrown on the fire before the eating begins (*Il.* 9.220). Wine is mixed and passed around generously, apparently customarily from left to right (*Il.* 1.597), for libation and drinking.

Ceremonial hand-washing is also standard, not only before the ritual of slaughter, but also before sitting down to a feast, when a golden jug (πρόχοος) and a silver basin (λέβης) are frequent washing equipment. Be-

---

12. It is interesting, however, that the only mention of pulses (in a simile) comes in a context that suggests they may be regarded primarily as agricultural weeds rather than a source of food (*Il.* 13.588–589). In this there is a strange parallelism with the Linear B texts, in which pulses are never mentioned—though we assume from the palaeobotanical remains that they were quite widely exploited at the time the texts were written (Halstead 2001, p. 38; de Fidio 1989, p. 199). A similar

sort of parallelism may perhaps be glimpsed in the treatment of olive oil in both the epics and the Linear B texts (see below). Cheeses and honey, however, as well as cereal, meat, and wine, are listed on Un 718 from Pylos, among ingredients for a feast in honor of Poseidon (Palmer 1963, pp. 215–216; Palaima, this volume; Bendall, forthcoming).

13. If barley is not available, oak leaves are pressed into service instead; see *Od.* 12.357–358. Similarly, in the

same passage, water is used to pour on the thigh bones instead of wine.

14. The only mention of boiling meat comes in a simile, where the rendering of pig fat in a cauldron (λέβης) is compared with the seething of the waters of the river Xanthos (*Il.* 21.362–364). Otherwise, cauldrons and tripod cauldrons are used only to heat water for ablutions (cf. *Il.* 18.343–350, 22.443, 23.40; *Od.* 8.433–437, 10.359).

fore joining the feast, individual heroic participants often bathe (or are bathed),[15] anoint themselves with olive oil (which, interestingly, never figures in a culinary context), and don fresh clothing.

A complex array of utensils and equipment is often used. In addition to the spits for cooking, we hear once of supports for the spits (*Il.* 9.214) and on two occasions of mysterious objects called πεμπώβολα (*Il.* 1.463 = *Od.* 3.460), usually translated as five-tined spits or, perhaps more plausibly, forks.[16] When circumstances allow it, the feasters sit on chairs of different types (κατὰ κλισμούς τε θρόνους τε: e.g., *Od.* 1.145 = 3.389 = 24.385, 10.233, 15.134, 17.86 = 17.179 = 20.249), often covered with cloth, at small, portable polished (stone?) or silver tables. Outdoors, or in Eumaios's hut, fleeces may substitute. Sometimes—but particularly if the feasters are divine or semidivine, guests of divinities, or overweening suitors—they place their feet on a footstool (*Il.* 14.241, 18.390; *Od.* 1.131, 4.136, 10.315, 367, 17.409–410, 462, 504, 19.57). The cooked meat may be placed on boards for serving, and bread may be served in baskets. Baskets are also used to hold the barley for the sacrificial ritual.

Wine is typically mixed in kraters, and drunk and libated from the epic δέπας (often qualified by the untranslatable epithet ἀμφικύπελλον), or less frequently from ἄλεισα or κύπελλα;[17] only once does anyone—Eumaios and Odysseus in the former's hut—drink from a σκύφος (*Od.* 14.112). Insofar as we are told, kraters are usually silver, and drinking cups are invariably gold. The importance of wine-drinking as a highly significant social activity is underlined by the custom of giving kraters and drinking cups as guest-friend gifts (*Il.* 6.220, 23.741–748, 24.233–234; *Od.* 4.591,

15. Bathtubs (ἀσάμινθοι) for this purpose seem to be available even to the Achaeans camped before Troy (*Il.* 10.576).

16. For the interpretation of these, see, e.g., LSJ, s.v. πεμπώβολον; Meier-Brügger 2001, p. 1147, s.v. πεμπώβολον (W. Beck); Chantraine 1968–1980, vol. 3, p. 771, s.v. ὀβελός; Kirk 1985, p. 101; cf. also Bruns 1970, p. 39; Buchholz, Jöhrens, and Maull 1973, p. 167, n. 614. The view that they represent five-tined instruments of tridentlike form is shared by virtually all ancient commentators and lexicographers. A different view is put forward by Kron (1971, pp. 131–144), who suggests that they represent bundles of five spits for roasting innards, partly on the grounds that forks or flesh-hooks would be inappropriate in the circumstances. While this idea perhaps finds a modicum of circumstantial support in the 10 spits associated with an Early–Middle Orientalizing burial in tomb 285 in the North Cemetery at Knossos (Snodgrass 1996, p. 591), it

has to be emphasized that it is not at all clear how the πεμπώβολα are used in the two Homeric contexts in which they occur. All we hear is that young men stand around with them in their hands while the thigh bones are burned (*Il.* 1.463 = *Od.* 3.460). Given the formulaic sequence, we might suppose that they are used to roast the innards, but this is not indicated either explicitly or implicitly. Metal forks or flesh-hooks of various designs, usually with two or three prongs, but also sometimes more, are relatively common in the Near East throughout the Bronze Age and Early Iron Age. They are also found in Late Bronze Age Cyprus (Catling 1964, pp. 65–66; Niklasson 1983, p. 174) and in Late Bronze and Early Iron Age Europe (see Duhn 1926, pp. 331–332, fig. 1, for a five-pronged example from an Italian hoard).

In the Aegean, a trident was discovered by Schliemann (1880, p. 255, no. 372) in shaft grave IV at Mycenae, a bident of Late Helladic (LH) IIA date comes from a tomb at Routsi

(Demakopoulou 1988, no. 261), and a six-pronged version is known from a tomb at Dendra (Persson 1942, p. 126; cf. Persson 1931, pl. XXXIV); for single-prong "flesh-hooks" of Early to Middle Bronze Age date, which may have served a similar purpose, see Branigan 1974, pp. 30, 173, pl. 15:1181–1184. As has often been pointed out, the most likely use for such implements in a feasting context is for spearing and extracting pieces of meat from a cauldron (E. Banou, in Demakopoulou 1988, p. 246, no. 261) —circumstances in which one might well envisage participants standing around waiting with these in their hands. If so, it is not impossible that the twice-repeated line preserves some fossilized echo of a cooking practice earlier than that ostensibly presented in the Homeric epics (see below, n. 50).

17. That δέπα and κύπελλα are regarded as virtually interchangeable is seen in *Il.* 1, where Hera's δέπας ἀμφικύπελλον of 1.584 morphs into a κύπελλον 12 lines further on.

615–619, 8.430, 9.203, 15.85, 115–119, 24.275). These vessels often have a long history of personal ownership, and are frequently regarded as their current owner's most prized possession. A final piece of equipment associated once with the preparation of a mysterious wine-based potion is a bronze grater used to grate goat's cheese (*Il.* 11.639–640).

The Homeric obsession with what one might characterize as emblematic feasting should alert us to the highly charged significance that this activity had for Homeric (and without doubt also pre-Homeric and post-Homeric) audiences. At its simplest and perhaps most superficial, there is its obvious dramatic significance. Feasts form the setting for the telling (or singing) of stories, whether to catch up on background history essential to the plot or to digress into anecdotes concerning offstage characters. They are also the prelude to important speeches in which intentions are announced or philosophies expounded. Moreover, feasts herald the beginning of an exciting action or development or the close of a successful or harrowing episode. They are, often, more or less formulaic punctuation points that, among other things, allow the bard to gather his thoughts and remember where he wants to go next.

Of perhaps greater significance is the reflective aspect of Homeric feasting, particularly as far as the close association between the feast and the singing of tales is concerned (cf. *Od.* 4.15–18, 9.5–10, 13.26–28, 17.358, 22.351–352; and for the association between feasting and lyres, or singing and dancing generally, see also *Od.* 1.144–155, 8.99, 248, 17.269–271, 21.428–430; *Il.* 1.473, 601–604, 24.62–63). In this, the Homeric epics might be said to mirror the contexts of their own performance, since, given the probability that they were elaborated and performed at festivals at some supraregional sanctuary such as Delos,[18] a context of large-scale religious feasting is almost assured. Indeed, at the risk of seeming flippant, it is hard to imagine how Homeric audiences could get through a performance of even a portion of the *Iliad* or *Odyssey* as we know them without a relatively free flow of wine to sustain them (cf., e.g., *Od.* 14.193–198, 15.390–400). For audiences at what may be described as epic occasions, the frequent epic scenes of heroic feasting, in which tales are sung, heroes' stories told, and important speeches of moral or philosophical exposition made, may well have served as a mirror in which they could glimpse themselves directly reflected. They allowed listeners to step through the looking glass to become one with the epic world.[19]

At a deeper level, Homeric feasting can be said to encapsulate values that are likely to have simultaneously created and confirmed a collective ideology: the values of companionship and commensality, equal sharing and individual esteem, reciprocity and the obligations of hospitality,[20] together with duties owed to the feasting community of which one is a member—and at least the potential for universal inclusion (if not always its actuality).[21] To a large extent, these are universal values in preindustrial societies (and remain at least ideals in almost all societies), but they are values that we particularly associate with an idealized notion of ancient Greece. The emphasis that the historical Greeks placed on such values as central to their own idea of themselves undoubtedly owes much to the pivotal part played by the Homeric epics, from the Archaic period on-

18. Taplin 1992, pp. 1–45.

19. In an even more reflexive mode, feasts themselves are subjects to be sung about at subsequent feasts down through the generations; to be present at a great feast assures one's participation in "history" (see, e.g., *Il.* 10.217).

20. See the expression ξενίη τε τράπεζα (*Od.* 14.158 = 20.230), which is used in the context of swearing an oath.

21. One of the most striking examples of exclusion from feasting (and perhaps the only occasion on which exclusion is ever made explicit in the epics) is the poignant passage in *Il.* 22.490–499 in which Andromache foretells the future plight of the orphaned Astyanax, driven from the feast by the sons of his dead father's companions because his father is no longer sharing their feasting. This, of all epic passages, is perhaps the one in which the sharing of the feast as an *exclusive* symbol of membership of an elite (and contingently constituted) warrior group is given most emphasis.

ward, as an accepted account of their earliest "history" and as the acknowledged basis for their educational system.

In this respect, aspects of the Homeric terminology that relate to feasting are particularly interesting. The most commonly used noun that we normally translate as "feast" is δαίς, which literally means a "share," "portion," or "division" (from the root verb δαίω, "divide" or "distribute"[22] [cf. *Od.* 5.61, 9.551]) and is often in fact more easily translated as such. There are numerous passages in the *Iliad* and the *Odyssey* where these principles underlying the notion of the word δαίς are made quite explicit. The noun-epithet combination δαίς ἐΐση occurs several times in both the *Iliad* and *Odyssey* in contexts where it is impossible to translate δαίς with either the single word "share" or "feast," since both are neatly wrapped up in it. In *Iliad* 4, for instance, Zeus declares his support for Priam and the Trojans against Hera's hostility, citing their punctiliousness in keeping him supplied with sacrifices:

οὐ γάρ μοί ποτε βωμὸς ἐδεύετο δαιτὸς ἐΐσης,
λοιβῆς τε κνίσης τε· τὸ γὰρ λάχομεν γέρας ἡμεῖς.

For never did my altar want for an equal share of the feast, of the libation and the fragrance; we obtained our due honor.
Il. 4.48–49; 24.69–70

The same phrase, δαιτὸς ἐΐσης, figures again in *Iliad* 9.225 when Aias reassures Achilles that he has no lack of his equal share of the feast either in the shelter of Agamemnon or in his own hut, in *Iliad* 15.95, and in the frequently repeated line

δαίνυντ', οὐδέ τι θυμὸς ἐδεύετο δαιτὸς ἐΐσης

They feasted, nor did any appetite feel the lack of an equal share.
Il. 1.468; 1.602; 2.431; 7.320; 23.56
Od. 16.479; 19.425[23]

Elsewhere, we find variations on the phrase δαίνυσθαι δαῖτα ("to share a feast") (e.g., *Il.* 9.70; *Od.* 3.66 = 20.280, 7.50, 11.185–186); and, indeed, the normal verbs to "give (or apportion) a feast" and to "feast" are the active and middle voices of δαίνυμι.

It is interesting that the word δαίς with the meaning "feast" is rarely used in later prose (except in specific Homeric references or allusions), though it does occur in tragedy.[24] It is thus a special "poetic" word, regarded as "archaic" and associated particularly with Homeric epic and (one assumes) with special Homeric and possibly quasi-religious connotations. Whether it is a word with a much earlier pre-Homeric history is hard to say. It does not, as far as I know, appear in the Linear B texts, where feasts or festivals are implied from the context or given specific proper names. However, the word *e-pi-de-da-to* (ἐπιδέδαστοι? [from δατέομαι],[25] "have been distributed"?) on Pylos tablet (PY) Vn 20, apparently in the context of the palatial distribution of wine to each of the nine centers of the Hither Province,[26] suggests the right kind of semantic association. In general, the texts' preoccupation with both meticulously measured palatial distribution and feasting (often together) makes it quite likely that the notions of

22. Cf. the verb δαίομαι and its synonym in this respect, δατέομαι.

23. Cf. also *Od.* 8.98, 11.185.

24. It also, as one might expect, occurs in Hesiod: cf. *Op.* 319–351, where several of the values associated with Homeric feasting are nicely expounded. In the phrase ἐπὶ δαῖτα καλεῖν ("to invite to a feast") in line 342, however, the word seems to have lost its frequent Homeric dual meaning of "portion or share" *and* "feast," and means simply "feast" (cf. also Hes. *Op.* 736, 742).

25. Ἐπιδέδαιτοι (from δαίομαι), the alternative suggested by Ventris and Chadwick (1956, p. 392; cf. also Lejeune 1958, p. 226; Lejeune 1971, p. 151; Gallavotti 1961, p. 173; Davies 1963, p. 87, s.v. *e-pi-de-da-to*) would be even better from our point of view, but now seems generally to be regarded as less likely (Palmer 1994, p. 74; Aura Jorro 1985, p. 223).

26. Palmer 1963, p. 369; Ventris and Chadwick 1973, pp. 348–349, no. 250; Palmer 1994, pp. 75–76.

"portion" or "share" and "feasting" were closely allied in at least Late Bronze Age ideology, and, indeed, built into much of the rationale behind palatial record-keeping.[27] In particular, the evidence from the tablets for palatial involvement in the direct apportionment of wine both to communities and individuals[28] might lead one to speculate whether the term δαίς could perhaps originally have acquired its secondary meaning of "feast" in the context above all of festal wine-drinking. If so, we should probably conclude that this development took place considerably earlier than the period of the Mycenaean palaces, since the use of the words δατέομαι and δασμός (*da-so-mo*: PY Wa 730) in the Linear B texts to mean "distribute or apportion" and "portion or share," respectively,[29] suggests that δαίνυμι and δαίς may already have acquired narrower and more specialized meanings than they appear to retain in the epics.[30]

Within this dominant notion of "sharing" and "equality" implied by the word δαίς, however, there is also scope for the concept of individual honor—the idea that some within the feasting circle may be (at least on occasion) a little more equal than others. Just as the gods always get their choice portions (typically the burned thigh bones of the animals, and the first taste of the wine in the form of libation), human participants can also be offered a "portion of honor," as when Agamemnon gives Aias the choice cuts from the back of the roasted ox (*Il.* 7.321–322) or when Menelaos sets before Telemachos and Peisistratos the same cuts that have been set aside as his own prerogative (*Od.* 4.65–66). The idea that a particular rank or status (including the status of honored guest conferred by the obligations of friendship or hospitality) may be singled out through apportioning the choicest meats or the first passing of the wine-cup (cf. *Od.* 3.51–53) is thus also built into the ideology and protocol of the feast.

Two other words used much more rarely in Homer to denote a "feast" are εἰλαπίνη (and its verb εἰλαπινάζω) (*Il.* 10.217, 14.241, 18.491, 23.201; *Od.* 1.226, 2.57, 11.415, 17.410; cf. *Il.* 17.577 [εἰλαπιναστής]) and ἔρανος (*Od.* 1.226, 11.415). Neither the precise meaning nor the derivation of the former is clear, and its epic derivatives seem to imply no more than generic feasting or reveling in company. On two occasions, however, the word itself is contrasted both with an ἔρανος and with a wedding feast (*Od.* 1.226, where it is, however, apparently more akin to a wedding; 11.415),[31] on one it is distinguished from a wedding (*Il.* 18.491), on one

---

27. Bendall, forthcoming; Palmer 1994, pp. 73–85.

28. Palmer 1994, pp. 73–85.

29. Palmer 1994, pp. 80–81, 85.

30. In the epics, not only does δαίς clearly retain its primary meaning of "share or portion" in places, but the verbs δαίω and δαίνυμι also on occasion retain a general sense of "distribute" well outside the semantic context of feasting (cf. *Od.* 3.309, 5.61; also perhaps *Od.* 9.551), despite the use elsewhere of δατέομαι (e.g., *Od.* 6.10, 14.208, 17.80; *Il.* 18.511, 20.394).

Conversely, the noun δασμός, which seems to mean "share or division" in general in the Linear B texts (Palmer 1994, p. 79; cf. also Classical Greek), occurs only once in the epics, in connection with the division of booty (*Il.* 1.166). This suggests that the Linear B use of δασμός as a general term for "share or portion" may postdate much of the original linguistic inheritance preserved in the Homeric epics, in which δαίς in its primary sense normally fulfills this less specific semantic function; and it further suggests that

the specialized use of δαίς meaning "feast" (and perhaps even primarily "feast," as in Hesiod) may already exist in the period of the Linear B texts. An older, primary sense of δαίς meaning "share or portion" may be reflected in a variety of Linear B titles and proper names, such as *da-i-ja-ke-re-u*, *da-i-pi-ta*, *da-i-wo-wo*, *da-i-ze-to* (Ventris and Chadwick 1973, pp. 178, 537; Mühlestein 1968, p. 113; Aura Jorro 1985, pp. 149–150).

31. In *Od.* 1.225–226 the implication is that εἰλαπίνη is a subspecies of δαίς.

from a δαίς (*Il.* 10.217), and on one apparently from drinking (*Od.* 2.57). This, together with its rarity, suggests a noun that originally had some fairly specific meaning, which it has already lost by the time that it is incorporated in the Homeric epics.[32] The observation that the parts of the lines in which it is differentiated from a wedding feast scan rather awkwardly (*Il.* 18.491; *Od.* 1.226) might hint that it is already an archaic word whose phonology has changed over time. As for ἔρανος, it occurs in Homeric epic only in the two lines in the *Odyssey* already cited. It is also found in a similar sense in Pindar (*Ol.* 1.38; *Pyth.* 5.77, 12.14), where it seems to mean no more than a generic feast or festival. Its later use to denote a club or mutual society (Dem. *Epistulae* 5.6.1, *In Aristogitonem* 1.22.1) has led to its usual translation in the *Odyssey* as a meal to which each contributes his share and thus as the proper Homeric technical term for the communal type of feast discussed above, and, although it is never explicitly applied in the epics to any of the more obviously communal type of feasts,[33] it may originally have had some such meaning.[34]

ARCHAEOLOGICAL AND HISTORICAL CONSTITUENTS OF HOMERIC FEASTING

There can be little doubt that the Homeric epics are not only creations of their own time, but that, precisely because of their ethnogenetic role (and probably also purpose) in creating a shared panhellenic "past," they reflect a complex accumulation of beliefs, concepts, and practices superimposed in popular consciousness over a long period and transmitted through different regional traditions. Indeed, this is certainly a necessary precondition for their immediate effectiveness in this respect, since the cumulative weight of what is "known" intuitively through narrative bardic song continuously generated, transmitted, and reinterpreted through successive generations in different places carries far more credence than any *ad hoc* creation contrived, however aptly or adeptly, out of nothing. Elements of chronological layering and, indeed, of linguistic and cultural transfer are evident in various aspects of the material culture and language of the epics, in some cases going back to at least the early Late Bronze Age, or earlier still, and covering an area that includes the Near East and Egypt as well as most of the Aegean. There is no reason to suppose that this sort of layering and transfer may not also apply to feasting practices and attitudes to feasting.

This combination of the integrative nature of the epics and the deep regional and historical accumulations that give effect to it means that, in terms of the definitions formulated by modern anthropologists, Homeric feasting behavior is likely to appear ambiguous and to resist clear classification. This ambiguity is characteristic of many of the social practices and institutions encountered in the epics. Indeed, it was arguably the deliberate ambiguity of Homeric epic, which like biblical scripture allowed it to be all things to everyone, that ensured its centrality to collective Greek identity from the beginning of the Archaic period onward. While in the archaeological record we may, given a certain amount of luck, be able to

32. Εἰλαπίνη is otherwise found only in later poetry (particularly epic) that consciously alludes to or is modeled on Homer. It is abundantly clear that late authors such as Athenaeus, as well as all the lexicographers and Homeric commentators, were as much in the dark as we are concerning its derivation and meaning. Cf. Frisk (1960, p. 455, s.v.) and Chantraine (1968–1980, vol. 2, p. 318, s.v.), who suggest that the term may have been a loanword.

33. Nor in Hes. *Op.* 722–723, where the term πολύξεινος δαὶς κοινός, meaning a feast with many contributory participants, is used.

34. Its etymology, like that of εἰλαπίνη, is obscure, though it has been suggested that it is closely related to Homeric ἦρα [= ϝῆρα] (cf. *Od.* 3.164; *Il.* 1.578), meaning "kindness" or "favor" (Frisk 1960, p. 455, s.v. ἔρανος; Boisacq 1923, p. 262, s.v. ἑόρτη). If so, the word *e-ra-ne*, which appears as the possible title of a functionary on Knossos tablet (KN Ch 902 (which lists cattle in association with various place names), almost certainly has no connection with ἔρανος.

identify detailed feasting practices that fall into well-defined and coherent categories of structure, motives, and practical benefits, the Homeric texts inevitably prove more elusive and ambivalent in this respect.

As it is, there is probably no limit to how far back into prehistory one can push feasting in general, either in the Aegean area or anywhere else. How far back (and from where) we can trace any of the specific ideologies and practices of Homeric feasting depends largely on archaeology, and particularly on what it can supply in the way of suitably contextualized artifacts, rarer representational art, and even rarer textual data.

We can start by looking at the cooking practices and equipment associated with feasting in the epics. The spits (ὀβελοί) that are used to roast meat (whenever we are given a description of the cooking process)[35] have usually been associated with the iron spits that appear in the Aegean area from the 10th century onward, occasionally accompanied by metal spit supports.[36] These seem to be a fashion that reached the Aegean from Cyprus, where spits of bronze closely followed by ones of iron occur already in 11th-century contexts, although the possibility that the idea of bronze spits together with a new, fashionable way of cooking meat may originally have reached Cyprus from the central or western Mediterranean in the closing centuries of the second millennium, along with imported examples of the artifacts themselves, cannot entirely be ruled out.[37] It has been argued that these spits are merely the translation into metal of wooden spits that already had a long history in the Aegean;[38] while this argument may perhaps gain some support from the possible identification of a bronze spit among unpublished objects from the 15th-century Vapheio tholos,[39] it leaves the puzzle of why they should not regularly have been translated into bronze at an earlier date and deposited much more frequently along with other bronze cooking equipment (for instance in Cretan tombs) or recorded in any recognizable form in the Linear B inventories. As it is, the

35. Explicit spit-roasting takes place both outdoors (*Il.* 1.465, 2.428, 7.317; *Od.* 3.462, 12.365) and indoors (*Od.* 14.420–430, 19.422). In some instances (e.g., *Il.* 9.468), spit-roasting is only implied.

36. For spits see Haarer 2000, 2001. For spit supports in the shape of ships, from Cyprus, Crete, and the Argolid, see Demetriou 1989, p. 66; Snodgrass 1996, pp. 591–592; Haarer 2000, pp. 50–52. Since extant examples of spit supports date predominantly from the later part of the eighth century, it may be significant that supports are mentioned only once in the epics (*Il.* 9.213–214). This passage does not recur in any other descriptions of feast preparation and to that extent is non-formulaic, but it gives us a more graphic description of how the spits are used than is provided by other accounts.

37. The precise chronology of the articulated bronze spits of western Mediterranean/Atlantic type is still uncertain, but they suggest a prior history of metal-spit development in the west, possibly of considerable duration. Examples of these occur in a tenth–ninth-century hoard at Monte Sa Idda on Sardinia and in a tomb of roughly similar date at Amathous on Cyprus (Karageorghis and Lo Schiavo 1989). As far as I know, however, no other bronze spits predating the Early Iron Age have been recognized in the central Mediterranean (see Haarer 2000, pp. 192–193). Nevertheless, the presence on the late-13th-century Gelidonya wreck of what seems to be a bronze spit (Bass 1967, p. 109, no. B 187, figs. 116, 117; but cf. Catling 1964, p. 99, where it is identified as the blade of a pair of smithing tongs) would place their eastern Mediterranean debut in an appropriate context for their import from the west to be considered (cf. Sherratt 2000a). The bundle of bronze spits associated with the bronze hoard from Anthedon in Boiotia (Catling 1964, p. 297), although almost impossible to date (Knapp, Muhly, and Muhly 1988, p. 248), may well be of Cypriot origin and could theoretically date as early as the 11th century. In this context, however, their main significance probably lies in the fact that they are bronze rather than in their artifactual nature. In other words, they cannot of themselves be taken as proof that bronze spits were used in Greece in a period immediately preceding the introduction of iron ones in the 10th century.

38. Cf. Karageorghis 1974, p. 171; Haarer 2000, p. 11.

39. Karageorghis 1974, p. 171, pl. XVIII:1.

regular appearance of metal spits only in the 11th century and later in Cyprus and the Aegean seems to indicate a new social or ideological emphasis on spit-roasting meat at this time, while the observation that spits often appear in tombs associated with male (warrior) burials suggests a context of male bonding through barbecuing, possibly mainly outdoors and associated particularly with hunting.[40] We are nowhere informed of the material of which Homeric spits are made, nor are we normally told precisely how they are used, which leaves room for the possibility that the recurrent passages in which spits are mentioned derive from contexts in which wooden spits, perhaps deployed in some other manner, were the norm. The ideology associated with Early Iron Age iron spits, however, as far as we can comprehend it, seems wholly in tune with their standard role in epic feast preparation, and with the general ethos associated with their use.

Another piece of equipment that also seems to belong in the Early Iron Age is the bronze grater used by Hekamede to grate goat's cheese into the curious potion she prepares for Nestor and Machaon in *Iliad* 11. Graters of bronze (and occasionally of iron) first turn up in Greece in tenth–ninth-century contexts, and have been discussed recently by David Ridgway.[41] The association at Lefkandi of three bronze graters with ninth-century graves furnished with weaponry, one of which also contained a number of iron spits,[42] brings these into the same general context, and suggests that they too are associated in some way with contemporary warrior feasting activity—though whether they were used only to grate cheese (as in the *Iliad*) or for a more exotic purpose is debatable. Given the general rule that elite activity is most susceptible to inclusion in elite-sponsored art, whether visual or verbal, at the time when it is newest and most novel (and therefore most elite), a date of around the tenth–ninth centuries for the initial incorporation of both spits and grater into pre-Homeric heroic song, with its probable emphasis in this period on the defining κλέα ("glorious deeds") of contemporary or near-contemporary individuals or small groups,[43] seems in principle quite likely.

The conclusion that Homeric cooking practices predominantly reflect those of Early Iron Age warrior elites finds support in the Bronze

40. Ample iconographic evidence exists for hunting and warrior groups and for feasting throughout the Late Bronze Age (Wright, this volume), and the presence of deer in the burned bone deposits from Pylos provides a further indication of this elite connection (Isaakidou et al. 2002; Stocker and Davis, this volume). The hunting scenes from the Palace of Nestor and possibly also from Ayia Irini on Kea, however, seem to point to a connection between the post-hunting feast and tripod cauldrons rather than spits (see below). The importance of the Early Iron Age spits lies in the indications they provide within the standard personal equipment of the warrior of a formal recognition of spit-roasting (and possibly, therefore, a new type of outdoor post-hunting feast). Inscriptions (one apparently a mark of ownership) on three bronze spits from a late-11th- to early-10th-century tomb (T. 49) at Palaipaphos-Skales in Cyprus further underline the notion that spits were at this time significant items of elite male personal equipment (Karageorghis 1983, pp. 61, 411–415, pl. A:2–4).

41. Ridgway 1997.

42. Popham, Touloupa, and Sackett 1982, p. 229, nos. 6–8; cf. Ridgway 1997, p. 325; Haarer 2000, p. 30.

43. Cf. Sherratt 1990.

Age archaeological record. Relatively deep tripod cauldrons (*ti–ri–po*, ideogram *201) are well represented in the Linear B texts (see below, Fig. 1:201), two of them occurring on a tablet (PY Ta 709) that lists decorated portable hearths and other palatial cooking equipment. They also appear in what is undoubtedly a feasting context in the hunting scenes that decorated the walls above megaron 46 at Pylos,[44] and possibly on a related type of scene from Kea.[45] Together with the absence of any objects identifiable as spits, they indicate the strong probability that ceremonial food (including meat for human consumption) was prepared in the Mycenaean palaces mainly by means of boiling or stewing.[46] No hint of this practice is found in the epics, where tripod cauldrons are used in heroic contexts exclusively to heat water for washing (*Il.* 18.344, 22.443, 23.40; *Od.* 8.434, 10.359). However, the reported results of recent organic residue analyses on clay versions of these tripod vessels (insofar as they may be reliable) seem to indicate that meat was frequently cooked in this way from at least the Middle to the Late Bronze Age in the Aegean area generally, and often, significantly, in ritual contexts.[47]

This method of cooking is much more economical than grilling or roasting, since the meat can be cut into smaller pieces and bulked out with liquids and other ingredients, and since boiling or stewing makes even the toughest bits edible. It is therefore inherently more appropriate for large-scale feasts than the Homeric practice of barbecuing.[48] Moreover, the suggestion, supported by traces of meat in tripod vessels from Armenoi, Thebes, and postpalatial Tiryns, that meat cooked in relatively humble clay pots may have become an item of diet of a progressively wide section of the population from the 13th century onward[49] gives us a plausible background against which to see the introduction of the exclusive warrior barbecue-feast with its distinctive equipment around the beginning of the new millennium as a new and deliberate form of elite differentiation. In light of this suggestion, the mysterious πεμπώβολα, which hover with no clear function in a repeated line in only two epic cooking scenes, might well be considered a fossilized remnant of the much older boiling or stewing practices that the Early Iron Age barbecue replaced.[50]

44. *Palace of Nestor* II, pp. 68–71, 107–108, pls. 122, M; Wright, this volume, p. 39, fig. 10.

45. Morgan 1998, fig. 6; Wright, this volume, p. 38, fig. 9.

46. Borgna 1997a.

47. Tzedakis and Martlew 1999, cf. esp. p. 183, no. 173 (a tripod vessel from Apodoulou, Middle Minoan IIB), p. 101, no. 70 (from Chania-Splanzia, associated with the remains of slaughtered animals, Late Minoan [LM] IB), p. 196, no. 181 (from room 31 of the cult area at Mycenae, LH IIIB), and for other tripod vessels that may have been used to cook meat, p. 115, no. 90; p. 116 no. 93 (from the LM IIIB cemetery at Armenoi), and p. 120, no. 96

(from a LH IIIB house at Thebes). Other cooking pots (not tripods) with signs that meat may have been cooked in them have been found in areas with evidence for ceremonial or ritual activity at Thebes, Mycenae, and Midea (Tzedakis and Martlew 1999, p. 121, no. 100; p. 122, no. 103; p. 127, no. 108; p. 131, no. 113; p. 186, no. 176). In the absence of detailed reports of the results, however, the interpretations suggested by Tzedakis and Martlew should be treated with caution. "Meat," for instance, means the presence of animal lipids, which may indicate no more than the presence of animal fat (and not necessarily flesh), as in *Il.* 21.362–364. Nevertheless, the doc-

umentary and iconographic evidence for the association of tripod cauldrons with feasting and hunting does seem to support the idea that boiling or stewing was the normal method of cooking meat in the Late Bronze Age.

48. For the presence of some 30 or so clay tripod cooking vessels in rooms 67 and 68 at Pylos, almost certainly associated with large-scale feasting in courts 63 and 88, see Whitelaw 2001, p. 57, figs. 2, 3; Bendall, forthcoming.

49. See n. 47 above; also Kilian 1985, p. 79.

50. See above, n. 16. It should be pointed out, however, that no word resembling πεμπώβολον has yet been found in the Linear B texts, nor have

The avoidance of any mention of olive oil in the epics for any culinary purpose may or may not be related to the above observations. Oil is not necessary for spit-roasting on an open fire, particularly since there is plenty of fat on the animals. It is probably not necessary for stewing or boiling either, but it greatly improves the taste of meat cooked in this way; and traces of olive oil are said to have been found in virtually all of the Bronze Age clay tripod vessels and other cooking pots with organic residues of meat,[51] as well as in a number of other cooking pots. This suggests that—as in the case of meat—olive oil may have been a fairly regular element of Bronze Age festal and other diets. It is interesting, however, that there is no clear evidence in the Linear B texts for the culinary use of oil,[52] although it figures largely in texts concerned with the manufacture of unguents and (usually in ready-perfumed form) in those concerned with ritual offerings, especially since oil in the epics (sometimes in a golden flask [*Od.* 6.79], and sometimes of vintage quality [*Il.* 18.351]) is used only for anointing. The consistent and positive emphasis in the epic poems on the preciousness of olive oil (which can hardly have escaped a Homeric audience) suggests that the absence of its mention in culinary contexts is not accidental; while it almost certainly reflects a continuation into later periods of the kinds of uses documented in Linear B, it may also indicate that olive oil generally (and perfumed oil in particular) was a relatively rare and expensive commodity throughout the Early Iron Age.

That feasts in the Mycenaean palatial period could be held on an impressively large scale—probably much larger than anything the normal Homeric barbecue would have been capable of coping with in reality—seems likely from various indications. The faunal evidence from Pylos, which has been discussed with great subtlety elsewhere,[53] provides reason for thinking that a feast in honor of Poseidon, with a number of suggestive similarities to that described in *Odyssey* 3.4–342, took place in the palace very shortly before its destruction. The 10 or more cattle involved[54] are a far cry from the 81 bulls contributed by the nine Pylian towns in the *Odyssey* (3.7–8), but probably enough, nevertheless, to feed over a thousand people at one time—perhaps the entire (male?) population of the town of Pylos, or a substantial number of representatives from each of the main Pylian centers. The picture envisaged of high-ranking diners feasting in pairs at small, fancy portable tables within the megaron, with a much larger gathering of their social inferiors in the southwest courts and a still larger

pronged forks or flesh-hooks been identified among feasting equipment listed on the tablets. The significance of the latter perhaps depends on whether such implements typically formed part of palatial equipment or were the private property of individuals—in which case, as with individual drinking cups (cf. below, n. 71), one would probably not expect to find them in palace inventories. All known Aegean examples come from tombs (see above, n. 16), which suggests

that they were indeed regarded as the personal possessions of the deceased.

51. Tzedakis and Martlew 1999, p. 108, no. 77; p. 115, no. 90; p. 116, no. 93; p. 120, no. 96; p. 122, no. 103; p. 127, no. 108; p. 127, no. 109; p. 131, no. 113; p. 183, no. 173; p. 185, no. 175; p. 186, no. 176; p. 196, no. 181; p. 198, no. 185.

52. Melena 1983, p. 120. Palmer (1994, p. 128), however, suggests that olive oil allotted to sanctuaries on the Fs tablets from Knossos was designed

for culinary use. See also Bendall 2001 for the argument that the palaces were dealing with much more olive oil than is allocated as offerings or for perfume manufacture on the tablets. The remainder, presumably, was intended for culinary use.

53. Isaakidou et al. 2002; Stocker and Davis, this volume.

54. See Stocker and Davis, this volume, p. 64, n. 21, where it is stated that the estimate of 10 cattle is likely to be low.

gathering of even lower ranks outside the area of the palace,[55] is one of which we clearly glimpse elements in the *Odyssey*.[56]

Much has been written over the last decade or so about the textual evidence for Mycenaean feasting,[57] and it has become abundantly apparent that feasts loom very large in the recorded activities of Mycenaean palaces. Because of the elusive "snapshot" nature of the texts, it is not always clear how such feasts were organized. We seem, however, to have evidence both for contributory feasts organized directly by the palaces, for which animals were brought in to the center from various surrounding (sometimes quite far-flung) communities, and for feasts at religious (and possibly also secular) centers elsewhere, to which the palaces themselves made contributions of wine, barley, honey, figs, or oil (the last perhaps principally for anointing garments offered to a deity).[58] Whether or not the latter were organized independently of the palaces, the very fact that we know about them indicates a close palatial interest, suggesting in turn that the palaces had a hand in most of the public or official feasts that went on in the localities with which they were concerned.

Despite the fact that we are concerned with subscription feasts, since most, if not all, of the ingredients were ultimately coerced from surrounding populations by one means or another, this close intertwining of palaces, religious centers, and other communities, in terms of the movement of feasting materials, appears to blur any clear distinction between the kinds of hosted and communal feasts discernible in the epics; moreover, it suggests that every official feast, no matter where it took place and who really bore the brunt of the expense, was meant to appear as a combination of communal effort and palatial beneficence.[59] Given what looks like the inherently precarious position of the palaces in the 13th, and probably also the 14th, century (effectively demonstrated by their sudden disappearance around 1200 B.C.), it may well have seemed a sensible strategy to involve as many as possible in the double obligations of commensality and clientage fuzzily merged in this way. The large numbers of animals and quantities of other materials sometimes involved[60] indicate that some feasts took place

55. Bendall, forthcoming; Whitelaw 2001; cf. also Borgna, this volume.

56. For the tables *(to-pe-za)*, many of them of stone and inlaid with precious materials, see PY Ta 642, Ta 713, Ta 715 (Palmer 1963, pp. 345–348; Ventris and Chadwick 1973, pp. 339–342, nos. 239–241), and cf. *Od.* 1.111, 138, 4.54, 5.92, 7.174, 9.8–9, 10.354–355, 370, 15.137, 466–467, 17.93, 333–334, 447, 19.61, 20.151–152, 259, 21.28–29, 22.19–21, 84–85, 438, and *Il.* 11.628–629. On the tablets, these are accompanied by equally fancy chairs *(to-no)* and matching footstools *(ta-ra-nu)* (Ta 707, Ta 708, Ta 712, Ta 714, Ta 722; Palmer 1963, pp. 348–353; Ventris and Chadwick 1973, pp. 342–346, nos. 242–246; cf. esp. for fancy chairs *Il.* 11.645; *Od.* 1.130–131, 7.162, 169, 8.65, 10.314 = 366, 16.408,

17.32, 20.150, 22.341, 438 = 452). If the *ta-ra-nu* truly are footstools (θρῆνυς), as are their Homeric verbal equivalents (though the word is also used once for the bench of a ship: *Il.* 15.729), there are a sufficient number to suggest that they were not merely provided for a divine or quasi-divine *wanax*. It is possible, however, that they were another form of seating equipment for palatial feasters (Di Filippo 1996; Palaima 2000, p. 237), perhaps equivalent to the κλισμοί with which θρόνοι are frequently paired in the *Odyssey* (for the κλισμός as a light chair without arms, see Hainsworth 1993, p. 294).

For a picture of the enclosures and the megaron of Odysseus's palace full of feasters, see *Od.* 17.604–605; for the neighbors and kinsmen of

Menelaos feasting in his house, *Od.* 4.15–16; for Eumaios's father's clients feasting in the forecourt of his house, see *Od.* 15.466–467. In *Od.* 19.60–62 we catch a glimpse of the clearing of the remains of the feast along with the tables and drinking cups—a reminder of the kind of process that resulted in the deposit in room 7 at Pylos.

57. E.g., Piteros, Olivier, and Melena 1990; Killen 1994, 1996; Wright 1995; Shelmerdine 1998; Bendall 2001, and forthcoming; Aravantinos, Godart, and Sacconi 2001. See also the chapters in this volume by Wright; Stocker and Davis; and Dabney, Halstead, and Thomas.

58. Shelmerdine 1995.

59. See Bendall, forthcoming.

60. Killen 1994, p. 78; 1996; Chadwick 1976, pp. 96, 100.

on a truly massive scale, increasing the probability that virtually everyone, regardless of social status, had a chance to share at some time in an official feast.[61]

That unofficial feasting, of which we naturally hear nothing directly, also existed outside the palace circles with some sense of at least tacit palatial benevolence is strongly hinted at by Halstead's observations that the constituent membership of palatial sheep flocks tended to be unusually fluid, suggesting that herders were free to remove fattened wethers for their own feasting requirements.[62] One can also glimpse this practice in the composite world of the epics, even if most clearly through its denial. When the swineherd Eumaios makes up his mind to slaughter the best of the pigs for Odysseus, who is disguised as an unknown stranger (*Od.* 14.414–417), he vents his feelings in words that ring not only with anger at the outrageous depredations made on his master's herds by the suitors, but also with the deeply felt personal grievance of one whose own accustomed rights (described by him in 15.373) have been arbitrarily and unjustifiably removed (cf. also *Od.* 4.87–88).

In general, however, as in the case of cooking practices, the glimpse that the Linear B tablets give us into palatial feasting equipment has little to offer the Homeric picture. It is particularly unfortunate that the shorthand nature of the texts does not often allow us to link ideograms and words, but despite this limitation, the proliferation of specialized forms and terminology probably indicates a degree of functional specialization adopted by the mainland palaces from Neopalatial Crete,[63] quite unlike anything seen in the epics. There are at least four names for jugs and at least four separate ideograms, with (in this case) three matches between them (Fig. 1:204–206).[64] Similarly, there are several ideograms for what we should probably recognize as drinking vessels—various forms of cups, goblets, kylikes, and chalices of gold or bronze, all of them with metal and ceramic counterparts in the archaeological record (Fig. 1:208, 215, 216, 218, 221).[65]

61. See Bendall, forthcoming; Dabney, Halstead, and Thomas, this volume.

62. Halstead 2001, pp. 41–44.

63. Borgna 1997b; also this volume.

64. Vandenabeele and Olivier 1979, pp. 246–258; Anderson 1994–1995, pp. 300, 302, 305, fig. 1. The four names are *qe-ra-na*, with *204 (KN K 93, PY Ta 711); *a-te-we*, with *205 (PY Tn 996); *ka-ti*, with *206 (PY Tn 996); and *po-ro-ko-wo*, without ideogram (MY Ue 611). Ideogram *303 (KN K 93), which looks like a beaked jug, has no identified name, but it appears in a collection of probable washing equipment (*226 [Fig. 1:226, 303], Vandenabeele and Olivier 1979, pp. 271–272). All are either certainly or probably of metal, in most cases bronze; and all occur in lists of vessels likely to be associated with feasting.

While the individual ideograms for the most part have plausible correlates in contemporary or earlier metal (and ceramic) types known from the archaeological record, among the names only *ka-ti* (cf. κάδος, a water jar or urn) and *po-ro-ko-wo* (cf. πρόχοος, a jug) can be identified with later Greek words. The word *qe-ra-na*, however, has also plausibly been connected with ritual washing (Aura Jorro 1993, p. 195, s.v. *qe-ra-na*; Anderson 1994–1995, p. 312), and the appearance of three *qe-ra-na* at the beginning of the sequence of Pylos Ta tablets (Palaima 2000), immediately followed by three *pi-je-ra₃* (with ideogram *200, a pedestaled basin [Fig. 1:200]), suggests that this was indeed the particular function of these jugs. Their ideogram (*204 [Fig. 1:204]) also appears with a basin (ideogram *305 [Fig. 1:305]) on KN K 93 (Vandenabeele and Olivier 1979,

pp. 271–273). That in general these are genuine ideograms, standing for more or less standardized types rather than "portraits" of individual jugs, is shown by their repetition on more than one document or by the plurality of individual vessels they represent.

65. Vandenabeele and Olivier 1979, pp. 200–205, 207–216: *208 (PY Tn 996), *215 (PY Tn 316), *216 (PY Tn 316), *218 (KN K 872), *221 (KN K 434). Of these, only *208 has a possible associated word (*po-ka-ta-ma*, though cf. Ventris and Chadwick 1973, pp. 338–339, no. 238; Anderson 1994–1995, p. 305). The word *[ku]-pe-ra* possibly occurs, without an ideogram, on MY Ue 611 (Ventris and Chadwick 1973, pp. 331–332, no. 234; Anderson 1994–1995, pp. 302–303; though cf. Palmer 1963, p. 364).

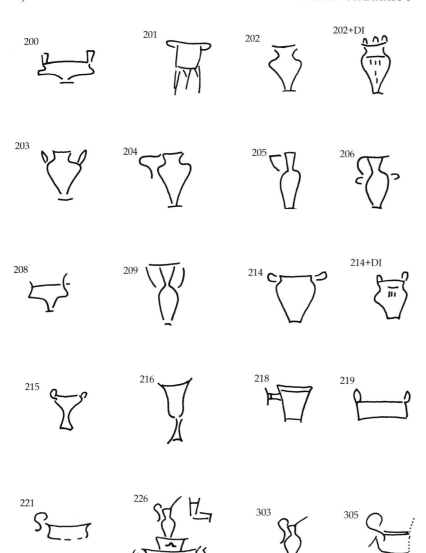

Figure 1. Selected Linear B ideograms for vessels. Adapted from Vandenabeele and Olivier 1979, passim

In each case, however, only two names (*po-ro-ko-wo* and possibly *ku-pe-ra*, both on Mycenae tablet Ue 611, and both, unfortunately, without ideograms) can be recognized as corresponding to the usual Homeric word for a jug from which water is poured for washing (πρόχοος: *Od.* 1.136, 7.172, 15.135, 17.91; *Il.* 24.301) and perhaps to one of the two less common words for a drinking cup (κύπελλον: *Il.* 1.596, 3.248, 4.345, 9.670, 24.305; *Od.* 1.142, 2.396, 4.58, 10.357, 20.253).[66]

66. There is no easily recognizable equivalent for the Homeric ἄλεισον, which is specified as gold in six of its nine mentions (*Il.* 11.774; *Od.* 3.50, 53, 8.430, 15.85, 22.9). However, the dative plural form *a-re-se-si* occurs on PY Ub 1318 preceded by the word *di-pte-ra* (skins), suggesting that the objects referred to are probably of leather (Voutsa 2001, p. 151). An

ἄλεισον may therefore originally have been a leather mug or wineskin (Ruijgh 1967, p. 159, n. 323, p. 356; Aura Jorro 1985, pp. 101–102, s.v. *a-re-se-si*).

Apart from the tripod cauldron and the δέπας (on which see below), other Homeric vessel words probably or possibly represented in the Linear B texts (some with ideograms; Fig. 1) are *pi-je-ra₃/pi-a₂-ra* (PY Ta 709 with

ideogram *200, Tn 996 with ideogram *219, Vandenabeele and Olivier 1979, pp. 221–224; cf. φιάλη, *Il.* 23.243, 253, 270, 616); *qe-to* (PY Ta 641 with ideogram *203, Vandenabeele and Olivier 1979, pp. 239–240; cf. πίθος, *Il.* 24.527; *Od.* 2.340, 23.305); *a-pi-po-re-we/a-po-re-we* (KN Gg series, PY Tn 996 with ideogram *209, Vandenabeele and Olivier 1979, pp. 259–263; cf. ἀμφι-

Particularly intriguing problems, from a Homeric point of view, arise with the ideograms *202 and *214 (Fig. 1:202, 202+DI, 214+DI), which accompany the noun *di-pa*, undoubtedly the same word as the Homeric δέπας (PY Ta 641; KN K 740, K 829, K 875).[67] On K 740, the 30 *di-pa* listed are clearly of bronze, and on Ta 641, where they are listed alongside tripod cauldrons, they are almost certainly also of metal. The regular ideogram *202, which is best described as looking like a jar, appears in three versions: one with four handles perched on top of the rim, one with three handles (Fig. 1:202+DI), and one with no handles (Fig. 1:202). These ideograms correspond to the written descriptions *qe-to-ro-we* ("with four ears"), *ti-ro-jo-we* ("with three ears"), and *a-no-we* ("with no ears"), respectively. As has often been remarked, this vessel hardly seems suitable for drinking, particularly with as many as four earlike handles protruding upward from the rim. Yet in *Iliad* 11.632–635, Nestor's famous gold-studded δέπας is described, improbably, as having four "ears" (οὔατα τέσσαρ') in addition to its eight gold doves (two around each "ear") and two stands or stems.[68]

The fact that on Ta 641 six assorted examples of *di-pa* occur alongside other vessels likely to be associated with feasting,[69] while on K 875 six handleless examples are assigned to six individuals probably of *basileus* (and therefore in some sense official) status, suggests that *di-pa* had a ceremonial function. The small number (six) listed on Ta 641—part of a series of tablets that seem otherwise to list the equipment needed for 22 feasters[70]—makes it doubly unlikely that they were intended as individual drinking vessels, and suggests a more communal function.[71] The ideogram itself cannot easily be reconciled with any ceramic form known from the archaeological record. Vandenabeele and Olivier identify it with a type of large bronze two- or three-handled "krater"-like vessel of Early Mycenaean date; this has a much wider mouth, however, than the vessels represented by most versions of the ideogram,[72] though it is not unlike ideogram *214 on KN K 740 (Fig. 1:214+DI), which appears to be associated with the

φορεύς, *Il.* 23.92, 170; *Od.* 2.290, 24.74 and passim); *ka-ra-te-ra* (MY Ue 611, Palmer 1963, p. 364; Ventris and Chadwick 1973, no. 234; Anderson 1994–1995, p. 301; cf. κρητήρ, *Il.* 1.470 and passim; *Od.* 1.110 and passim); and perhaps *ke-ni-qa* (KN Ws 8497, Vandenabeele and Olivier 1979, p. 177; Dialismas 2001, p. 128; cf. χέρνιβον, *Il.* 24.304). That in the Pylos texts (though not in the epics), *pi-je-ra₃* (φιάλαι) are basins for ritual washing is indicated by their position in the sequence of Ta tablets, brilliantly reconstructed by Palaima (2000; see above, n. 64). It thus seems likely that they have a similar function to the Homeric λέβης in such passages as *Od.* 1.137 = 4.53 = 7.173 = 10.369 = 15.136 = 17.92, 3.440, 19.386, 469. See also Anderson 1994–1995, pp. 319–320, for

other possible Homeric vessel words in Linear B, either uncertain (*a-ke-a₂*? = ? ἄγγος [e.g., *Od.* 2.289], *a-ma*? = ? ἀμνίον [*Od.* 3.444]); oblique (*ka-ne-ja*, cf. κάνεον [e.g., *Od.* 1.147, 17.343], *ke-ra-me-u*, cf. κέραμος [e.g., *Il.* 9.469, cf. 5.387]); or less directly concerned with feasting (*a-sa-mi-to* = ἀσάμινθος [e.g., *Il.* 10.576; *Od.* 4.48], *re-wo-to-ro* = λοετρόν [cf., e.g., *Il.* 14.6]).

67. Vandenabeele and Olivier 1979, pp. 234–239; cf. Gray 1959, pp. 50–51, pl. VII; Anderson 1994–1995, p. 300.

68. That the handles on Nestor's δέπας are called (literally) "ears" need not imply any uniquely special relationship between it and the Linear B *di-pa*, since the word for "ears" is often used to denote handles on vessels in later (including modern) Greek (see Gray 1959, p. 50). It is also used elsewhere

in the *Iliad* (18.378) for the handles on Hephaistos's wheeled tripods. What it does imply in the Linear B and Homeric cases, however, are particular sorts of handles that project upward like ears, typically from the rim of a vessel.

69. Killen 1998; Palaima 2000.

70. Palaima 2000.

71. The absence of identifiable drinking vessels in the Ta series may suggest that elite palatial feasters used their own personal drinking cups—a practice with good epic analogies (cf., e.g., *Il.* 16.225–227). If so, they may have kept them (or left them behind) in the central megaron (see Bendall, forthcoming).

72. Vandenabeele and Olivier 1979, pp. 236–239, figs. 161, 162. Cf. Matthäus 1980, pp. 150–157, pls. 22, 23.

word *pa-ko-to* on PY Ta 709 (Fig. 1:214).[73] This identification, insofar as it is convincing,[74] might be thought interesting in view of the emphasis put on the size and weight of Nestor's uniquely described δέπας in *Iliad* 11.638. As it is, it is clear from Ta 641 that *di-pa* come in different sizes, since three of the examples listed there are described as *me-zo* ("larger") and the other three as *me-wi-jo* ("smaller").

Also of interest in this connection is that the word *di-pa* on the tablets not only seems to be associated with two rather different-looking ideograms, but also invariably needs to be qualified with a specific description, relating either to size or the number of handles or both. In this respect, an analogy can be drawn with the Homeric δέπας, which is regularly tied to the epithet ἀμφικύπελλον—even though the nature of the descriptions is quite different. Even in the 13th century, then, the term itself—unlike other contemporary forms of vessel terminology—was apparently a relatively generic one, which, though it may have been associated with a specific function, had less precise specificity of form than is suggested by other noun-ideogram combinations. This in turn suggests that it was probably already an old, well-established term. Indeed, the possibility that it was originally a Luwian loanword[75] hints at its much greater antiquity.

By the eighth century, as its variant Homeric forms show, the word was firmly entrenched in the artificial language of epic where it seems to denote a generic drinking-cum-libation vessel, with the emphasis perhaps above all on libation.[76] By this time, however, it seems evident that any clear sense of a specific meaning (or function) for the word, and for its standard qualifier ἀμφικύπελλον, had been lost irretrievably. On balance, it seems likely that the epic δέπας is the cumulative and confused result of a very long and varied history for the term and its application, going back well before the Late Bronze Age. It may well have had its origins in a ritual vessel, possibly for libation or other form of offering—a function with which the *di-pa* may still have been associated in the 13th century. Indeed, it is not impossible that Nestor's unique two-stemmed δέπας, which (apart from its four "ears") sounds nothing like the Linear B *di-pa*, preserves traces of a much earlier ritual form that had disappeared or changed beyond recognition by the period of the palaces.[77]

73. Vandenabeele and Olivier 1979, p. 235, pl. CXXIII:5 [= Fig. 1:214+DI], cf. pp. 240–241, pl. CXXIV:2 [= Fig. 1:214]. There is a great deal of confusion in the literature over the classification of ideogram *214. Palmer (1963, p. 342) gives the ideogram associated with *pa-ko-to* on Ta 709 as *234, while Anderson (1994–1995, p. 303) gives no number for this ideogram (though cf. her fig. 1, where it is shown as *214). For the view that the ideogram on KN K 740 should not be associated with *di-pa*, see Gray 1959, p. 50.

74. Though cf. Matthäus 1980, p. 157, n. 7.

75. Palmer 1963, p. 487; cf. Janko

1992, p. 237; Anderson 1994–1995, p. 313.

76. Cf. the repeated lines *Il.* 1.471, 9.176; *Od.* 3.340, 7.183, 21.272. See also, e.g., *Il.* 3.295, 7.480, 23.196, 219, 24.285; *Od.* 3.46, 63, 7.137, 8.89, 18.418, 21.263.

77. The description ἀμφικύπελλον, which is often, and particularly after Schliemann's pronouncements (1880, pp. 237–238), translated as "double-handled" (cf. ἀμφιφορεύς), ought to mean probably (by analogy with ἀμφιφορεύς) "with cups (or hollows) on both (or all) sides" (cf. Arist. *Hist. an.* 642a.9, where it is compared with the cells of a honeycomb). One might,

in this case, envisage cups (κύπελλα) arranged around something like the Linear B *di-pa*, which might be assumed to have served as a central vessel from which wine was dispensed. What it also brings to mind, however, are some of the multiple vessels found in clay (and almost certainly also produced in metal) from the Early Bronze Age onward (cf., e.g., Buchholz and Karageorghis 1973, pp. 67, 298, no. 858), particularly the late Early Bronze Age to early Middle Bronze Age Cycladic "kernoi," with a single large vessel in the center surrounded by small cups (e.g., Renfrew 1972, pl. 11:1; Sherratt 2000b, figs. 116–118, pls. 254–

In general, as we move back in time beyond the reach of the Linear B texts, the possibility of positively identifying elements of practice or equipment that have a direct bearing on Homeric feasting becomes understandably slighter. There can be no doubt, however, that feasting took place in earlier times and that it was almost certainly as important a social institution as in the palatial and later periods. The emphasis on drinking vessels in graves of the Early Mycenaean period combines with the emphasis on weaponry, chariotry, hunting, and glittering items of personal adornment to suggest that the feast was an important bonding mechanism for the kind of active elite warrior band that we can probably see, for instance, in the Mycenae shaft graves—and one might hazard that its importance in this respect was directly commensurate with its exclusivity. At the same time, the spotlight directed on the individual at the time of the funeral, which the frequent practice of covering the body with lavish gold ornament betrays, suggests that the esteem and honor of individuals within the group was also an important preoccupation.

The large and heterogeneous range of (often unique) precious metal drinking cups found in the shaft graves and other tombs of the prepalatial period[78]—clearly items of portable, personal wealth—also leads one to suspect that, as in the epics, these vessels were frequently guest-gifts, many of them perhaps with their own long histories of previous distinguished ownership. It seems likely, in view of the absence of drinking cups from the Pylos Ta series, that individual ownership and use of prized drinking vessels remained a feature of palatial elite society three centuries or so later. The golden kylikes and chalices listed on Tn 316 as having been given by the Pylos palace to various divinities may thus represent an institutionalized adaptation to a religious context of the practice of giving such objects as guest-gifts.[79]

The exclusive, mutually supportive ethos of the warrior band in the earliest Mycenaean period (and probably also of its feasting practices) is hinted at above all by the symbolism of the circle, seen in tangible form not only in the two grave circles at Mycenae, but in contemporary tumuli and perhaps also the earliest tholos tombs. Some of this symbolism survived into the palatial period in the form of the fixed circular hearths that are a feature of mainland palace megara, and it is tempting to suppose that those who feasted around these hearths inside the megara were principally the e-qe-ta, in whom (complete with their patronymics) one can probably see a residual hereditary element of the earlier warrior band.[80]

256). These vessels, rather than the two-handled Anatolian "depas" with which the name has long been fancifully associated by archaeologists, arguably more closely resemble Nestor's double-stemmed δέπας. The original concept of a δέπας, which in the 13th century was associated with the vessel type(s) shown on the Linear B ideogram(s), and which eventually fed into the Homeric epics in a vague and shadowy form overlaid (particularly in Nestor's case) by elements of the palatial "variable-eared" di-pa, is

likely to extend back as far as the third millennium.

78. Wright, this volume.

79. Palaima 1995, p. 628. The divinities (or their human representatives) presumably would not only appreciate them for their bullion value, but also use them for the kinds of feasting or quasi-feasting purposes with which they are associated in some representations (see, e.g., Wright, this volume, p. 42, fig. 12, p. 45, fig. 16).

80. One might speculate that the number 22, highlighted by Stocker

and Davis (this volume) as possibly the number of feasters within the megaron (see, earlier, Palaima 2000, p. 237), bears some relationship to the number of members of the e-qe-ta band at Pylos, 15 of whose names have been identified (Jasink 1976). The same number (22) seems to apply, for instance, to pairs of wheels assigned to chariots on the Sa tablets (Chadwick 1976, p. 170), i.e., those assumed to be ready for regular use, rather than those kept for purely ceremonial occasions. Almost as intriguing are the 10 sets of

Traces of a similar symbolism of the circle can be glimpsed in epic feasting contexts. It can be seen in the way in which animals for slaughter may be placed in order around the altar (*Il.* 1.447–448),[81] or, alternatively, the prospective feasters may arrange themselves around a single animal (*Il.* 2.410).[82] It may also be seen in the arrangement of the feasting party, implied by the placing of Demodokos on a chair in the middle of the feasters who are seated in order (ἐξείης) in Alkinoos's palace (*Od.* 8.65–66 = 473; cf. 9.8), by Antinoos's peremptory words to Odysseus and the manner in which the latter goes round the feasters in order (*Od.* 17.447, 450), and by the way the feasting suitors take turns stringing the bow, in order from left to right in the same direction that the wine is circulated (*Od.* 21.141–142; cf. *Il.* 1.597). This symbolism can also be seen in the epics in other archetypically heroic contexts, as when the Achaean heroes stand in a circle around "godlike" Menelaos in his hour of need (*Il.* 4.211–212), hunters encircle a lion (*Od.* 4.792), or the elders on Achilles' shield sit in a sacred circle on polished stones (*Il.* 18.504).

ASPECTS OF HOMERIC DRINKING

One or two aspects of, and attitudes toward, wine-drinking in the Homeric epics are of special interest in relation to the history of drinking in the Aegean. Here, the epics are particularly valuable in that contexts of use, descriptions of wine, and social and ideological attitudes toward wine emerge much more explicitly from them than from the archaeological record or even from the Linear B texts alone. As with other aspects of the *Iliad* and *Odyssey*, the epics provide a freeze-frame of the accumulated strands of attitudes and practices involving wine that had built up over a very long period, forming part of a generalized Greek consciousness around 700 B.C.

In the first place, the epics have two words for "wine": the usual one, (ϝ)οῖνος, and another one, μέθυ, which appears in only two places in the *Iliad* (7.471, 9.469; cf. also μεθύουσαν ["soused"] in *Il.* 17.390) and in 15 instances in the *Odyssey*. Almost half of the references in the *Odyssey* occur in a single recurring line:

ἥμεθα, δαινύμενοι κρέα τ' ἄσπετα καὶ μέθυ ἡδύ

We sat, feasting on unlimited meat and sweet wine.
                    Od. 9.162, also 9.557, 10.184, 468, 477, 12.30[83]

This sounds very like a proverbial expression of plenty, similar to the biblical expression "a land flowing with milk and honey."[84] From the contexts in which μέθυ appears in the epics, it is clear that it is indistinguishable

body armor listed on the Sh series from room 7 as newly repaired (Palaima 1996; Dialismas 2001, p. 132). If we add to these the minimum of 11 *e-qe-ta* (10 of them with preserved names) on the *o-ka* tablets, whose armor (if any) is presumably in good condition, we return to nearly the same number. To speculate further, is there any connection between the pairing of sets of

armor on the Sh tablets and the pairing of feasters at individual tables (Palaima 2000, p. 237; Stocker and Davis, this volume)? Was the renovated armor to be ready for collection at the time of the feast, the equipment for which was recorded and debris of which was deposited in the same room?

81. Cf. Kirk 1985, p. 101.
82. Cf. Kirk 1985, p. 159.

83. The other instances of μέθυ occur in *Od.* 4.746 (the same phrase in 7.265; cf. also 17.533), 7.179 = 13.50, 9.9, 45, 12.362, 14.194, with a single instance of μεθύοντι ("drunkard") in 18.240.

84. Exod. 3.8, 13.5; Lev. 20.24; Num. 13.27; Deut. 26.9; Jer. 11.5; Ezek. 20.6.

from οἶνος, but the word itself, cognate with English "mead," almost certainly had a rather different meaning in an earlier form of Greek, probably referring to a drink made from fermented honey.[85] In this connection, it is particularly interesting that the word also appears once on the Pylos texts in the phrase *me-tu-wo ne-wo*, apparently as the name of a festival ("of the new wine [or mead]") (Fr 1202)[86]—precisely the sort of context in which names may persist long after they have lost their original meaning and specific significance (just as "Yuletide" is still used to refer to the Christmas festival).

While μέθυ in the epics is sweet (ἡδύ or γλυκερόν: *Od.* 14.194), οἶνος is most often gleaming or sparkling (αἶθοψ: *Il.* 1.146 and passim; *Od.* 2.57 = 17.536 and passim), though it can also be red (ἐρυθρός: *Od.* 5.165, 9.163, 208, 12.19, 327, 13.69, 16.444) or black (μέλας: *Od.* 5.265, 9.196, 346), like life-giving blood, in a few cases in what might be thought of as symbolically suggestive contexts. Οἶνος is also described as sweet—either straightforwardly sweet (*Od.* 3.51, 10.519 = 11.27, 20.69; cf. also *Il.* 2.340; *Od.* 3.391, 15.507), which could mean sweet in a metaphorical sense, or literally sweet—or described by compounds of the word for honey (μέλι) as "honey-sweet" (μελιηδής, μελίφρων: *Il.* 4.346, 6.258, 264, 8.506, 546, 10.579, 12.320, 18.545, 24.284; *Od.* 3.46, 7.182 = 13.53, 9.208, 10.356, 14.78 = 16.52, 15.148, 18.151, 426, 21.293). Accompanying this is an implication that the sweeter the wine the higher the quality and—in notable instances—the greater the strength, like the ultra-sweet, ultra-strong wine given by Maron as a gift to Odysseus (*Od.* 9.196–215). Though these compounds are also used in a metaphorical sense to describe such abstract concepts as life, sleep, and homecoming, and are applied to other sweet things such as grapes and the fruit of the lotus, their frequent use to qualify wine suggests that honey may have been added to it to increase the sugar content, either at the time of manufacture or later, a procedure that would enhance both its strength and its keeping qualities. Though there is no explicit indication of this in the epics, the appearance of the adjective *me-ri-ti-jo* ("honeyed") on the back of a sealing nodule recording a wine delivery at Pylos[87] suggests that, at least in the 13th century, certain wines may have been treated in this way. Honey is explicitly mixed with wine for drinking on one or two occasions in the epics, but in circumstances that indicate that mixing of this sort is unusual—certainly not normal practice for heroes who (it is implied) always drink their wine mixed with water.[88]

It seems that almost anyone can drink wine in the epics, with the possible exception of women (apart, that is, from goddesses or semi-goddesses). The entire Achaean army is kept well supplied at Troy (*Il.* 9.71–72); Eumaios has plenty of wine in his humble hut; and even plowmen drink wine to refresh themselves in the course of their work (*Il.* 18.545). At the same time, there is a strong suggestion that the kind of formal drinking party that takes place in the Homeric palace is, like the Classical symposium, for men only. In these contexts wine is described as εὐήνωρ ("manly") (*Od.* 4.622); Odysseus, disguised as a beggar, is invited by Telemachos to sit and drink wine at a table and chair "with the men" (μετ' ἀνδράσιν: *Od.* 20.262); and we are told that, after his bath in Alkinoos's palace, Odysseus goes to join the men in their wine-drinking (*Od.* 8.456). This sort of drinking is often accompanied by the songs of the bard (*Od.* 1.340). The association

85. Referred to as ὑδρόμελι by Classical and later authors. For the precedence of mead over wine in Greek mythology, see Kerenyi 1976, pp. 35–38. Kerenyi (p. 37) points out that the μελίκρητος (used first in sequence with wine, water, and barley to summon the dead in *Od.* 10.518–520, and cf. 11.26–28), though usually thought of as honey mixed with milk, probably denotes mead. See also Kerenyi 1976, pp. 37–38, for the particular suitability of leather vessels as containers for fermenting mead—perhaps indicative of the original associations of the Homeric ἄλεισον (see above, n. 66).

86. Palmer 1963, p. 434; Palmer 1994, pp. 63–64.

87. Palmer 1994, p. 63.

88. See below for more detailed discussion.

of wine with "manliness" may be further reflected in the number of masculine proper names derived from the root οἰνο- in the epics. We have two Oinomaoses in the *Iliad,* one Oineus, and one Oinops, all of them heroes themselves or the fathers or grandfathers of heroes; and one Oinops, the father of an excess-hating diviner, in the *Odyssey.* Possibly in a similar sort of connection, wine may also be associated with freedom (*Il.* 6.528).[89] Finally, that there is a perceived parallelism—if not blurring—between divine and kingly consumption of wine is suggested by the picture of Alkinoos sitting on his throne drinking his wine "like an immortal" (ἀθάνατος ὥς: *Od.* 6.309). One wonders whether, at this point, one should think of the megaron at Pylos with the throne of the *wanax* flanked by its libation channels.

Although wine is a normal component of hospitality and refreshment from the palace to the humblest dwelling, along with the other staples of bread and water (and, like them, part of the standard provision when setting out on a journey), wine also figures quite largely in princely gift-giving. The Kikonian Maron gives Odysseus, along with seven talents of gold and a silver krater, a gift of 12 jars of wine of exceptional sweetness and strength; while Euneos king of Lemnos sends a gift of a thousand measures of wine to his compeers Agamemnon and Menelaos at Troy, along with an unspecified number of shiploads of wine for sale to lesser members of the Achaean contingent (*Il.* 7.467–475). What appear to be distinctions in qualities of wine implied by such gifts also occur elsewhere in the epics, and may have applied in Bronze Age palatial times.[90] The wine stored in pithoi in Odysseus's palace storeroom is of more than one sort (*Od.* 2.340–352): the best wine is stored for Odysseus's homecoming; the second-best is that which Telemachos asks Eurykleia to draw off for him for his journey to Pylos; one might presume the existence of a third quality offered (at least initially) to the suitors whom Telemachos complains have consumed all of Odysseus's wine along with his flocks of sheep and goats (*Od.* 2.56–58). Elsewhere we hear of wine reserved for the elders (*Od.* 13.8), and the "choice" (ἔξαιτος) wine enjoyed by Sarpedon and Glaukos as leaders of the Lycians (*Il.* 12.318–320). Vintage wine is also appreciated. The special wine stored in Odysseus's palace against his return is described in approbatory fashion as "aged" (*Od.* 2.340); and the wine that Nestor brings out in honor of Telemachos is, we are told, 11 years old (*Od.* 3.391–392). There is the same sense of enhancement through long keeping as there is with the unguent used to anoint Patroklos's body, which has been kept for nine years (*Il.* 18.351).

Wine is apparently produced in many different places, at least in some cases on a small scale. Laertes has his vineyard plot, no more than a small holding (*Od.* 1.193, 11.193), and even the Cyclopes produce an admittedly strife-stirring kind of wine from wild vines (*Od.* 9.111, 358). At the same time, there are suggestions, particularly in the "Catalogue of Ships," that certain localities may be especially famed for wine production or the quality of their wine. Epidauros, Arne, Histiaia, and Pedasos are all singled out as famous for their vineyards. Apparently particularly prominent in this respect is the North Aegean region, the home of Maron and Euneos's special gift-worthy wines and of the Thracian wine brought daily to Troy

89. On the other hand, the obscure phrase κρητῆρα ἐλεύθερον may simply be a reference to one of the epithets of Dionysos (Ἐλευθήρ) (cf., e.g., Puhvel 1964, p. 164; but see also Palmer 1963, p. 419; Antonelli 1996, p. 172).

90. See Palmer 1994, pp. 62–63, 89.

on Achaean ships for the Achaean army (*Il.* 9.71–72). The regional reputation for specialization in wine that this may imply may be a relatively late feature, datable to no earlier than the 10th century, when evidence for long-distance transport of amphoras, possibly containing North Aegean wine, begins to appear.[91] Although there may be some evidence for export of wine from Crete in the Neopalatial period, there is little clear sign that wine was transported in significant quantities by ship around the Aegean in the Late Bronze Age. This is suggested by the failure of the Aegean world generally to adopt their own version of the Canaanite jar (the forerunner of the Classical amphora).[92]

Wine for heroic drinking is usually explicitly "mixed" (the verb used is κεράννυμι) and invariably served from mixing-bowls or kraters (κρητῆρες, from the same verb), though—perhaps surprisingly—on only two occasions are we specifically told that it is mixed with water (*Od.* 1.110, 9.209). Nevertheless, the general epic ethos, in which drunkenness is seen as not only a dangerous but also a shameful condition (*Od.* 14.466, 18.240, 331, 19.122, 21.293–294), strongly suggests that dilution of wine with water is what a Homeric audience would have understood, particularly in view of the Polyphemos episode in *Odyssey* 9. Those who drink unmixed wine (like the Cyclops) tend to come to grief;[93] and in general any suggestion of not being able to take one's wine, along with its misuse in unmixed form, is regarded as decidedly nonheroic. Characters associated with drunkenness include Polyphemos, Elpenor (who is otherwise portrayed as a rather ineffective warrior and a bit simple-minded: *Od.* 11.61), and the centaur Eurytion ("the first who found his own evil in heavy drinking": *Od.* 21.304). There is also a strong implication that suitors in the *Odyssey* might well be capable of committing such a solecism (*Od.* 16.292 = 19.11, 18.406–407), while one of the worst and foremost insults that Achilles in his quarrel with Agamemnon can think to hurl at him is to call him a drunkard (*Il.* 1.225).

This raises the question of when the practice of mixing wine with water, well attested in the Classical symposium, first made its appearance in Greek lands. It is not a question readily susceptible to direct archaeological investigation. Moreover, some confusion results from conventional archaeological terminology, in which the term "krater" is extended to prehistoric vessels of roughly the same size or shape as Classical kraters, with an unspoken assumption that both were used in the same way. Nevertheless, despite these difficulties, it is possible to offer suggestions.

The shaft graves at Mycenae and other Early Mycenaean graves contain bronze vessels of a suitable size and shape to have fulfilled the functions of epic κρητῆρες, and which are, indeed, often called "kraters."[94] Not only is their general function unclear,[95] however, but they occur only in bronze—in contrast to the wealth of precious metal drinking cups from the same and other contemporary graves. The only possible example of a precious metal "krater" known from this early period is the unique silver "battle krater" from shaft grave IV, which is sufficiently large and, in its restored shape, most closely resembles a relatively wide-mouthed, medium to large, amphoroid (or "Palace Style") jar of the type known from the contemporary ceramic repertoire.[96] Whatever the function of this vessel,

91. Catling 1996, p. 126.

92. Palmer 1994, pp. 187–188. Recently, Rutter (2000) has suggested that a type of short-necked amphora of the LM IIIA–B period might be regarded as an equivalent of the Canaanite jar. The jar is so far known mainly from Kommos, however, and there is as yet no clear evidence that it traveled widely (Rutter 2000, pp. 182–183). The absence of clear evidence for the long-distance transport of wine in the Aegean Late Bronze Age contrasts with the case of oil in LM/LH IIIB, associated with the large transport stirrup jars of mainly Cretan origin.

93. A symptom of Polyphemos's uncouthness seems to be that he even drank milk unmixed (*Od.* 9.297).

94. Matthäus 1980, pp. 150–157, pls. 22, 23, 24:202–204.

95. Matthäus 1980, pp. 154–155.

96. Sakellariou 1974; cf., e.g., Müller 1909, p. 316, fig. 16; and for smaller versions of the shape, Karo 1930–1933, pl. CLXVII; Mountjoy 1986, p. 12, fig. 3.

however, it is significant that no general class of precious metal vessels can be identified as "kraters," nor are there any large, sufficiently wide-mouthed, kraterlike vessels in the decorated ceramic repertoire of the Early Mycenaean period. Such vessels first appear in clay in the form of enlarged goblets in LH IIIA1,[97] when, as James Wright points out elsewhere in this volume, a few precious metal vessels of comparable size and identical shape also occur in tombs.[98] The form these vessels take in both media strongly suggests that a concept of "kraters" as a distinct functional class did not exist before this period, but was "invented" by enlarging an existing form of drinking vessel in the early 14th century.[99]

This is not to say that the function or functions served by the LH IIIA1 and later vessels were necessarily also entirely inventions of these periods, since any mixing of wine with other substances could easily have taken place in individual drinking vessels, as in Nestor's famous δέπας (*Il.* 11.631–639). Nor can we assume that these vessels were called "kraters," which would at least confirm that they were used for mixing something.[100] The appearance of these enlarged drinking vessels does suggest, however, the formal recognition of a new, or more regularly occurring, practice. If what we call "kraters" can indeed be regarded as true κρητῆρες, their scale seems to indicate substantial mixing rather than merely the inclusion of additives, and dilution with water is a reasonable possibility.[101] The timing of the first appearance of "kraters" in the ceramic repertoire strikes me as potentially significant, since it coincides with the appearance of the Mycenaean palaces on the Greek mainland, and thus raises the possibility that the regularized practice of substantially diluting wine with water may have been a direct result of the deliberate inclusion of wider elements of society in official feasting in this crucial period.[102] Moreover, the persistence of ceramic "kraters" from this period into the eighth century suggests that this practice thereafter continued without a break.[103]

97. Or in LH IIB at the very earliest (see Mountjoy 1999, p. 214, no. 89). Cf., however, French 1964, pp. 248–249, 256; Mountjoy 1986, p. 61, table IV.

98. See, e.g., Persson 1942, pp. 87–88, fig. 99:1.

99. The commonest form of the LH IIIB–C "krater," at least in some regions, is the deep bowl krater (Furumark [1941] shapes [FS] 281–282), an enlarged version of the contemporary deep bowl, which probably also acted as a drinking vessel. For kraters of pedestal type from palatial pottery assemblages at Pylos—possibly a regional feature—see Bendall, forthcoming. The amphoroid kraters (FS 52–55) that form such a prominent feature of Argive pottery exports to the eastern Mediterranean appear to have been ceramic versions of a metal form already well integrated into eastern Mediterranean Late Bronze ceramic reper-

toires (Furumark 1944, p. 238; Matthäus 1985, pp. 228–232, pls. 66–68; Kling 1989, p. 130; Morris 1989; Karageorghis 1990, pl. XXIV; Sherratt 1999, p. 188; cf. Steel, this volume).

100. The absence of clearly recognizable kraters on the Linear B texts (with the probable exception of one *ka-ra-te-ra* on MY Ue 611, listed, without ideogram, alongside equipment plausibly associated with feasting: Palmer 1963, p. 364; Ventris and Chadwick 1973, no. 234) is possibly not as significant as it seems. The failure of the Pylos Ta series, for instance, to mention kraters is comparable to the omission of drinking vessels, about whose existence we have no doubt. It is possible that, as in the epics (cf., e.g., *Il.* 23.741–748; *Od.* 15.115–119), precious metal kraters, like drinking cups, were prized personal possessions, often perhaps heirlooms or the objects of

guest-gifts, and would therefore not figure in lists of communal feasting equipment held in the palace.

101. One need not assume that the 20 measures of water to one δέπας of wine required by Maron's exceptional vintage was the normal ratio. In Classical times, a ratio of 2:3 for wine and water, respectively, seems to have been typical.

102. Dabney, Halstead, and Thomas, this volume.

103. Very few contexts in the epics can be cited in which unmixed wine is explicitly used: libations of unmixed wine are poured at the swearing of solemn oaths in regard to the proposed single-combat duel between Menelaos and Paris (*Il.* 2.341 = 4.159) and in connection with the final preparation for burial of Achilles' cremated bones (*Od.* 24.73). Both of these are very solemn, ritual occasions, and in the first

As already mentioned, wine can be mixed with substances other than water in the epics, but only rarely and in rather interesting contexts. Apart from villains (who may think of it—or at least think others capable of it: cf. *Od.* 2.329–330), only women do it, and, it seems, only certain sorts of women. Though men can drink the results, mixing wine in this way is not a normal part of male, let alone heroic male, culture in the epics, and one detects an implication that it is not a regular part of a Greek cultural ethos or even a particularly commendable use of wine. Its effects can be either good or bad. The most famous instance is provided by Circe, the enchantress and seductress, who mixes Pramneian wine not only with barley, cheese, and honey, but also with certain malignant (perhaps hallucinogenic) substances that turn Odysseus's companions into pigs and destroy their memories (*Od.* 10.234–240).[104] The antidote for this is the mysterious herb moly (*Od.* 10.305)—perhaps not wild rue *(Ruta graveolens)* or garlic *(Allium nigrum),* with which it was variously identified by the ancients,[105] but the maritime squill *(Urginea maritima),* which also has a white flower and was used medicinally in Classical times. The associations of this plant, as Peter Warren has pointed out, are not only apotropaic, but may have been linked, from at least as early as the middle of the second millennium, with certain manifestations of the Mistress of Animals.[106]

Another instance of wine mixed with a psychoactive substance—though this time to more benign effect—is found in the scene in the *Odyssey* in which Helen mixes a potion of wine with νηπενθὲς ἄχολον, a sedative with a euphoriant effect, which, we are told, was given to her by Polydamna of Egypt:

τῇ πλεῖστα φέρει ζείδωρος ἄρουρα φάρμακα, πολλὰ μὲν ἐσθλὰ μεμιγμένα, πολλὰ δὲ λυγρά

Where the grain-giving earth brings forth the greatest number
of drugs, many good in the mixing, and many malignant.

Od. 4.229–230[107]

The effects of this drug suggest a liquid preparation of opium, for which there is evidence in the Aegean and the eastern Mediterranean from at least as early as the middle of the second millennium, but whose use is

of these cases the "unmixed libations" (σπονδαί τ' ἄκρητοι) are contained in a formulaic line that has the ring of a very ancient, ritualized saying—as ancient and ritualized as the single combat in the general context of which it arises (the reference to "right hands" in the same formulaic line recalls the kinds of rituals typically associated with swearing blood brotherhood). See also Kirk 1985, pp. 302–303, on the problems caused to later commentators by the use of a krater during the oath-sacrifice in *Il.* 3, to which 4.159 ostensibly refers; and pp. 347–348, on the absence of any mention of "right hands"

in the account given of it. It is also interesting that in *Il.* 9.202–204, when the delegation including Odysseus arrives at Achilles' shelter, Achilles tells Patroklos to mix a stronger (ζωρότερον) drink, since it is for the men who are dearest to him.

104. It has been suggested that the hallucinogen is *Datura stramonium* (the thorn-apple), which contains the alkaloids hyoscyamine, atropine, and hyoscine, and whose properties were known in antiquity: Philipp 1959, p. 513; Hijmans 1992, p. 30; cf. Polunin 1969, pp. 372–373.

105. Theophr. *Hist. pl.* 9.15.7;

Gal., *De temperamentis* 12.82, 19.124; Dioscorides, *De materia medica* 3.46.1. Dioscorides tells us that the word was still in use in Cappadocia and Galatia, which suggests that it may originally have been of Anatolian (and perhaps non-Greek Aegean) origin.

106. Warren 1984; cf. also Hijmans 1992, p. 30.

107. Another woman "who knew of all the drugs that the broad earth nourishes" (though without any mention of either "good" or "malignant" ones) is Agamede, a figure of the long-gone days when Nestor was a young man (*Il.* 11.741).

probably considerably older.[108] In a third instance, the ancient hero Nestor's Trojan captive, Hekamede, again mixes Pramneian wine with cheese and barley in Nestor's enormous δέπας (*Il.* 11.637–639). In this case, although there is no mention of any other substance added, one might suspect that the cheese is a Homeric substitute for something else.[109] Nutritious though cheese and wine may be for elderly kings and wounded warriors, it is hard to believe that the bronze graters, of which ninth-century Euboian warriors appear to have been so proud,[110] were regularly used only for the ceremonial grating of a mundane item such as cheese, which can just as effectively be scraped with a knife.

The significance of the Pramneian wine offered by Circe and Hekamede is a bit of a mystery—and clearly was also to the commentators and lexicographers of later antiquity.[111] That it indicates a very special sort of wine is suggested by the comparison of Hekamede to goddesses as she stirs it in Nestor's δέπας (*Il.* 11.638),[112] and by the fact that it was apparently not mixed with water. It is referred to only twice in the epics, both times in association with mixtures (either with or without the explicit addition of mind-altering drugs), which suggests that it was a type of wine that was regularly doctored,[113] that it had special medicinal properties in its own right, or possibly that it was made from an ingredient other than the grape, rather than a simple toponymic description as suggested by some later scholiasts.[114] The occasional presence of such wine-based mixtures deep in the heart of the epics suggests that the spread of "civilized" wine use in early Greek culture from the East in the third millennium may have subsumed preexisting customs of drinking other psychoactive substances.[115] At the same time, the exclusive association of these types of wine-based mixtures with foreign, foreign-connected, or otherwise strange and exotic *women* suggests that, by the time of the Homeric epics, this use of wine for other than purely medicinal purposes may have been actively excluded from the normal Greek perception of wine use—and that wine had effectively supplanted the social and cultural use of other substances, at least at any level of society that counted.[116]

On what may be a related point, we can turn to a particularly intriguing type of epic drinking vessel, not yet mentioned, which occurs only

108. Kerenyi 1976, pp. 23–28; Sherratt 1995, p. 32; cf. also Tzavella-Evjen 1983, p. 188.

109. Tzavella-Evjen (1983, p. 188) suspects that the "something else" is ergot on the barley.

110. As were their seventh-century Etruscan successors: Ridgway 1997, pp. 331–338. One wonders whether these graters combined with some gratable narcotic substance might have been the equivalents of the morphine packs carried by First World War officers.

111. Chantraine 1968–1980, vol. 3, p. 933, s.v. πράμνειος.

112. Circe, of course, is an actual goddess—even if a somewhat suspect (and essentially foreign) one (Hes. *Cat.* 46).

113. Cf. Hippoc. *Mul.* 1–2.

114. Ridgway 1997, pp. 327–328.

115. For varying views about the spread of wine-drinking in the Aegean area, see, e.g., Renfrew 1972, pp. 281–285; Hamilakis 1996; Maran 1998, pp. 251–255. For arguments that an ideology of wine-drinking as a symbol of elite lifestyle "arrived" from the East no later than the mid-third millennium, see Sherratt 2000b, pp. 51, 355. See also Sherratt 1995 for discussion of

the use of a wide variety of psychoactive substances in addition to grape-based wine in Old World prehistory, including that of the Aegean.

116. It is noticeable in the Homeric epics that, with the exception of Circe's and Helen's φάρμακα, and the φάρμακα that the suitors fear Telemachos may add to their wine, virtually all φάρμακα, such as the ἤπια φάρμακα in the hands of a "blameless healer" (ἀμύμων ἰητήρ) like Patroklos in *Il.* 11.822–835, are applied externally (*Il.* 4.218, 5.401 = 900, 11.514–515, 15.394, 16.28–29).

twice in the *Odyssey*. This is the strange κισσύβιον, a word often translated—for want of a better term—as "ivy bowl."[117] It is in a κισσύβιον that Eumaios (in a recurrent line) mixes the honey-sweet wine when entertaining the disguised Odysseus and later Telemachos in his rustic hut (*Od.* 14.78, 16.52). But even more strikingly, it is a κισσύβιον from which the Cyclops Polyphemos drinks three bowls of the extra-strong unmixed wine that makes him so drunk that Odysseus is able to outwit him (*Od.* 9.345–346). The association with ivy is, of course, familiar from the Dionysiac symbolism of the Archaic period onward; but, once we recall the "sacral ivy" patterns painted on pottery jugs and drinking vessels, and decorating embossed metal cups and other feasting equipment already in the centuries around the middle of the second millennium, it becomes apparent that an association of ivy with drinking may well go a very long way back in the Aegean.[118] It could perhaps be argued that the epic κισσύβιον simply preserves a dim recollection of ivy-decorated vessels of the Late Bronze Age, themselves merely fashionable manifestations of a partly understood motif borrowed deferentially by Neopalatial Crete from Egypt;[119] although this may be part of the story, the contexts in which it is used suggest that there is more to it than this.

Dionysos himself, now clearly demonstrated as a deity of considerable antiquity in the Aegean with deep roots in Crete,[120] may well have been associated with ivy long before his association with the vine.[121] In a Frazerian view of early religion, ivy makes perfect sense as an attribute of an epiphanic vegetation god, since it is not only an evergreen that grows mysteriously both upward and laterally without the apparent need of soil, but also has a curious dual cycle of growth that allows it to flourish in shade and cold.[122] At the same time, from a structuralist point of view, ivy in Dionysiac symbolism

117. The alternative—a bowl (or cup) made of ivy wood (LSJ s.v.)—makes no sense, since ivy does not produce wood suitable for this purpose (cf. *RE* V.2, 1905, cols. 2826–2847, s.v. Epheu [F. Olck]).

118. For the "sacral ivy" pattern (Furumark motif 12) on ceramic jugs, drinking vessels, and other shapes (including Palatial-style jars and rhyta), particularly of LH I–IIIA date, see Furumark 1941, pp. 268–274. For the same motif on contemporary Cretan clay vessels (including cups, goblets, jugs, a pedestaled cauldron, and jars), see *PM* II, p. 476, fig. 284, p. 485, fig. 291:e, p. 486, fig. 292; *PM* IV, p. 361, fig. 301:c–e; Popham 1967, p. 338, fig. 1:10–11, p. 346, fig. 5:11, pls. 77:d, 83:b, 84:c; Betancourt 1985, p. 129, fig. 98:B, D, F, p. 137, fig. 103:B, p. 141, fig. 105:H, p. 146, fig. 109, pls. 17:G, 21:E, 24:B. Ivy

leaves are a relatively frequent motif on metal vessels with probable feasting associations: cf., e.g., *PM* II, p. 481, fig. 288:c (a bronze cup from Mochlos), p. 642, fig. 408 (the handle of a bronze basin from Knossos); Persson 1942, p. 75, fig. 88, p. 89, fig. 101, pl. IV (a gold cup and silver spoon from Dendra chamber tomb 10); Persson 1931, p. 95, fig. 67, pls. XXXI:3, 6, XXXIII:5 (a bronze spouted bowl, a bronze jug, and a silver cup from Dendra chamber tomb 2); Åström 1977, p. 53, figs. 16, 18, 19, pls. XXV, XXVI:1, XXVII:1, 2, XXVIII (a bronze basin and bronze jug from Dendra chamber tomb 12); Matthäus 1980, pl. 55:466 (a bronze brazier from Kato Zakros). They are also found decorating stone pedestal lamps from Crete (*PM* II, pp. 480–481, figs. 287:g, 288:a; Buchholz and Karageorghis 1973, pp. 92, 355, nos. 1149–1150).

119. *PM* II, p. 480.

120. Kerenyi 1976; Antonelli 1996.

121. It is not clear, for instance, that Dionysos is linked with wine in the Linear B texts; at Chania, perhaps significantly, gifts to him take the form of honey (Palmer 1994, p. 62; *OCD*³, p. 479, s.v. Dionysus [A. Henrichs]; Godart and Tzedakis 1991; cf. Kerenyi 1976, pp. 29–37). He was certainly strongly associated with wine by the time of Hesiod, however, and almost certainly by the time of the Homeric epics (cf. Hes. *Op.* 614; *Il.* 14.325, where he is described as "a source of joy to mortals"). For Kissos as one of the names by which he was known in the deme of Acharnai in Attica, see Paus. 1.31.6. For the antiquity of his association with ivy, see also Kerenyi 1976, pp. 61–64.

122. Otto 1965, pp. 153–155, quoted in Kerenyi 1976, pp. 63–64.

may be seen as a symbolic inversion of the cultivated vine;[123] and in the *Odyssey*, too (especially where the land of the Cyclopes is concerned), we might be tempted to see it as representing the antithesis of the vine and civilized norms of wine use—an anti-vine, characteristic of the wild (or ἄγριος) domain beyond the bounds of the civilized world.[124]

But could such clever (and fleeting) symbolism have impressed Homeric audiences unless the ivy that gave its name to this vessel also formed an intimate and pervasive part of the Greek cultural experience of drinking? Was ivy, in fact, part of the varied inheritance of drinking practices of an earlier "untamed" world that wine, as a symbol above all of "civilization," first subsumed and ultimately displaced in Aegean culture over the course of several millennia?[125] If so, in this as in other respects,[126] the Homeric epics set the agenda for a new, ideal, "civilized" world, exclusively characterized by universal (and predominantly male) wine use with the closely regulated social norms that we see in them, and in which the drinking of other psychoactive substances, either on their own or mixed with wine, is relegated to strictly medicinal use, or to the twilight realms of female "witches" (or "witch"-goddesses) and foreigners.[127] As with other components of the ideal new Greek world delineated by the epics, it was an ideal that probably far outshadowed any actual practice. Inherited by the post-Roman West and given new life at the Reformation, it is an ideal that nevertheless still casts a long shadow.[128]

123. Otto 1965, pp. 153–155; Kerenyi 1976, p. 63; Ruck 1986a, pp. 185–186.

124. Perhaps the antithesis, too, of the light-loving flowers that adorn purification basins and kraters (*Od.* 3.440, 24.273).

125. Ivy's medicinal uses were widely acknowledged in antiquity (Polunin 1969, p. 848; *RE* V.2, 1905, cols. 2826–2847, s.v. Epheu [F. Olck]; and see also Ruck 1986a, p. 183). Among other things, it was regarded as a useful analgesic, and as having particular applications for a variety of gynecological and obstetric disorders. In addition, the sap or berries drunk in small quantities in wine were thought to promote conception, while the umbels, ground and added to wine in much larger quantities, were regarded as a contraceptive. The leaf stalks mixed with honey and applied to the womb externally were believed to act as an abortifacient. Whether or not they were effective, these perceived applications in the manipulation of female fertility probably marked it as a socially dangerous ("women's") plant whose use needed careful social control. That it

was also regarded as having psychoactive properties is clear from the belief that the sap and fruit, if drunk, caused weakness and befuddling of the senses, and that any part of the plant had the ability to attack the nerves (no doubt in large enough quantities it could also induce blindness).

Ivy may well have many of the properties attributed to it by the ancients. It is still a component of several proprietary medicines in continental Europe, and the toxicity of the berries when ingested in significant quantities is well known. In general, it is likely that it was used from a very early period, along with other better-documented plants such as cannabis, henbane, and poppy, to spice up various lightly fermented fruit-based brews that preceded, and probably continued to form more readily available substitutes for, the elite use of grape-based wine (Sherratt 1995; see also Ruck 1986a and 1986b for a much more ambitious attempt at tracking the use of a wide variety of psychoactive plants in the hidden recesses of Greek cultural history).

126. See Sherratt 1996.

127. From this point of view, the story of Lykourgos in *Il.* 6.130–140, with its portrayal of atavistic (and ultimately doomed) opposition to the young, fragile, wine-associated god and his "fosterers," has a certain logical consistency. Whether or not the stories (Apollod. *Bibl.* 3.5.1; Plut. *Quomodo adul.* 1) of Lykourgos's crazed attacks on vines themselves (in the belief that their wine was pernicious) were already current by this early date, this kind of rationalization gives a vivid insight into antiquity's own perceptions of what his opposition was about. In Greek myth, Lykourgos is merely one of a series of figures punished with madness (or, in his case, also with blindness) for their opposition to Dionysos, the most famous of whom is Pentheus in Euripides' *Bacchae,* in which the virtues of wine are given a glowing account (Ruck 1986a, p. 179). Significantly, perhaps, others include women, such as the daughters of Minyas (Ov. *Met.* 4.1–40) and the daughters of Proitos (Hes. *Cat.* 18).

128. See Goodman 1995, p. 143, n. 66.

CONCLUDING REMARKS

There can be no doubt that feasting is an integral part of the *Iliad* and *Odyssey* and plays a very important role in them. It provides not only the most likely setting for the creation and elaboration in performance of the Homeric epics themselves, but also the consistent setting in which their content was perceived as having been rehearsed over many generations, thus providing the notion of continuity with the past essential to bind the identity of the present to its "history" (cf. *Il.* 10.217). That this was not just a perception but a historical reality also seems beyond doubt. Feasting in the various forms glimpsed in the epics (including religious, funerary, nuptial, aristocratic, warrior, community, and more general social feasting) did indeed, over a very long period, provide the occasions for the creation, transmission, and re-creation of the kinds of heroic songs and cycles of songs that constituted the prehistory of the epics and provided much of the material for their specifically Homeric form. Feasting can be seen to be deeply embedded in this prehistory in a number of different ways, from the values and practices glimpsed in the epics to their associated equipment and terminology.

The most prominent values of Homeric feasting—the ideals of equal sharing, mutual obligation, and individual esteem within the collective, and the potential for universal inclusion, together with the drinking exclusively of wine according to well-defined social rules and the "taming" of the Olympian gods by making them co-feasters at a relatively safe distance—may be seen as among the conscious props of a new sense of Greek collective identity and ideology that was shaped in the later eighth century, and which the epics themselves were specifically designed to foster. This is not to say, however, that these ideals were simply or entirely creations of this period. Rather, as seems likely from the contradictory or anomalous elements we occasionally glimpse behind their facade, they represent an accumulation of historical values, attitudes, and practices encapsulated in a wealth of story-patterns, formulaic genre scenes, motifs, and vocabulary inherited from an extended past.[129] The various elements of this blending of different relics of past and present are often not easy to disentangle—a tribute in itself to the wholly organic processes of imaginative creation that produced the Homeric epics as we know them. When it comes to the more nebulous sphere of values, these can often reinforce each other relatively seamlessly. A Mycenaean palatial anxiety to ensure that all those sectors of society on which it relies for its continuation should believe that they have the opportunity to feast with the aid or blessing of palatial munificence, for instance, can end up being harnessed to produce a more generalized notion of universal inclusion. An original and obvious duality in the meaning of the word for "feast," preserved in certain formulaic phrases, can reinforce the notion of equal sharing at a time when the word itself has lost this more general connotation; and the symbolism of the elite circle of feasters, traceable in various forms throughout the Late Bronze Age, can continue or reemerge in new forms.[130] Only occasionally do we glimpse values that seem to jar with the predominant ones: Aithon's compulsory subscription feast in *Odyssey* 19.194–198 (which contrasts with

129. Cf. Sourvinou-Inwood 1981, p. 18, on the similarly composite, cumulative nature of Homeric attitudes to death.

130. As it may have done, perhaps under Homeric influence, in the 5th century "tholos" attached to the Prytaneion in Athens (Miller 1978).

the contributory feast for all of Menelaos's Spartan townsfolk), or the misery predicted for the orphaned Astyanax in *Iliad* 22.490–499 (which contrasts with the notion that even shepherds and reapers can feast on meat). While these examples might reflect a much older vision of feasting as the privileged preserve of ruling elites or close-knit warrior bands, they might equally well be telling us about contemporary attitudes to Cretans and non-Greeks.[131]

Similar observations can be made for the material cultural field of feasting practices and equipment. We now know (if we did not guess it before) that feasting was an important activity for Aegean societies almost as far back as we can trace them. We know more particularly, thanks to a decade of often inspired textual studies, that feasting loomed large in the concerns of the Mycenaean palaces, and at 13th-century Pylos, at least, we can combine the Linear B texts with the archaeological record to obtain a remarkably full picture of the nature of such feasting: the occasions on which it happened, who took part, where they did so, what was consumed, and what equipment was used.[132] Thanks to the preservation of frescoes (and their imaginative reconstruction), we can see these feasts in action with their bardic accompaniments, and perhaps even glimpse something of the songs that were sung on such occasions.[133] We also know, thanks to sophisticated faunal analyses, that at Pylos and elsewhere selected bones of animals slaughtered for feasting were burned in a manner reminiscent of rituals described in the epics.[134] Suggestive though all this may be, however, I am not sure how far it helps illuminate the prehistory of epic feasting without running the risk of precipitating us back into the kind of Homeric fundamentalism that once saw the epics as a transmitted reflection of 13th-century history retained (as far as the vagaries of transmission allowed) in a 13th-century setting.[135] What it does is to make it increasingly likely that the Homeric epics preserve elements that originated in bardic creations many centuries earlier; to go any further than this, however, we need to seek clues in the epics themselves.

It is above all the tantalizing glimpses of anomalies or contradictions in the material cultural field of practices and equipment that most suggestively hint at the thick past of aoidic inheritance underlying the epics.[136] Though feasting, because of its very nature, may not be as revealing in this respect as other aspects of epic material culture, it is perhaps still possible on occasion to detect the effects of the mingling of different chronological contributions. For instance, the unmixed libations and right hands by which oaths are sworn in the ancient-sounding formula of *Iliad* 4.159 (= 2.341) seem to have no part in the ceremony to which they ostensibly refer, in which a krater plays a prominent part (*Il.* 3.269); one might, therefore, suggest that the libating (and perhaps also drinking) of unmixed wine fossilized in this formula derives from a very early period, perhaps before the regular appearance of kraterlike vessels in LH III (see above). Similarly, while the invariable Homeric practice of cooking on spits can probably be assigned a terminus post quem of around 1000 B.C., it is conceivable that the curious πεμπώβολα, which occur in a single repeated line and whose function is unexplained, preserve traces of an older festal practice of boil-

131. Sherratt 1996.
132. Palaima, this volume; Bendall, forthcoming; Stocker and Davis, this volume.
133. Shelmerdine 1996, p. 477; Davis and Bennet 1999; Wright, this volume.
134. Isaakidou et al. 2002; Stocker and Davis, this volume; Dabney, Halstead, and Thomas, this volume.
135. Isaakidou et al. (2002, p. 90) make a similar point.
136. Sherratt 1990.

ing or stewing meat in tripod cauldrons, which is otherwise conspicuous by its absence. Again, it seems curious that the bronze grater that, like spits, formed part of the equipment of ninth-century warriors, should be reduced in *Iliad* 11.639–640 to grating nothing more exciting than goat's cheese into the Pramneian wine that is elsewhere given more colorful additives; one might suspect that its original warrior associations and purpose had meanwhile changed. Wine is drunk and libated from a completely interchangeable trio of δέπα (often ἀμφικύπελλα), κύπελλα, and ἄλεισα, which must originally have had different forms and functions, and whose precise significance (in some cases) was almost certainly no longer evident to Homeric bards and their audiences. Nestor's highly improbable δέπας in *Iliad* 11.632–635, complete with its four "ears," which must have been as impossible to envisage in the eighth century as it is now, seems more likely to preserve a confused (and confusing) memory of a much earlier form (or forms) of δέπας, which had passed in the course of its very long aoidic history through the songs of a Mycenaean palatial bard, than to have been specially invented for the occasion.[137] Similarly, the strange κισσύβιον, though woven into a neat structural contrast that is particularly well designed to fit an eighth-century context of Greek ethnogenesis, nevertheless itself recalls vessels (and also perhaps hints at drinking practices) that have roots in a much deeper and probably rather different past.

Over 120 years after Schliemann excavated Tiryns and Mycenae with a copy of the *Iliad* in his hand, and over 60 years after Blegen first put spade to earth at his Palace of Nestor at Pylos, the wheel has begun to turn full circle. The idea of a long prehistory of aoidic inheritance that ultimately fed into the epics, once uncritically championed (not to say exaggerated) and subsequently dismissed as pure wishful thinking, is becoming respectable once more, as several of the contributions to the present volume attest. That it is so is in large part tribute to the sophisticated and painstaking work of archaeologists at Pylos and elsewhere who, by studying the evidence in a wholly contextual manner, can read between the lines of Linear B texts, reconstruct the circumstances in which animal bones were deposited, and reveal something of the complexity and ideology of Aegean feasting practices at a very early period. Their results tell us nothing about the historicity of Homeric epic, with which earlier scholars were often concerned, but they are beginning to indicate with increasing persuasiveness that certain elements of the epics (including elements of epic feasting) themselves have a long history, which, moreover, extends back well beyond any conventionally imagined setting for a "historical" Trojan War.

137. *Pace* Hainsworth 1993, p. 293.

REFERENCES

Anderson, D. 1994–1995. "Mycenaean Vessel Terms: Evaluating the IE Evidence," *Minos* 29–30, pp. 295–322.

Antonelli, C. 1996. "Dioniso: Una divinità micenea," in De Miro, Godart, and Sacconi 1996, pp. 169–176.

Aravantinos, V. L., L. Godart, and A. Sacconi. 2001. *Thèbes: Fouilles de la Cadmée* I: *Les tablettes en linéaire B de la Odos Pelopidou, édition et commentaire,* Pisa.

Åström, P. 1977. *The Cuirass Tomb and Other Finds at Dendra* 1: *The Chamber Tombs* (*SIMA* 4), Göteborg.

Aura Jorro, F. 1985. *Diccionario micénico* 1, Madrid.

———. 1993. *Diccionario micénico* 2, Madrid.

Bass, G. F. 1967. *Cape Gelidonya: A Bronze Age Shipwreck* (*TAPS* n.s. 57.8), Philadelphia.

Bendall, L. M. 2001. "The Economics of Potnia in the Linear B Documents: Palatial Support for Mycenaean Religion," in *Potnia: Deities and Religion in the Aegean Bronze Age. Proceedings of the 8th International Aegean Conference, Göteborg* (*Aegaeum* 22), ed. R. Laffineur and R. Hägg, Liège, pp. 445–452.

———. Forthcoming. "Fit for a King? Hierarchy, Exclusion, Aspiration, and Desire in the Social Structure of Mycenaean Banqueting," in *Food, Cuisine, and Society in Prehistoric Greece* (Sheffield Studies in Aegean Archaeology 5), ed. P. Halstead and J. C. Barrett, Sheffield.

Betancourt, P. P. 1985. *The History of Minoan Pottery,* Princeton.

Boisacq, E. 1923. *Dictionnaire étymologique de la langue grecque,* Paris.

Borgna, E. 1997a. "Kitchen-Ware from LM IIIC Phaistos: Cooking Traditions and Ritual Activities in LBA Cretan Societies," *SMEA* 39, pp. 189–217.

———. 1997b. "Some Observations on Deep Bowls and Kraters from the 'Acropoli Mediana' at Phaistos," in *Late Minoan III Pottery: Chronology and Terminology. Acts of a Meeting Held at the Danish Institute at Athens,* ed. E. Hallager and B. P. Hallager, Athens, pp. 273–298.

Branigan, K. 1974. *Aegean Metalwork of the Early and Middle Bronze Age,* Oxford.

Bruns, G. 1970. *Küchenwesen und Mahlzeiten* (*ArchHom* II, Q), Göttingen.

Buchholz, H.-G., G. Jöhrens, and I. Maull. 1973. *Jagd und Fischfang* (*ArchHom* II, J), Göttingen.

Buchholz, H.-G., and V. Karageorghis. 1973. *Prehistoric Greece and Cyprus: An Archaeological Handbook,* London.

Catling, H. W. 1964. *Cypriot Bronzework in the Mycenaean World,* Oxford.

Catling, R. W. V. 1996. "A Tenth-Century Trade-Mark from Lefkandi," in *Minotaur and Centaur: Studies in the Archaeology of Crete and Euboea Presented to Mervyn Popham* (*BAR-IS* 638), ed. D. Evely, I. S. Lemos, and S. Sherratt, Oxford, pp. 126–132.

Chadwick, J. 1976. *The Mycenaean World,* Cambridge.

Chantraine, P. 1968–1980. *Dictionnaire étymologique de la langue grecque: Histoire des mots,* 4 vols., Paris.

Davies, A. M. 1963. *Mycenaeae Graecitatis Lexicon* (Incunabula graeca 3), Rome.

Davis, J. L., and J. Bennet. 1999. "Making Mycenaeans: Warfare, Territorial Expansion, and Representations of the Other in the Pylian Kingdom," in *Polemos: Le contexte guerrier en Égée à l'âge du Bronze. Actes de la 7e Rencontre égéenne internationale, Université de Liège* (*Aegaeum* 19), ed. R. Laffineur, Liège, pp. 105–120.

de Fidio, P. 1989. "Dieta e gestione delle risorse alimentari in età micenea," in *Homo edens: Regimi, miti e pratiche dell'alimentazione nella civiltà del Mediterraneo,* ed. O. Longo and P. Scarpi, Milan, pp. 193–203.

Demakopoulou, K., ed. 1988. *Das mykenische Hellas: Heimat der Helden Homers* (Exhibition Catalogue, Staatliche Museen Preussischer Kulturbesitz), Athens.

Demetriou, A. 1989. *Cypro-Aegean Relations in the Early Iron Age* (*SIMA* 83), Göteborg.

De Miro, E., L. Godart, and A. Sacconi, eds. 1996. *Atti e memorie del secondo Congresso internazionale di micenologia, Roma–Napoli* 1: *Filologia* (Incunabula graeca 98), Rome.

Dialismas, A. 2001. "Metal Artefacts as Recorded in the Linear B Tablets," in *Manufacture and Measurement: Counting, Measuring, and Recording Craft Items in Early Aegean Societies* (*Meletemata* 33), ed. A. Michailidou, Athens, pp. 121–143.

Di Filippo, M. C. 1996. "L'ideogramma *220 nei testi micenei," in De Miro, Godart, and Sacconi 1996, pp. 245–248.

Duhn, F. von. 1926. "Pempobolon (zu *AA*. 1925, 282–86)," *AA* 1926, pp. 331–334.

French, E. 1964. "Late Helladic IIIA1 Pottery from Mycenae," *BSA* 59, pp. 241–261.

Frisk, H. 1960. *Griechisches etymologisches Wörterbuch* 1, Heidelberg.

Furumark, A. 1941. *Mycenaean Pottery: Analysis and Classification*, Stockholm.

———. 1944. "The Mycenaean IIIC Pottery and Its Relations to Cypriote Fabrics," *OpArch* 3, pp. 194–265.

Gallavotti, C. 1961. "Note sulle lessico miceneo," *RivFil* 39, pp. 160–179.

Godart, L., and Y. Tzedakis. 1991. "Les nouveaux textes en linéaire B de la Canée," *RivFil* 119, pp. 129–149.

Goodman, J. 1995. "Excitantia: Or How Enlightenment Europe Took to Soft Drugs," in *Consuming Habits: Drugs in History and Anthropology*, ed. J. Goodman, P. E. Lovejoy, and A. Sherratt, London, pp. 126–147.

Gray, D. H. F. 1959. "Linear B and Archaeology," *BICS* 6, pp. 47–57.

Haarer, P. 2000. "Obeloi and Iron in Archaic Greece" (diss. Univ. of Oxford).

———. 2001. "Problematising the Transition from Bronze to Iron," in *The Social Context of Technological Change: Egypt and the Near East, 1650–1050 B.C.*, ed. A. J. Shortland, Oxford, pp. 255–273.

Hainsworth, B. 1993. *The Iliad: A Commentary* 3: *Books 9–12*, Cambridge.

Halstead, P. 2001. "Mycenaean Wheat, Flax, and Sheep: Palatial Intervention in Farming and Its Implications for Rural Society," in *Economy and Politics in the Mycenaean Palace States* (Cambridge Philological Society, Suppl. 27), ed. S. Voutsaki and J. Killen, Cambridge, pp. 38–50.

Hamilakis, Y. 1996. "Wine, Oil, and the Dialectics of Power in Bronze Age Crete: A Review of the Evidence," *OJA* 15, pp. 1–32.

Hijmans, B. L. 1992. "Circe on Monte Circeo," *Caeculus* 1, pp. 17–46.

Isaakidou, V., P. Halstead, J. Davis, and S. Stocker. 2002. "Burnt Animal Sacrifice in Late Bronze Age Greece: New Evidence from the Mycenaean 'Palace of Nestor,' Pylos," *Antiquity* 76, pp. 86–92.

Janko, R. 1992. *The Iliad: A Commentary* 4: *Books 13–16*, Cambridge.

Jasink, A. M. T. 1976. "L'e-qe-ta nei testi micenei," *SMEA* 17, pp. 85–92.

Karageorghis, V. 1974. "Pikes or Obeloi from Cyprus and Crete," in *Antichità cretesi: Studi in onore di Doro Levi* 2 (*CronCatania* 13), Catania, pp. 168–172.

———. 1983. *Palaepaphos-Skales: An Iron Age Cemetery in Cyprus* (Ausgrabungen in Alt-Paphos auf Cypern 3), Konstanz.

———. 1990. *Tombs at Palaepaphos*, Nicosia.

Karageorghis, V., and F. Lo Schiavo. 1989. "A West Mediterranean Obelos from Amathus," *RStFen* 17, pp. 15–29.

Karo, G. 1930–1933. *Die Schachtgräber von Mykenai*, Munich.

Kerenyi, K. 1976. *Dionysos: Archetypal Image of the Indestructible Life*, trans. R. Manheim, London.

Kilian, K. 1985. "La caduta dei palazzi micenei continentali: Aspetti archeologici," in *Le origini dei Greci: Dori e mondo egeo*, ed. D. Musti, Rome, pp. 73–115.

Killen, J. T. 1994. "Thebes Sealings, Knossos Tablets, and Mycenaean State Banquets," *BICS* 39, pp. 67–84.

———. 1996. "Thebes Sealings and Knossos Tablets," in De Miro, Godart, and Sacconi 1996, pp. 71–82.

———. 1998. "The Pylos Ta Tablets Revisited," pp. 421–422, in F. Rougemont and J.-P. Olivier, eds., "Recherches récentes en épigraphie créto-mycénienne," *BCH* 122, pp. 403–443.

Kirk, G. S. 1962. *The Songs of Homer*, Cambridge.

———. 1981. "Some Methodological Pitfalls in the Study of Ancient Greek Sacrifice (in Particular)," in *Le sacrifice dans l'antiquité* (*EntrHardt* 27), ed. J. Rudhardt and O. Reverdin, Geneva, pp. 41–80.

———. 1985. *The Iliad: A Commentary* 1: *Books 1–4*, Cambridge.

———. 1990. *The Iliad: A Commentary* 2: *Books 5–8*, Cambridge.

Kling, B. 1989. *Mycenaean IIIC:1b and Related Pottery in Cyprus* (*SIMA* 87), Göteborg.

Knapp, A. B., J. D. Muhly, and P. M. Muhly. 1988. "To Hoard Is Human: Late Bronze Age Metal Deposits in Cyprus and the Aegean," *RDAC* 1988, pp. 233–262.

Kron, U. 1971. "Zum Hypogäum von Paestum," *JdI* 86, pp. 117–148.

Lejeune, M. 1958. *Mémoires de philologie mycénienne* 1, Paris.

———. 1971. *Mémoires de philologie mycénienne* 2 (Incunabula graeca 42), Rome.

Lorimer, H. 1950. *Homer and the Monuments*, London.

Maran, J. 1998. *Kulturwandel auf dem griechischen Festland und den Kykladen im späten 3. Jahrtausend v. Chr.: Studien zu den kulturellen Verhältnissen in Südosteuropa und dem zentralen sowie östlichen Mittelmeerraum in der späten Kupfer- und frühen Bronzezeit* (Universitätsforschungen zur prähistorischen Archäologie 53), Bonn.

Matthäus, H. 1980. *Die Bronzegefässe der kretisch-mykenischen Kultur* (Prähistorische Bronzefunde 2.1), Munich.

———. 1985. *Metallgefässe und Gefässuntersätze der Bronzezeit, der geometrischen und archaischen Periode auf Cypern: Mit einem Anhang der bronzezeitlichen Schwertfunde auf Cypern* (Prähistorische Bronzefunde 2.8), Munich.

Meier-Brügger, M., ed. 2001. *Lexikon des frühgriechischen Epos* 19: *Lieferung, πασιδίκη–πλέω,* Göttingen.

Melena, J. L. 1983. "Olive Oil and Other Sorts of Oil in the Mycenaean Tablets," *Minos* 18, pp. 89–123.

Miller, S. G. 1978. *The Prytaneion: Its Function and Architectural Form,* Berkeley.

Morgan, L. 1998. "The Wall Paintings of the North-East Bastion at Ayia Irini, Kea," in *Kea-Kythnos: History and Archaeology* (*Meletemata* 27), ed. L. G. Mendoni and A. I. Mazarakis Ainian, Athens, pp. 201–210.

Morris, C. E. 1989. "The Mycenaean Chariot Krater: A Study in Form, Design, and Function" (diss. Univ. of London).

Mountjoy, P. A. 1986. *Mycenaean Decorated Pottery: A Guide to Identification* (*SIMA* 73), Göteborg.

———. 1999. *Regional Mycenaean Decorated Pottery,* Rahden.

Mühlestein, H. 1968. "Deutung einiger Linear-B-Wörter," in *Studia Mycenaea. Proceedings of the Mycenaean Symposium, Brno,* ed. A. Bartonek, Brno, pp. 113–116.

Müller, K. 1909. "Alt-Pylos II: Die Funde aus den Kuppelgräbern von Kakovatos," *AM* 34, pp. 269–328.

Niklasson, K. 1983. "A Shaft-Grave of the Late Cypriote III Period," in P. Åström, E. Åström, A. Hatziantoniou, K. Niklasson, and U. Öbrink, *Hala Sultan Tekke* 8: *Excavations 1971–79* (*SIMA* 45.8), Göteborg, pp. 169–213.

Otto, W. F. 1965. *Dionysos: Myth and Cult,* trans. R. B. Palmer, Bloomington.

Palace of Nestor II = M. Lang, *The Palace of Nestor at Pylos in Western Messenia* II: *The Frescoes,* Princeton 1969.

Palaima, T. G. 1995. "The Last Days of the Pylos Polity," in *Politeia: Society and State in the Aegean Bronze Age. Proceedings of the 5th International Aegean Conference, Heidelberg* (*Aegaeum* 12), ed. R. Laffineur and W.-D. Niemeier, Liège, pp. 623–633.

———. 1996. "'Contiguities' in the Linear B Tablets from Pylos," in

De Miro, Godart, and Sacconi 1996, pp. 379–396.

———. 2000. "The Pylos Ta Series: From Michael Ventris to the New Millennium," *BICS* 44, pp. 236–237.

Palmer, L. R. 1963. *The Interpretation of Mycenaean Greek Texts,* Oxford.

Palmer, R. 1994. *Wine in the Mycenaean Palace Economy* (*Aegaeum* 10), Liège.

Persson, A. W. 1931. *The Royal Tombs at Dendra near Midea,* Lund.

———. 1942. *New Tombs at Dendra near Midea,* Lund.

Philipp, H. 1959. "Das Gift der Kirke," *Gymnasium* 66, pp. 509–516.

Piteros, C., J.-P. Olivier, and J. L. Melena. 1990. "Les inscriptions en linéaire B des nodules de Thèbes (1982): La fouille, les documents, les possibilités d'interprétation," *BCH* 114, pp. 103–184.

Polunin, O. 1969. *Flowers of Europe: A Field Guide,* London.

Popham, M. R. 1967. "Late Minoan Pottery: A Summary," *BSA* 62, pp. 337–351.

Popham, M. R., E. Touloupa, and L. H. Sackett. 1982. "Further Excavation of the Toumba Cemetery at Lefkandi, 1981," *BSA* 77, pp. 213–248.

Puhvel, J. 1964. "Eleuthèr and Oinoâtis: Dionysiac Data from Mycenaean Greece," in *Mycenaean Studies. Proceedings of the Third International Colloquium for Mycenaean Studies Held at Wingspread,* ed. E. L. Bennett Jr., Madison, pp. 161–170.

Renfrew, C. 1972. *The Emergence of Civilisation: The Cyclades and the Aegean in the Third Millennium B.C.,* London.

Ridgway, D. 1997. "Nestor's Cup and the Etruscans," *OJA* 16, pp. 325–344.

Ruck, C. A. P. 1986a. "The Wild and the Cultivated: Wine in Euripides' *Bacchae,*" in R. G. Wasson, S. Kramrisch, J. Orr, and C. A. P. Ruck, *Persephone's Quest: Entheogens and the Origins of Religion,* New Haven, pp. 179–223.

———. 1986b. "The Offerings from the Hyperboreans," in R. G. Wasson, S. Kramrisch, J. Orr, and C. A. P.

Ruck, *Persephone's Quest: Entheogens and the Origins of Religion,* New Haven, pp. 225–256.

Ruijgh, C. J. 1967. *Études sur la grammaire et le vocabulaire du grec mycénien,* Amsterdam.

Rutter, J. B. 2000. "The Short-Necked Amphora of the Post-Palatial Mesara," in *Πεπραγμένα Η΄ Διεθνούς Κρητολογικού Συνεδρίου. Ηράκλειου* 3, ed. A. Karetsou, Herakleion, pp. 177–188.

Sakellariou, A. 1974. "Un cratère d'argent avec scène de bataille provenant de la IVe tombe de l'acropole de Mycènes," *AntK* 17, pp. 3–20.

Schliemann, H. 1880. *Mycenae: A Narrative of Researches and Discoveries at Mycenae and Tiryns,* New York.

Shelmerdine, C. W. 1995. "Shining and Fragrant Cloth in Homer," in *The Ages of Homer: A Tribute to Emily Townsend Vermeule,* ed. J. B. Carter and S. P. Morris, Austin, pp. 99–107.

———. 1996. "From Mycenae to Homer: The Next Generation," in De Miro, Godart, and Sacconi 1996, pp. 467–492.

———. 1998. "Where Do We Go from Here? And How Can the Linear B Tablets Help Us Get There?" in *The Aegean and the Orient in the Second Millennium. Proceedings of the 50th Anniversary Symposium, Cincinnati* (*Aegaeum* 18), ed. E. H. Cline and D. Harris-Cline, Liège, pp. 291–299.

Sherratt, A. 1995. "Alcohol and Its Alternatives: Symbol and Substance in Pre-industrial Cultures," in *Consuming Habits: Drugs in History and Anthropology,* ed. J. Goodman, P. E. Lovejoy, and A. Sherratt, London, pp. 11–46.

Sherratt, E. S. 1990. "'Reading the Texts': Archaeology and the Homeric Question," *Antiquity* 64, pp. 807–824.

Sherratt, S. 1996. "With Us But Not of Us: The Role of Crete in Homeric Epic," in *Minotaur and Centaur: Studies in the Archaeology of Crete and Euboea Presented to Mervyn Popham* (*BAR-IS* 638), ed. D. Evely, I. S. Lemos, and S. Sherratt, Oxford, pp. 87–99.

―――. 1999. "*E pur si muove:* Pots, Markets, and Values in the Second Millennium Mediterranean," in *The Complex Past of Pottery: Production, Circulation, and Consumption of Mycenaean and Greek Pottery (Sixteenth to Early Fifth Centuries B.C.),* ed. J. P. Crielaard, V. Stissi, and G. J. van Wijngaarden, Amsterdam, pp. 163–211.

―――. 2000a. "Circulation of Metals and the End of the Bronze Age in the Eastern Mediterranean," in *Metals Make the World Go Round: The Supply and Circulation of Metals in Bronze Age Europe,* ed. C. F. E. Pare, Oxford, pp. 82–98.

―――. 2000b. *Catalogue of Cycladic Antiquities in the Ashmolean Museum: The Captive Spirit,* Oxford.

Snodgrass, A. M. 1996. "Iron," in *Knossos North Cemetery: Early Greek Tombs* (*BSA* Suppl. 28), ed. J. N. Coldstream and H. W. Catling, London, pp. 575–597.

Sourvinou-Inwood, C. 1981. "To Die and Enter the House of Hades: Homer, Before and After," in *Mirrors of Mortality: Studies in the Social History of Death,* ed. J. Whaley, London, pp. 15–39.

Taplin, O. 1992. *Homeric Soundings: The Shape of the Iliad,* Oxford.

Tzavella-Evjen, H. 1983. "Homeric Medicine," in *The Greek Renaissance of the Eighth Century B.C.: Tradition and Innovation. Proceedings of the Second International Symposium at the Swedish Institute in Athens* (*SkrAth* 4°, 30), ed. R. Hägg, Stockholm, pp. 185–188.

Tzedakis, Y., and H. Martlew, eds. 1999. *Minoans and Mycenaeans: Flavours of Their Time,* Athens.

Vandenabeele, F., and J.-P. Olivier. 1979. *Les idéogrammes archéologiques du linéaire B* (*ÉtCrét* 24), Paris.

Ventris, M., and J. Chadwick. 1956. *Documents in Mycenaean Greek,* Cambridge.

―――. 1973. *Documents in Mycenaean Greek,* 2nd ed., Cambridge.

Voutsa, K. 2001. "Mycenaean Craftsmen in Palace Archives: Problems in Interpretation," in *Manufacture and Measurement: Counting, Measuring, and Recording Craft Items in Early Aegean Societies* (*Meletemata* 33), ed. A. Michailidou, Athens, pp. 145–165.

Warren, P. 1984. "Of Squills," in *Aux origines de l'Hellénisme: La Crète et la Grèce. Hommage à Henri van Effenterre présenté par le Centre G. Glotz,* Paris, pp. 17–24.

Whitelaw, T. M. 2001. "Reading between the Tablets: Assessing Mycenaean Palatial Involvement in Ceramic Production and Consumption," in *Economy and Politics in the Mycenaean Palace States* (Cambridge Philological Society, Suppl. 27), ed. S. Voutsaki and J. Killen, Cambridge, pp. 51–79.

Wright, J. C. 1995. "Empty Cups and Empty Jugs: The Social Role of Wine in Minoan and Mycenaean Societies," in *The Origins and Ancient History of Wine* (Food and Nutrition in History and Anthropology 11), ed. P. E. McGovern, S. J. Fleming, and S. H. Katz, Philadelphia, pp. 287–309.